*Confronting Animal
Exploitation*

D1564138

Confronting Animal Exploitation

Grassroots Essays on Liberation and Veganism

Edited by KIM SOCHA *and* SARAHJANE BLUM

Afterword by pattrice jones

McFarland & Company, Inc., Publishers
Jefferson, North Carolina, and London

LIBRARY OF CONGRESS CATALOGUING-IN-PUBLICATION DATA

Confronting animal exploitation : grassroots essays on liberation
   and veganism / edited by Kim Socha and Sarahjane Blum ;
   afterword by pattrice jones.
      p.   cm.
   Includes bibliographical references and index.

   ISBN 978-0-7864-6575-0
   softcover : acid free paper ∞

    1. Animal rights movement.   2. Animal rights.
  3. Veganism.   4. Animal rights movement—Minnesota.
  5. Animal rights—Minnesota.   6. Veganism—Minnesota.
  I. Socha, Kim.   II. Blum,
Sarahjane.
HV4708.C66 2013
179'.3—dc23   2012050323

BRITISH LIBRARY CATALOGUING DATA ARE AVAILABLE

On the cover: cattle photograph (Design Pics/Thinkstock);
soybean field (iStockphoto/Thinkstock)

Manufactured in the United States of America

McFarland & Company, Inc., Publishers
  Box 611, Jefferson, North Carolina 28640
  www.mcfarlandpub.com

Contents

ACKNOWLEDGMENTS vii

PREFACE *Sarahjane Blum* 1

INTRODUCTION: HALLWAY CONVERSATIONS ON ANIMAL
LIBERATION AND VEGANISM *Kim Socha* 3

Section I. Theory for Praxis

Turning Our Heads: The "See No Evil" Dilemma *Dallas Rising* 11

Anti-Capitalism and Abolitionism *Travis Elise* 22

"Just tell the truth": A Polemic on the Value of Radical Activism
Kim Socha 44

Literary Analysis for Animal Liberation: Stephen King's
Animal Kingdom *Patrick McAleer* 66

Section II. Veganism in Action

Vegan Parenting: Navigating and Negating Speciesist Media
Al Nowatzki 89

On Cheese, Motherhood and Everyday Activism
Chelsea Youngquist Hassler 112

Till Vegan Do Us Part? Personal Change, Interpersonal
Relationships and Divorce *Elizabeth Cook* 129

Section III. Narratives of Change

Introducing Speciesism to the Rescue Community
Melissa E. Maaske 139

Tales of an Animal Liberationist *Dallas Rising* 155

An Oral History of the Animal Rights Coalition: Thirty Years
of Grassroots Activism *Mary Britton Clouse, Charlotte Cozzetto,
Heidi Greger* and *Vonnie Thomasberg* 175

Section IV. Moving Toward Revolution

Killing Them Softly: Marketing a Movement, Marketing Meat
    M. Ryan Leitch   191

How "Humane" Labels Harm Chickens: Why Our Focus as
    Advocates Should Be Egg-Free Diets, Not Cage-Free Eggs
    Melissa Swanson   204

The "Dreaded Comparisons" and Speciesism: Leveling the
    Hierarchy of Suffering   *Kim Socha*   223

Animal Enterprise Acts and the Prosecution of the "SHAC 7":
    An Insider's Perspective   *Aaron Zellhoefer*   241

Some Things Get Better, Some Get Worse: On Being Scared,
    Being Around, and Trying to Be Kind   *Sarahjane Blum*   255

AFTERWORD: FLOWER POWER   *pattrice jones*   263

ABOUT THE CONTRIBUTORS   281

INDEX   283

Acknowledgments

We earnestly thank all of those who helped this book come together, from the behind-the-scenes support of our families and friends to the active support of our authors. Special notice must be given to this book's un-credited editors: M. Ryan Leitch was integral in encouraging activists to begin thinking of themselves as authors and become part of this project; and Al Nowatzki ably assisted us with last minute edits and revision suggestions as we prepared the final manuscript. Without them, we shudder to think what you'd be holding in your hands. Thank you to astute readers David Meyer and Charlene Yin and to pattrice jones for her thoughtful Afterword. Also, special thanks to Daniel and Lily-Belle, Patrick and Siouxsie for their patience and morale-boosting kindnesses.

We are so pleased with the authors who have contributed to this book, as they each offer their own inimitable "take" on the broad concepts of animal liberation and veganism. Thanks to all of you for your daily work as animal advocates and for being willing to share that work with the reading public. We offer special thanks to grassroots activists across the world advocating for animals in their local communities — every day you contribute to the movement and inspire people to see through an objective that often seems unobtainable: the cessation of animal suffering caused by humans. This book is written for you and by those like you. *Let's never stop until the cruelty ends.*

Preface

SARAHJANE BLUM

Confronting Animal Exploitation: Grassroots Essays on Liberation and Veganism is filled with the great courage and challenging opinions of sixteen of the most enthusiastic activists I have worked with on behalf of our world's other-than-human animals. Along with the great privilege of helping Kim Socha edit this anthology, I leaned upon the guidance of these authors as I learned the Midwest way of helping animals. As much as there is "a movement" filled with vigorous debate and grand coalitions, every community offers its own style of movement. This book explores the styles which have developed in the Twin Cities over the past thirty years. Some readers may be surprised to see the conflict-avoidant "Minnesota Nice" ethic mixed with radical challenges to American society. But culture shock is part of embracing any new community, as I learned years ago.

In 2000, I lived on the island of Maui, worked at a vegetarian health food store, and tried living off the grid. Six months into my stay, news broke that plans were in the works to build a new shopping center with a dolphinarium as its main attraction. Along with my fellow transplant activist Ryan Shapiro, I got involved in the effort to stop this from coming to pass. We would teach the locals all the up-to-the-minute trends in non-violent civil disobedience. We'd get hundreds of people to lock themselves to the doors of the city council, and if it got that far, to stand arm in arm blocking the paths of bulldozers. It likely wouldn't get to the point where anyone would smash a window, but I had picked up a few pointers on doing that too.

As the first step of planning, I met with Steve Sipman, a long time activist for cetacean rights. (In 1977, he executed the first reported animal liberation in America when he rescued two dolphins from a University of Hawaii laboratory and set them free in the Pacific ocean). I couldn't have gotten thirty seconds into my pitch before he stopped me — "not so fast, *haole*, that's not how we do things here." I was skeptical of his plans to print petitions, get them signed, and deliver them to the county council. Six months later, however, not only was the shopping mall idea off the agenda (a double win), but a statute was instituted banning cetacean captivity on the four islands that comprise Maui county. There are undeniable gains made by talking to people about how "we do things here" and asking "Why?" that can never be replaced by manuals for activism or the thread of a blog post. It's possible they can't be captured in a book, but my hope springs eternal.

As animal activists, we know better than anyone that people don't want to know how the sausage gets made. As the essays in this volume show, industries, laws, and deeply rooted personal defense mechanisms get triggered when we try to expose the truth behind what on the surface seems a clean, smooth, and even natural process.

This book is the baby of Kim Socha. Without her, it would not exist. In January 2011, I sat in Kim's living room and looked around at my colleagues, cohort, and activists I had never met before, and watched as Kim got people — many of whom had never written anything for publication — enthusiastic about research, hard unpaid labor, and exposing themselves to an often dismissive public. The collection of excited, bashful, and slightly terrified folks in the room were in many ways self-selected, as activist communities so often are. Looking into their faces, I took a snapshot of our community: primarily under forty, virtually all white, and dominantly heterosexual and female; these are the humans we have been able to engage to come to meetings, write emails, stand in the cold to protest injustice against animals and risk damage to marriage, family, and friendships to speak out about their own agency in personal choices.

When we called out for authors from our community, these were the people who answered, and we are eternally grateful to each and every one of them. Not only do I hope this volume be read for the insights each essay offers, I also hope readers will come away with a sense of the conversations that flow within our community. And then ask: What have we missed? Because while there is much that is new about our book, there is much that looks and sounds like the old voices as well, for better and worse.

Read this book, carefully, with compassion, and with my hopes that down the line when someone else as brave and magnetic as Kim manages to get a room filled with overworked, underappreciated scribes to write a book, the room will reflect the diversity we have not yet brought into the movement in Minneapolis.

Please enjoy this anthology filled with the lives, reflections, and hopes of a few of the activists who are proud to call these Twin Cities home.

Introduction

Hallway Conversations on
Animal Liberation and Veganism

KIM SOCHA

The idea for this essay compilation was sparked in 2010 during a protest in St. Paul, Minnesota. I was speaking with a fellow activist about the state of the animal rights/liberation movement (AR/L), and he happened to mention that major AR/L conferences have become tiresome in recent years because the same people are saying the same things, while alternative, more radical ideas are censored or watered down. When I asked why he still bothers going to such conferences, he explained that he enjoys the "hallway conversations" that take place amongst grassroots activists from across the nation and beyond. As we spoke, I thought of my own impressions when I pick up the latest AR/L anthology and see the same names appear in book after book. Thankfully, *Sistah Vegan*, edited by A. Breeze Harper, and *Sister Species*, edited by Lisa Kemmerer, have offered refreshing alternatives to that trend.

But still, I was waiting for a collection that was more locally grounded, springing from the community as opposed to a national call for papers. Rather than wait for a time when impassioned, locally-active grassroots volunteers get more of a voice in global animal liberation dialogues, I realized my position, and *duty*, as an activist and scholar to help move these "hallway conversations" about animal liberation and veganism to the podium. Thus, the arguments, ideas, opinions and counsel in this book are developed, supported and informed by scholars, activists and scholar/activists who have yet to be heard within an already marginalized movement.

Within my community, I regularly engage in my own conversations with people willing to dedicate their time, brainpower and financial resources to the cessation of animal suffering at the hands and consumer demands of human beings. Although we all maintain our unique ideologies about and methods of animal advocacy, I, my co-editor Sarahjane Blum, and the authors represented in this text believe that animals exist for purposes other than human use, and they should be left to those purposes without human interference. Therefore, interrogation of protectionism and incrementalism is to be found within the following pages, as are theories, musings and narratives meant to inspire and galvanize readers to action. I believe that the intensity of ideological differences about the "right way" to save animals should never be used to silence grassroots activists who hold what may be perceived as radical, unyielding messages. In *Aftershock*, pattrice jones eloquently emphasizes the need for community and respect amongst factions of divided movements that ultimately share a common objective: "There just aren't enough of us — any of us in any movement — for us to afford the price of demoralization that divisiveness brings. We can disagree, even vehemently, without tearing each other down or our movement apart" (148). Ultimately, whether we build up or tear down our sometimes divided movement depends on all of us, and the ways in which our decisions will impact animals must be held up for consideration.

Who We Are and Why This Book

This collection is written by sixteen activists local to the Twin Cities area in Minnesota, yet the issues we write about are not geographically bound. There is no single shared affiliation among us, nor are we a collective who regularly meet. Some of us work more independently, not affiliating ourselves with any organization. We are individuals who work together to varying degrees; some of us see each other multiple times per week; others see each other by happenstance at local events; some of us are good friends; others are acquaintances, and some have never met, but together we provide one "snapshot" of what animal rights, liberation and advocacy looks like from the perspective of grassroots activists from the Twin Cities. We believe that our position mirrors dynamics in other cities throughout the world, and we look forward to seeing books from activists throughout the country sharing their own grounded perspectives.

As an interdisciplinary scholar and social justice activist, I would be remiss if I did not comment on another element of this "snapshot," one that counters the diversity of individuals recognized in the paragraph above. I've looked for ways to make the following statement in an eloquent way; however, such rhetoric undermines the truth of the observation. Therefore, I'll just say it, just as Sarahjane acknowledges in the Preface: *We are all white.* This is not an apology, but a reality that is problematic, yet expected. In 1998, Wesley Jamison noted in "A Profile of Animal Rights Activists": "Anecdotal and ethnographic accounts of the racial composition of the movement suggests that it consists of white activists. This speculation is confirmed by the various research projects" (65). More recently in 2011, Emily Gaarder reaffirms Jamison's earlier account of racial disparity in her own exploration of why so many women are drawn to the animal rights movement (15). Part of this lack of diversity, at least as far as this book goes, can be explained by the region from which we write, as Minnesota is approximately eighty-five percent white (U.S. Census Bureau). However, this demographic cannot be used to excuse our lack of diversity, nor should it diminish the work of animal advocates who are not white. Rather, I hope that it empowers the animal advocacy community with which I work to continue to look for ways to be more inclusive, as it is something that we regularly discuss but to which there are no immediate answers. We do not want to fill a quota, but to find ways to connect with oppressed groups that can make both us, as animal proxies, and them, as culturally marginalized, a more dynamic presence both locally and globally.

With that noted, we as author/activists come together to inform and inspire a culture that is often hostile to our views and/or misinformed about our goals. As the tenor of this book will show, our ultimate objective is to change people's perceptions of nonhuman animals. As ethical vegans, we all purposefully avoid animal products, byproducts, items tested on animals, and venues that exploit animals. Veganism is a foundation of these essays, even those that do not openly address it. This, in part, explains the book's title. While *we* see veganism as an inherent part of animal liberation, not everyone chooses veganism for those same reasons.

The authors of this text are vegan animal activists, advocates and liberationists who have experienced the joys and disappointments of outreach. The essays we have written spring from those moments of elation, frustration, encouragement, failure, success, shame and strength. Therefore, while theories of animal liberation, animal rights and critical animal studies factor into these essays to differing degrees, experience is the principal research that informs this collection. As termed by feminist-vegan scholar Carol J. Adams, this style of writing is aptly viewed as "engaged scholarship," or theory in praxis. As used in this text, "engaged scholarship" indicates studies by those who are allied with social issues on a street level, fully connected with the ideas, theories and struggles of which they write. With no keys to the ivory tower and limited access to the microphone, these are the voices that most need to be sounded.

Additionally, I wanted to develop this book project because so many divisions within the AR/L movement seem to spring from human ego and ideology clashes. To some extent, the derision is beneficial, as debates can help us determine best practices, which is at the very heart of a movement that seeks to expose cruelty and oppression. Too often, however, egos and fixed strategies overshadow the emphasis on animal liberation. We may "win" (or "lose") arguments with what we perceive as the opposition here and there, but these are pyrrhic victories if the cage doors remain soldered shut. In sum, we cannot let our differences with other activists distract us from our ultimate objective — *the cessation of animal suffering as sanctioned, overseen and administered by human beings.*

The authors of *Confronting Animal Exploitation: Grassroots Essays on Liberation and Veganism* were approached with a simple question: "If you could say one thing about your veganism and/or animal advocacy to the world, to those both within and outside of the animal liberation movement, what would it be?" The varied responses can be found within the following pages. No one was told what topic to write about to fill gaps in a pre-conceived agenda. However, we did ask that those who label themselves from a specific philosophical animal liberation viewpoint explain the position from which they write. For many, this means explaining the contentious term "abolitionist," a label that others in this book reject.

Fortuitously, each author provided his/her own distinctive take on that initial question, resulting in an array of essays that vary in theme, tone, and approach. And they all demonstrate courage from a group of advocates many of whom, prior to this book, did not consider themselves writers. As the book project progressed, Sarahjane and I were not sure if we would divide the book into sections. However, as the essays came in, we noticed four diverse areas into which each could fit: "Theory for Praxis," "Veganism in Action," "Narratives of Change," and "Moving Toward Revolution."

"Theory for Praxis" begins with Dallas Rising's "Turning Our Heads: The 'See No Evil' Dilemma." She uses psychology, scholarship and personal experience to help activists understand why the public refuses to look at animal suffering and how, by recognizing that, we can help them see the evil inherent in animal industries. Travis Elise's "Anti-Capitalism and Abolitionism" follows, proposing challenges to ownership of the term "abolitionism" (in an animal advocacy context) by law professor Gary Francione and considers the ways in which an assessment of capitalism, an inherently violent economic system, must be integrated into a new definition of the word. My following essay, "'Just tell the truth': A Polemic on the Value of Radical Activism," also argues against capitalist ideology, but with focus on veganism as a spinoff of the diet-industrial complex and the limits of reform and rights. Ultimately, I argue for all who agree with my theoretical premises to embrace the terms "vegan" and "radical" without fear or artifice. Finally, Patrick McAleer, Stephen King scholar, offers "Literary Analysis for Animal Liberation: Stephen King's Animal Kingdom," innovatively showing how popular fiction, analyzed within the parameters of the burgeoning academic discipline of critical animal studies, can open space for consideration of nonhuman animals as beings with inherent value, not as tropes for humans.

The next section, "Veganism in Action" explores challenges to and strategies for going — and staying — vegan for life, offering ideas for what the concept of veganism in action looks like. Herein, Al Nowatzki adds to the growing cultural focus on vegan parenting in a unique way. "Vegan Parenting: Navigating and Negating Speciesist Media" considers how to steer through the cultural obstacles of raising vegan children when they are consistently bombarded with speciesist media, even that which is putatively animal-friendly. Chelsea Youngquist Hassler follows with "On Cheese, Motherhood and Everyday Activism." The personal journey that Chelsea describes offers a list of ways that one can integrate vegan activism into her life when dealing with friends and family whose responses to veganism range from curious to hostile. And she writes this essay as a new mother in a geographical region known for its love of cheese. Elizabeth Cook's "Till Vegan Do Us Part? Personal Change, Interpersonal Relationships and Divorce" tackles the difficult issues one faces when deciding to become vegan, or, more specifically and importantly, an animal activist. She also addresses the uncomfortable topic of how one's lifestyle changes can lead to marital discord and divorce.

Melissa E. Maaske's "Introducing Speciesism to the Rescue Community" is the first essay in the section "Narratives of Change." Therein, she recounts her paradoxical experiences of working with those who love animals enough to rescue certain species while still consuming others. She also offers practicable ideas for introducing speciesism to animal rescue organizations, as they may be more open to understanding speciesism than those who are not concerned with any animal issues. In Dallas Rising's second essay of this section, she uses "Tales of an Animal Liberationist" to present snapshots of what daily animal liberation activities look like, from rescuing stray dogs to saving fish from suffocation by the lakeside. These are potent stories meant to guide and inspire those who feel overwhelmed by the depths of animal suffering with which they are daily surrounded. Rounding off this section is "An Oral History of the Animal Rights Coalition," through which Mary Britton Clouse, Charlotte Cozzetto, Heidi Greger and Vonnie Thomasberg explore three decades of local abolitionist activism and how they have been able to maintain a consistent message against challenges both within and outside of the animal liberation movement.

This book's final section, "Moving Toward Revolution," contains identifications of and potential remedies for the obstacles that the authors see preventing the animal advocacy movement from liberating nonhuman animals, which will surely take a revolution. M. Ryan Leitch's "Killing Them Softly: Marketing a Movement, Marketing Meat" assesses how animal rights and so-called humane meat are marketed to their respective audiences, calling for both critical analysis of marketing terms and authenticity in how advocates represent themselves and their beliefs. With the recent rise in backyard farming and animal organizations cooperating with animal industries, Melissa Swanson offers the timely essay "How 'Humane' Labels Harm Chickens: Why Our Focus as Advocates Should Be Egg-Free Diets, Not Cage-Free Eggs," showing the ways in which there is no such product as a humane egg and resounding the call that those concerned about animal (mis)treatment become vegan. In my second essay of this collection, "The 'Dreaded Comparisons' and Speciesism: Leveling the Hierarchy of Suffering," I consider the potential for and pitfalls of making comparisons of suffering between "racialized" human and nonhuman animals. With two classic animal rights studies as a foundation, I historicize and analyze the outcomes of these comparisons, proffering ideas for both when they should cease and how they can be beneficial. Aaron Zellhoefer's "Animal Enterprise Acts and the Prosecution of the 'SHAC 7': An Insider's Perspective" offers a firsthand account and critical assessment of governmental acts that specifically protect animal industries while also demonizing animal liberation activists. With explicit focus on the "SHAC 7" legal case, Aaron exposes the blatant unconstitutionality of legislation that targets the First Amendment rights of animal advocates. Sarahjane Blum writes the concluding essay of this section, "Some Things Get Better, Some Get Worse: On Being Scared, Being Around, and Trying to Be Kind." Sarahjane uses stories from her extensive history within the AR/L movement and wide range of strategies to consider where the movement has been, how it has changed and how it needs to change if it is to be less conflict-ridden and more effective.

Finally, pattrice jones — long time activist, friend and inspiration to many of us who developed this book — writes the Afterword. Her body of work has given the world a consistent message of peace, parity and defiance in the face of injustice. For all of these reasons, we are honored that she has agreed to offer this text's closing thoughts. More importantly, pattrice ends this collection of challenging essays with her own challenges to those who've penned them. She offers support for and critique of the "snapshot" we've developed as one that should be more diverse and less divisive. Her concluding message demonstrates how much work is left to be done, yet also how much compassionate effort and important work is currently being accomplished by the authors of this collection.

Before concluding, a word about language is required. The authors of this collection see themselves as animals; thus, we are all torn by the too easy binary of humans/animals or humans/nonhuman animals. In Joan Dunayer's preface to her book *Speciesism*, she notes this quandary: "Even the word nonhuman divides all animals into two, seemingly opposed categories: humans and everyone else. With equal validity we could recognize all animals as robins or nonrobins" (xi). However, because there are millions of animal species apart from humans, the authors of this book will variously use the terms "animal," "nonhuman," "other-than-human animal" and "nonhuman animals" to designate those beings who are not *Homo sapiens*. As human animals are writing this book, we make these designations for the sake of simplicity and look forward to a day when, perhaps, we can find terminology that won't continually reinforce the human/animal binary that causes so many of the problems discussed within this volume.

In sum, we put forth these essays to inform, educate, persuade, inspire, enrage and enlighten. We see this book as a start to a broader dialogue amongst grassroots activists, scholars and the community. This collection is written for our supporters, our dissenters and the merely curious. Most importantly, it is written for the untold number of animals who continue to be manipulated, exploited and slaughtered by human beings who, to varying degrees, do not see their value. We hope this book will inspire change as it opens people's eyes to uncomfortable and violent truths that underlie our culture, and sometimes even our movement.

Can we read ideas we don't agree with but understand the passion that prompts those ideas? Can we sit with someone who shares our compassion for animals but challenge their liberatory methods? Can we honestly believe that another's ideas are misguided, even counterproductive, yet still call that person a companion in the battle for the hearts and minds of a mainstream public who overtly and covertly partake in animal abuse? I cannot speak for all the authors in this book, so I'll answer for myself: "I hope so."

Let the dialogues begin.

Works Cited

Adams, Carol J. "The Sexual Politics of Meat." Indiana University of Pennsylvania Women's Studies Organization. Indiana, PA. 22 Apr. 2009. Lecture.

Dunayer, Joan. *Speciesism.* Derwood, MD: Ryce, 2004. Print.

Gaarder, Emily. *Women and the Animal Rights Movement.* New Brunswick, NJ: Rutgers University Press, 2011. Print.

Guither, Harold D., Ed. *Animal Rights: History and Scope of a Radical Social Movement.* Carbondale: Southern Illinois University Press, 1998. Print.

Jamison, Wesley. "A Profile of Animal Rights Activists." Guither 60–72. Print.

jones, pattrice. *Aftershock: Confronting Trauma in a Violent World—A Guide for Activists and Their Allies.* New York: Lantern, 2007. Print.

U.S. Census Bureau. "State & Country Quick Facts." www.census.gov, 17 Jan. 2012. Web. 4 June 2012.

Section I. Theory for Praxis

Turning Our Heads
The "See No Evil" Dilemma
DALLAS RISING

I'm standing in the basement of Coffman Union at the University of Minnesota next to a television playing a looped DVD of the slaughterhouse documentary *Meet Your Meat*. The TV is visible to a group of students through a glass wall of a small market where they are waiting in line to purchase energy drinks and pre-wrapped deli sandwiches. Several of the students glance for a few moments at the screen, watching as a cow hanging upside down by one leg is having her throat slit, and her blood flows out of her to the rhythm of her still beating heart. Some of the students stiffen, some flinch, some of their eyes widen at the sight. But within a couple of moments, most of them turn away, make their purchase, and take off for somewhere else. I remain at the table with the video and my piles of leaflets and continue to wait for the bravest of them to stop and *really* watch. I pray that some of them have heard what the animals are saying in their squeals and moans and squawks. In her story "Am I Blue?" Alice Walker writes: "The animals have not changed. They are in fact *completed* creations (at least they seem to be, so much more than we) who are not likely to change; it is their nature to express themselves. What else are they going to express? And they do. And, generally speaking, they are ignored" (5). My experiences at the U of M prove her assessment to be true.

Having spent much of the past thirteen years bearing witness to these magnificent "completed creations" and working to get the public's attention focused on what they are trying to express, I have felt firsthand the sting of being ignored both personally and on their behalves. I find it curious that my anger is directed at the people who ignore the violence being done to animals more often than it is actually toward the people committing the crimes. To me, the act of turning away and pretending not to see is just as offensive as the violence itself. Walker's words resonate with me and resound questions about why my species continues to close their ears to other animals' cries. It is clear that the animals' expressions are not enough to stop the viciousness of humankind against them. When I started to speak on the animals' behalves, it didn't take me long to learn that the same people who are content to ignore what animals have been attempting to communicate directly to them are not easily reached by my ambassadorship either. Indeed, feeling ignored is a constant experience of animal rights activists, as I imagine it is for the animals themselves.

Abolitionist activists are especially apt to be ignored and censored, even by other animal rights activists. As abolitionists, we refuse to look away from the hanging cow having her throat slit, and we challenge the idea that animal exploitation is acceptable as long as we do it "humanely," as we know that is an impossibility. As abolitionists, however, rather than remain angry at those who turn their heads, we need to understand why they do so, further contemplating how to make them stop, look and take action. We need to go beyond thinking that people who do not agree with us are evil, even while we contend against their "see no evil" stance. Through such understanding, we may better be able to give new voice to and cease the suffering of our fellow creatures.

After reading Walker's story, I started to wonder: what, exactly, are the reasons behind people ignoring what animals are trying to say, and, by extension, what animal rights activists are trying to say, even when they recognize that animal cruelty and animal suffering at human hands are wrong? While I do not feel that I have found complete answers to these questions, I surmise that people ignore animal misery for three primary reasons: (1) we have divorced ourselves from other animals and the natural world, (2) we are terrified to risk alienation from our social groups, and (3) we are constantly being persuaded by cultural forces to forget the violence we inflict on animals because it is traumatic for us to face those realities. While all of these reasons work in tandem, I will deal with them singly within the sections below.

Divorced from Nature

Before the beginnings of human civilization, before human beings physically and mentally sequestered themselves from the rest of the global community of other animals, we lived in relative concord with the rest of the natural world, taking what was needed to survive as a species. We traveled to find food and warmth and lived in close proximity to other animals, rivers, and trees. Even a popular creation story in our culture starts out with humans in nature: Adam and Eve in the Garden of Eden. But recently, in relative terms, we have divorced ourselves from nature and distanced ourselves from almost every other animal species. Not only have we distanced ourselves, but we have elevated ourselves to be "masters" over all other life on Earth. This domination of life has caused untold pain, suffering and destruction for all life on our planet. Not one form of life has escaped the terror with which we have flooded the world.

In *Eternal Treblinka*, a comparison of our treatment of animals and the Holocaust, Charles Patterson writes, "In the first century B.C.E., Cicero, the Roman philosopher and statesman, maintained that everything in the world was created for the sake of something else," with "a character in one of his writings declar[ing] that 'men can make use of the beasts for their own purposes without injustice'" (19). Patterson later points out Plato's notion of the "Great Chain of Being," which was prevalent throughout the population of Greece, as being especially relevant within the development of Western culture. This worldview benefited the Greeks, as it presumed that they "ranked higher than non–Greeks, women, slaves, and, of course, animals [...D]ifferent beings ranked hierarchically on a chain that descended from the immortal gods on high, down through humans to animals, plants, stones, and dust at the very bottom" (21). While humans have begun to shift toward a more holistic view of the world, we still take this self-appointed power for granted and hold onto our presumed supremacy.

During this complex process of inflicting human will on the rest of the Earth, humans have universally adopted an ethnocentric view of all things. In *Animal Rights/Human Rights*, sociologist David Nibert explains ethnocentrism as "the view of things in which one's own group is the center of everything, and all others are scaled with reference to it" (12). The ethnocentric view that our species holds makes it difficult for us to consider nonhuman animals as beings independent from our own needs and wants. In "Am I Blue?" Walker uses various forms of human oppression to help her reader connect the dots to see the suffering of a horse named Blue. That is an effective way to get people with an ethnocentric viewpoint to recognize animal suffering, but it does little to address the root problem of ethnocentricity, which is why humans cause animal suffering in the first place. This way of thinking has been the norm for our species for so long, that it has been culturally packaged as reality without alternative.

Writer and political cartoonist Vance Lehmkhul opens his article "The Decline and Fall of Human Supremacy" by illustrating this very point. He states,

> From antiquity up to a few hundred years ago, it was understood by nearly all human beings that the sun revolved around the earth. This made sense because as we were the center of consciousness, creation and the universe itself, the cosmos should logically be set up as a backdrop to humanity. Thinking otherwise was heresy for some and discouraged for all [6].

Just as people were discouraged — by threat of death, in some cases — from proposing that our planet was not, in fact, the center of the galaxy, those working to dispel the myth that human beings are superior to nonhumans, and that we inherently deserve control and power over other life forms, are ignored, ridiculed, and threatened. Consequently, adopting an abolitionist perspective that attempts to mend the rift with nature opens one up to threat of social ostracism.

Terrified of Alienation

Throughout my years of working to educate the public about animal issues and encouraging people to adopt a vegan lifestyle as a way to reduce animal suffering, I have noticed that those who are most likely to stick with the changes they make in their diets are the ones who have the most social support. Definition of the word "vegan" has come under scrutiny recently due to increased interest in animal issues, so any discussion of the lifestyle should be supported with a definition of what the term even means. Jack Norris, RD, director and co-founder of Vegan Outreach, has this to say on the issue of defining veganism: "Being vegan to me means one thing: an attempt to reduce the intense suffering of nonhuman animals. To me, saying 'I'm vegan' is synonymous with saying, 'I have decided to live a lifestyle that does not support animal exploitation.'" This is all well and good, and it seems a noble ethical path, but strangely, when one makes the decision to limit suffering in the way Norris describes, s/he is very often met with hostility from friends and family.

Elizabeth Cherry confirms my observations on social support in "Veganism as a Cultural Movement," which summarizes a study she conducted that looked at what influences people who are vegan but *not* vegan activists. Cherry affirms that "maintaining a vegan lifestyle is not dependent on individual willpower, epiphanies, or simple norm following; it is more dependent on having social networks that are supportive of veganism" (157). In fact, in my experience, it is a lot easier to find a substitute for dairy than it is to feel like you are suddenly separated from and misunderstood by close friends and family members. The feeling of being different than and apart from dominant culture is worse than any craving for cheese or ice cream could ever be.

Someone who has experienced or witnessed unspeakable violence often undergoes resulting feelings of being disconnected from his or her peers who have not been a part of that violence. Judith Herman, trauma expert and clinical professor of psychiatry at Harvard Medical School, describes the conflict a victim or witness experiences in the aftermath of violence in this way:

[S]he often comes into conflict with important people in her life. There is a rupture in her sense of belonging within a shared system of belief. Thus she faces a double task: not only must she rebuild her own "shattered assumptions" about meaning, order, and justice in the world, but she must also find a way to resolve her differences with those whose beliefs she can no longer share [178].

I have been familiar with this dynamic from a very early age. For example, when I was in fourth grade and learned about animal testing and how animals are killed to make meat, I was horrified. Knowing that my mother loved our guinea pigs and rabbits at home, and remembering how she had pet the cows with me at the State Fair, I thought that all I would have to do would be to tell her what I had learned, and she would want to become vegetarian with me.

However, my mother did not respond to the terrible news about what was happening to animals on farms and in laboratories in the way I had wanted her to. Suddenly, I was not only distraught about the animal cruelty I was still trying to wrap my young brain around, but also about how my mom could say she cared about animals but not enough to make any changes in her diet. That was the moment I decided I didn't want to be just like my mom anymore. There were only parts of her I wanted to emulate. Not only did I lose my faith in my own species, but I lost the image of my mom as a perfect being as well. It was painful, confusing and, as Herman notes, isolating.

One instinct we have yet to stifle in ourselves is the need to be accepted by others of our kind. We have survived in the wild by working within social groups, and the desire to belong is primal and powerful. Rejection actually occurs as an innate danger to us on a gut level, so going against the status quo is perceived as a real risk to our feelings of safety. The connection between alienation and shame may shed some light on why many people who feel sympathetic toward animal suffering will not take the risk of speaking out against it. It may also be why potential abolitionists take the path of welfarism — attempting to regulate animal abuse, rather than working to abolish it. In *Aftershock*, long time activist pattrice jones explains the connections between shame and alienation. She states, "Our bodies are programmed to respond to that feeling of aloneness with shame in order to motivate us to do whatever we need to do to regain the safety of the social group," and she wisely notes that feelings of shame can often be intolerable (28). In short, being accepted and not "rocking the boat" trumps compassion for many people, and they have an arsenal of ethnocentric reasons and excuses to defend their choices to turn away from the suffering they see.

Admittedly, I sound angry and arrogant in that last sentence, and one could accuse me of adopting a "holier than thou" attitude. However, I won't deny that I am angry. I'm furious, and I will no longer be ashamed of it. That said, I admit that I have fallen prey to the same way of thinking that I critique above. I too have turned my head and bitten my lip so that I would not risk rejection, and I have been ashamed of myself as a consequence. For example, I kept silent when my husband's mother organized a second wedding reception for us and served meat. The reception was supposed to be a celebration in our honor, and my husband and I (who met at an animal rights meeting, no less) didn't say anything about it. I spent the duration of the party in the garage so that I wouldn't have to smell the dead animals being cooked in the house. In an attempt to absolve my guilt, I tried passing the blame to my husband, arguing that he should have been the one to confront his mother. However, the truth is that I was too afraid of being rejected by his family to risk voicing my distress about the meat at the reception. To this day, I regret staying silent. Consequently, I have learned that turning our heads doesn't only harm the animals; it harms us as well.

Confronted by Trauma and Violence

Judith Herman's *Trauma and Recovery*, as noted on the book jacket, is lauded as being "universally recognized as a classic in the field of psychology." And while her book is not animal specific, I find that it applies to my experiences bearing witness to animal suffering and cruelty. Animals who endure violence and abuse are victims of suffering and trauma as well. Therefore, it is quite natural to adopt and adapt her theories directly within consideration of violence toward animals and of the people who are exposed to that trauma within the role of activist, as I will in this section.

People often assume that there are only two parties involved in violence: the victim and the perpetrator. We forget that there is often a third party to a violent episode: the witness. However, this witness need not be present to observe the violence. Anyone who listens to the victim is a witness. Anyone who sees a photograph or a video image of a crime after it has been committed is a witness. Anyone who has seen the scars and the psychological damage of a victim is a witness. Here, Herman explains the choice every witness to violence needs to make:

> It is morally impossible to remain neutral in a conflict. The bystander is forced to take sides. It is very tempting to take the side of the perpetrator. All the perpetrator asks is that the bystander do nothing. He appeals to the universal desire to see, hear, and speak no evil. *The victim, on the contrary, asks the bystander to share the burden of pain.* The victim demands action, engagement, and remembering [8].

I would be hard pressed to come up with a more concise and eloquent way to describe the dilemma that a person exposed to the realities and scope of animal suffering is thrust into. It is tempting to look the other way and ignore what is happening, especially when looking the other way seems so much easier than trying to help the vulnerable and weak, and especially when you may become alienated for caring too much.

Herman goes on to further explain the dilemma in which the witness is placed and how the perpetrator tempts the witness into turning her head away: "In order to escape accountability for his crimes, the perpetrator does everything in his power to promote forgetting. Secrecy and silence are the perpetrator's first line of defense. If secrecy fails, the perpetrator attacks the credibility of his victims. If he cannot silence her absolutely, he tries to make sure that no one listens" (9). The fact that slaughterhouses, factory farms, animal research facilities, fur farms and other horrors that animals are subjected to are hidden behind closely guarded doors or in out of the way locations points to one level of secrecy.

Animal advocates are generally forced to obtain photos and video of these operations by conducting undercover investigations because our requests for tours are repeatedly denied, even when we offer to cover any costs incurred and meet at the convenience of the perpetrator. This emphasizes the perpetrator's determination to keep his actions secret and out of the view of the public. In fact, the animal-industrial complex is so determined to keep animal activists from exposing the trauma and violence inherent in their industries, that they are trying to pass so-called "ag gag" bills across the country that will penalize such investigations. For example, as noted on Will Potter's blog, in my state of Minnesota, "House File 1369 was introduced to criminalize production of an 'image or sound' of animal suffering in a sweeping list of 'animal facilities,' including factory farms, animal experimentation labs, and puppy mills." Perpetrators thrive on secrecy, and these bills support the abuse they want to hide.

When animal rights activists have been able to obtain photos and video footage documenting the abuse of animals, our credibility and evidence are routinely challenged. Herein, my suppositions about issues of trauma for both victim and witness are confirmed by Herman. She concludes, "It is not only the [victims] but also the investigators of [traumatic] conditions whose credibility is repeatedly challenged" (9). Defending one's credibility to a hostile audience, especially about issues of such great importance, is something most people would rather avoid, especially when the perpetrator — in this case, the animal-industrial complex — is so powerful.

In *Why We Love Dogs, Eat Pigs and Wear Cows*, Melanie Joy, social psychologist and professor, explains the concept of carnism (the ideology of meat eating) as a coercive cultural system "in which eating certain animals is considered ethical and appropriate" (30). In my interview with Dr. Joy, she explained that the reason well-intentioned people who are "generally kind to animals" turn away from animal cruelty (particularly when it comes to how they respond to information about animals being made into meat) is because

> people do care about animals, and don't want them to suffer — and yet the thought of not eating animals can feel daunting and overwhelming. So, people turn away from information that puts them in a position where they have to choose between knowingly violating their integrity (harming an innocent being) or make a dramatic lifestyle change they may not be ready for.

Joy punctuates this theory by explaining, "Babies are eating animals before they can even talk." Another primary reason people turn their heads to the realities of systemic animal cruelty is that they fear the distress they may experience as a result of the betrayal of trusted people and systems. They choose to ignore reality because it may feel uncomfortable to experience the pain of being lied to by people who were supposed to have taught them right from wrong. Further, they choose not to experience the psychological and emotional consequences of realizing they have unknowingly been made a victim *and* a perpetrator of torture and violence. Instead, they just look the other way and pretend they don't see. Life is just easier that way.

But not really. It only seems easier for the time being. In reality, turning our heads in an effort to avoid dealing with the messiness of our horror, guilt, and impious treatment of other animals offers only a false sense of serenity. The truth doesn't go away, and it cannot be suppressed forever; it is always there, and we cannot avoid it indefinitely. The role of the abolitionist activist is to hasten this cultural confrontation with the truth. Martin Luther King, Jr. makes a beautiful, startlingly revealing and pointed distinction between this false sense of peace and true justice in his classic "Letter from Birmingham City Jail":

> I must confess that I have been gravely disappointed with the white moderate. I have almost reached the regrettable conclusion that the Negro's greatest stumbling block in the stride toward freedom is not the White Citizen's Counselor or the Ku Klux Klanner, but the white moderate who is more devoted to "order" than to justice, who prefers a negative peace [which is] the absence of tension to a positive peace which is the presence of justice.... We will have to repent in this generation not merely for the vitriolic words and actions of the bad people, but for the appalling silence of the good people.

The animal liberation movement struggles with the same obstacles to justice that Dr. King describes in his letter. There is no shortage of good people who recognize that what our species is doing to other animals is unconscionable, but the vast majority of them insist on ignoring the issues to avoid the discomfort and risks that go along with challenging them. Simultaneously, others make compromises that result in slightly bigger cages and a couple more centimeters of wing-span space. Ultimately, however, this posturing amounts to nothing more than "the appalling silence of good people."

Regardless of all of these strong social forces, it is imperative that we challenge the accepted nature of human supremacy and speciesism. To understand speciesism, one need not go any further than *Merriam Webster's Online Dictionary*; simply put, speciesism is defined as "1. prejudice or discrimination based on species; *especially* discrimination against animals 2. The assumption of human superiority on which speciesism is based." Our challenge as abolitionists is a challenge against the speciesism within ourselves and that manifests in others, including other people who claim to care for animals. While it is never easy to be that person who voices an unpopular belief, it is crucial that we do so when it comes to animal exploitation. In fact, it is morally imperative.

A local folksinger and songwriter, Ellis, wrote a song called "Take A Risk" that encourages people to speak out for what they believe. I find the words so inspiring, that I offer them here as an anthem for abolitionist activists: "Take a risk / Find yourself in the middle / There are others like you working to make things right / ... You can't rely on the world to change for you / You can start to use your voice and that's the best that you can hope to do." While I appreciate these lyrics, I also contend that we can do more than use our voices — and we must by taking deliberate and consistent steps to end animal oppression. That said, I don't believe one can get very far or last very long if she is afraid to speak the truth, however unpopular that truth may be. And we certainly aren't likely to inspire others to join the animal liberation movement if we stay silent. If you care about animals but eat them and/or their byproducts, if you abhor animals in cages but work to get them bigger cages, you are staying silent.

Conclusion: The Abolitionist Pledge to Help Others See

My husband occasionally performs wedding ceremonies for non-religious friends. One afternoon we arrived early for a wedding so he could prepare himself and the couple for a ceremony. I told the bride how beautiful the backyard looked, and she said that the groom was nervous about someone sinking into a mole hole in the yard and getting hurt. She went on to tell me how much he hated the moles and was threatening to kill them. I promised her I would look into humane mole removal and get some information to her soon.

A few minutes later, I saw the grass near my feet start to shift and quake. "Oh no," I thought, "Stay down there, little guy!" I glanced around nervously, hoping the groom wouldn't notice the shifting grass. But he did, and he erupted in fury. He shouted to another man to go to the shed and get his shovel. He looked at me and said, "You're not going to want to watch this." I looked at him and said, "I'm not going to let you do this." I was terrified. He was angry. It was his yard and his wedding day, and here I was telling him what he can and can't do. However, I would be damned before I would let him kill that mole if I could prevent it. I took a few steps and placed my feet on either side of the moving grass. For the moment, the groom was still. He wasn't challenging me, though his buddy was coming up behind him with the requested shovel.

I saw a piece of plywood and pointed to it, saying, "If you bring me that piece of wood, I'll lay it down over the mole and stand on it the whole afternoon. You have my word that this mole will not ruin your wedding day." I felt like I was shaking inside, so I was surprised at how clear and calm my voice sounded. "You can turn around and put that shovel away now," I said to his buddy. The groom stayed silent and just looked at me for a few moments. I could tell he was angry, but he eventually turned to his friend and said, "Put it away." I stood guarding the mole for the next forty five minutes or so, until the ceremony was over and the groom came up to me and apologized for being "such a jerk." He said he was just really stressed out and he was sorry I had to meet him like that. A few weeks later, I ran into the bride, and she reported that her husband's attitude toward the moles had changed since their wedding day. "He's not going to kill any of them," she said with a smile.

I have wracked my brain trying to come up with better or more eloquent advice to budding activists than "use your voice," but nothing else has materialized. You may be skeptical of the promised impact of speaking the truth and standing up for what is right. Sure, the mole story is nice, but it's just anecdotal. Even as I write this, I wish there was something more substantial and measurable that I could offer as a solution. However, I do know that words carry tremendous power, and it takes courage to speak up when you aren't repeating socially accepted sentiments. My thought is that there are many, *many* people who care about animals, enough so that if they all acted according to their consciences, the amount and depth of animal suffering and death would dramatically lessen. Right now, however, not enough people are giving voice to what they *really* believe because they are blocked by the issues of nature, alienation, culture and trauma that I have explored in this essay.

Animal abolitionism begins with breaking through those obstacles and being honest about what we find when the myths are exposed. Then we can have faith in something better, a something better on which *we will not compromise.* If we can put our faith in words and back them up with appropriate actions, we have a shot at creating our vision of the world we want to live in, rather than just surviving this one.

Works Cited

Cherry, Elizabeth. "Veganism as a Cultural Movement: A Relational Approach." *Social Movement Studies* 5.2 (Sept. 2006): 155–170. *Academic Search Premier.* Web. 11 Oct. 2007.

Ellis. "Take a Risk." *Blueprint Live.* Rubberneck Records, 1998. CD.

Herman, Judith. *Trauma and Recovery: The Aftermath of Violence—from Domestic Abuse to Political Terror.* 14th Ed. New York: Basic Books, 1992. Print.

jones, pattrice. *Aftershock: Confronting Trauma in a Violent World—A Guide for Activists and Their Allies.* New York: Lantern, 2007. Print.

Joy, Melanie. Personal Interview. 19 Oct. 2007.

_____. *Why We Love Dogs, Eat Pigs and Wear Cows: An Introduction to Carnism.* San Francisco: Conari, 2010. Print.

King, Jr., Martin Luther. "Letter from a Birmingham Jail." *African Studies Center.* University of Pennsylvania. Web. 2 Jan. 2011.

Lemkuhl, Vance. "The Decline and Fall of Human Supremacy." *Vegetarian Voice* 28.2 (2005): 6–7. Print.

Nibert, David. *Animal Rights Human Rights: Entanglements of Oppression and Liberation.* New York: Rowman & Littlefield, 2002. Print.

Norris, Jack. "One Thing." *Defining Vegan.* VeganOutreach.org. Web. 2 Jan. 2011.

Patterson, Charles. *Eternal Treblinka: Our Treatment of Animals and the Holocaust.* New York: Lantern, 2002. Print.

Potter, Will. "'Ag Gag' Bills and Supporters Have Ties to ALEC." greenisthenewred.com, 26 Apr. 2012. Web. 26 May 2012.

Walker, Alice. "Am I Blue?" *Living by the Word: Selected Writings, 1973–1987.* Reprint. New York: Houghton Mifflin, 1989. 3–8. Print.

Anti-Capitalism and Abolitionism

Travis Elise

The most contentious issue presently within the animal rights movement is without question the debate over strategy. There are some who advocate for promoting incremental animal welfare legislative reform, others who advocate for boycotts, others for vegan education, some for sabotaging private property and directly liberating animals from spaces where they are exploited, and yet others advocate strict non-violent pacifism. Gary L. Francione, a law and philosophy professor at Rutgers University, may currently be the author who has drawn the largest amount of attention and criticism from within the movement. Francione describes his theory of strategy as abolitionism. After examining the strengths and weaknesses of Francione's theory and its major critics, I will lay out a revised and expanded theoretical framework for the abolition of animal exploitation.

I will focus primarily on the criticism of Robert Garner, a philosopher from the University of Leicester specializing in political theory. Garner is not the only critic of Francione's, but he co-authored a book with Francione — *The Animal Rights Debate: Abolition or Regulation?*— and, as such, has contended in most length with Francione's theories (as opposed to strategies). I will also analyze criticism offered by Norm Phelps, Bruce Friedrich, and Peter Singer.

Francione's Abolitionism

The basis of Francione's theory of abolition is laid out his book *Animals, Property, and the Law*. In it, he argues that as long as animals are property, they are theoretically unable to have rights. Those who try to regulate animal use engage in a "balancing" act of interests between those of the animal (as property) and those of the human (as property owner). In the end, the interests of the human property owner — no matter how trivial comparable to the interests of the animal — will win out. This normative theory of rights parallels

22

our society's legal theory as well. As Francione explains: "It is a fundamental premise of our property law that property cannot itself have rights as *against* human owners and that, as property, animals are objects of the exercise of human property rights [emphasis mine]" (4). By extension, efforts to regulate "animal use [do] not, as a general rule, transcend that level of protection that facilitates the most economically efficient exploitation of the animal" (5). Dubbing these efforts legal welfarism, he investigates the way laws aiming to reduce animal harm recast concepts like "humane" and "unnecessary suffering" to represent drastically different ideas than they do in everyday use (5). These laws and phrases exist because we, normatively speaking, regard animals differently than mere inanimate objects. However, because legally property rights trump animal interests in our society, and due to common law's social purpose being wealth maximization, animal welfare legislation protects animals only insofar as it coincides with economic interests (5).

Because of this, Francione finds problematic any strategy based on regulating animal use through legal reform. First and foremost, the strategy is inconsistent on a theoretical level in Francione's view. If a practice is morally wrong, it should not be campaigned and/or advocated for even if it would result in reduced suffering. For instance, if it is morally wrong to torture and murder someone, one not should advocate for murder without torture (Francione, *Rain* 141–146). Second, the primary motivating force behind animal welfare legislation is not a concern for animal well-being but rather profit incentive. Most so-called "improvements in animal welfare" are really just more economically efficient forms of exploitation and only incidentally reduce exploitation. Market forces make industry and legislators reluctant to enact changes which would create a competitive disadvantage, and regulating bodies such as the World Trade Organization (WTO) that prohibit trade barriers for moral reasons also prevent meaningful reforms from taking place. Third, Francione argues that such reforms ameliorate the public's uneasiness with animal exploitation, thus counteracting the work of vegan education campaigns which attempt to educate the public about the intrinsic value animals have and the immorality of animal exploitation. Fourth, animal advocacy groups benefit from such reforms even when they are hollow since they can prop them up as victories in order to ensure a steady flow of donations from supporters (*Vegan Freak Radio*).

Francione argues welfare reforms are most often changes in production that would have happened anyway and are frequently more economically efficient forms of production. This is not a new phenomenon; 1958's Humane Slaughter Act required the stunning of cattle prior to them being shackled in the slaughtering process in order to protect workers from being injured by being hit by animals struggling and swinging in midair. Rendering cows immobile also limits carcass damage and, thus, product loss. Therefore, the Humane Slaughter Act resulted in improved economic efficiency and better profit margins for animal exploiters (Francione, *Rain* 95–98).

A more current example involves the slaughtering of poultry. Animal welfare advocates have been promoting an alternative to dipping the heads of chickens into electrified water to stun them. The new method promoted by People for the Ethical Treatment of Animals (PETA) and the Humane Society of the United States (HSUS) is called "control atmosphere killing" (CAK) or a similar alternative "control atmosphere stunning" (CAS) which involves gassing birds before they are shackled and hoisted. One of the main selling points used by PETA and HSUS for CAK/CAS is that they reduce production costs by "decreasing carcass downgrades, contamination and refrigeration costs; increasing meat yields, quality, and shelf life; and improving worker conditions" (Francione and Garner 33).

In a 2007 podcast hosted by Erik Marcus, Francione claims that industry reforms ameliorate public concern over animal treatment in a few key ways. First, voluntary industry reforms touted by companies like Whole Foods Market and approved by groups like HSUS give the public the idea that such products are ethical to consume. Second, campaign victories such as those in Florida and California have a similar affect. Due to this, a "happy meat" movement distracts from the movement's true message, the abolition of animal exploitation. The result is a theoretically confused agenda and message.

Garner as Critic

One of Francione's most significant critics is Robert Garner, a philosopher from the University of Leicester specializing in political theory. He believes Francione's thesis is exaggerated. Garner argues that since animals have more protection in certain places than others (e.g. in Britain and Europe generally more than the U.S.) and since the property status of animals is more or less universal, there must be other factors which cause this discrepancy. These factors are varying societal values and public opinion, the dominance of animal exploiters as an interest group in politics, and the prevalence of a certain form of liberal ideology in society. Garner does concede the property status of animals is incompatible with a genuine animal rights or liberation agenda, but maintains that significant changes in animal well being can be achieved while animals are regarded as property.

To support his claim, Garner cites a number of British legislative moves. A recent ban on fox hunting with hounds has widespread public support. Additionally, the National Trust, an owner of land and historical sites in

Britain, has banned deer hunting on its property as a result of pressure from animal protection groups. Furthermore, veal crates, sow stalls and tethers have been banned in Britain since 1968. Since the property status of animals is the same in Britain and the rest of Europe as it is in the U.S., Garner maintains there must be an alternative explanation for the difference in animal status in the U.K.

Garner cites public opinion as one aspect of his alternative theory. Vegetarianism, for instance, is much more common in Europe and Britain, especially compared to the U.S. As stated above, there is widespread disapproval of hunting, though the actual effect of the laws Garner cites is disputed. Garner finds Francione's claim that "animals have only one right, the right not to be treated as property" to be inconsistent with a genuine animal rights agenda since animals can be exploited when they are not property. For instance, most animals who are hunted are not property, and throughout history, property has not always existed as a concept. Garner maintains the abolition of the property status of animals is not only unnecessary to end animal exploitation but also insufficient ("Political Ideology" 77).

Critiquing Garner

The validity of Garner's critique of Francione's thesis rests on several questions. Has animal welfare reform been successful? How does one measure success? Is animal suffering being reduced? Are the profits of animal exploiters being affected negatively or positively? Has the demand for animal products reduced or increased? Do the effects on demand result in an effect on the vegan movement and is this effect sustainable? In other words: do people go vegan due to welfare reforms, do they just reduce their consumption, or neither? Throughout his books, as well as on his blog, podcasts, and in various interviews, speeches, and others essays, Francione cites countless examples of reforms which do very little for making animals lives better; in fact, they help animal exploiters become more profitable, while fattening the bank accounts of animal welfare nonprofits. And all of this occurs while sending an overall confused message to the public about the movements' views of the moral status of animals and the implications of that status. Francione confidently states that animal welfare has been a complete and total failure. As he notes in his debate with Garner:

> You (Garner) appear to think that a heavy burden rests on the opponent of welfarism to demonstrate that it is ineffective and the abolitionist approach which focuses on nonviolent vegan education, would be better. You *assume* that welfarist reform is effective and that the abolitionist approach would not work [206].

While Garner admits many welfare reforms have the effect of improving productivity for animal exploiters, he nonetheless believes this not to be true in every situation (Francione and Garner 208–209). However, even with the ban on fox hunting with hounds that Garner cites as an example of successful legislation, Francione finds loopholes which are publicly known and used by hunters. Fox hunting with hounds is still legal. More hounds are registered for hunting than ever before and hunting is on the rise. Garner concedes that the law isn't perfect, but argues it accomplished its purpose by reducing suffering. However, when one's litmus test for success is simply a reduction in suffering, success becomes much easier than the eventual and incremental abolition of the exploitation of animals.

Another issue to examine is Garner's view of the role of public opinion and the influence of animal exploitation industries on the state. Like many critics, Garner seems to think Francione's whole solution is to promote veganism and nothing else. This is a mischaracterization of Francione's view. What he fails to see is Francione's assessment of the present movement and how vegan and animal rights education is simply a first step. Francione believes that had the animal rights movement begun promoting a consistent vegan message from its early days, it would already have a significant base from which it could then use to push for real legislative changes to incrementally chip away at the property status of animals. Without such a base, change is impossible. Garner argues vegan education is necessary but should be paired with political action, yet he is unable to show that current political action is not, as Francione describes, a total failure.

At another point in Francione and Garner's *The Animal Rights Debate*, they discuss the merits of the Humane Slaughter Act, with Garner asking Francione if the movement should not have supported the legislation (208–209). However, Francione had already analyzed this dilemma in *Rain Without Thunder* through his discussion of the "thirsty cow" scenario (141–146). The thirsty cow scenario, offered by Ingrid Newkirk of PETA, asks whether one should offer water to a thirsty cow on her way to the slaughterhouse. For Newkirk, this scenario refutes the abolitionist position since suffering reduction (giving water to the thirsty cow) and abolition (maintaining the position that the cow has a right not to be exploited) are not in opposition to one another.

Francione disputes Newkirk's analogy by drawing a distinction between macro and micro activity. Giving water to a thirsty cow on the way to slaughter may be the morally correct thing to do for the individual is such a situation (the micro) but that does not equate to designing a strategy to which a social movement should orient itself (the macro). Garner makes the same sort of error as Newkirk does. He fails to acknowledge several key realities regarding macro-based legislative reforms. One is that such legislative demands take up a monumental amount of time, energy, and resources. Does one choose to spend enormous amounts of time, money, and energy in lobbying efforts which, in the end, make animal exploiters stronger, more respectable in the public eye, and more profitable, all while only marginally improving the lives of animals? For Francione, the answer is an obvious no. Instead, abolitionists should articulate why such reforms are farces and the reason why animal exploiters often agree to them (it makes them more profitable) and why animal welfare organizations campaign for them (it gives them campaign victories to tout when fundraising). Francione argues that abolitionists should do this while also articulating a consistent and coherent animal rights message to the public instead of using debatable and inexact buzz words like "cruel," "compassionate," and "humane." In sum, abolitionists should be principled in their message by conveying an honest vision of how animals should be morally viewed and treated by humans.

Bruce Friedrich and Norm Phelps as Critics

Aside from Garner, Francione has been critiqued by both Bruce Friedrich and Norm Phelps. Friedrich is the former vice president for policy for PETA and is currently senior director of strategic initiatives for Farm Sanctuary. Norm Phelps is a writer, the former spiritual outreach director of the Fund for Animals, and a founding member of the Society of Ethical and Religious Vegetarians (SERV).

In an article with the *Huffington Post* and another for *Satya* Magazine (co-authored with Peter Singer), Friedrich lays out his critiques of Francione's abolitionism. In "Getting from A to Z: Why Animal Activists Should Support Incremental Reforms to Help Animals," Friedrich argues (similarly to Garner) that since countries with stronger animal welfare laws also have higher rates of veganism and vegetarianism, this refutes Francione's claim that such laws ameliorate public uneasiness about consuming animals. Friedrich's claim is difficult to assess since he doesn't cite any examples. So let us hypothesize what he is referring to.

If Friedrich is referring to the lack of welfare legislation in other parts of the world such as the Global South and other less industrialized parts of the world, it would be disingenuous to suggest this is solely due to lack of an animal rights movement. Both factory farming and animal experimentation are staples of the industrialized Western world. One will not find laws regulating the treatment of animals in institutions in places where such institutions don't exist. Also, historically, vegetarianism, veganism, and the animal movement emerged in the industrial age within the middle class. Many parts of the world have not reached such a stage of industrial development.[1]

The question over the effects welfare reform has on animal product consumption and the popularity of veganism has drawn much dialogue amongst Francione, Garner, Phelps, Friedrich and Singer. Francione acknowledges the absence of any empirical data on the matter, but claims his position can be supported intuitively. Garner counters by rephrasing Francione's evidence as anecdotal. At one point in their *Satya* article, Friedrich and Singer state:

> If one were to believe what those who oppose welfare campaigns are saying, one might imagine before these reforms, large numbers of people were refusing to eat meat, but now they have decided that, because animals are not treated so badly, they can eat meat again. That is not the case, of course. Rather than salve consciences, passage of the AWA [Animal Welfare Act] and HSA [Humane Slaughter Act], as well as the advance of the fast food campaigns, have placed the issue of cruelty to farmed animals before millions of people as an important societal issue. That can only help to advance the day we're all striving toward.

Friedrich and Singer don't provide any evidence for this claim. However, in a later article, Friedrich cites Norm Phelps's elaboration on their claim as supporting evidence.

Phelps's essay "One-Track Activism: Animals Pay the Price" portrays Francione's position as a two-prong argument. The first argument is that the "'welfarist' message undercuts the 'abolition' message and it makes it easier for the public to eat animal products with a clear conscience." The second of Francione's arguments is that such reforms "reinforce the legal status of animals as property and does not challenge that status directly" and is therefore "counterproductive." What Phelps fails to cite as an underlying argument in Francione's position is the economic efficiency of such reforms. Phelps argues that such campaigns are resisted by animal exploiters because they will cause demand to decrease as production and consumer costs rise. He cites the Center for Consumer Freedom, a well known public relations organization used by corporations and industry groups like United Egg Producers and the Animal Agriculture Alliance, as evidence that the industry opposes welfare reforms. In truth, however, corporations oppose *all* reform, for it creates a situation in which demand for regulation may become stronger, more challenging and more threatening in the future.

The study cited by Friedrich and Phelps in support of welfare reform came out of Kansas State University,[2] stating the following: "As a whole, media attention to animal welfare has significant, negative effects on U.S. meat demand" (quoted in Phelps, "Science Weighs In"). Citing that sentence, Phelps declares that "the findings (of the study) are clear and unequivocal."

Are they? After examining Phelps analysis, it becomes clear that his claim is overstated. The study finds that animal product consumption is affected negatively by media attention focused on animal welfare. Specifically, the consumption of eggs, poultry, and pork are affected negatively. Beef consumption was unaffected. Phelps argues that the reason beef was unaffected is because cattle are "the least horrifically treated of all factory farmed animal" and because the welfare campaigns focused on pigs, egg laying hens, broiler chickens, and turkeys and "did not, by and large, deal with cows" ("Science Weighs In"). Phelps also says the study concluded that consumers who reduced their consumption of pigs, chickens, and turkeys did not switch to consuming cattle.

He ultimately decides that media attention on animal welfare was caused by welfare reform campaigns. However, he doesn't speculate on whether it was merely the media attention on the issue which caused the drop in consumption (as the study claims) or whether the success or failure of such campaigns had any effect or, if there was one, how long the effect lasted. Imagine if all the campaigns initiated by PETA, HSUS, and Farm Sanctuary had failed. Would the effect on consumption be the same? Perhaps, perhaps not. I can speak from anecdotal experiences that the "happy meat" movement (as it is called) has made many vegetarians and even vegans go back to consuming animals. It would be interesting to see a study examining the recidivist rates of former vegans and vegetarians and the reasons they give for going back to consuming animal products.

Once done lauding that study, Phelps undermines his own position. He claims veal consumption dropped during the height of the anti-veal campaigns of the 1980s and '90s, only to rise again when the campaigns subsided. Phelps notes Francione's position that the increase in veal consumption arose from ostensibly better treatment of veal calves. Phelps, of course, counters Francione's position by claiming that veal consumption rose because of the aforementioned decline in welfare/reform campaigns and the surge in media attention that arose from said campaigns. There are two main problems with Phelps's argument.

First, Phelps fails to correctly cite Francione's blog post "What Battle Are We Winning?" Francione specifically states that reforms in the veal industry, according to animal welfarists and the industry itself, has led to increased consumption of calves because the public feels better about how the animals are treated. Citing from Farm Animal Net, a website sponsored by major animal welfare organizations such as PETA, HSUS, Farm Sanctuary, and the Animal Welfare Institute (AWI), Francione notes: "Strauss (the main veal producer in the United Sates) asserts that veal consumption rose in Europe, where individual veal stalls are now illegal, during the 5 to 10 year conversion process there" (quoted in "What Battle").

Second, Phelps does not address Francione's claim (made in the very post Phelps references) that the new production model in Europe is beneficial to the producer. In HSUS's article "Strauss Veal and Marcho Farms Eliminating Confinement by Crate," Texas A&M animal scientist Dr. Ted Friend is cited during his testimony before Congress in 1989: "[T]he crated calves required approximately five times more medication than those in the less confining environments." Phelps and Friedrich ignore Francione's commentary that most animal welfare reforms actually make the animal exploitation industry *more profitable* and *more efficient*, as proven by Friend's statement.

Finally, Phelps fails to see how the decline of the veal campaign and its effect on veal consumption is problematic as support for his theory. To suggest that negative media attention on animal exploitation industries through welfare reform campaigns have a negative effect on consumer demand for animal products is not a surprising revelation, nor does it blow a hole in the abolitionist position. Is simply reducing demand for a product really the type of strategy the movement should be pursuing, especially when there is no sign of the consumer downturn in demand being sustainable? The movement and its goals should not be measured in animal product consumption associated with a particular single issue campaign at a particular period of time, but should be measured by the number of ethical vegans in society and their organizing capacity to expand the vegan movement, which could eventually reach critical mass and threaten animal exploitation as a whole.

There are three final points that need mention in support of Francione's thesis. The first concerns voluntary industry standards such as the Certified Humane Raised & Handled label endorsed by such groups as HSUS and the American Society for the Prevention of Cruelty to Animals (ASCPA) and rising popularity of local, grass-fed, organic and similarly labeled animal products. This phenomena does not increase the market price of animal products because they are voluntary regulations and are not imposed by the government. As such, the industry does not resist them. They exist because they supply a niche market of conscientious omnivores who are willing to pay a premium price for such products, some of whom are former vegans and vegetarians. Since these products are actively promoted by groups like HSUS and ASCPA, it is quite clear that the animal movement is sending the message that such products are ethically acceptable.

The second point touches on Francione's view of the property status of animals. A common mischaracterization of Francione's views consists of claiming that, according to his theory, regulating animal use is impossible as long as animals are property. This is not Francione's view. According to him, we could in theory regulate animal use all we wanted to, including banning certain practices and so on. But we don't because animals are property and as such their social and individual purpose is often to make profit and, therefore, the property status of animals militates against regulating animal use.[3]

Finally, to fully understand Francione's abolitionism, one must comprehend his notion of opportunity cost. Every dollar and minute spent on one campaign equals one dollar and one minute which cannot be spent on another. Given the enormous amount of energy and funding spent on welfare reform campaigns and how little money is invested in vegan education campaigns, the movement's direction is clearly that of welfare. Moreover, there is no sign that such campaigns are successful, nor that a decline in animal product use is sustainable due to negative media attention. If the movement had decided to invest in vegan education campaigns back in the 1980's instead of welfare reforms, it is likely we would be in a much stronger place today.

A General Critique of Francione

The first critique of Francione's thesis, which I share with Garner, is skepticism toward Francione's insistence that the only right which animals have is the right not to be used as property. While Garner claims that the abolition of the property status of animals in neither sufficient nor necessary, I argue it is necessary but not sufficient. It is necessary for the reasons Francione argues, namely that the property status of animals militates strongly against any serious protection of animal interests since the interests of property are discounted when weighed against the interests of property owners. The abolition of the property status of animals is not sufficient since one can easily imagine situations in which animals are exploited yet are not considered property. Hunting is a classic example. The hunted animal is not necessarily the property of anyone. The harm done to wild animals by never ending human expansion such as deforestation, mining, oil drilling, and urban sprawl is another example of this. Respecting the most basic interests of animals is the end goal of the animal rights movement. The most basic interests which animals have are not to be killed, enslaved, or deprived of basic needs, not to be relieved of property status.

An Anti-Capitalism Critique of Francione

Another difficulty with Francione's thesis is his apparent lack of a defined political ideology. As such, I will present an anti-capitalist analysis to be paired with Francione's abolitionism. While Francione does not openly embrace capitalism and even praises the work of anti-capitalists such as Bob Torres[4] and

David Nibert,[5] Francione nonetheless neglects to incorporate an anti-capitalist analysis into his theory. Since animals are private property and are exploited primarily as commodities with profit value, another avenue of strategy for ending animal exploitation would be to abolish private property and, thus, the profit motive. In other words, abolish capitalism.

Capitalism is an economic system in which the means of production are owned and controlled by a class of non-producers called the bourgeois or the capitalist class. Meanwhile, a much larger class of producers actually produce the goods and services of society. They are called the proletariat or the working class. The working class must survive by selling their labor power to the capitalists for a wage. The wage is not a full return for the value of the worker's labor power. When the product is sold to a consumer, the rest of that value, minus the labor power, goes to the capitalist in the form of profit. Karl Marx refers to this as surplus value.[6]

To illustrate, imagine a group of workers who labor in a factory making widgets. The workers churn out widgets all day long for their wages. The capitalist then sells the widgets to consumers and takes in, say, one million dollars in revenue in a given month. About thirty percent of the revenue goes to cover the cost of supplies and overhead costs of the factory. Another five percent goes to pay interest on loans and twenty five percent goes to paying the workers' wages. Where does the remaining forty percent of the revenue end up? Profit! That's surplus value. The surplus value goes to provide the capitalist with a luxurious life free of want or need while the rest is reinvested so the capitalist can accumulate more profit and further invest in capital.

To continually increase capital, capitalists must keep finding new commodities to sell, even things that, in the past, were never seen as commodities but as natural resources, such as water. Most nonhuman animal exploitation occurs when animals are commodified. Whether for food, scientific research, clothing, entertainment or any other use, animals are bought and sold as commodities, with the profit extracted reinvested into more capital to be used for producing more commodities (i.e., more animals).

As the profit-incentive of competition causes capital to expand more and more, living and working conditions are sacrificed and capitalism becomes a nightmare for human animals, nonhuman animals and the environment. The following consequences make up that nightmare: increased work production without increased wages, poverty wages, unemployment, slashed benefits, wars for oil and other resources, enslavement of cheap labor and resource theft in the Global South, inner city housing gentrification that displaces the urban poor, urban sprawl into rural areas, chronic health conditions caused by unhealthy commodities and a toxic environment, massive consumerism, education and health care debt, and the prison industrial-complex through which capitalists use public funding for profit.

The profit incentive militates against any attempt to control capitalism. While the working class can force capital to retreat and reorganize, it cannot control it. A humane form of capitalism is impossible. The only solution is to abolish it.

Many in the animal advocacy movement argue that capitalism is not a fundamental obstacle for the abolition of animal exploitation. This belief contains the hidden premise that the abolition of capitalism is not necessary for the abolition of human exploitation either. Yet, as critics of capitalism have demonstrated, this is not the case. For any abolition of animal and human exploitation to occur, capitalism must also be abolished. As Susan Finsen asks so eloquently in her essay, "Obstacles to Legal Rights for Animals," "Is it likely that this massive system, which has so far ignored the most basic interests of human beings around the globe, can be bent to consider the interest of animals?" (quoted in Nibert 246).

Sociologist David Nibert argues in *Animal Rights/Human Rights: Entanglements of Oppression and Liberation* that working toward abolishing capitalism is a necessary step towards the liberation of humans and other animals. Nibert, a socialist, confidently declares, "The social system that is most conducive to the liberation of both devalued humans and other animals is socialism — a *true* socialism that reconfigures contemporary technological and productive capacity to meet the material needs of the world's inhabitants without oppression" (251).[7]

In an exchange between Garner and Francione in their book, Garner likens the abolitionist ideology to that of a particular radical left strand of thought which believes that social revolution is closer to reality when the conditions of the working class are at their worse. The view that class oppression furthers revolutionary potential is a common view held by many on the revolutionary left. The rationale is that when conditions get bad enough, the agitation of the working class will reach a breaking point and revolution will follow. Conversely, when capitalists grant concessions to the working class, it fosters a climate of class peace, and revolution is not seen as an advantageous option.

Francione objects to the analogy by arguing that workers have a certain level of moral worth and are not treated merely as means to an end, whereas animals are. While I agree with Francione, I think it misses Garner's point. Regardless of the moral status of animals or workers in society, Garner is saying the abolitionist position for ending animal exploitation demands that things get worse before they get better. However, I do not believe that things have to get worse for animals, or for humans, for a revolution to occur. Building the vegan movement, as Francione argues, works to make things better in the here and now.

It is also useful to construct a more accurate analogy between the animal rights movement and the radical left and/or the broad socialist movement.[8] It is valuable to find common trends between human animal and nonhuman animal liberation movements, especially for younger, less experienced activists so that they can draw lessons from the past instead of making similar mistakes and thinking they must reinvent the wheel to liberate animals. That said, there is no question that the animal rights movement is different and unique from all other human struggles primarily because humans possess a degree of social organizing ability which most animals lack.[9] This key distinction between the animal rights movement and other movements should be kept in mind when making such comparisons.

Continuing with the analogy, if the broad socialist movement represents the animal rights movement, then clearly socialism or the abolition of capitalism represents animal liberation or the abolition of animal exploitation. Additionally, the main group of people in need of liberation are animals and the working class (or all of humanity as some might argue). The enemies are the animal exploiters and the capitalist class.

From an abolitionist perspective, one can see similar patterns of movement development between the two causes. One is the prevalence of class collaboration between capitalists and labor or working class "leaders" on the one hand and collaboration between animal exploiters and animal welfare, or so-called "animal rights" groups, on the other. In a particular historical period in the class struggle, representatives of the working class have engaged in forms of class collaboration which served to benefit themselves (the representatives) as well as the capitalists at the expense of the workers whom they were supposed to represent. A classic example of this is the emergence of no-strike pledges, dues check-off, grievance procedures, the closed shop, and the rise of bureaucratic unionism.

In past labor struggles, high points of strikes, sit-down strikes, massive picketing, boycotts and engaged union membership would dwindle after any given fight subsided, whether it ended in a victory or a loss. This occurred in the Lawrence (Massachusetts) Textile strike in 1912 led by the Industrial Workers of the World (IWW). Twenty five thousand textile workers went on strike under the banner of the IWW, yet within a year of the strike ending, there were only about 700 dues paying members left in Lawrence (Lens 159). The same happened to the Congress of Industrial Organization (CIO) and the United Auto Workers (UAW) during the sit-down strike wave of 1937. In late 1937, after the sit-down strikes at the Fisher Body plant in Lansing, Michigan, workers began to flock to UAW. The local had 8,027 dues paying members at its peak. In less than a year, it only had 1,078 (Wetzel).

After these cycles, unions struck deals with capitalists, agreeing to no-strike pledges in exchange for dues check-off (Burn 55–57). The no-strike clause forbid workers from striking during the duration of a contract, thus removing the workers' greatest weapon. Dues check-off consists of employers taking dues out worker's paychecks and passing them along to the union. This allows unions to sustain its dues income and not waste the resources to collect the dues from members individually. It also resulted in the union or closed shop. The union shop or closed shop requires workers to pay union dues. Refusal to pay dues could result in termination of employment (Wetzel). In cases such as this, the capitalists got what they wanted: a benign workforce unable to strike to halt production. The smooth flow of commerce was ensured and future capitalist profit secured. The union bureaucrats got guaranteed dues income to maintain their salaries. Meanwhile, laborers became subjected to a bureaucratic grievance procedure in which their grievances were negotiated and dealt with by management and union representatives often without worker input. In other words, workers were abandoned by the unions who were supposed to advocate for them.

These historical lessons bear striking similarities with the current animal rights movement. As Francione has pointed out countless times, welfare reforms actually result in improved productivity and higher profits for animal exploiters. These reforms are supported and campaigned for by animal protection organizations. Francione argues these campaigns benefit animal organizations because they are propped up as victories which are used in fundraising drives. The animal exploiter, like the capitalist, gets better productivity and more profit, and the animal protection organization, like the bureaucratic union, gets a steady flow of income to maintain salaries. Due to this opportunism, the interests of animals and more effective strategies to serve their interests are disregarded to serve the economic interests of bureaucratic animal organizations.

In light of these commonalities between the animal rights and socialist movements, Francione's opposition to mainstream corporate nonprofits animal welfare organizations needs a constructive critique. Francione's strategy for dealing with opportunistic animal welfare organizations is to ignore them. While I do share the same view of these organizations as Francione, I would recommend a more proactive approach. The most effective way of diminishing the influence these organizations have is to create alternative organizations which can challenge the organizational and ideological supremacy of groups like PETA, HSUS, and Farm Sanctuary.

The blueprint for an alternative organizing model is radically different than that of the large corporate nonprofits and substantially different than that of the traditional small, more democratic, grassroots organizations as well.

Based on mass organizing models from other social movements, this structure is more egalitarian and democratic than that of most animal advocacy groups. In large corporate nonprofits, members typically have no power or influence. Those in power, including the board of directors, are usually self-appointed and have no accountability to the membership. The bureaucracy sees only the revenue supplied by members and the free labor that comes from them in the form of volunteer and internship hours. Even more progressive grassroots organizations don't have very democratic structures, though they typically do better work and are more principled in their politics than larger groups. Still, power generally lies in the hands of a select few people.

In contrast, the alternative structure used by many mass political organizations would place the general membership in control of the organization. Any executive officers that do exist would be answerable to the general membership. The general membership would, through democratic and participatory decision making, steer the direction of the organization in terms of both campaigns and ideology. For instance, campaign proposals, positions statements, funding allocations and so on would be decided by the general membership and not the officers. The role of officers becomes merely administrative.

This paradigm breaks down the barrier between an organization's membership and its bureaucracy, allowing members to develop a sense of ownership and control of the organization. It also fosters individual growth within the organization, allowing for members to develop leadership and organizing skills in order to build them into more effective animal advocates. These organizers can then go out and win campaigns and pass along their skills to others. By winning campaigns, organizers develop confidence in themselves and the movement.[10] By passing along their skills to others, organizers, in a sense, reproduce themselves. This makes it possible to build a base more rapidly.

Confident organizers can protect groups from the typical rates of burnout, disillusionment, and attrition that are common in all social movements but rampant in the animal rights movement. The stability which this organizing model offers can aid the movement in weathering social crises which have traditionally been disastrous for the animal advocacy and vegetarian movements. Historically, for instance animal advocacy and vegetarian organizations have prospered in times of peace and prosperity and have declined in times of crisis such as wars and economic downturns. A strong, member-empowered organization can be a source of institutional memory which can preserve collective knowledge instead of having to start all over again after every downturn of movement momentum.

In addition to animal liberation, such an organization should place anticapitalism and human struggles on its agenda as well. The movement can gain insight from the more mature human struggles of social movements which have a greater wealth of collective knowledge about organizing than does the animal rights movement, which has been held back through its corporate organizing structures thus far. By participating in human struggles, the abolitionist animal rights movement can foster respectful relationships across a range of issues, win converts to the cause of animal rights, and build unity around basic points of agreements with other movements and organizations. This coalition building can become a basis for campaigns which may begin to erode the property status of animals. Nibert argues for such cross movement solidarity. He proclaims, "[A] view (held by mainstream animal advocates) that ignores the possibilities that socialism may offer for liberation of other animals unduly limits visions and strategies for political alliances and social change" (243).

A Critique of Francione on Violence

One very controversial position of Francione is his condemnation of groups and individuals who promote violence and property destruction, such as the Animal Liberation Front (ALF). In "Commentary #5: On Violence," Francione makes three arguments for his rejection of violence. First, he rejects violence on ethical grounds, though he avoids discussing his pacifist views. Instead, he makes two practical arguments against the use of violence.

First, he argues violence is a useless strategy since it doesn't affect the demand for animal products. If, for instance, a factory farm, fur farm, or animal experimentation lab closes because of property destruction, another will simply take its place. Only by reducing the demand for animal products, argues Francione, can abolition of animal exploitation occur. Therefore, vandalism and property destruction, like legislative welfare reform, are a waste of activist time and resources. Only through "creative, nonviolent vegan education" can the demand for animal products ever be chipped away. His other practical critique of violence is that it is alienating to the general public. Vandalism and property destruction make an average person view the perpetrators as terrorists and criminals rather than freedom fighters.

Let us examine these two practical critiques before delving into a philosophical deliberation on violence. Francione argues that violent strategies do not affect the demand for animal products. However, he is forgetting that violent methods are often not intended to reduce demand for animal products but are used to liberate individual animals. Liberating these individual animals is a justified and a worthy goal in its own right. He also declares that violence is alienating and off putting to the general public, but I contend against the empirical claims of this argument. Do violent methods make others look upon the movement in an unsympathetic light? For some, it surely does. But for others, I am equally sure this is not the case.

When violence is used, such as highly-publicized ALF actions, animal exploiters are exposed to the public. This exposure can have positive results for the movement. Individuals may be exposed to visual depictions of animal exploitation which they have never encountered before. Thus, some may begin to think about animal exploitation differently. Francione's argument assumes all violent acts used against animal exploiters have the same goal in mind (financial damage), which is not always the case, as their acts can be seen to expose the horrors of animal industries as well. He also assumes the public uniformly looks upon such acts negatively.

Another possible example to counter Francione's claims are open rescues, which involves liberating an animal from a place of exploitation (such as a factory farm), filming the rescue and being open about the motive behind it (to help the animal). The media is often alerted and veterinary care is provided for the rescued animal. No vandalism or any other property damage is done other than trespassing and theft (i.e., taking the animal from his/her confinement). Would Francione take issue with this form of action since it does involve violence in the sense that property rights are being violated?

Even without deciding the merits of ALF activity, open rescues, or any other form of property destruction, Francione needs to take the issue more seriously. Furthermore, he should seriously consider the implications of his long-term movement strategy. If the vegan movement grows to a point where it has a significant base and legislative action becomes a viable possibility for abolishing the property status of animals (which Francione acknowledges is a goal of his strategy), then he is, in fact, endorsing the use of violence. The violence he endorses is the violence of the state. Since Francione endorses the use of state violence, a critique of his general pacifist ideology is required.

As a pacifist, Francione claims violence only begets more violence and cannot be a strategy for establishing peace. As he put it:

> The reason that we are in the global mess that we are in now is that throughout history, we have engaged and continue to engage in violent actions that we have sought to justify as an undesirable means to a desirable end. Anyone who has ever used violence claims to regret having to resort to it, but argues that some desirable goal supposedly justified its use. The problem is that this facilitates an endless cycle of violence where anyone who feels strongly about something can embrace violence toward others as a means to achieving the greater good and those who are the targets of that violence may find a justification for their violent response. So on and on it goes ["A Commentary on Violence"].

Francione's rejection of violence raises some challenging questions. How does Francione advocate pacifism and still endorses government legislation? After all, any endorsement of state intervention in society is an endorsement of violence. The state can be defined as an entity which has a claim to the monopoly of the legitimate use of physical force or violence in its territory (Weber). Francione's advocacy for nonviolence is usually accompanied by examples of social reform coming about due to nonviolent means such as the U.S. Civil Rights Movement in the 1950's and '60's. The Supreme Court decision Brown v. Board of Education in 1957, which ruled segregated public schools to be unconstitutional, resulted in clear state intimidation. The case of the Little Rock Nine involved President Eisenhower ordering federal troops to escort nine black children into school in order to enforce desegregation against a non-compliant school district as well as a racist and possibly violent white citizenry. Francione and other pacifists ignore the fact that this was a form of state violence in which the violence of the state was used against the potentially violent racist white community of Little Rock, Arkansas.

Francione's pacifist ideology also prevents him from acknowledging that his position in society is protected and ensured by violence. As an American citizen in the twenty-first century where the United States uses violence throughout the world to guarantee the subjection of the people of the Global South, Francione is a privileged subject of a violent empire. By failing to realize how his social status in society is enabled by violence, Francione also fails to realize the implications of his pacifism. He sees the use of violence in a vacuum devoid of circumstances or historical context. History has demonstrated that violence is a natural and completely reasonable response from the oppressed against the oppressor.

For example, it is reasonable and expected for a woman to respond violently towards a man who attempts to rape her. Francione acknowledged this on the *Michael Medved Show*. But it would seem to follow that, on a larger scale, a group of oppressed people could reasonably resist their oppressors through armed struggle. Yet Francione seems to condemn this, a condemnation that is hard to defend. There are countless historical examples of armed struggle being the only rational choice when the oppressed are faced with violent opposition. Peter Gelderloos, in *How Nonviolence Protects the State*, makes this point in a very polemical yet still convincing way. He writes:

> Nonviolence declares that the American Indians could have fought off Columbus, George Washington, and all the other genocidal butchers with sit-ins; that Crazy Horse, by using violent resistance, became part of the cycle of violence, and as "as bad as" Custer. Nonviolence declares that Africans could have stopped the slave trade with hunger strikes and petitions, and that those who mutinied were as bad as their captors; that mutiny, a form of violence, led to more violence, and, thus, resistance led to more enslavement. Nonviolence refuses to recognize that it can only work for privileged people, who have a status protected by violence, as the perpetrators and beneficiaries of a violent hierarchy [24].

It is a contradiction for Francione to advocate for legislative reform in the distant future when a serious vegan movement has been established as a political base and yet condemn any form of what he sees as violence. If Francione has no moral qualms with forcing the general population to respect the interests of animals through the violence of the state, why does he have a problem with a group of animal liberationists from doing so on their own? Even though Francione believes the movement needs to involve a "revolution of the heart," he can't really expect everyone to be won over with persuasion. After all, there are still white supremacists in our society. How can he expect there will not always be speciesists in society? People of color are protected from white supremacists by the violence, or threat of violence, from the state as well as by their own communities and anti-racist allies. Does Francione condemn these examples of violence? If Francione doesn't condemn such an example of violence, while still condemning the use of violence when used against animal exploiters, he is acting hypocritically.

In general, Francione's criticisms of violent tactics is one devoid of nuance and is often paired with tactics many find disturbing. He has censored people on his website's forum (Battuello), and he publicly outed individuals who support illegal tactics, encouraging others to inform the authorities about such individuals (Potter). Further, he has engaged in an ongoing war of words with Steven Best, a professor at University of Texas, El Paso who supports ALF-like methods. Consequently, Francione's tactics have made many look upon him negatively as a movement leader (Yates). From my experience, some have completely written off his views of movement strategy due to his problematic personality. In many discussions within the movement, Gary Francione the person receives more attention than Gary Francione the theorist. He appears to condemn others who write off his abolitionism as being "divisive," "fundamentalist," "utopian" as a way to avoid seriously addressing the substance of his arguments. His ability to do this comes from a position of power and privilege.

Francione's brushes off his own critics in similarly broad strokes. While his views on welfare reform may be accurate and his views on building a solid political base through vegan education may be the correct path for the movement, as a movement leader, Francione's ability to persuade others in the movement is compromised by his problematic and, some might argue, authoritarian personality.

Conclusion

Gary Francione has impressively documented that the animal advocacy movement's strategy has been one of total, epic failure through its refusal to consider the property status of animals and how it militates against any effective legislative reform. The narrative Francione has constructed depicts welfare reforms as counterproductive wastes of activists' time, which serve to make animal exploitation more economically efficient. These reforms are promoted by an opportunistic animal welfare advocacy bureaucracy which upholds such reforms as victories in fundraising campaigns to maintain their bureaucracies and their healthy executive salaries. This strategy has done very little for the well being of animals and has helped animal exploiters become more profitable. Further, welfare and reform have sent a confused and contradictory message to the public about the moral status of animals which has helped to ease the collective guilt of an animal-exploiting citizenry. Francione has convincingly defended this narrative against critics like Robert Garner, Bruce Friedrich, and Norm Phelps. His critics have failed to provide a convincing counter-narrative that demonstrates the effectiveness or even the potential effectiveness of the current strategy of the animal advocacy movement.

While Francione's thesis holds up to its critics, it also needs revision and expansion. His strategy for the movement is, first and foremost, to expand the base of the movement (which one could say is the real measure of the movement, as opposed to the movements supposed claims of "victories"). Also, Francione's solution to abolishing animal exploitation is to simply abolish the property status of animals. There are problems with both his means of achieving animal rights/liberation and his strategies for expanding the movement's base. Francione supports increasing a foundation for animal advocacy via nonviolent vegan education. However, his opposition to violent tactics is inconsistent with his long term strategy of then using a political ideology to enact legislative change. His personal behavior toward others in the movement, particularly those who are supportive of what he considers to be violent tactics, is problematic and compromises the influence his theoretical contributions may have on the movement.

Additionally, the means of his strategy are not elaborated upon. Democratic, collectively controlled organizations which build members into confident, skilled organizers and leaders is a proven method — commonplace in historical social movements — which can contribute to expanding and strengthening the animal rights/liberation movement.

Francione's solution to abolishing animal exploitation is to abolish the property status of animals. This is not only an insufficient strategy, but it also fails to account for the economic implications of private property and the destructive nature of the capitalist mode of production which accompanies it. In addition to abolishing the property status of animals, the other most effective means of achieving animal liberation is abolition of private property itself. This means the abolition of capitalism.

NOTES

1. This is not to imply that only middle-class people can be animal rights advocates nor that only in an industrialized society can such a movement develop. I am merely showing a historical pattern.

2. For the full report, see Glynn T. Tonser and Nicole J. Olynk's "Impacts of Animal Well-Being and Welfare Media on Meat Demand" in *The Journal of Agricultural Economics* 62.1 (February 2011): 59–72.

3. Francione attributes this view to Cass Sunstein in his interview on *Vegan Freak Radio,* Episodes 94 and 95.

4. See Bob Torres, *Making a Killing: The Political Economy of Animal Rights.* (Oakland, CA: AK Press, 2007).

5. See David Nibert, *Animal Rights/Human Rights: Entanglements of Oppression and Liberation.* (New York: Rowman & Littlefield, 2002).

6. For Marx's discussion of surplus value, see *Capital Vol. 1: A Critique of Political Economy.* (London: Penguin Classics, 1992)

7. Here the word socialism can be interpreted in a broad sense: a society in which the means of production are owned and controlled socially and things are produced for use and not profit. This use of the word socialism is shared by Marxists, anarchists, and other socialists alike. For Garner's critique of a socialist theory of animal liberation, see *The Political Theory of Animal Rights* (Manchester, UK: Manchester University Press, 2005). For a Marxist view, see Ted Benton, *Natural Relations: Ecology, Social Justice, and Animal Rights.* (London: Verso, 1993)

8. Broad socialist movements can include democratic socialists, communists, anarchists, libertarian Marxists, as well as other variations of socialism.

9. This is not to suggest animals lack agency or autonomy. For an excellent analysis of animal agency see: Jason Hribal, "Animals, Agency, and Class: Writing the History of Animals from Below." *Human Ecology Review.* 14.1 (2007).

10. A similar point is made by Nate Hawthorne in "Mottos and Watchwords: A Discussion of Politics and Mass Organizations."

WORKS CITED

Battuello, Patrick. "Banned by Fellow Vegans." examiner.com. Clarity Digital Group, n.d. Web. 28 May 2012.

Burn, Joe. *Reviving the Strike: How Working People Can Regain Power and Transform America.* Brooklyn: Ig Publishing, 2011. Print.

Francione, Gary L. *Animals, Property, and the Law.* Philadelphia: Temple University Press. 1995. Print.

_____. "A Comment on Violence." *Animal Rights: The Abolitionist Approach,* 13 Aug. 2007. Web. 22 May 2012.

_____. "Commentary #5: On Violence." *Animal Rights: The Abolitionist Approach,* 22 Aug. 2009. Web. 22 May 2012.

_____. "More on Violence and Animal Rights." *Animal Rights: The Abolitionist Approach,* 22 Mar. 2009. Web. 22 May 2012.

_____. *Rain Without Thunder: The Ideology of the Animal Rights Movement.* Philadelphia: Temple University Press, 1996. Print.

_____. "What Battle Are We Winning?" *Animal Rights: The Abolitionist Approach,* 28 Mar. 2007. Web. 22 May 2012.

Francione, Gary L., and Robert Garner. *The Animal Rights Debate: Abolition or Regulation?* New York: Columbia University Press, 2010. Print.

Friedrich, Bruce. "Getting from A to Z: Why Animal Activists Should Support Incremental Reforms to Help Animals." *Huffington Post Blog.* The Huffington Post.com, Inc., 21 Feb. 2011. Web. 22 May 2012.

Friedrich, Bruce, and Peter Singer. "The Longest Journey Begins With a Single Step: Promoting Animal Rights by Promoting Reform." *Satya*, Sept. 2006. Web. 22 May 2012.

Garner, Robert. "Political Ideology and the Legal Status of Animals." *Animal Law* 3 May 2002: 77–91. Web. 29 May 2012. PDF.

Gelderloos, Peter. *How Nonviolence Protects the State.* Cambridge, MA: South End Press, 2007. Print.

Humane Society of the United States. "Strauss Veal and Marcho Farms Eliminating Confinement by Crate." abolitionistapproach.com. 22 Feb. 2007. Web. 28 May 2012. PDF.

Lens, Sidney. *The Labor Wars: From the Molly Maguires to the Sit-Downs.* Chicago: Haymarket Press, 2008. Print.

Marcus, Erik. "Erik Marcus Debates Professor Francione on Abolition vs. Animal Welfare." *Erik's Diner*, 25 Feb. 2007. Web. 22 May 2012. Podcast.

Michael Medved Show. "Wesley J. Smith Debates Professor Francione on Animal Rights, Part 1." medvenmedhead.com, 16 Apr. 2010. Web. 22 May 2012. Podcast.

_____. "Wesley J. Smith Debates Professor Francione on Animal Rights, Part 2." medvenmedhead.com, 3 May 2012. Web. 22 May 2012. Podcast.

Nibert, David. *Animal Rights Human Rights: Entanglements of Oppression and Liberation.* New York: Rowman & Littlefield, 2002. Print.

Phelps, Norm. "One-Track Activism: Animals Pay the Price." *Advocacy Essays and Articles.* Vegan Outreach, n.d. Web. 22 May 2012.

_____. "Science Weighs in at Last: Campaigns for 'Welfarist' Reforms Cause People to Buy Significantly Less Meat." *European Vegetarian and Animal News Alliance.* 2011. Web. 22 May 2012.

Potter, Will. "ALF to Vegan Death Threats?" greenisthenewred.com. 1 Sept. 2009. Web. 22 May 2012.

Torres, Bob, and Jenna Torres. "Bob and Jenna Torres Interview Professor Francione on His New Book, 'Animals as Persons: Essays on the Abolition of Animal Exploitation,' Part 1." *Vegan Freak Radio*, 20 June 2008. Web. 22 May 2012. Podcast.

_____. "Bob and Jenna Torres Interview Professor Francione on His New Book, 'Animals as Persons: Essays on the Abolition of Animal Exploitation,' Part 2." *Vegan Freak Radio*, 26 June 2008. Web. 22 May 2012. Podcast.

Weber, Max. "Politics as a Vocation." *ne.jp.* n.d. Web. 22 May 2012.

Wetzel, Tom. 1988. "The Origin of the Union Shop." libcom.org. 12 Jan. 2012. Web. 27 May 2012.

Yates, Roger. "'The Abolitionist Approach' Is Not Fit for Purpose." *On Human-Nonhuman Relations: A Sociological Exploration of Speciesism.* human-nonhuman.blogspot.com, 21 Apr. 2011. Web. 22 May 2012.

"Just tell the truth"

A Polemic on the Value of Radical Activism

KIM SOCHA

There is nothing more corrupting than compromise. One step in that direction calls for another, makes it necessary and compelling, and soon it swamps you with the force of a rolling snowball become a landslide. — Alexander Berkman

Radicals do not limit their goals to reforms. It is not their business to make concessions with victimizers to bring about an alleviation of oppression's resulting misery. — Brian A. Dominick

In *Imperial Ambitions*, a series of post–911 interviews with Noam Chomsky, journalist David Barsamian quotes early twentieth-century Marxist Antonio Gramsci, asking how revolutionaries are to subvert, in Gramsci's terms, the "hegemonic ideology." Chomsky, with his inimitable temperance, replies to this question by stating, "I deeply respect Gramsci, but I think it's possible to paraphrase that [question] — namely, just tell the truth.... It's something any one of us can do.... How complicated is it to understand the truth or to know how to act?" (64–65). Chomsky's simple response solidifies the reasons I have adopted a radical animal advocacy position: I cannot accept the use of nonhuman animals to suit human purposes. As a moderately new activist and long time student of animal rights/liberation (AR/L) theory, I herein critique compromise and pretense in the AR/L movement not only for the animals' sakes, but to set a place at the cultural table for animal advocates as broad scale political thinkers and savvy social critics.

Some of this essay's arguments are familiar, but they demand reiteration as mainstream animal proxies continue striking deals with exploiters and killers. Albeit a case of semantics, I use the terms radicalism and reformism to avoid the movement's contested terms: abolition and welfare. That word war inevitably devolves into impossible equations meant to determine who cares more about nonhumans. All activists care, and I have no interest in fueling word wars based in human ego. The arguments I make herein are not meant to widen the chasm between the too easy binaries of abolitionism and welfarism. Rather, I have come to view the movement as, to use the terminology of Steven Best and Anthony J. Nocella II, an "ecosystem" through which "the strength of the movement lies in its diversity, so long as there is mutual respect, understanding and solidarity" (45). I accept this, but I also feel an ethical obligation to explore the limits and dangers of working with systems of oppression — reform, rights and corporate ideology — because I don't think them capable of helping animals. Respect and vehement disagreement can indeed coexist, and that forms the groundwork for this essay.

"Radicalism" and "reformism" hold different connotations for individuals, and no niceties on my part will lessen the weight of those implications. As I define them, radicalism seeks the root of a problem, uproots it and replaces it with something new; reformism takes a problem and alters it into something more acceptable, *re*forming it with the same materials. (There is also radical reformism, explained below.) While the radical refuses to compromise for animals in activist contexts, the term should not designate presumption of ethical perfection or untainted rebellion. As I use the term, "no compromise" simply means that there is no acceptable exploitation and slaughter of non-human animals in industrialized Western culture. On a personal level, to live in contemporary American society as a radical requires continued negotiation of ethics, as animals and their byproducts are everywhere. Even if vegans eradicate most animal products from their lives, human rights violations and environmental destruction continue to underlie our commodities. However, I do not need to shun contemporary culture to be radical. In fact, radicals are most effective when a part of the world, not apart from it. For the animals, radicalism means refusing to champion cage-free eggs and free-range cows if we as activists do not eat eggs or cows. This is where the truth comes in. To paraphrase Chomsky, this essay is an argument for telling the truth, no matter how uncomfortable to the listener.

Radicalism is unyielding and unwilling to work with oppressive institutions. Radicals garner less tangible victories such as changes in law or surges in demand for "humane" animal commodities, and this poses difficulty for activists who do not negotiate the use of animal bodies with animal exploiters in a culture that demands instant results and concrete outcomes quantified on charts, graphs, financial bottom lines and new laws. Radical activism may initially seem idealistic, utopian and stagnant. Yet there is *always* work to do by exposing and subverting speciesism. In contrast, reform assuages animal suffering to moderately lesser degrees that would still be unacceptable for humans, thereby maintaining the speciesist standard. Accordingly, an argument for radical activism is an argument against reform through analysis of its limits.

The Limits of Reform and a
Defense of Radical Vegan Activism

During 2009's Animal Rights Conference, Dallas Rising defined radical abolitionist activism as "rooted in eliminating animal cruelty and not only regulating it," positing a point of harmony amongst activists: a three-pronged purpose to "expose, address and intervene" for nonhuman animals. We unveil the realities of animal exploitation, speak of that exploitation, and attempt to stop the abuse. However, we approach the prongs differently. All animal activists agree that animals matter to some extent. To reformers, this means making use of nonhumans more humane. Many stop there, feeling that while animals are less significant than humans, that is no reason to entirely disregard their capacity to suffer. Next, radical reformers argue for progressing in steps toward complete liberation. Therefore, the path to freedom includes making animal exploitation less egregious along the way. This is an attractive idea, but it is also paradoxical because those who promote it support complete eradication of the animal-industrial complex while also supporting corporations and industries that maintain that very complex.

Radical reform promises the best of both worlds: immediate decrease in animal suffering and the eventual elimination of that suffering at human hands. Radicals who do not support reform are accused of utopian thinking and of indirectly causing animal cruelty because we do not support making animals more comfortable before they are slaughtered. These arguments are short sighted. In Norm Phelps's "One-Track Activism: Animals Pay the Price," a case against radical tactics and ideology, he recounts the triumphs of reform: a three percent decline in battery cages, promised eradication of veal crates by 2012, etc. And he plaintively states, "Suffering matters, and I cannot turn my back on it. I hope you can't either." However, he does not report a decline in animal slaughter resulting from those "victories" because that proof does not exist. He cites a rise in vegetarianism, but vegetarianism is not a sufficient model for it includes animal byproducts, and people may choose a meatless diet for health reasons only. They may see no problem with supporting other forms of animal exploitation. Finally, as Phelps acknowledges, many who call themselves "vegetarian" still consume chicken and fish, if only rarely.

Not only are animals still dying for human use, but their deaths are intensifying according to current estimates and future prognoses. Brian Halweil of the Worldwatch Institute reports that meat and animal byproduct consumption is increasing, and by "2050 nearly twice as much meat will be produced as today, for a projected total of more than 465 million tons." Further, Phelps is hasty when proposing that rising meat and animal byproduct costs (resulting from more humane farming practices) will deter people from buying those products. Halweil asserts that higher meat costs simply mean consumers will find less costly sources of animal protein. Likewise, in a study of the Western world's meat eating patterns, Vaclav Smil argues that

> reduction of high Western meat intakes due to higher costs of beef, pork, and chicken is not very likely in a world where commodity prices have experienced a long secular decline. But even suddenly rising prices would make little difference in societies where disposable incomes are now generally so high that demand for such desirable items as meat or gasoline is highly price-inelastic [629].

Further, more "animal-friendly" farming practices can never be sustainably replicated on the massive scale that will satiate American desire for cheap meat. In current cultural contexts, so-called "humane" meat will always be the province of the wealthy.

In essence, the rising popularity of locavorism, a component of "humane" farming, may only assist in further class divisions in the United States, with moneyed consumers feeling proud for eating high-end animal flesh, while those struggling financially will logically seek the most calories for their buck by eating low-end animal flesh from fast food dollar menus. As Vasile Stănescu explains, the "essence of the locavore argument is that because it is harmful to the environment to transport food over long distances (referred to as 'food miles'), people should instead, for primarily environmental reasons, choose to consume only food that is grown or slaughtered 'locally.'" The outcome of the locavore movement, once all of the arguments are made, is that to save the planet, we have a moral imperative to eat meat.

Indeed, Stănescu, in "'Green' Eggs and Ham? The Myth of Sustainable Meat and the Danger of the Local," ultimately shows that locavore theory, if not interrogated, leads to "unreasonable attacks on vegetarianism" and veganism. Locavorism is enticing to those who care about the environment and treatment of nonhuman animals, and it attempts to convince the prosperous few who can afford "sustainable" meat that they can have their animal flesh and be ethical too. Consequently, radical, non-reformist vegans are patronizingly posed as utopian thinkers and/or dangerous threats to environmental justice. In fact, Stănescu notes "Vegan Utopia" as a "dismissive subheading" in Michael Pollan's popular book *The Omnivore's Dilemma* (while significantly noting that vegans can be locavores too).

This term "utopia" is commonly used to dismiss the concerns of radical/abolitionist vegan activists, so it demands some consideration. The easiest way to debase a perceived opponent's perspective is to use patronizing terms to make that adversary seem utterly naïve and misguided. To illustrate, a recent book by Lierre Keith, a former vegan food activist, poses the suggestion that the radical (and illogical) vegan agenda is to end *all* animal suffering, even amongst species. As proof, she summarizes a random online vegan discussion board post in which a participant argues that "[s]omeone should build a fence down the middle of the Serengeti, and divide the predators from the prey. Killing is wrong and no animals should ever have to die" (7).

Keith later asserts that vegan animal liberationists attempt to hold themselves apart from the cycle of life and death and from the reality that, even as vegans, living organisms die so that we may continue living, whether it be plant life, small organisms and other species that live in the soil tilled for our vegetables or insects killed by the windshields of trucks that deliver organic produce to farmers' markets (79). This is, without doubt, a purposefully false depiction of radical activists, and though there may be some who hold such impossible ideas, they are most definitely the minority of an ethical movement that seeks to reduce, not eradicate, suffering. To be clear, veganism is not grounded in utopian thinking, and most vegans know that life itself continues only because once-living organisms die. We accept this, and there is no way to personally avoid it until we ourselves expire.

As Vegans for Sustainable Agriculture contend against what they term Keith's "straw man" arguments, the "goal of veganism is to eliminate direct, unnecessary suffering at the hands of humans — not to magically end all death." Although the mistreatment of animals has never been acceptable, we have fortunately reached a position in human evolution where alternatives to animal exploitation are plentiful in the industrialized world, so there is no longer sound justification for the violence against animals that is *de rigueur* in contemporary Western culture. As Matthew Scully writes in *Dominion*, "What were once 'necessary evils' [hunting, wearing animal skins, eating meat] [have] become just evils" (43). The Serengeti, aside from those areas where humans have destroyed habitat, is just fine the way it is.

Pushback from environmental meat eaters is expected, but the utopian label is often used by reform-supporting vegans as well. Phelps states, "Devising strategies and tactics that work in the *real world* is the most challenging part of animal rights advocacy" (emphasis added). This is accurate, but his statement unfortunately follows an accusation that what he terms "abolitionist" activism is filled with "noble platitudes" not sufficiently supported by practicable ideas and strategies (a.k.a. utopian). Perhaps this perception exists because very few have looked for answers "in the trenches" among activists who are doing the hard work of changing minds. Such perceptions ignore the value of veganism as a serious political statement with broad social and cultural ramifications that extend beyond nonhuman animal oppression. It is a remonstration against domination and violence, not only of nonhuman animals, but of exploited humans and the environment.

Phelps' arguments, and those like his, sound reasonable, but when critically assessed, they fall short of their long-term liberational promises. Similarly, such posturing is ideologically unstable, a dilemma that those outside of and/or new to the movement observe when animal advocates cooperate with industry. (I have been that "wanna be" activist compelled to consider confusing and contradictory messages from established organizations.)

Activist handbooks regularly encourage advocates to consider how they represent their cause, asking us to think about what we wear and how we handle conflict. However, ethical consistency is an equal if not more important representational concern, but it does not get nearly as much emphasis. If image does matter, then working toward slighter better treatment for non-humans (compromise) is a precarious representation. Rather than try harder to meet a social norm, the AR/L movement should try harder to normalize the idea that animal exploitation is not open to discussion. In a book that challenges notions of what constitutes animal welfare in the sciences, Richard P. Haynes concludes the following on reformism in the animal research field,

> What is typically ambiguous about this middle position ... is that it waivers between arguing that working for reform, as opposed to abolition, is strategically more effective for improving the lot of animals used exploitatively ... and arguing that appropriately reformed exploitative practices are ethically acceptable [80].

Along with being "ambiguous," the ideological contradiction inherent in radical reformism is also speciesist. If organizations that presume to speak for animals settle for some forms of animal utilization, even with the hope of eventual emancipation, they are saying that humans matter more than non-humans, for they are accepting — albeit begrudgingly — treatment of animals that would never be acceptable if applied to humans. But if we don't believe this on the inside, we should not say it on the outside nor reward the endeavors of animal exploiters with praise and support.

For example, approximately five years ago, Smithfield Foods, Inc. reported that it would "phase out gestation stalls or crates at all 187 sow farms it owns in eight states and replace them with 'more animal-friendly' group housing pens over the next decade" ("Pork Giant"). In response, the Humane Society of the United States (HSUS), the self-declared "largest and most effective animal protection organization" in the nation, encouraged other meat producers to "emulate" Smithfield. In kind, Bruce Friedrich, then with People for the Ethical Treatment of Animals (PETA) and now with Farm Sanctuary, the former widely viewed as the most radical animal liberationists, stated, "Kudos to Smithfield for doing it, whatever their reasons" (quoted in "Pork Giant").

Kudos to Smithfield? They have not changed their product line, and sloughing off the reasons for Smithfield's decision is a specious choice. PETA itself reports that within the United States alone, 65 million pigs are captive on factory farms, and 112 million pigs are killed each year worldwide ("Pigs: Intelligent Animals"). Smithfield's industry contributes to this gruesome statistic. The pig industry generates its "products" exclusively to slaughter them for human consumption. Smithfield's pledge to phase out gestation crates is not a promise to lessen the number of pigs slaughtered. Just the opposite. As a profit-making entity, their objective is *always* to make more profit, and this means selling more pig's body parts. Their public relations scheme disguised as a humane resolution helps consumers feel better about eating pig products, for the pigs they are eating lived in "animal-friendly" environments before slaughter. In truth, however, and every activist knows this, there is nothing remotely animal-friendly about Smithfield Foods, Inc., and their use of that deceitful terminology would be laughable if it was not so lamentable.

Smithfield's actions are not surprising, but HSUS and PETA's are. These groups inarguably hold the most financial and media power in the U.S. of all animal interest organizations; this is why news outlets consulted them when Smithfield made their announcement. HSUS and PETA are the mainstream media's go to groups when they are seeking sanction or condemnation of the latest AR/L controversy.[1]

Consequently, their endorsement of inhumane practices affects how animals are viewed by the majority of an under-informed public that is rarely, if ever, introduced to less elastic responses to corporate pronouncements such as Smithfield's. HSUS and PETA are undoubtedly comprised of passionate advocates who have helped mainstream the AR/L movement. But in this case, they used their power recklessly by giving kudos and asking others to emulate a corporation that profits from the confinement, torture and slaughter of pigs. As Bob Torres more forcefully affirms, "[HSUS and PETA] make Faustian bargains with industry that condemn animals to maintain their status as property and commodities of a bloody capitalist machine" (93). This Smithfield/PETA/HSUS case study exemplifies the reasons for Torres's condemnation.

When animal proxies bargain on animals' behalves, they are giving power to animal exploiters to determine what constitutes acceptable use. With this power in the hands of those who will profit from animal use, the eradication of animal industries is effectively off the agenda. When animal welfare is the issue, there will necessarily be experts to determine what constitutes fair use. The problem, as Haynes defines it, "is that the alleged experts are either the same people that use animals in research or that are employed by institutions who have a major financial interest in using animals for research" (67). The most chilling application of this logic is apparent in the standard conclusion of experts that "death does not count as harmful to the interests of animal[s], nor prolonged life a benefit" (Haynes ix). To repeat, "experts" on animal welfare have determined that death is not harmful to animals' interests. Smithfield would agree; people who care about animals should not.

The disturbing judgment of animal "experts" in the sciences sets the tone for other animal industries as well: "Who decides what is considered a customary practice [in the use of animals raised for food production]? Seemingly, the definition of an inhumane practice is determined by the average farmer" (Wolfson 31). Like the researcher who determines that death is not harmful to animals, the farmer must come to the same "expert" determination to ensure profit. The world over, any industry or institution tasked with marketing, researching or monitoring nonhumans opposes animal liberation, and this includes government bureaucracies.

To illustrate, the U.S. Fish and Wildlife Service (USFWS) is headed and administered at federal and state levels predominately by hunters and "pro-hunting" bureaucrats (Spiegel 64). The following verbiage is from their Web site:

> Since the late 19th century, hunters concerned about the future of wildlife and the outdoor tradition have made countless contributions to the conservation of the nation's wildlife resources. Today, millions of Americans deepen their appreciation and understanding of the land and its wildlife through hunting. Hunting organizations contribute millions of dollars and countless hours of labor to various conservation causes each year ["Hunting"].

This romanticized view of wildlife conservation and hunting cunningly elides the reasons people hunt — for sport, fun and trophies — and it is based upon suspicious premises. For instance, USFWS commonly paints deer hunting as necessary to control overpopulation, proposing it as necessary for ecological balance and suggesting that hunting cessation would consign thousands of deer to slow, agonizing deaths through starvation. This is a common assertion, but wildlife overseers have been known to "manipulate flora, exterminate natural predators, regulate hunting permits, and even at times breed and release deer, all in order to maintain herd sizes large enough to ensure what they call a 'harvestable surplus' of the animals men [and women] most like to kill" (Luke 140). USFWS runs nature as a corporation, and terms such as "conservation" and "wildlife preservation" are marketing tools, much like the phrase "animal-friendly."

The lauded conservation work of wildlife-loving hunters is evident in USFWS's response to the question "What do hunters do for conservation"?: "A lot. The sale of hunting licenses, tags, and stamps is the primary source of funding for most state wildlife conservation efforts." The images of rural simplicity and stewardship that arise when hearing "conservation work" is belied by this truth: conservation means people are buying the right to kill animals. This is a twisted state of affairs, but it works well for medical researchers, government bureaucracies and corporations, all of which claim some concern for animals even as they determine that prolonged animal lives are not of benefit to the animals their industries exploit.

The establishments against which animal activists contend are vast; they have immense financial resources, media power, governmental sanction and public support. There are so many of them and so few of us. When advocates sustain and approve of these monolithic animal exploiters, the movement is not progressing toward freedom but preserving a tyrannical hierarchy with nonhumans on the lowest rungs of consideration. This is the tragedy of compromise. It is tragic whenever animal bodies are made products to be negotiated in terms of who has the right to do what with nature, and much like compromise, legal rights are not necessarily friends of the animals either.

The Limits of Legal Rights

The battle for legal rights for nonhumans has long been at the forefront of the AR/L movement. However, I remain suspicious of the twinning of law and rights because of its history in human culture. Rights are an arbitrary concept that have not always served humanity well, so it is imprudent to think that animals could benefit in a long-term way from a concept that carries the heavy burden of a classist, racist and sexist history. Rights and the law have distinctive characteristics, and it is not my purpose to explain those distinctions. When I discuss the law and rights as a combined entity, I mean *legal rights*: entitlements and dispensations determined, regulated and enforced by systems of law. And the law, including its association with rights and government, is not able to speak to the objectives of the AR/L movement. For proof, one needs only to look at how it has (dis)served humanity. In 1892, Peter Kropotkin critiqued rights in *The Conquest of Bread*, the tenor and truth of which holds just as much validity today as it did 120 years ago. He argues that

> all that is necessary for production ... have been seized by the few in the course of that long story of robbery, enforced migration and wars, of ignorance and oppression, which has been the life of the human race before it learned to subdue the forces of Nature ... [and this occurred because the few have] tak[en] advantage of *alleged* rights acquired in the past [4, emphasis added].

Rights are human constructs that have been and continue to be used to justify the enslavement, torture and slaughter of human and nonhuman animals. The idea of rights is problematic because it implies an ultimate truth and a natural hierarchy that delegates privilege for some, not for others and *never for all.* To rephrase bluntly, I defer to the late comedian George Carlin: "Folks, I hate to spoil your fun, but there's no such thing as rights. They're imaginary. We made them up. Like the boogie man.... Rights are an idea. They're just imaginary." Consequently, rights and the law — the tools of reform and regulation — are unlikely to liberate animals.

From an alternate perspective, Thomas Kelch, after cataloguing the positions of anti-rights theorists, eventually concludes that rights should not be abandoned because they "are such an ingrained aspect of our legal system that it seems unlikely they could be purged without the demolition of the current structure of society" (262). Gary Francione rejects rights criticism as the province of feminists who support what is most commonly theorized as a feminist care ethic, and he associates this ethic with reformist ideology, concluding that "rights are not inherently patriarchal," but "simply a way of protecting interests" (20). Neither of these critiques is satisfactory, as they refuse to consider new paths to liberation apart from the status quo and to acknowledge whose "interests" are most often served in the U.S. and beyond. Kelch and Francione's assumption that rights of any kind could ever be unmoored from the financial interests of dominant groups within a capitalistic, patriarchal and speciesist culture is both naïve and circumscribed. If rights have any value, those benefits are incapacitated when applied in an intrinsically corrupt system.

Legal rights and legislation are a start, but of limited potential for absolute liberation. As to rights, Mary Midgley concisely argues that they should be better seen as a concept "used in a wide sense to draw attention to problems, but not to solve them" (quoted in Kelch 262). While I am not asserting that all activists should abandon every legal option in the course of their advocacy, especially when faced with immediate instances of animal mistreatment, we should recognize the law's inadequate potential to challenge widespread, institutionalized cultural standards that give human beings the natural, and by extension legal, right to use animals.

When the government establishes guidelines for how humans may use animals, even in the spirit of social evolution, they are more firmly establishing control over animals, albeit in the guise of compassion. It is troubling that animal activists, as representatives of nonhumans, are giving that control to those who have financial stakes in the continued use of animals as machines. Meat, dairy and other corporatized animal industries are more closely allied with the U.S. government than ever before (we are on the verge of plutocracy, if not already there), and representatives of those industries comprise the bureaucracies that determine our nation's laws and food standards. In a decades old critique of the plutocratic system, Alexander Berkman makes the following statement that should continue to encourage radical activism:

> They will see to it that no legislation is passed against their interests. Now and
> then they will make a show of fighting certain laws and favoring others, else
> the game would lose interest for you. But whatever laws there be, the masters
> will take care that they shouldn't hurt their business, and their well-paid
> lawyers know how to turn every law to the benefit of the Big Interests, as daily
> experience proves [72].

Now and then, the animal-industrial complex will "make a show" of improving/reforming animals' lives so that advocates feel they are still in "the game." However, in the end, Big Business will do nothing that will "hurt their business," and their business is killing animals. They don't ever deserve kudos from the AR/L movement, but condemnation. As David J. Wolfson concludes in *Beyond the Law*, the goal of federal legislation has been and will always be to protect "farming interests" and the interests of other animal exploiters (44). The government, the legal system and corporations will not solve the problem of animal exploitation, no matter how much money welfare/protectionist organizations spend on their campaigns and no matter how much they pursue the path of negotiation. As Brian A. Dominick tersely observes in "Animal Liberation and Social Revolution," "The politician will never understand why the state should protect animals" (12). They've barely helped humans, so stop looking to politicians for help.

In the introduction to *Terrorists or Freedom Fighters?*, Best and Nocella observe that "human struggles for freedom — especially those of gender, race, or sexual 'identity politics' — can easily be co-opted and absorbed" by dominant institutions, rendering "their critical edge ... blunted. Similarly, animal welfare advocacy is easily absorbed by current systems of domination" (13). As with humans, the absorption of animal issues into mainstream reformist establishments will not allow the "radical transformations" of mind, tradition and habit that are necessary to save nonhumans from their continued exploitation, nor will it do anything to challenge exploitative "social institutions and economic systems" (Best and Nocella 13–14). Certainly, there are economic, cultural, political, social and gender issues that account for welfare's failure to free humans from financial and cultural bondage, issues that do not readily apply to nonhumans. However, although human/animal welfare analyses do not a perfect analogy make, the outcomes and critiques are similar.

Although laws regulating mistreatment of animals in the Western world have existed for 400 years, about 200 years in the U.S., animals still suffer and die in unpardonable numbers. Approximately 10 billion animals per year are slaughtered for food in the U.S. (50 billion worldwide) (Ernst). This is *just* for food, not factoring in animals held captive on fur farms, in laboratories, entertainment venues, etc. Even Norm Phelps, within his argument *against* no-compromise activism, admits that "we cannot dismiss the fact that forty-seven years after the beginning of the vegan movement and twenty-two years after the birth of the modern animal rights movement, the number of animals slaughtered for food in the United States is continuing to rise." This comes after years of reforms that all who care about animals wanted to be successful. In some cases, the reforms were successful, and they may have alleviated the suffering of nonhumans to an extent of which we can never be aware. But one must wonder, does a few more feet of space within a pig's confinement stall constitute an achievement? It may be cause for humans to pat themselves on the back, but that pig is still confined and headed to slaughter.

AR/L activists who want to improve the conditions in which animals are exploited should rethink the promise that liberation awaits at the end of a new bill, law or list of regulations that the government asks animal exploiters to follow. Those who work for animals occasionally want to claim triumph. This is understandable, but activists must honestly ask themselves if they would rather convince people to eat grass-fed cows for the rest of their lives (and again, this is not a sustainable goal) or inspire them to completely give up eating cows. This is not a rhetorical proposition but something to answer candidly so that we are not wasting our resources on campaigns we don't believe in. Billions of animals are tortured and slaughtered each year for human pleasure, entertainment, scientific inquiry and other base reasons. However, conceding to these exploitative institutions will not end exploitation. Accordingly, a radical approach to liberation must assess one of the most inequitable systems in human history: capitalism, a system whose treachery lies in its ability to look so much like freedom.

The Limits of Corporate Subterfuge: A Feminist Critique

In "Effective Advocacy: Stealing from the Corporate Playbook," Bruce Friedrich acknowledges that animal rights outreach is a style of marketing, and "[a]s hard and as smart as people on Wall Street work to sell stocks, and advertisers work to sell the latest SUV, we need to be working that hard in our cause" (187). While I agree in terms of fervor, I am wary of using manipulative tactics, specifically because of their effects on women. Feminists have long critiqued PETA's use of eroticized female bodies to sell animal liberation, whereby PETA mirrors the compromise that commonly arises during social revolutions when "the woman question" is put aside or only partially answered for the broader cause of the rebellion. Specifically, animal rights organizations have negotiated women's self worth to sell veganism as a get-thin-quick scheme.

In *Vegan Freak: Being Vegan in a Non-Vegan World*, Bob and Jenna Torres speak directly to women who might adopt an animal-free diet in the hopes of becoming skinny: "Authors far craftier than us have sold millions of books by convincing women that going vegan is a fantastic way to squeeze into that little black 'fuck me' dress" (102). The authors identify an emerging distortion of the AR/L movement, one that has been appropriated by the same media and advertising monolith that consistently tells women they are substandard. It is from this cultural arena that I explore the detrimental effects of "stealing from the corporate playbook."

Rory Freedman and Kim Barnouin's *Skinny Bitch* book weight-loss series is an example of this AR/L distortion. Though not marketed as vegan- and animal rights–centered, the books contain graphic descriptions of how animals become food. In addition, the authors use derogatory comments to the reader as "thinspiration" to get and stay skinny. A 2008 Salon.com review concisely summarizes the problem here: "Thanks to 'Skinny Bitch,' women who hate their bodies no longer need rely on their own self-loathing to stoke the flames of what seems like motivation but is actually self-flagellation — penance for the sin of being too fat" (Klausner). This book also peddles the myth that veganism equals thinness, and considering the rates at which diets fail, dabbling in veganism to meet a Madison Avenue ideal will likely fail as well.

The authors, formerly of the modeling industry and current PETA spokeswomen, home in on women's culturally-imposed weaknesses — fear of food, especially fatty foods. *Salon*'s Julie Klausner reports a reader's response to the malicious discourse in *Skinny Bitch*, "It was a formerly anorexic friend of mine who nailed it when she read excerpts from the book. 'When you have an eating disorder,' she told me, 'that's the voice you hear in your head all the time.'" Freedman and Barnouin also play the tired rhetorical trick of deprecating nonhuman animals in their diatribes against overweight women. Use of the word "bitch" eases this text into a tradition of the oppressed adopting negative terms within a radical agenda of disempowering the oppressor who so named them. However, *Skinny Bitch* is hardly a feminist tract, nor is it wholly animal-friendly.

More alarming than their use of "bitch" is their reliance on phrases such as "being a fat pig will hinder you" (12), "gluttonous pig" (39), "bloated pig" (40) and "[d]on't be a pig anymore" (184). The authors enforce a negative image of pigs as overweight, slovenly creatures who deserve to be maligned. We all make the occasional speciesist slip up, but using speciesist rhetoric in casual conversation is different than publishing a book that relies on animal-hating metaphors that will be familiar to the authors' self-loathing target audience. The harmful commentary in *Skinny Bitch* allows for our culture's continued consumption of creatures deemed unworthy of compassion.

At an animal rights presentation in 2011, I asked the audience why dogs are family and pigs are food in Western culture, despite their similar characteristics in terms of intelligence and friendliness. Melanie Joy's response in *Why We Love Dogs, Eat Pigs and Wear Cows: An Introduction to Carnism*, is appropriate here: "The answer to these questions can be summed up by a single word: *perception*. We react differently to different types of meat not because there is a physical difference between them, but because our perception of them is different" (12). However, the average person is not aware of Joy's concept of carnism. Thus, a respondent honestly, though disturbingly, explained that dogs are cute and lovable and pigs are "filthy animals." In other words, one species is worthy of our compassion and the other is not. *Skinny Bitch* supports the latter sentiment by continuing the deception that being a pig is damnation as much as is being a "large" woman. With animal activists maintaining this commodity culture mindset of the diet-industrial complex ("anything to sell a book") we cannot hope for something better for women and nonhuman animals.

More than offensive, however, *Skinny Bitch* has a major identity crisis. There *is* valuable information in it. The authors reveal the truth behind the animal food industry and the financial relationships between governmental agencies such as the Unites States Department of Agriculture (USDA), Food and Drug Administration (FDA), and Environmental Protection Agency (EPA) and companies who deal in animal bodies and byproducts. Freedman and Barnouin reveal the truth in *Skinny Bitch*, but they encase the truth in lies — women must be skinny to be attractive and being attractive should be a priority — via the typical verbiage of female disempowerment. Rather than seek new modes of animal liberation, they borrow from our culture's lies about women and attempt to reform them into an argument for animals. Most strangely, they seem aware of the book's shortcomings.

The very last page of *Skinny Bitch* offers a cautionary post script: "Wait! We have a confession to make. We really couldn't care less about being skinny.[2] Don't get scared or upset; you will definitely lose weight if you adopt the *Skinny Bitch* lifestyle. However, our real hope is for you to become healthy. We don't want anyone to be obsessed with getting skinny" (224). First, I'm hesitant to buy this public service announcement–style qualifier as anything more than preemptive damage control for those sensitive readers who might yell "foul" at the authors' continued proclamation that women should put being skinny high on their priority lists. Secondly, with a few sentences, the authors attempt to counteract the unscrupulous messages endemic to the title, content, and imagery of their book. This attempt fails, but it speaks strongly to the character of our culture that even a book that earnestly wants to be about saving animals must resort to destroying women.

A recent comment to a vegan Q & A advice column sums up the frustration ethical vegans feel when their concerns are peddled as a diet. "Chubby in Calistoga" expresses frustration over "'vegan activists' using sexism and fat oppression to spread what is really a compassionate lifestyle" ("Ask Laura" 79). As much as AR/L activists want veganism to increase, no truly compassionate person wants another living being to live or die painfully, and to hate oneself and one's own body is to live in pain. Compassion is the foundation of this movement, and

> [a]s a movement that fights exploitation and oppression, we should refuse to be exploitative and oppressive. We can't legitimately use arguments that oppress and exploit women through ridiculous and unachievable notions of beauty and body size to argue that we should not be exploiting another group that is vulnerable to deep and pervasive social injustice [nonhuman animals] [Torres and Torres 103].

In sum, exploiting women is an unethical and callous way to market animal liberation. When women tell me that *Skinny Bitch* made them go vegan, my appreciation of the book's purpose is tainted by a sadness that their self-worth had to be bartered to make that choice. The truth in *Skinny Bitch* is true whether it is couched in woman-hating messages or not. Empathetic activists can do better than to play upon women's fears in an attempt to liberate animals. I chose *Skinny Bitch* as an example of corporate subterfuge because the diet industry is enormous, and it plays with people's fears of inadequacy, encouraging them to buy products and concepts that will make them lifelong consumers and keep them distanced from reality. This books epitomizes the ways in which certain factions of the AR/L movement are willing to reposition oppressions (in this case women and animals) on the hierarchy ladder to sell animal liberation.

Despite our differing perspectives, animal advocates of all kinds contend against oppression, making it imperative that we consider all aspects of a speciesist culture, including the economy. In the U.S., this means that "we're going to need to fight the heart of the economic order that drives these oppressions. We're going to have to fight capitalism" (Torres 11). Capitalism is an innately tyrannical system through which parity is not possible. It is built upon a slave/master dichotomy with the bulk of a nation's resources in the hands of a moneyed few. If animals will not be liberated though the industries that exploit them via reforms and laws, as argued in the previous sections, then they will not be liberated by a corporate ideology that exchanges impossible ideals for money. This is especially true of the diet industry, which is kept aloft by the constant failure of its customers.

Skinny Bitch represents a trend in which veganism is being absorbed into corporatized culture by making animal liberation a product for purchase.

Therein, the AR/L movement's radical political message could easily be marketed away if veganism becomes/remains a Euro-American bourgeois lifestyle choice. *This matters.* In "The Rise of Critical Animal Studies," Steven Best admonishes Leftists for refusing to acknowledge animal exploitation as a serious social concern while also asserting that the AR/L movement is rightfully seen as "politically naïve," "single-issue" and currently incapable of seeing, much less articulating, the connections between animal exploitation and global capitalism. While not arguing that the free market invented speciesism, which it did not, Best sees it as exponentially ramping up the destruction of "people, animals and nature. It cannot be humanized, civilized or green-friendly"; rather, it needs to be "transcended through revolution" on all levels. Veganism is more than just a food alternative or, as it is more commonly seen, as a list of food prohibitions that lead to malnourished bodies — which are also marketed as desirable to women — and neurological disorders. It is a protest against domination, exploitation and oppression.

Best also observes that "privilege rots the soul and weakens the will." Culturally and financially, the AR/L movement is predominately comprised of the socially privileged who can benefit from and take advantage of the ostensible benefits of a capitalist system. And while many in the movement lament this reality, I have yet to hear anyone deny it. This does not necessarily have to be a negative assessment either. For example, other social movements such as the Underground Railroad and Freedom Summer needed those with more social liberty to see through the projects' goals. Still, my own social advantages, meager as they may look to some, are in consistent combat with my worldviews and a source of frustration even as they offer me security and the leisure time to be an activist. My current response, unrefined as it may be, is to continue investigating the ways in which I and others are hindered by this capitalist system founded upon disparity and to refuse to be a "single-issue" activist.

With veganism as part of the commodity system, capitalism will give us cookbooks, diet books, pleather, faux fur, "cheeze," mock meat, and t-shirts and bumper stickers that declare our veganism to passersby. Yet although these are things that I and others may enjoy, they are *human* indulgences available only to those who have the financial means to buy them. Meanwhile, if all goes as planned, meat consumption will continue to rise, especially in historically unindustrialized countries that want to mirror America's mass-consumption-of-cheap-food model. As evident as the benefits of commodity veganism are for *me*, market-based economies do not encourage emancipation for animals. The truth is that capitalism will always give us "more cages, and until we destroy the *social* machine which produces those cages ... the closest we can expect to come to liberation is momentary and relative freedom"

(Dominick 20). Many of us want something more. We want enduring and absolute animal liberation, and this will not happen without considering alternatives to reform, rights and corporate dogma.

A Radical Search for New Tools

My concerns about animal liberation have led me to look at human emancipation movements as points of comparison, and the works of key feminist writers have fueled my move toward activism rather than mere armchair agreement. (In fact, I applied the work of these women to the animal liberation movement in another book project entitled *Women, Destruction and the Avant-Garde: A Paradigm for Animal Liberation*.) These author/activists, although their conditions and historical perspectives were different, observed the limitations of standard forms of rebellion in the struggle for freedom. In poet and artist Mina Loy's 1914 "Feminist Manifesto," she negates the idea that gender emancipation means women will have the opportunity to be like men, to have men's jobs, rights and social opportunities. Rather, she declares that women have had enough with "scratching on the surface of the rubbish heap of tradition ... the only method [for liberation] is Absolute Demolition" (153). To paraphrase, Loy was demanding that women cease seeking integration into the world that subjugates them. Explore something new, for freedom can only come from outside the system, a system that needs to be destroyed.

Fast forward approximately forty-five years, and radical activist, poet and feminist Audre Lorde famously echoes Loy through her use of the human slave trade analogy. In critique of white liberal feminists seeking success in the cultural spheres created by patriarchy and white privilege, Lorde declared, "The master's tools will never dismantle the master's house" (quoted in De Veaux 249). Her critique was a challenge to women to cease using the means of the oppressor within the fight against that oppressor because he designed the tools, honed them, developed the rules and regulations for their use and set up the institutions that oversee their execution. When you use the master's tools, he is in always in control, whether or not you see him.

Loy and Lorde's sentiments are essential to understanding radical animal liberation activism. In kind, activism that negotiates the use of animal bodies is "scratching on the surface of the rubbish heap of tradition," and it is using the master's tools in a futile attempt to dismantle his house. To presume that humans, animal advocates or otherwise, have the "right" to barter usage of so-called lesser beings is arrant speciesism. While all activists claim to speak on the animals' behalves, which always entails presumption, radicals are not presuming that animals want a bit more space in which to suffer on the factory farm; they are presuming a truth that animals don't want to be confined and slaughtered, tormented and disposed of. Seems a fair presumption.

Rather than look to industry, law, government and corporate tactics to alter treatment of nonhumans, activists must reflect on how to undermine industry, law, government and corporate tactics to save animals from any human handling. The Vegans of Color Web site declares in its tagline: "Because we don't have the luxury of being single-issue." As they voice concern for nonhumans, advocates from historically oppressed groups have continued obstacles to overcome in a racist, classist, sexist culture. However, regardless of ethnic identity, *all* animal activists must look at oppression more holistically because none of us have the luxury of being single issue anymore. This focus will allow for alliance building with putatively non-animal-friendly groups who rally against globalism, corporate culture and plutocracy, among other issues. This is not the only area for growth, but such coalitions may assist the AR/L movement in becoming more focused on foundational social and political transformation even as some of us maintain our distinctive focus on nonhuman animals.

As activists seek new tools, we must ponder the benefits of and limits to the theories and concepts of human oppression. While coalition building is vital, there are limits therein. First, animal exploitation is unethical regardless of its connection to human oppression. Secondly, animal liberation is not only about social justice, an innately *human*-centered concept that, while it lends itself to consideration of animal issues, is about humans coexisting as social animals. Nonhuman animals are better off when apart from human beings. In other words, we should just leave them alone. Finally, even among social justice theorists, "justice" is an ambiguous term, and while it most often refers to dispensations of the law, "equality," "*entitlement, merit* and *desert* [in the end,] most people's views about justice are *indeterminate*" (Commission on Social Justice 51). For the human animal, the benefits of justice theory, as with law and rights, are circumscribed by the term's uncertainty. Hence, justice theory is even more unlikely to help animals, as it is ill-advised to think of nonhumans in terms of "merit" or an earned right to humane treatment. However, justice theory is not without its uses.

When the Commission on Social Justice determines that parity must be "based on a basic belief in the intrinsic worth of every human being" (61), it provides a catalyst for conceptualizing nonhumans. The many manifestations of the AR/L movement would seem to agree with the Commission's conclusion, while extending "intrinsic worth" to include nonhuman animals. When applied to animals, this principle of justice "implies that humans ought not to interfere in an animal's ability to flourish," meaning to live as they would without human interference (Haynes 146). There is no more basic or effective starting point for understanding the radical animal activism that I have explored in this essay. Brian Luke boils down this AR/L perspective to "terms of caring" (125). Our work is to make people care about animal suffering, both the apparent and the hidden. Our starting point is to be honest about how much we care and not to be ashamed that our care knows no middle ground. There needs to be some of us, more of us, who will be gently inflexible and comfortable with the phrase, "That just isn't good enough."

Negotiations, half truths, untruths and exploitation cannot be the answer to the animal question. If you want humans to cease consuming the reproductive secretions of nonhumans, don't campaign for cage-free eggs but for the eradication of human demand for eggs and the egg industry. If you think that women are animals with multi-faceted capabilities and worth beyond weight, don't use their bodies and culturally-imposed self-loathing to sell animal liberation. If you oppose the hierarchy and authoritarianism that demands subjugation, cease looking to the law, government and corporations to liberate animals. If you want people to be vegan, don't ask them to be vegetarian.

This uncompromising approach need not necessitate rage, riots and direct action, though they are not without value. Rather, radicalism can manifest in less dramatic ways. For example, my activist organization stages regular legal and peaceful protests in front of a store that sells animals who may come from puppy and kitten mills, but regardless of where they come from, our main concern is that the store sells animals bred for profit. When the store owner asked to sit down with a representative from our group, we refused because he would not consider the option of no longer selling live animals. If we had no possibility of getting what we want, there was no purpose in negotiating the animals' lives. We are following the model of activists around the U.S. who have successfully closed this chain's franchises in different cities.

Imagine if those activists had accepted a compromise such as the franchise owner would still sell "pets," but also coordinate occasional adoption days with local shelters. With the negotiation made, the protesters would have gone away, puppies and kittens would have continued to be produced as "products," and animals would continue to languish in shelters, albeit, *maybe*, to slightly lesser degrees. As things stand now, thanks to a more radical approach, animal merchants of this national chain are closing up shop and going away. This is radicalism.

As an interpersonal example, I met a woman at an outreach event who proudly explained that she only eats grass-fed cows. She also volunteers with the poor in Guatemala, and it would be problematic for activists to expect such individuals to stop eating one of their only food sources. (Her intent, it seems, was to prove that the situation in Guatemala justified meat eating the world over.) I lauded the work she was doing in Central America, though kindly explained that while Guatemalans have limited food options in a subsistence economy, she lives in a country with ample alternatives to animal products. Although my gut reaction was to applaud her more ethical food choice with the approval she sought, I refuse to applaud behaviors I don't endorse. I would not accept her justification for eating sentient beings killed for human pleasure, no matter their pre-slaughter diet. That was it. No angry diatribe. No violence. Just a well meaning woman who left me that day with a "thank you" and a packet of vegan recipes in her handbag that she promised to try. *This is radicalism,* and it is about being true to ourselves and to the animals we so desperately want to unshackle.

Radical animal advocacy is about telling the truth. Anyone can do it, and more of us need to. As Chomsky asks, "How complicated is it to understand the truth or to know how to act?" (65). My desire to write this essay springs from interaction with activists who want the same thing I do — cessation of animal exploitation in every way imaginable — but who choose the reformist route. I really like these people. Some have been in the movement longer than me, and I admire their compassion, but I do not understand their tactics. Consequently, I cannot help but wonder what would happen if everyone who *really* wants total animal liberation took animals off the negotiation table. Critics might say that this idea, much like complete liberation, is hopelessly utopian in the world we currently live in. I agree, so I reiterate that liberation is not possible without a radical and practicable revision of that world. This is hard work, much harder than lobbying politicians or integrating veganism into the diet industry. However, it is also honest work, the results of which can lead to bodily integrity for all. *Finally.*

NOTES

1. As anecdotal proof of PETA's influence, the Minneapolis-based activist group with which I work is often assumed to be PETA for seemingly no other reason than we are showing concern for animals.
2. Incidentally, they are both skinny.

WORKS CITED

"Ask Laura." *VegNews.* Sept./Oct. 2010: 78–79. Print.
Berkman, Alexander. *What Is Anarchism?* 1929. Edinburgh, UK: AK Press, 2003. Print.
Best, Steven. "The Rise of Critical Animal Studies: Putting Theory into Action and Animal Liberation into Higher Education." *State of Nature* Summer 2009. Web. 30 July 2011.
Best, Steven, and Anthony J. Nocella II, eds. *Terrorists or Freedom Fighters? Reflections on the Liberation of Animals.* New York: Lantern, 2004. Print.
_____. "Behind the Mask: Uncovering the Animal Liberation Front." Best and Nocella 9–63. Print.
Carlin, George. *You Have No Rights.* 12 Mar. 2008. *YouTube.* Web. 30 Oct. 2010.
Commission on Social Justice. "What Is Social Justice?" *The Welfare State Reader.* 2nd Ed.

Eds. Christopher Pierson and Francis G. Castles. Cambridge, UK: Polity, 2006. 50–61. Print.

Chomsky, Noam, and David Barsamian. *Imperial Ambitions: Conversations on the Post–9/11 World*. New York: Macmillan, 2005. Print.

De Veaux, Alexis. *Warrior Poet: A Biography of Audre Lorde*. New York: Norton, 2004. Print.

Dominick, Brian A. "Animal Liberation and Social Revolution." 3rd Ed. Syracuse, NY: Critical Mess Media, 1997. Print.

Donovan, Josephine, and Carol Adams, eds. *The Feminist Care Tradition in Animal Ethics*. New York: Columbia University Press, 2007. Print.

Ernst, Stephanie. "Animal Use and Abuse Statistics: The Shocking Numbers." Change.org. 5 Oct. 2009. Web. 17 Aug. 2011.

Francione, Gary L. *Animals as Persons: Essays on the Abolition of Animal Exploitation*. New York, Columbia University Press, 2008. Print.

Freedman, Rory, and Kim Barnouin. *Skinny Bitch*. Philadelphia: Running Press, 2005. Print.

Friedrich, Bruce. "Effective Advocacy: Stealing from the Corporate Playbook." Singer 187–195. Print.

Halweil, Brian. "Meat Production Continues to Rise." *Vital Signs Online*. Worldwatch Institute. 20 Aug. 2008. Web. 31 Dec. 2010.

Haynes, Richard P. *Animal Welfare: Competing Conceptions and Their Ethical Implications*. New York: Springer, 2010. Print.

Humane Society of the United States. Homepage. Web. 19 Nov. 2010.

"Hunting." *U.S. Fish and Wildlife Service*. 22 March 2010. Department of the Interior. Web. 21 Nov. 2010.

Joy, Melanie. *Why We Love Dogs, Eat Pigs and Wear Cows: An Introduction to Carnism*. Newbury Port, MA: Conari Press, 2011. Print.

Keith, Lierre. *The Vegetarian Myth: Food, Justice and Sustainability*. Crescent City, CA: Flashpoint, 2009. Print.

Kelch, Thomas G. "The Role of the Rational and the Emotive in a Theory of Animal Rights." *The Feminist Care Tradition in Animal Ethics*. Adams and Donovan 259–300. Print.

Klausner, Julie. "Hey, skinny bitch!" Salon.com. 11 Feb. 2008. Salon Media Group. Web. 22 Aug. 2010.

Kropotkin, Peter Alekseevich. 1892. *The Conquest of Bread*. New York: Putnam, 1907. Print.

Loy, Mina. "Feminist Manifesto." 1914. *The Lost Lunar Baedeker*. Ed. Roger L. Conover. New York: Farrar Straus Giroux, 1996. 153–156. Print.

Luke, Brian. "Justice, Caring and Animal Liberation." *The Feminist Care Tradition in Animal Ethics*. Adams and Donovan 125–152. Print.

Phelps, Norm. "One-Track Activism: Animals Pay the Price." *Advocacy Essays and Articles*. Vegan Outreach. Web. 31 Dec. 2010.

"Pigs: Intelligent Animals Suffering in Factory Farms and Slaughterhouses." Peta.org. People for the Ethical Treatment of Animals. Web. 29 Oct. 2010.

"Pork Giant to Phase Out Gestation Crates." *Food Inc. on MSNBC.com*. MSN, 25 Dec. 2007. Web. 29 Oct. 2010.

Rising, Dallas. *Animal Rights Conference 2009 in Los Angeles*. 30 Sept. 2009. *YouTube*. Web. 29 Oct. 2010.

Scully, Matthew. *Dominion: The Power of Man, the Suffering of Animals, and the Call to Mercy*. New York: St. Martin's Griffin, 2002. Print.

Singer, Peter, ed. *In Defense of Animals: The Second Wave*. Malden, MA: Blackwell, 2006. Print.

Smil, Vaclav. "Eating Meat: Evolution, Patterns and Consequences." *Department of Ecology*. Colorado State University. 29 Nov. 2005. Web. 31 Dec. 2010.

Spiegel, Marjorie. *The Dreaded Comparison: Human and Animal Slavery*. New York: Mirror Books/IDEA, 1996. Print.

Stănescu, Vasile. "'Green' Eggs and Ham? The Myth of Sustainable Meat and the Danger of the Local." *United Poultry Concerns*, 10 Dec. 2010. Web. 15 May 2012.

Torres, Bob. *Making a Killing: The Political Economy of Animal Rights*. Oakland, CA: AK Press, 2007. Print.

_____, and Jenna Torres. *Vegan Freak: Being Vegan in a Non-Vegan World*. 2nd Ed. Oakland, CA: PM Press, 2010. Print.

Vegans for Sustainable Agriculture. "Words Not Pie: The Vegan Response to Lierre Keith at the Upcoming VegetarianMyth.com." Indybay.com. San Francisco Bay Area Independent Media Center. 15 Mar. 2010. Web. 23 Nov. 2011.

Vegans of Color (Homepage). Wordpress.com. 2011. Web. 11 Aug. 2011.

Wolfson, David J. *Beyond the Law: Agribusiness and the Systematic Abuse of Animals Raised for Food or Food Production*. Watkins Glen, NY: Farm Sanctuary, 1999. Print.

Literary Analysis
for Animal Liberation

Stephen King's Animal Kingdom

PATRICK MCALEER

Nonhuman animal oppression is easily visible, as is the low status that nonhuman animals often have in the eyes and minds of most humans. Although it is perhaps unnecessary to note the power and hierarchical structures erected that separate man and "beast" in the modern world, it is necessary to examine these relationships alongside numerous examples of abuse, torture and mistreatment of nonhumans so that change can be enacted. Change, of course, is a necessity as the overarching public mindset concerning nonhuman animals is disturbing. Animals, for most, are mere objects, items of consumption and spectacles for entertainment; these "norms" facilitate violence towards them, and this violence is all too often ignored. Zoos, for example, are locales of abuse, especially as "teasing [nonhuman animals] is endemic at zoos, and is perpetuated by both children and adults.... People hurl rocks, coins, bottles cans.... Cigarette butts have been founds in cages ... [and] even needles, pins, nails, razorblades, and shards of glass find their way into exhibits" (Hribal 106). Aside from this troubling overview of nonhuman animal mistreatment, even the term "exhibit" clearly identifies the animals in zoos as objects, as property to be displayed and ogled rather than admired and treated with care and compassion. Moreover, there are countless examples of "wild" or "escaped" nonhuman animals who are demonized and then killed because of purported transgressions against humans. From "attacks" on circus trainers by tigers and elephants to "attacks" on campers by bears, most nonhuman animal actions that are directed at humans, and that do not display unflinching obedience, are considered to be abhorrent and thereby necessitate dramatic if not deadly action. Of course, this needs to change, and although change is not always easy, there are many means through which we can begin to envision, or re-vision, nonhuman animals as living beings who deserve sympathy and autonomy. And perhaps one means of promoting change comes from re-examining popular culture: in the case of this essay, the fiction of Stephen King.

Perhaps it is strange to consider Stephen King's fiction as an arena of social change, especially concerning nonhuman animals. Yet the critical eye is able to learn from most any forum or medium, and King's fiction (in the eyes of animal rights activist or vegans) provides many compelling examinations of the nonhuman animal kingdom. King's fiction is generally horrific, troubling, and frightening, and yet for all the terrors of which King writes, there is a sense of sadness. The gloom and melancholy that populate King's canon are often found among the human social circles of which King writes, from broken families like the Torrances in *The Shining* to matters of racial injustice in *The Green Mile*. But if we look past King's human characters and examine his nonhuman ones, we encounter various instances of what appears to be a grotesque imagination at work, an imagination that, according to James B. Twitchell, is simply a matter of King composing fiction that is frightening but in a safe way: "[King's fiction] is violence contrived not to be taken seriously, not to be believed, but to shock and to be endured. It is violence drawn not from life but from fairy tales filtered through gothic conventions. As in fairy tales, the usual trigger for violence is outside the natural world" (106–7). Twitchell's commentary suggests that the preponderance of the unnatural or supernatural within King's canon is a heavy veil of fiction that simply serves the purpose of entertainment, albeit through disgust. Twitchell seems to claim that there is no potential for symbolism, allegory or moral/ethical discussion and transformation within King's fiction — it is, for lack of a better phrase, one dimensional. It is fiction aimed at a single goal to capture readership through spectacle, violence and fear. Moreover, as Twitchell implies, the spectacle, violence and fear of which King writes results in *temporary* effects upon the reader; any "endurance" associated with a King text is simply a matter of enduring the violent onslaught of the plot rather than King creating an enduring, lasting impression upon the reader concerning issues that extend well beyond disturbing corpses or monsters in the mist. Yet reading the King canon with a gaze towards the well-being and survival of his nonhuman characters reveals a horror more frightening than the fictitious monsters or the human travesties for which King is largely known.

Stephen King is often relegated to the role of a "Master of Horror," and the generic labeling might be difficult for some to navigate regarding animals. In other words, we can surmise that many see nonhuman animal consumption, death or even torture as completely non-horrific. But such perceptions do not erase the actual horror of animal abuse that populates the real world. With that said, King's fiction does indeed magnify the horrors nonhuman animals face every day. And this magnification is not necessarily a matter of

King foregrounding nonhuman animal abuse to simply add instances of horrific spectacle to his fiction. As one King scholar, Amy Canfield, says, "True horror, though, occurs when the terror we read is mimicked in real life in ways that make novels seem tame" (391). Although Canfield is referencing domestic abuse, her words echo clearly within the field of critical animal studies and regarding King's fictions that present the abuse, torture and death of nonhumans: for every dead cat of which King writes (such as Church from *Pet Sematary*), there are thousands of other cats in the real world who die at the hands of humans, whether by accidental means (like Church's demise as he is run over by a semi-truck), or by the hands of humans who find pleasure in animal suffering.

Moreover, continuing to use domestic abuse as a doorway into the discussion of animal rights within the King canon, Canfield explores domestic abuse and the invalid, socially-constructed rationalizations behind the perpetuation of such abuse. She states that "[t]his social order and the belief in the sanctity of marriage, at any cost, is also reinforced by communities, law-enforcers, friends, and family" (395). In other words, as marriages often break down and become abusive, there are many who support the perpetuation of all marriages simply for the sake of maintaining this social norm so that the cultural institution of marriage may remain untarnished and looked upon favorably.

The same holds true for nonhuman animal abuse: we can easily see that abuse is unwarranted and unethical, but social norms that rely on animal subjugation for entertainment, clothing, or food promote ignorance and indifference towards nonhuman animal suffering so that such common or profitable practices remain customary. Additionally, as "[w]omen who are abused rarely suffer their abuse in silence," so to do animals suffer loudly and within circles that hear their cries for help yet perpetually ignore these calls for help (Canfield 395). And, again, just as the "sanctity of marriage" propels some women to stay within abusive relationships, various social norms (or abnormal social codes, from the perspective of the animal rights activist) dictate that nonhuman beings are of lesser importance than their human counterparts and are to be relegated to the status of pet, sport, entertainment, food or even literary trope.

The belief in the normalcy and *righteousness* of established social norms compels individuals to continue with harmful and abusive relationships with nonhumans, primarily because such is merely acceptable to a large number of people. As a result, views that stem from animal rights circles are often seen as abnormal, no matter how intelligent or rational such messages are, as these perceptions contradict what the larger group determines to be "right" while alternative ideologies that favor animal well-being are, by simplistic contrast, "wrong." But perhaps the "Master of Horror" can help us to re-vision the nonhuman animal world and literally see that which many have purposefully chosen to be ignorant.

Critical Animal Studies: A Revolutionary Reading Perspective

Before exploring and analyzing the animal kingdom through a selection of King's fiction, it should be noted that this essay is not an attempt to put words into the mouth of the "Master or Horror" or to simply identify the numerous examples of animal suffering (and/or succor) in his works. Rather, this essay considers the effects that veganism and an empathetic alliance with the animal rights movement has on one's perspective of the world. So, as we approach the fiction of Stephen King with a critical eye cast towards the nonhuman animal characters that populate his fiction, we must read these texts with the intention of doing more than simply observing the presence of nonhuman animals. Much as how critical race studies are concerned with more than the mere presence of non-white characters in literature and other artistic expressions, the overarching theories of Critical Animal Studies (CAS) helps us to critically read and analyze the work of Stephen King and other forms of popular culture from an animal rights perspective so that, perhaps, action and positive change may occur.

Quite possibly, some of the more telling instances of animal rights discourse are found in comedy. For example, Bill Watterson, author of the comic strip *Calvin and Hobbes*, drew a transparent strip in which a man walking through cubicles of an office is suddenly shot by a pack of deer who are walking erect (like humans) and equipped with hunting rifles. These anthropomorphic deer then gather around the corpse of the dead man and share (typical) congratulations when "game" has been killed: "You got him"; "He's a big one, too!"; "Nice shot, Bambi"; and "Somebody get the camera" (5/160). Although this particular scene is the imagined fantasy of Watterson's titular character, Calvin, and is explained as an alternative view to overpopulation in which humans are hunted by animals to "thin out the herd" (and perhaps lessen the drastic effects that humans have on the Earth), the undertones are quite clear.

Further, the late George Carlin has provocatively weighed in on issues surrounding nonhuman animals: "I think people have a lot of nerve locking up a tiger and charging four dollars to let a few thousand worthless humans shuffle past him every day. What a shitty thing to do. Humans must easily be the meanest species on Earth" (237). Additionally, Carlin notes,

I do not torture animals, and I do not support the torture of animals, such as that which goes on at rodeos: cowardly men in big hats abusing simple beasts[1] in a fruitless search for manhood. In fact, I regularly pray for serious, life-threatening rodeo injuries. I wish for a cowboy to walk crooked, and with great pain, for the rest of his life [237].

These commentaries on the nonhuman animal condition from Watterson and Carlin are relatively easy to understand and interpret, but ignorance and indifference often mitigates the affect of critical (and comical) discourse surrounding nonhuman animals.

For instance, when we read Stephen King's novel *Cell* and of the characters' intentions to kill the zombies who populate this novel, we read "'it wouldn't be murder, not really; it would be extermination,'" encountering dialogue that represents more than a "survival plan" (193). The simple substitution of "extermination" for "murder," or even "zombie" for "animal," carries some difficulty in terms of fully understanding King's fiction. If we simply accept that zombies are "lesser beings," or disposable beings, there's a problem. Zombies, like nonhuman animals, are not necessarily entities to be automatically relegated to a position lower than that of humans; yet within *Cell*, the zombies are indeed automatically placed into a position of subordination through which the human characters justify murder. This reflection of zombies as animal-like creatures who are lesser beings than humans needs to be examined, challenged and changed. To (re)read *Cell*, or any other Stephen King text, in which humans are presumed to be superior beings while other animals are relegated to roles as pests to be exterminated is essential. The burgeoning field of CAS is but one way that we can critically view nonhuman animals and perhaps find sympathy as well as enact change.

A CAS reading of nonhuman animal suffering in popular culture helps us to maneuver past what Steven Best calls "the distorting lens of speciesism." Speciesism, according to Joan Dunayer, "is a failure to empathize with those outside one's group," and this cornerstone term for CAS reminds us that (re)reading any text involving nonhuman animals cannot be done critically unless we shed any biases we have concerning them (10). If we read a text and defer to the prevailing social norms concerning nonhuman animals, we will fall into the trap of speciesist readings and, quite often, look upon nonhuman animal suffering with indifferent eyes. Moreover, we must understand that CAS is not necessarily a cure-all, or even an easy way of reading texts. As Best notes, "The term 'animal studies,' in fact, is a misnomer that impedes understanding from the start, for the field is not about nonhuman animals in isolation from human animals, but rather about human-nonhuman animal relations."

On the heels of Best's overview of the power and difficulties of CAS,

Dunayer further reminds us of the obstacles that need to be overcome, especially regarding language. She notes that "even the word *nonhuman* divides all animals into two, seemingly opposed categories: humans and everyone else" (xi). But when we become aware of these difficulties in language and the overwhelming inability for humans to look towards animals/nonhumans with a critical eye (or even with a sense of equality), we realize that even with the problems involved in CAS, a willingness to look at animals/nonhumans as more than subservient entities is a move in the right direction. With CAS a broad guide for "reading" the world, and reading King's fiction, we are equipped to do more than simply gloss over or ignore any images or references to those who populate the animal kingdom besides humans.

Now we arrive at the core of this essay's overarching topic of Stephen King's fiction and its potential to sharpen one's senses and sensibilities concerning nonhuman animals. To start, one of the best examples of re-visioning that I have experienced concerning King and the animal kingdom, aided by the CAS lens, comes from hearing King speak in Seattle in November 2006 for the tour of his book *Lisey's Story*. During this event, King described a scene in which his main character, Lisey Landon, discovers a dead cat in her mailbox:

> At first she saw only a darkish shape and a green glimmer, like light reflecting off marble. And wetness on the corrugated metal floor of the mailbox. The darkish shape grew fur, and ears, and a nose that probably would have been pink in the daylight. There was no mistaking the eyes; even dulled in death, their shape was distinctive. There was a dead cat in her mailbox. Lisey began to laugh. It was not exactly normal laughter, but it wasn't entirely hysterical, either. There was genuine humor in it.... What made it funny was that Lisey didn't *own* a cat [King, *Lisey's Story* 216].[2]

After reading this scene, King paused and interrupted his narrative with the following comment: "Who thinks of this sick shit?" At the time, King's sarcasm seemed funny to me. Upon review, I realize that King's question, although tongue-in-cheek, suggests that animal abuse and torture is almost unheard of, and that it takes a "Master of Horror" to imagine the cruelty that even a single nonhuman animal may endure within the realm of *fiction*. This is, of course, not the case.

The "sick shit" of animal torture, abuse, and death is a reality that people certainly think about, but in ways that are rarely helpful or progressive. Indeed, several years removed from King's discussion of dead nonhuman animals, and now equipped with a new means of re-viewing the commonplace plights of them, I no longer laugh at King's query. Animals who are killed for consumption, or to disturb other people (whether a dead cat in a mailbox or a severed horse's head in one's bed *à la The Godfather*), is no laughing matter. In light of this altered perspective, and while thinking of King's musings, I am pushed to ask the question, "Who *doesn't* think of this sick shit?" The answer? Seemingly, almost everyone doesn't think, or think critically, of the "sick shit" surrounding the plight of nonhuman animals.

Seriously, *why* do many people *not* take the time to seriously think about and imagine the cruelty and suffering that nonhuman animals face, both in fiction and in reality? Interestingly and disturbingly, just about everyone I know (my vegan/animal rights activist friends and colleagues aside) seems to consciously choose to *not* think about the "sick shit" of animal death and suffering. These are the individuals who may look at a cow grazing in a field and equate this animal with dinner rather than think about what must happen in order for that living being to be reduced to a piece of meat. These are the same individuals who may pet a pig at the local zoo and not see that pink face looking up from their plates of bacon and pork chops.

In short, few people actually think of the "sick shit" surrounding nonhuman animals, or, rather, the food that they eat and the clothes that they wear. To say the least, this "sick shit" is everywhere; it is merely waiting to be discovered, or re-discovered, And this is my experience with the fiction of Stephen King that has surrounded my academic life for some time — new lenses of reading have helped me to discover what I should have known all along: that nonhuman animal suffering is all around us, even in the pages of a King novel. This suffering is hardly a matter of course or a simplistic plot device; it is a reflection of horror, especially the horror of indifference. Therefore, the goal of this discussion is to consider the powers, and challenges, in and of literature to help shape our collective consciousness and consciences regarding the use and abuse of nonhuman animals in today's world through the fiction of Stephen King.

Horror "Goes to the Dogs"

Stephen King, whether by design or not, writes into his fiction a particular sensitivity to nonhuman animals and how the nearly-unimaginable tortures that they endure warrant not just attention, but also action. This is almost hard to believe as, for example, the opening pages of his 2009 novel *Under the Dome* begin with a woodchuck being gruesomely "cut in two. Then he fell apart on the edge of the road. Blood squirted and pumped; guts tumbled into the dirt; his rear legs kicked rapidly twice, then stopped" (5). This scene in *Under the Dome* appears to be little more than an insensitive passage that highlights nonhuman animal death and which is, strangely, appealing to the reader as a violent hook to capture interest. Despite the disturbing and disgusting image of "road kill," I would argue that most readers tend to be indifferent, or even humored, by the death of this animal.

However, the careful reader who looks beyond the distasteful spectacle of nonhuman animal death sees that King is not necessarily promoting a hierarchical treatment of nonhuman animals. Indeed, King says of the unfortunate woodchuck, "[h]is last thought before the darkness that comes to us all, chucks and humans alike [was]: *What happened?*" (5). King's attribution of a gender to the woodchuck, rather than the dismissive pronoun "it," along with equating the woodchuck's death as something that is comparable and *equal* to that of a human's death, is something that casual readers might ignore, miss, or even dismiss. King's history, or perceived image as a writer who aims to "gross out" his reader, makes it difficult to pay attention to the subtleties of his writing. But, of course, we would do well to set King's reputation aside if we are to genuinely engage with his rhetorical treatment of nonhuman animals.

To be sure, many of King's earlier fictions seem to make it easy for readers to avoid critical and sensitive readings of King's nonhuman animal characters, but there is much to learn from King and these characters, from the titular *Cujo* to the oft-forgotten "billy-bumbler"[3] named Oy in King's *Dark Tower* series. In a broad sense that can be extended to the treatment of nonhuman animals, some scholars view King as a writer who treads the grounds of justice and claim that, "[King] forces us to condemn all forms of abuse, mental and physical, and to welcome the violent end of the abuser" (Kelley 107). This is, of course, only partially true in that most of King's abusers who earn the ire of the reader (from Jack Torrance of *The Shining* to Annie Wilkes of *Misery*) are *humans* who have little to no compassion and act out in inappropriate ways towards other humans. As noted King scholar Tony Magistrale says, "[T]he real monsters in King's canon are always human, and more often than not, they take the form of adult males who erect and maintain elaborate bureaucratic systems of control" (52). When we look at these broad criticisms of King's work and his treatment of "monstrosity," an exposure to CAS prompts us to analyze King's work more deeply and examine human transgressions *and* the nonhuman animal victims of such inhumanity. There are certainly obstacles to overcome when sifting through King's fiction to engage his treatment of nonhuman animals, especially as readings and criticism focused on his constant examinations of abuse and injustice in his fiction are largely relegated to the suffering of humans, not nonhumans. This is not to discount or deny the terrible horrors of domestic abuse in King's writing, but this does implore us to consider that there is more than human suffering occurring in his fiction.

However, much King criticism nonetheless tends to look towards human relations with other humans and is often accompanied by a sense of optimism.

In one instance, Susan M. Kelley claims that "[King] is an author who punishes transgressors" (108). Perhaps this is true when it comes to humans who abuse other humans, but King's fiction is not always aimed at retribution or justice. Leland Gaunt from *Needful Things* proves that evil is not always vanquished, as Mr. Gaunt may unwillingly leave Castle Rock at the end of this novel, yet he finds a new home and new people to torture at the tale's conclusion.

Of course, there *are* examples in King's fiction of evil and abusers finding justice or death: George Stark from *The Dark Half,* Annie Wilkes from *Misery,* and even Jack Torrance from *The Shining.* But for every defeat of an evil human threat, readers find a Randall Flagg from *The Stand, The Eyes of the Dragon* and the *Dark Tower* series, enduring temporary setbacks only to instigate more chaos. To say the least, evil is not always punished or eliminated, and the endurance of evil and unethical behavior is intimately tied to the existence of most nonhuman animals. Still, justice does have a place in King's fiction at times, especially as it concerns nonhumans, and one of the only means of justice regarding animal torture comes in *It* with the death of the character Patrick Hockstetter.

Hockstetter is a disturbed young boy who kills his little brother, Avery, and also kills cats, dogs, and birds by leaving them locked in an abandoned refrigerator. With this brief overview of Patrick's transgressions, we might be justified in assuming that most readers would consider that the death of a human is of greater importance and leads to more "appropriate" sorrow than the death of nonhumans that Patrick causes. However, King's treatment of Patrick does not leave off with a mere glimpse into Patrick's "secondary" transgressions. King carefully goes into disturbing detail regarding the emotions (as disturbing as they may be) surrounding Patrick's twisted actions against nonhumans:

> excitement — that feeling of color and sensation — was simply too powerful and too wonderful to give over entirely. Patrick killed flies. At first he only smacked them with his mother's flyswatter; later he discovered he could kill them quite efficiently with a plastic ruler. He also discovered the joys of flypaper ... and Patrick sometimes stood for as long as two hours in the garage, watching the flies land and then struggle to get free [791].

This description is not to be taken lightly. Although some readers might consider King's examination of Patrick as just another example of the author's verbose prose, it is an important exposure to the indifference to suffering that many embrace. Patrick's treatment of insects and mammals are detailed to disturb readers on two fronts: to remind readers that people like Patrick actually exist and to show readers that abuse of nonhumans is not only commonplace but also receives little afterthought. Like much of King's perceived audience, Patrick does not view abuse and torture as wrong — he finds joy and pleasure in such actions, and while it is a bit of an exaggeration to say that most readers are complicit with Patrick's deeds, their dismissal of abuse suggests a common ground of indifference and ignorance towards nonhuman animal abuse. This speculation is put forth as King's readers do not necessarily have to visually witness Patrick's evils. Although the audience is asked to visualize and imagine the torture Patrick enacts, imagination is only so powerful. In many cases, imagination can become impotent or controlled, especially if the individual who might be asked to imagine disturbing events like animal torture is willing to close his/her mind's eye.

For those who approach Patrick Hockstetter and his actions through CAS, they find an example of an author attempting to communicate (but not necessarily cure) the everyday evils of human actions. And although It, the main villain[4] of *It*, kills Patrick, providing some sort of relief (and perhaps joy) for those who find this animal abuser to be a prime candidate for death, the most revealing aspect of Patrick's existence within *It* is how Patrick turned to animal abuse in the first place.

As mentioned, Patrick kills his infant brother, but this murder is not the end game of a psychopath who begins to exercise power over life and death through the torture and abuse of animals. Unlike many murderers or sociopaths, Patrick begins his murderous impulses by killing his brother and *then* moves on to killing insects and animals. Most psychological profiles on murders and serial killers point towards a reverse order of death as the transformation into a murderer often begins with small animals and then moves towards human victims. This inversion of the typical growth of a killer within King's novel suggests that humans and nonhumans are, especially in the eyes of a psychopath, of equal status. And perhaps this is the horror of *It*: only Patrick, a troubled if not deranged human, is able to see value in nonhuman animal life. Further, although it is troubling to read of his deeds, this character can help King's readers come to the realization that killing is killing no matter *who* (not "what") dies.

Cujo offers another testing ground for the powers of reading King's canon with the aid of CAS. First and foremost, we must remember that *Cujo* is not entirely about the title character — this story is a Castle Rock yarn, pulling from the history of a fictional town that King creates in *The Dead Zone* and continues with *The Dark Half* and *Needful Things*. Moreover, the fiction mainly focuses on the disintegrating marriage of Vic and Donna Trenton, with their son, Tad, finding himself caught in the crossfire of a failing marital union. Yet when we focus on the main nonhuman character in this text, we find that there is a particular duality involved.

For some readers, Cujo is a sentient being capable of thought, which is partially evidenced by King's attempts to provide inner dialogue for Cujo as he (not *it*) looks towards his young companion Brett Cambers as "THE BOY" (21). Therefore Cujo, as a sentient individual who feels pain and possesses a clear intelligence, rudimentary or otherwise, becomes much more than "just an animal" or a "dumb beast." However, according to John R. Woznicki, "we are meant to confuse Cujo and his human counterparts. King intentionally blurs the division between animal and human" (128). On one hand, Woznicki suggests that any semblance of equality that Cujo has with humans is accidental or a mere trick of the fiction. On the other hand, Woznicki also suggests that any instances in which Cujo is seen as more than an animal are certainly present in the text. Still, this suggestion that Cujo is more than a "mere" animal is easily ignored or dismissed by readers and even the characters in the novel.

Cujo, like the rabies that he contracts, becomes an *evil* to be vanquished; as Donna Trenton says when she and her son Tad are trapped by the Saint Bernard, "*It's a sick dog and that's all it is*" (163, emphasis added). If we apply Donna's words to humans, suggesting that sickness is an excuse to vanquish or eliminate humans who are deemed abnormal (or sick), we are left to wonder what the results might be. But because Cujo is "just an animal," or a monster of sorts, it seems that his suffering is tolerable and his death justifiable. Indeed, as Woznicki also claims, "Cujo must learn to deal with pain; but *as a lower form of animal*, his coping mechanisms involve escape, and, ultimately, when escape is not an option, violence" (128, emphasis added). King seems to establish Cujo as a monster, as a violent "other" to be mastered and conquered, despite any efforts to the contrary. Moreover, as the early pages of *Cujo* discuss Tad's extreme fear of monsters, it is no surprise that Cujo becomes one of the "monsters" of which Tad is afraid.

As *Cujo* opens, Tad, like most any child, suspects that monsters live in his closet. This fear is ultimately mitigated, but not erased, as his father pens "The Monster Words." These words begin with the declaration, "*Monsters, stay out of this room! You have no business here*" (60). This mantra, or pseudo-catechism, foreshadows the eventual stand-off between Cujo against Donna and Tad. But, more importantly, these words can be read as an oppressive dismissal of nonhuman animals like Cujo. When "The Monster Words" state that monsters have no business in Tad's room, we can substitute the word "monster" for "animal." This suggests, again, that animals are lesser beings and that humans have an inherent right to dominate them, especially within "civilized" domestic settings. King may even have Donna declare of Cujo that, "'It's [*sic*] not a monster ... it's [*sic*] just a *dog*,'" but her empty classification is challenging as well as indicative of a tendency to view nonhuman animals as lesser beings, even if they are clearly non-monstrous (184). This is reflective of a constant push-and-pull within *Cujo*: the title character receives some sympathy in that we realize Cujo needs help because he has contracted rabies and is not a monster; however, when readers and critics relegate Cujo to the status of *dog* (translation: lesser being), this negates the intellectual progress CAS asks us to embrace. But this constant return to the realm of perceiving nonhumans as lesser beings, as inferior to humans, is a normal practice that can be challenged.

When we further analyze *Cujo* and the veiled layers of meaning and complexity involving animal rights, we would do well to look at Cujo's death and witness the disturbing and deliberate content. Among the darkly compelling content, especially for readers who are attuned to Cujo's ascendancy beyond "monster" or "animal," we all must come directly face-to-face with Cujo's murder: "She [Donna] slammed the door on Cujo's head again and again ... The dog's head was plastered with thick, sticky blood, as black as insect blood in the chancey starlight" (229). King goes on to describe the final moments of Cujo's life as Donna completes his death: "She swung the bat like Mickey Mantle going after a high fastball. She missed Cujo's head but the bat struck him in the ribs. There was a heavy, dull thump and a snapping sound from somewhere inside Cujo. The dog uttered a sound like a scream and went sprawling in the gravel" (287). These descriptions, it should go without saying, are not exactly constructed to be pleasurable; indeed, the details of Cujo's death serve a clear purpose. They present an almost natural predilection of violence towards nonhuman animals, from those who pose a threat or even to those hunted down as sport for some. To wit, although Donna survives Cujo's rabid advances, her son Tad dies.[5]

After Tad's death, and after Cujo has been killed, Donna finds it fitting, natural and acceptable to brutalize Cujo's corpse: "She went for the baseball bat. She picked it up and began to bludgeon the dog again. The flies rose in a shiny green-black cloud. The sound of the ball bat making contact was heavy and terrible, a butcher-shop sound. Cujo's body jumped a little each time she struck it" (293). Donna blames Cujo for her son's death when, of course, it is not that simple; Cujo may be the easy target for anger and hatred, or the convenient underlying cause behind Tad's death, but Cujo's disease and Donna's decision to leave her home in a mechanically unsound vehicle are the more logical underlying causes. However, to Donna, Cujo is simply a lesser being, and while her compassion for her son naturally outweighs her compassion towards another individual, her slanted views of Cujo are but few among many others that populate the King canon. This overarching dismissal of the well-being of nonhuman animals is certainly familiar and is also revisited in King's short story "Premium Harmony,"[6] published in *The New Yorker* in 2009.

While the name of this short story refers to a fictional brand of cigarettes,

it also refers to the solace that the main character, Ray, feels at the story's conclusion upon learning that his wife, Mary, has died. Additionally, the harmony
that Ray seems to embrace at the end of the story comes with yet another
death — the death of his dog, Bizness. The story takes Ray, a cold and heartless
character, and his wife to a convenience store into which she goes to purchase
a gift for her niece and a pack of cigarettes for Ray. Mary has a heart attack
while in the store. When Ray learns of what happens to Mary and leaves his
car to check on her, the story takes a proverbial turn for the worse. But what
could be worse than a man losing his wife to a heart attack?

In this story, the more disturbing death involves the forgotten character,
Biz, who also dies, and not as quickly as Mary. King foreshadows Biz's death
as he notes, "Ray locks the car" and goes to investigate his wife's condition
(70). This minor note becomes of key importance for readers attuned to the
well-being of the tale's nonhuman, Biz. As Ray leaves his car, locked and
with the windows rolled up, it becomes clear that an extended amount of
time away from the vehicle is more than just imminent doom for Biz. It is an
example of humans constantly ignoring the presence of nonhuman animals
as well as a plot device that increases tension for readers who fear for Biz's
well being. Indeed, Biz's "master" Ray is anything but a poster child for compassion.

One early instance of Ray's callousness towards Biz comes after Mary
depicts Biz as if he were their child, their baby: "Ray hates it when she calls
Biz the baby. He's a dog, and he may be as bright as Mary likes to boast when
they have company, but he still shits outside and licks where his balls used to
be" (69). Ray, like many humans, finds that canine bathing habits — defecating
outdoors and cleaning (not necessarily licking) their genital areas — are "sub-
human," and as Ray views Biz as a creature necessarily beneath him, it is no
surprise that Ray takes Biz's death rather lightly:

> When he [Ray] opens the door, heat rushes out at him, and when he puts his
> hand on the steering wheel to lean in he pulls it back with a cry. It's got to be
> a hundred and thirty in there. Biz is dead on his back. His eyes are milky. His
> tongue is protruding from the side of his mouth. Ray can see the wink of his
> teeth. There are little bits of coconut caught in his whiskers. That shouldn't be
> funny, but it is. Not funny enough to laugh at, but funny.... Great sadness and
> amusement sweep over him as he looks at the baked Jack Russell. That any-
> thing so sad should be funny is just a crying shame [73].

For some readers, this aspect of "Premium Harmony" is simply a climax with
which King ends the story to ruminate upon Ray's insensitivity, at least for
those who do not find much horror surrounding Biz's death. Other readers,
however, are troubled by Ray's cold-heartedness; indeed, who can read of a
nonhuman animal, or any animal for that matter, forced to endure such a

painful death? With the primary example of indifference to nonhuman animal suffering in *Cujo*, and the secondary example of indifference towards nonhuman animal well-being within "Premium Harmony," we see that for every step King and his readers may take forward, there are characters and startling realities that take us right back to the start. And at this starting point, we find that nonhuman animals are continuously treated as second-class citizens and that the horrors surrounding nonhuman characters of which King writes are not always discovered or considered by his readers.

Even when King "humanizes" his nonhuman animal characters or writes of animal torture and suffering, his audience remains ignorant. This, of course, reflects the common double-standard we witness in the world at large concerning the constructed human/animal divide. When humans hurt, attack, and oppress animals, it is normal; but when animals hurt, attack, or somehow "oppress" humans, such is often perceived as genuine horror. Yet the real horror of which King writes is found within the constant dismissal of any being who does not fit within the worthy category of "human."

Every Dog ... and Cat ... and Billy-Bumbler Has His/Her Day

Beyond *Cujo*, when it comes to the "horrors" of animals attacking humans, we have several examples of feline mistreatment in King's fiction that further remind us of the obstacles that nonhuman animals must face. One of the most well-known cats in King's oeuvre is Church from *Pet Sematary*. In short, Church is brought back from the dead to appease the sorrow of his owner/master/companion Ellie Creed, a young child who has yet to learn of death's inevitability. As such, we must ask: Is it fair to Church that he is brought back from the dead? Readers, or people like Ellie's father Louis Creed, seem to be more concerned with the emotional well-being of Ellie, who must eventually learn that all creatures die, rather than the well-being of Church, who has been buried, reanimated, clawed through the earth, and has returned as a shadow of his former self. Yet the horror of *Pet Sematary*, it seems, is not Church's reanimation. Rather, the horror appears to come from Church's changed persona — a cat who was once a loving family member has been transformed into a monster who no longer provides joy or solace to the Creed family.

Once Church turns away from the role that he had fulfilled for humans, or that had been prescribed to him by humans, he is no longer a beloved pet. He becomes a monster, an outsider like Cujo, who only finds relatively open arms from Louis Creed, a fellow monster who buried Church in the pet cemetery and loses his humanity throughout the rest of the novel. Here we cry "foul" regarding the mistreatment of Church as a beast, as a monster, when he no longer plays according to the rules and role demanded of him. Perhaps Louis' son Gage Creed, also a reanimated monster later in the novel, says it best in the film version of *Pet Sematary*: "No fair!"

No fair, indeed. The double-standard that exists concerning human expectations and treatments of nonhuman animals is, to say it again, ubiquitous yet often remains unnoticed and a plot device to the more important interactions amongst humans. Sometimes the mistreatment of nonhuman animals in the world outside of fiction and in the Stephen King canon does not go unnoticed. This is especially true in King's novella "Apt Pupil," as former Nazi officer Kurt Dussander captures several stray cats so that he can slowly kill them in his oven. But beyond clear discussions of animal torture that elicit compassion and even anger from some readers, another example of feline horror in King's canon presents the argument that there is little wrong with showing compassion and respect for nonhuman animals from a more indirect perspective. King's short story "The Cat from Hell," despite its slightly offensive title, provides plenty of subtext that shows careful readers that nonhuman animals deserve our respect and compassion.

Within "The Cat from Hell," King suggests that when animals attack, it is either natural or justified. As to the broad plot of the story, a rich man named Drogan believes his cat, who almost unsurprisingly remains nameless, as the cat is "just an animal," has killed several people. Drogan's ultimate response to these paranoid thoughts is to hire a contract killer who is supposed to, "'Kill it. Bury it ... Bring me the tail,' he [Drogan] said. 'So I can throw it in the fire and watch it burn'" (364). On one level, the notion of a human hiring another human to kill an animal in the form of a mob hit seems ridiculous. Then again, it is not entirely ridiculous when we think of factory farms where people are paid to kill nonhuman animals and other people pay to consume their mutilated corpses. Still, in "'The Cat from Hell," there seems to be a glimpse of nonhuman animal empowerment.

The possible empowerment is found in the prospect that a nonhuman animal has exerted a semblance of autonomy and power in such a way that his/her oppressor — Drogan — is frightened enough of the new power relationship that he will do anything to recapture his previous position as "master." Seeing a nonhuman animal "push back," like the deer with hunting rifles in the aforementioned *Calvin and Hobbes* comic strip, is an example of hushed nonhuman animal histories. As Jason Hribal discusses the numerous examples of nonhuman animal resistance against zookeepers and circus trainers in *Fear of the Animal Planet*, he says of nonhuman animals who fight their human oppressors, "Resistance is not a psychological disorder. Indeed it is often a moment of distinct clarity" (151). This is important to note, as nonhuman animal resistance to human oppression in "The Cat from Hell" is troubling as Drogan's schemes remind us that humans will do almost anything to maintain the power structures that they have erected, especially concerning nonhumans. Further, while the prospect of hiring someone to kill a cat is hardly inspiring or amusing, "The Cat from Hell" should not be seen as a story entirely comprised of insensitivity or as a target of scorn by those within the animal rights movement. Above all else, this is a tale in which the good guy, the cat, wins.

One of the early victories for the nameless cat in "The Cat from Hell" arises when King describes the hit man, named Halston, showing a noticeable hesitancy towards killing the cat. King writes, "Halston liked cats. They were the only animals he did like, as a matter of fact. They got along on their own. God — if there was one — had made them into perfect, aloof killing machines. Cats were the hitters of the animal world, and Halston gave them his respect" (354). Although this respect that Halston feels is misplaced, it is nonetheless intriguing that a murderer can see the value of a life, especially that of a nonhuman animal. The respect, however misguided, is overshadowed by Halston's allegiance to human institutions and emotions, namely money, greed, and "honor": "He [Halston] felt a kinship [with the cat], but no urge to renege on the hit" (365). Halston may not necessarily have any ill will towards the cat he is supposed to murder, but his mindset is all too familiar as many humans also do not hold any ill will towards the nonhuman animals whom they consume.

To say the least, Halston's inability to embrace what little compassion or respect that he feels towards the cat is his undoing. As the story progresses, the nameless cat attacks Halston, and it is not unreasonable to feel excitement and joy as the cat fights back against a human predator whose only real desire is to kill him/her:

> It [the cat] rammed into his [Halson's] mouth, a furry projectile. He gagged on it. Its front paws pinwheeled, tattering his tongue like a piece of liver. His stomach recoiled and he vomited. The vomit ran down into his windpipe, clogging it, and he began to choke.... The cat was forcing its way into his mouth, flattening its body, squirming, working itself further and further in.... Somehow, it had gotten its entire body into his mouth [372].

Later, after Halston has died, the cat literally emerges from the story (and Halston) victorious in his fight against human oppression: "Above Halston's navel, a ragged hole had been clawed in his flesh. Looking out was the gore-streaked black-and-white face of a cat, its eyes huge and glaring" (374). This re-birth of sorts is a bit disgusting, but is also liberating. For once, a nonhuman animal has provided King's constant reader with a taste of justice outside of the human realm. But before we consider King as a true friend to the non-human animal, we look towards his *magnum opus*, the *Dark Tower* series, and see that even in King's largest work, the role of the nonhuman animal reverts to that of a dismissed entity whose feelings and intelligence are ignored.

Of all the nonhuman animal references and inclusions in King's canon, perhaps Oy of the *Dark Tower* series stands tallest among the rest. This individual not only receives the most attention in terms of word count compared to other nonhuman characters in King's corpus, but also receives the most characterization among all of King's nonhuman (and non-fantastical) creations; Oy possesses the capability of rudimentary speech, can count by tapping his paw on the ground a certain number of times to represent his understanding of arithmetic, and he is seen shedding tears on several occasions. Further, Oy has more than a name, of course — he is a member of a group of questers who comprise the core cast of *The Dark Tower*, and he directly contributes to the outcomes of the numerous adventures this group (or, in King's words, *ka-tet*) have. While Oy is familiarly utilized by humans for his sense of smell to track people, and even speaks to his comrades through broken speech akin to that of a parrot, he is also largely disregarded by the four human members of his family — Roland Deschain, Eddie Dean, Susannah Dean and Jake Chambers (although Jake, Oy's "boy," has a special bond with Oy; Jake is almost never without Oy's company and considers Oy to be a friend). But Oy's status with this group receives inconsistent and dismissive treatment that critical readers should find troubling.

As mentioned, there are numerous instances in which Oy is forgotten, perhaps because he is not human. For example, in the third book of the *Dark Tower* series, *The Waste Lands*, the cast of characters that King creates must cross a dilapidated bridge, and as they begin their perilous trek across the broken bridge, the group forgets that Oy, too, must cross the bridge. As the group begins to cross, the character Eddie Dean, who takes up the rear, almost falls off the bridge as Oy attempts to cross. Oy darts towards the front of the group where his friend, Jake Chambers, is walking, and as the forgotten member of this group runs past Eddie, causing Eddie to lose his balance and almost fall into the river below the bridge, Eddie angrily mutters, "'Fucking dumb animal'" (291). Of course, had Eddie or his other companions given due attention to their nonhuman companion (rather than nonhuman pet), Eddie's undue anger would not have been vocalized. Had this group remembered the presence of their nonhuman animal companion, Oy would likely have been carried carefully across the bridge rather than forced to fend for himself. Moreover, because this group does not account for Oy's safe passage across the bridge, at one point Oy loses his own footing and begins to fall off the bridge. While Jake dives towards Oy to rescue the "billy-bumbler," Jake's human companions admonish him for risking his life to save Oy. Although Jake shows compassion for Oy, the others show very little interest in him, and the same can be said for the narrator of these tales, who often refers to the five-member group of this story as a quartet rather than a quintet.

Further, readers are constantly reminded of Oy's "beastly" existence as he is often distanced from his companions because he is only a "small, furry animal" (398). Amusingly, and perhaps tellingly, the only character in *The Dark Tower* who consistently acknowledges Oy's existence is a computer known as Blaine. To see a nonhuman in the form of a computer consistently acknowledge the existence of another nonhuman reminds us of much more than Oy's mercurial status within the *Dark Tower* series: we are reminded that dismissal of nonhuman animals is commonplace, even when they are family "pets," which mirrors Oy's role in the group. But King, once again, shows that ignorance towards nonhuman animals is more complex than mere forgetfulness.

At a late stage in the *Dark Tower* series, the main character, the gunslinger Roland Deschain, is journeying towards the Dark Tower. During his adventure, he loses his human companions Eddie, Susannah and Jake, but he maintains company with Oy. And although Roland mostly forgets Oy's existence, Oy does not forget his love for and allegiance towards Roland. To clarify, within the seventh and last book of this series, Roland's illegitimate son, Mordred, is on the gunslinger's trail, and aims to kill his father. And when Mordred finally catches up to Roland, Mordred's eventual ambush is halted by Oy who attacks him. Oy's selfless act distracts Mordred and allows Roland just enough time to react to the ambush and to then kill his would-be killer. However, Oy loses his life in the process as Mordred, before his own death, flings Oy into the branches of a dead tree where the billy-bumbler is impaled. If there is anything positive to glean from this scene, it is that as "[Mordred] had left Oy out of his calculations, and was now paying the price," readers see that the love a nonhuman animal can have for another animal is clear, and that ignoring the presence of nonhuman animals can have disastrous results, especially for Mordred (769).

Indeed, had Mordred considered that Oy is anything but a simple creature, perhaps Mordred would have kept his life. Also, with Oy's sacrifice, we witness, through Roland's grief, a genuine love that is not always given to nonhuman animals. In his sadness, Roland reflects upon Oy's death and reveals a familial bond alongside a deep-seated sense of grief: "Here was another one he [Roland] had killed, and if there was consolation to be had, it was this: Oy would be the last. Now he [Roland] was alone again ... *I only kill my family*, Roland thought, stroking the dead billy-bumbler" (772). Oy's death, like the deaths of many nonhuman animals not labeled "companions," is surrounded by forgetfulness and dismissal: Roland, despite his cries of pain, actually shows a level of indifference towards the death of his friend. In *Wizard and Glass*, the fourth book of the *Dark Tower* series, Roland has a vision in which he sees a billy-bumbler impaled on a tree branch; and this billy-bumbler is, of course, Oy. But this premonition of Oy's death is forgotten as Oy does indeed die (and by way of impaling, just as Roland foresaw).

Roland never stops to think that his friend, his *family*, will endure the agonizing end he knows is forthcoming. Roland displays a willingness to forget about the survival and well-being of Oy, suggesting that his quixotic human endeavors — to find the Dark Tower, and only to find this tower — are of more value than the life of a nonhuman animal. Such forgetfulness, pride and arrogance may be common when it comes to nonhuman animals, but that is the troubling reality that King's fiction conveys. If Roland had true compassion, rather than just regret, perhaps his nonhuman animal companion could have avoided death. But we cannot re-write King's fiction; what we can do, however, is learn from the mistakes and transgressions of which King writes.

Even after Oy's death, and the deaths of countless other nonhuman animals in King's fiction, there is hope. Such hope, and perhaps compassionate re-visioning of the subservient existence of many nonhuman animals, is horrifically gained through fictional representations of nonhuman animal death and mistreatment that reflects pressing social issues that extend well beyond the pages of Stephen King's fictional universe.

Putting the "Human" in "Inhumanity": Where Is Stephen King Pointing Us?

Throughout this exploration of Stephen King's canon and the numerous instances of nonhuman animal suffering and human indecency, the goal has been to critically examine rather than passively observe King's treatment of nonhumans in his writing. Through this critical analysis, we discover that although King may not be an animal rights activist himself, he is an exceptional chronicler of the human condition, especially that which relegates nonhuman animals to lowly statuses and inhumane treatment. As things stand, the conversation is simmering, and in order to reach a metaphorical boil, we can look to King as but one vessel of change from the realm of popular culture: "We need his uncanny ability to give form to these inexpressible fears because we cannot speak them. Perhaps it is finally that in King's works we find not just our fears but ourselves" (Lant and Thompson 4). The mirror that King holds up to his audience, more often than not, casts a rather hideous reflection.

For example, as King muses upon the nature and complexity of the cosmos in *The Gunslinger*, his examination of God (who can function as a substitute for humankind) suggests that passivity towards nonhumans is, well, natural: "'If God watches over it all, does He actually mete out justice for a race of gnats among an infinitude of races of gnats? Does his eye see the sparrow fall when the sparrow is less than a speck of hydrogen floating disconnected in the depth of space? And if he does see ... what must the nature of such a God be?'" (223). In other words, what must the nature of such a *human* be if justice is not sought for all creatures, big and small? Rather, how can we begin to find justice, compassion and understanding for *everyone*?

All things considered, one of the ways we further the causes of animal rights is to approach this issue through many of the same vehicles used by equal rights advocates of the last 150 years, which is exposure and situating it into the everyday psyches of the people. While the attention given to certain issues can reach somewhat overbearing levels, such as the linguistic transformation of rhetoric known as "politically correct language," there is something to be said for a movement that has resulted in a move from indifference to actual attention. And the action that is sought is not necessarily an eternal struggle: "Once people recognize speciesism's inherent cruelty and injustice, there's no further need to argue issue by issue" (Dunayer 161). In other words, the unintentional connection between King's literature and animal rights activism is not a matter of self-interest or aimed at forging secure financial futures through a perpetual presence. The goals of animal rights activists are purposefully aimed at self-destruction: once the world is made aware of animal suffering *and* takes action to halt further needless killing, there will be no further need for these groups. What can be nobler than an institution or movement whose primary goal is its self-destruction?[7]

As we close the current conversation on nonhuman animals through the fiction of Stephen King, we leave with the hope that change can be achieved through, at the very least, careful reading. And while King is much more than just a popular, or hack, writer, we nonetheless face obstacles with his fiction and its typical readers. Twitchell suggests that many of King's readers are immutable and often have a non-transformative experience with his fiction. Specifically, Twitchell comments:

> Certain audiences want to be shocked, and since most visceral shock is visual, they want images, scenes, and scenarios which turn their stomachs and make their eyes roll. They want violent turns and rapid descents. They want to lurch. They want to be "grossed out." They want cartoon action [128].

This "cartoon action" is almost synonymous with the seemingly unreal, and therefore unimportant, aspects of King's corpus that portray nonhuman animals as either victims of extreme human behaviors or as mythically heroic characters. Yet fiction is but one vehicle through which we find at least some clues, suggestions and tools to use in the worthwhile endeavor of re-visioning and embracing equity and compassion for nonhuman animals. As Susan M. Kelley states of King:

> [He] urges us to embrace decency.... He declares abuse to be evil and inexcus-able for a rational, responsible [person]. His moral judgments may strike us as too simple, maybe too black-and-white, but his understanding of the com-plexity of human behavior negates that assumption. He understands how hard it is to be decent [113].

But decency, according to King, is actually almost impossible:

> At bottom, you see, we are not *Homo sapiens* at all. Our core is madness. The prime directive is murder. What Darwin was too polite to say, my friends, is that we came to rule the earth not because we were the smartest, or even the meanest, but because we have always been the craziest, most murderous moth-erfuckers in the jungle [*Cell* 206].

But this Earth and its animals, human and nonhuman alike, are not beyond saving. We are not in Dante's hell where we are asked to abandon all hope. And we are not in a fairy-tale world or a world that can reasonably accept the assertion that "[a] key to understanding the attraction of Stephen King's violence is that it is *never* the result of human will" (Twitchell 107). King's violence, especially towards nonhuman animals, is more often than not vio-lence that is enacted and perpetuated by humans. Yet, with new eyes with which to view nonhumans, readers may become willing to realize that Stephen King's fiction is a powerful ally for nonhuman animals as King creates pur-poseful and necessary stigmas associated with the words *humane* and *human-ity.*

NOTES

1. Carlin's language here is revealing-while he is forward with his views on animal rights, he is not necessarily an animal rights activist, and his language reveals a certain bias, or at least stratification, regarding humans and nonhuman animals. Still, his words are noteworthy because he indicates a logical dissonance concerning "normal" practices regarding nonhuman animals that others would do well to adopt.

2. King's emphasis of the word "own" highlight's Lisey's disconnect from the dead cat, which rationalizes the absence of grief and disgust. Moreover, emphasizing ownership of another living being, especially a nonhuman animal, is likely not a concern for many readers whereas others with a sensitivity to animals would likely take offense to the notion of cat ownership.

3. This nonhuman animal, "look[s] like a combination raccoon and woodchuck, with a dash of dachshund thrown in for good measure" (*The Waste Lands* 221). According to one of King's characters, this being looks more like "'a fucked-up weasel,'" which is a generally dismissive view of nonhuman animals that many people hold (*Wizard and Glass* 636). This

nonhuman animal, despite being named and treated rather humanely through most of King's *Dark Tower* series, is often forgotten and set aside from the group of human characters that make up the main cast, suggesting a clear separation between humans and nonhuman animals.

4. Denoting It as a villain might be problematic, especially for the discussion at hand. It is ultimately portrayed as a large, female spider in the conclusion of the story, and demonizing It (despite the numerous murders for which It is responsible) should not necessarily be the automatic response readers have. While we may find many of It's actions to be despicable, judgment should not be immediate or automatic for an individual that is nonhuman and does not observe human codes of conduct.

5. In the film version of *Cujo*, Tad survives Cujo's advances and the immense heat that he and Donna must endure while trapped in their Ford Pinto. This happy-ending, however, is not to be found in the actual text, which is interesting to note as Tad dies from being trapped inside of a car on a hot day, which is a notable and perhaps ironic twist as most animals who die in cars because of immense heat are typically canines.

6. Many thanks to Sarahjane Blum for pointing out the importance of this story as it relates to King's fictional treatments of nonhuman animals. Indeed, with hundreds of short stories and dozens of novels to King's name, recalling all the stories that can be useful for analyzing King's unwitting involvement in animal rights is sometimes difficult.

7. Many thanks to Kim Socha who discusses this notion of "purposeful self-defeat" regarding animal liberation. As she discusses in *Women, Destruction and the Avant-Garde: A Paradigm for Animal Liberation*, the most genuine means of animal liberation is to seek total liberation so that the movement does not need to exist once its goal is met. To say the least, an organization whose ultimate goal is, essentially, its own destruction is noteworthy, noble, and, of course, decidedly non-capitalist.

Wᴏʀᴋs Cɪᴛᴇᴅ

Best, Steve. "The Rise of Critical Animal Studies: Putting Theory into Action and Animal Liberation into Higher Education." Stateofnature.org. n.d. (originally published in *The Journal for Critical Animal Studies*, 7.1, 2009). Web. 30 July 2011.
Canfield, Amy. "Stephen King's *Dolores Claiborne* and *Rose Madder*: A Literary Backlash Against Domestic Violence." *The Journal of American Culture* 30.4 (Dec. 2007): 391–399. Print.
Carlin, George. *Brain Droppings*. New York: Hyperion, 1997. Print.
Dunayer, Joan. *Speciesism*. Derwood, MD: Ryce, 2004. Print.
Hribal, Jason. *Fear of the Animal Planet: The Hidden History of Animal Resistance*. Petrolia, CA: Counter Punch, 2010. Print.
Kelley, Susan M. "Stephen King's Cases Against Child Abuse: *Carrie* and *The Shining*." *Censored Books II: Critical Viewpoints*. Ed. Nicholas J. Karolides and Nat Hentoff. Lanham, MD: Scarecrow, 2002. 107–114. Print.
King, Stephen. "The Cat from Hell." *Just After Sunset*. 2008. New York: Pocket Books, 2009. 352–374. Print.
_____. *Cell*. 2006. New York: Pocket Star Books, 2006.
_____. *Cujo*. 1981. New York: Signet, 1982. Print.
_____. *The Dark Tower*. 2004. New York: Scribner, 2005. Print.
_____. *The Gunslinger* (Revised and Updated Edition). New York: Plume, 2003. Print.
_____. *IT*. 1986. New York: Signet, 1987. Print.
_____. *Lisey's Story*. 2006. New York: Pocket Books, 2007. Print.
_____. "Premium Harmony." *The New Yorker*. 9 Nov. 2009: 68–73. Print.
_____. *Under the Dome*. 2009. New York: Gallery Books, 2010. Print.
_____. *The Waste Lands*. 1991. New York: Plume, 2003. Print.
_____. *Wizard and Glass*. 1997. New York: Plume, 2003. Print.

Lant, Kathleen, and Theresa Thompson. "Imagining the Worst: Stephen King and the Representation of Women (Introduction)." *Imagining the Worst: Stephen King and the Representation of Women.* Eds. Kathleen Lant and Theresa Thompson. Westport, CT: Greenwood, 1998. 3–8. Print.

Magistrale, Tony. *Stephen King: The Second Decade,* Danse Macabre *to* The Dark Half. New York: Twayne, 1992. Print.

Pet Sematary. Dir. Mary Lambert. Perf. Dale Midkiff, Fred Gwynne, Denise Crosby and Miko Hughes. Paramount, 1989. DVD.

Twitchell, James B. *Preposterous Violence: Fables of Aggression in Modern Culture.* New York: Oxford University Press, 1989. Print.

Watterson, Bill. *There's Treasure Everywhere.* Kansas City, MO: Andrews and McMeel, 1996. Print.

Woznicki, John R. "Keep *Cujo* Unleashed." *Censored Books II: Critical Viewpoints.* Ed. Nicholas J. Karolides and Nat Hentoff. Lanham, MD: Scarecrow, 2002. 126–137. Print.

Vegan Parenting
Navigating and Negating Speciesist Media
AL NOWATZKI

Elmo and Zoe race against the clock to find healthy foods of different colors. They've already found a red food: peppers. Next up is white. They approach Gina, who is eating lunch outside. Unfortunately, her bread is pumpernickel — "Brown!" — and inside the sandwich is baloney — Pink!" — and mustard — "Yellow!"

"We need healthy *white* food!" Zoe laments.

From stage right, we hear clanking bells and the clip clopping of hoofs. Up trots a farmer and a cow, both of them Muppets.

"Did I hear ya say white food, little monsters?" the farmer asks in an Scottish accent, "Aye, well I've got some right here," he says, gesturing toward the cow. He takes Gina's glass, bends down toward the cow's udders and enthusiastically says, "All right Gladys, it's milkin' time!"

We hear several squirts and Gladys blissfully moves her head back and forth to the rhythm they make. The farmer brings up a full glass of milk. "Here you go," he says, "straight from the cow!"

"Milk! Milk! Yeah!," Elmo and Zoe gleefully exclaim.

"Did I mention that I'm proud to be a cow?" Gladys adds, "Not everyone can make food that's chock full of vitamin D."

Childhood is saturated in media[1] and this saturation begins before children even become cognizant of it. The National Association for the Education of Young Children encourages certain forms of media exposure, reminding parents that they should read books to their children even in infancy (9). And while many parents follow the American Academy of Pediatrics' recommendation to keep television away from children until age two, after that point most parents plant their kids in front of the TV to watch, on average, three hours of television a day (1). Children consume on average, per day, nearly five and a half hours of media of all types — computers, books, television, etc. — combined (Kaiser Family Foundation 78).

It's unfortunate and sobering that *Sesame Street*, a program known for being a progressive beacon of acceptance and feel-good liberalism, is so entrenched in speciesism that they lie to children to promote the supposed benefits of consuming cows' milk. It either doesn't register to the professionals who produce *Sesame Street* that cows' milk is, in fact, *fortified* with vitamin D, or they intentionally gloss over reality. They are either ignorant or wantonly dismissive of the fact that the vast majority of dairy cows suffer the theft of their calves year after year, bellow out for them for days after they're taken, are hooked up to machines that irritate their udders and cause infections and are killed once they are deemed "spent."

It should be no surprise that *Sesame Street* reflects speciesist norms. The creators of the show live, as we all do, within an overwhelmingly speciesist society. And while it's possible that the sponsors of *Sesame Street*—among them, the animal exploiting companies Earth's Best and the Good Egg Project—have some influence, I'm willing to give *Sesame Street* the benefit of the doubt and assume that content is not directly and explicitly affected by sponsors. But while there may be no causation, the correlation is too important to ignore: speciesist companies sponsor a speciesist show. It's a package deal.

In this one short clip described above, *Sesame Street* not only unquestioningly reinforces the questionable idea that cows' milk is a human health-food, but they also firmly plant the cow in what speciesist society has deemed her rightful place: her job is to give us milk. *Sesame Street* tells the kids she does it with a proud smile.

Vegan parents should be aware of the ways in which speciesism is transmitted via children's media and should formulate ways to talk about these messages with their children. Later in this essay, I'll detail three different forms of speciesist media: overt, easygoing and unintentional. Vegan parents will undoubtedly come across these forms while raising their children.

There are no concrete numbers about vegan children, but according to a 2000 Zogby poll, roughly .9 percent of the population of the United States is vegan (quoted in Vegetarian Resource Group). It's conservative to estimate that vegans now, over a decade later, make up one percent of the population. One percent of 300 million U.S. residents means there are about three million vegans in the United States alone. If we assume that most of them are adults and that only thirty percent of them will raise children, then conservatively, one million vegans will raise children. Further, we'll assume that vegans only raise kids with other vegans, or that children are raised vegan only when both parents are vegan — not true, I know, but I'm trying to err on the conservative side. Five hundred thousand couples with an average of two children each equals one million vegan kids in the United States alone.[2]

A generation of vegan children is being raised in a pervasively speciesist society. And though it may seem like a lot of pressure, the job that vegans do as parents will, in part, determine the size of vegan generations to come.

Some Notes on Attitudes Intended to Undermine Vegan Parents

Before exploring the issues of speciesism in children's media, it may be instructive to touch on the other aspects of vegan parenting which are of concern to non-vegan parents and the public at large. Various concerns, objections and obfuscations may be made by non-vegans who are coming to terms with — or arguing against — how vegan parents choose to raise their children. The speciesist messages portrayed in all media make it easier for these objections to proliferate, producing an echo chamber that reinforces the status quo at every turn.

The first of these concerns is nutrition. It is sometimes assumed by non-vegans that vegan kids will, at some point in their lives, choose to consume animal products because their bodies will need some elusive nutrient that is contained therein. The myth that animal products, especially cows' milk, are needed for human health is nowhere as pervasive as it is in regard to child nutrition. Posters of celebrities wearing milk moustaches, many with their children on their laps, hang in nearly every public school cafeteria in the country. Talking cows gush about how great their milk is for you on *Sesame Street*.

Vegan parents know better. They know because they've read up on it from reputable sources that cows' milk, in addition to other products of exploitation, is not necessary for human health and it's not needed for children to thrive. Considering that approximately 70 percent of humans are lactose intolerant (Heyman 1280), it should be a given that one doesn't need mammalian milk past infancy to be healthy.

I offer my two children as an anecdotal example, both of whom have eaten a vegan diet their whole lives. At their regular check-ups, they are consistently around and above the fiftieth percentile for measurements of weight and height. And yet my wife and I are, time after time, asked by pediatric nurses how much cows' milk our children drink and where they get their protein if they don't get it from animal flesh.

If one does a search for vegan children on the internet, he will find a plethora of robust, healthy kids who don't consume any animal products. If this anecdotal evidence doesn't do it for those concerned, they may be convinced by the American Dietetic Association's position that appropriately planned vegetarian diets, including total vegetarian or vegan diets, are healthful, nutritionally adequate, and may provide health benefits in the prevention and treatment of certain diseases. Well-planned vegetarian diets are appropriate for individuals during all stages of the lifecycle, including pregnancy, lactation, infancy, childhood, and adolescence, and for athletes [1266].

Ideally, vegan parents won't need to tell their children that eating vegan is healthy. They'll know it because they'll be healthy. When they get sick, parents can tell them that kids just get sick. If someone tells a child that they're sick because they're vegan, parents can tell their children that that person doesn't know what they're talking about. There are roughly three million vegans in the United States alone who are a testament to the fact that veganism is at least as healthy as non-veganism. Many of them are children. It can be concluded that the challenge to raising vegan children on the nutrition front is null and void.

Another reason children of vegan parents will inevitably choose to eat non-vegan foods, according to some, is that they will rebel against their parents when they reach their teens. They will become ardent meat eaters, much to the joy of the meat-eating majority. It's an interesting claim, but it's one that doesn't warrant much concern from vegan parents.

Vegan parents who are vegan for the reason of respecting the interests of other-than-human animals will likely pass that respect down to their children. An analogous example would be children who are raised as anti-racists. When a person learns from the get-go that oppression is wrong, it's hard to lose that knowledge. If parents teach their children about the oppressive ideology of speciesism, the oppression of other-than-human animals, and sentience and the interest in living that it entails, then there's no compelling reason to believe that the kids will someday unlearn that.

Of course, there is still a probability that children of vegan parents will decide that they shouldn't respect other-than-human animals, or that respecting them means something other than being vegan. On the flip side, there's also a chance that all the kids of non-vegans out there will come to veganism later in life. Parenting is full of unknowns. All parents need to make peace with that fact.

Vegan parents will also come across the charge that they're brainwashing their kids into being vegan. This claim could only be made by someone who doesn't have a grasp of the concept of speciesism, someone who hasn't recognized that they were unwittingly indoctrinated with that ideology as a child. The brainwashing charge comes from the perception that vegan parents are teaching their kids fundamental principles which are counter to dominant culture. But don't most non-vegan parents teach their kids to respect animals as well?

The late Stanley Sapon, professor of psycholinguistics at the University of Rochester, said that "we typically raise children from birth to five or six years in a kind of fantasy-land of ideal behavior on the part of the world's inhabitants ... a 'land of goodness and mercy,' a land where the animals are our friends, and we are the friends of the animals." Children under a certain age are not taught that other-than-human animals are here for us to exploit and kill. Instead, representations of these beings are used in children's media to illustrate life lessons, as in books like *Chicken Little* and *The Three Billy Goats Gruff.* Other stories also teach us that other-than-human animals should be spared suffering and death — as in the case of Bambi — and should live free from captivity and have their intrinsically valuable lives respected by others — a major theme of, for example, the children's movies *Free Willy* and *Rio.*

Vegans parents take these lessons to their logical conclusions and teach their children to not only say that animals are our friends, but also *act* as if they are. It's not enough to say, "Be nice to animals." We need to actually *be* nice to all animals. Chicken dinner, steak on Fridays and eggs for breakfast run counter to this message.

Framing the Conversation

Vegan parents can stack the deck against the possibility of their children choosing to not be vegan later in life by instilling in their children a sense of justice and the critical thinking tools needed to make decisions for themselves once they reach the appropriate age.

Vegan parents would do well to occasionally talk to their children about why others aren't vegan, about the reasons non-vegans give for continuing to participate in the exploitation of animals. These discussions may be about grandparents, friends, or even a child's non-vegan parent or caregiver. By discussing the arguments for animal exploitation, and reinforcing the fact that our loved ones employ these arguments, vegan parents not only give their children the tools to defend veganism, but also to empathize with and understand those who have not chosen veganism. No, this doesn't mean that parents need to defend the choice of others to exploit animals. It does mean, however, that parents pass along a basic respect for others and an understanding of others' positions on what we owe other-than-human animals. This can only help vegan children in their future interactions with a non-vegan world that won't always be accepting of their views on other-than-human animals.

It's understandable that vegans get pushback from family, friends and society at large. Vegans challenge something that has been seen as one essential aspect of humanity: namely, that we are wholly separate from other-than-human animals, so much so that we don't even consider ourselves animals. So much so that we can enslave, torture and kill other animals without any thought to how they wish to be treated, without asking ourselves the very basic question of whether or not they have an interest in continuing to live.

We all live in a speciesist society, so it makes sense that speciesist norms get transmitted through the media we consume and that these norms are transmitted to children at a young age. Sapon said:

> Somewhere around the age of kindergarten ... [comes] time for the beginning of some serious disillusionment, to carry out a culturally sanctioned program of systematic desensitization. The animals in the picture books change from fantasy friends, who have feelings, and behave just like people, to objects of utility.

Although I will show later how speciesist norms are subtly and not-so-subtly reinforced at a much earlier age, even in the picture books portraying fantasy friends, Sapon makes the relevant point that once children reach a certain age, there is a shift in how they regard other-than-human animals. A shift in perception will happen within vegan children as well. They may not change from animal-lovers to animal-eaters upon entry to kindergarten, but they will, in all likelihood, begin to regard other-than-human animals differently.

"Animals are our friends," is a phrase often repeated in many vegan homes, and with good cause. It's a simple, age-appropriate way to teach our children about kindness to all animals. But this can't be the only thing children are told because they will eventually become adolescents who realize that all animals are not, in fact, their friends. Indeed, they never even meet the chicken who was turned into the nugget at their friend's house. In what way was that chicken their friend? The cow whose skin was turned into leather shoes was not their friend. The elephant who suffers the blows of her torturers at the circus is not their friend. Bees aren't their friends, and they may even have had the stings to prove it!

A hungry tiger is not their friend.

While "animals are our friends" works well for toddlers and preschoolers, it needs to be promptly followed by the larger lessons of equal consideration. Vegan parents need to let their children know that all animals are deserving of justice and respect from us, regardless of our personal feelings toward them. Veganism is not a matter of compassion any more than being anti-racist is a matter of compassion. It's not a matter of being nice to our friends any more than being a feminist is a matter of being nice to our friends. Veganism, like feminism and anti-racism, is an expression of justice and anti-oppression. Being vegan is being fair. Parents will serve their children and other animals well to phrase it that way.

This isn't to say that there's no room for lessons on compassion. We're compassionate when we console a suffering family member, when we bring an injured squirrel into a wildlife rehabilitation center, or when we help push a stranger's car out of the snow. Compassion is essential in an imperfect world. Without a firm grounding in justice, acts of compassion are either one-time undertakings of charity or band-aids for larger structural problems which deserve to be examined and rooted out. If compassion is helping out those who are suffering, then justice is refraining from actions which cause harm in the first place. A sense of justice is integral to the understanding and embrace of animal rights. Lessons in justice can be as easy as saying, "We don't hit," and as complicated as expounding upon the finer points of sentience, egalitarianism and equal consideration.

It's tempting to shy away from discussing complex ideas like these with children. We tend to assume that since they won't understand everything we say, it's no use saying anything. A voice from the world of sexual education is instructive here. In *From Diapers to Dating: A Parent's Guide to Raising Sexually Healthy Children*, Debra W. Haffner writes:

> Some parents have asked me why it is important to answer preschoolers' questions about where babies come from.... Avoiding this question may get you off the hook for the moment, but it also gives your child the message that you don't want to talk to them about sexuality issues. Answering this question simply now lays the foundation for future conversations, and it tells your child that you will teach them about this important subject [73].

When educating children about sex, parents may use words children don't understand and a large percentage of what they say may go over children's heads. It's true that children probably won't retain knowledge of what a fallopian tube is when they're three years old, but it doesn't hurt to include that information in the discussion. They'll take what they need from the conversation and another similar conversation will take place again in a few months, at which point they'll absorb more information.

Veganism and animal rights should be treated in a similar fashion. If parents are serious about animal rights and passing respect for all animals down to their children, then they should speak matter-of-factly about animal interests, animal minds, social justice and equal consideration. Thankfully, this does not mean that vegan parents should convey to their children every gory detail of what happens on farms and in slaughterhouses — that would be more akin to teaching young children about rape, as opposed to imparting to them a healthy view of sexuality. Knowledge of those horrors is not necessary for a firm grounding in animal rights.

As far as praxis goes, vegan parents should, at the very least, tell their kids about the things they're expected to do and not do in regard to animal products and actions toward other animals. Giving children a basic knowledge about how they're expected to act is necessary to avoid confusion and stressful social situations.

A child who has been told what they are and are not expected to eat, for example, is less likely to feel hurt when they're told they can't eat scrambled eggs at Grandma's house. Parents shouldn't wait for an awkward situation like that to explain to their kids what they do or don't eat and why. Instead, they should be having these discussions early, often and in the comfort of their own homes without the presence of a non-vegan audience.

Vegan parents should strive to be anti-speciesist in the home and limit, to a reasonable degree, the amount of speciesism their young children come into contact with in their everyday lives. Even when this is accomplished, speciesist messages still end up being conveyed to children through the media they consume. It is for this reason that vegan parents need to carefully choose media for their young children and navigate and negate, when possible, the speciesist media they do come into contact with.

On Media Restriction and Selection

It's important to note briefly that the effect that media has on children can often be overstated. In the book *Killing Monsters: Why Children Need Fantasy, Super Heroes and Make-Believe Violence*, Gerard Jones writes,

> Even if a child's attention is mostly focused on a TV show, it won't be the show that will make the deepest impression on her idea of how she is sup-posed to behave — it will be the way mom or dad behaves while the show is on. Expressing anger or anxiety about a child's entertainment won't make her like the entertainment less — but it *will* model anger and anxiety for her. She's not likely to shape her real behavior around what she sees characters do on the glass screen. But if she sees parents allowing entertainment violence but treat-ing others lovingly, she will get the message, "An adult is supposed to be okay with make-believe violence but not make it real" [186].

This isn't to say that parents should let their young children watch ultra-violent television shows or read to them a picture book about slaughterhouses. When parents have unquestioned control over media selection, i.e., in the preschool years, there's no compelling reason to choose violent media over non-violent media. But there's also not a lot of cause to worry if some media violence — including speciesism, which perpetuates violence — makes its way through.

When my daughter was three years old, she pretended to eat the monkeys from her Barrel of Monkeys game. At first, I was shocked and told her not to pretend to eat animals. But after more thought, I realized that she was probably just trying to process the idea of people eating animals. Her make-believe violence was harming no one. Indeed, it was developmentally appropriate and beneficial. I ended up telling her that it was okay to pretend to eat animals if she really wanted to. She did it a few more times and then moved on to something else. (I originally wrote about this incident in a blog post titled "My Daughter the Monkey Eater." See Nowatzki.)

If kids, once they're old enough to read and choose their own media, want to watch speciesist television or read a book about life on a farm, even one that depicts that farm in a positive light, parents should let them. By not allowing children to choose their own media, parents give that media power over them. The underlying message that is conveyed when children aren't allowed to choose violent media is that there's something wrong with merely *reading* about violence, that it's as bad as violence itself (Jones 117). If kids aren't allowed to read a book about Old MacDonald's farm, parents teach them that even *thinking* about the farming of animals is on the same scale of wrongness as eating farmed animals. This doesn't mean that parents need to be silent about their objection to harmful messages. Jones writes, "Saying, 'I don't like that show,' or 'I don't want that hateful song to be played in my house,' models decisiveness and moral courage" (186).

The lessons children learn from and about media come largely from their parents. Whether parents watch television with their children and explain the difference between the images on the screen and reality, or simply state that they feel uncomfortable with books portraying animal exploitation, kids are watching how parents react to media and act, toward them and others, in everyday life. Fortunately, the values taught by parents cannot so easily be undone simply by being exposed to media that runs counter to them.

When children are exposed to speciesism in media, parents can either choose to ignore it or address it. What parents do will depend largely on the type of media and the age of their child. It's also possible — in the baby, toddler and pre-school years — to restrict speciesist media. But shutting it out completely is an impossible task; one that, if it were possible, would be ultimately stifling and counterproductive.

Vegan parents have an especially difficult task ahead of them. Speciesist messages will make their way to our children's eyes, ears and minds, often within brightly colored books, television shows and movies that appear to be nothing more than wholesome fun. To effectively navigate and negate these messages, it helps to first understand their forms. The remainder of this essay will focus on the three major forms that speciesism takes in children's media: overt, easygoing and unintentional. In conclusion, I'll offer a couple examples of media that refreshingly transcend these forms of speciesism.

Overt Speciesism

In *Animal Equality: Language and Liberation*, Joan Dunayer writes, "Deceptive language perpetuates speciesism.... Bigotry requires self-deception. Speciesism can't survive without lies" (1). Nowhere is the bigotry of speciesism more obvious than in the media that ostensibly educates our children about the animal exploitation industry. Overtly speciesist media explicitly reinforces and bolsters the social norm of speciesism.

Out and About at the Dairy Farm, a book geared toward kids aged four to eight, paints this rosy picture: "A cow can't make milk until she has a baby. Most cows are two years old when they have their first calf. After that, cows have a baby every year, and they continue to give milk. A healthy milk cow gives milk about ten months out of every year" (Murphy 7). Contained within this paragraph is horrible violence, but you won't see it unless you look between the lines, and children won't see it unless it is pointed out to them. Cows "have a baby every year," but no mention is made of the routine rape — euphemistically known as artificial insemination — which takes place on the vast majority of dairy farms. Cows' milk isn't "given," it's taken by us. And all of this is done to those they call "milk cows," relegating their entire being to the substance for which they are exploited (Dunayer 146). Finally, nowhere is the connection made that the biological reason cows lactate is to feed their calves.

The book does, however, give mention to the supposed fate of the calves: "After calves are born, they stay with their mothers for a few hours. Then we move the female calves into their own pens in the calf barn. We sell the male calves to farmers who raise them as bulls" (14). It's true that female calves may be raised to adulthood for breeding and milking purposes, but most males born into the diary industry are killed for their flesh (a.k.a. veal) when they're only calves; rarely are they sold to farmers who "raise them as bulls."

In the book *Where Do Chicks Come From*, children are told about the fertilization, pregnancy and birth of chicks. The first few pages seem innocent and unbiased enough. The rooster and hen mate, the egg is fertilized and starts to grow. But at this juncture, the book points out that, "[t]he egg you eat for breakfast could never grow into a chick because it was never fertilized" (Sklansky 11). Why is this information included in a book about where chicks come from? There's no reason to involve the fact that chickens are exploited for their eggs. Perhaps the author felt that children would be disgusted if they thought that the eggs they ate for breakfast had fetal chickens contained within. Maybe she wanted to assure them that there aren't any baby chicks in there and so assure them that it's perfectly acceptable to eat eggs.

The book continues on, presenting an idyllic view of a mother chicken hatching her egg:

"Inside the eggshell, the chick pecks a hole into the air space at the end of the egg. It takes its first breath and goes, 'Cheep! Cheep!'"

"'Cluck, Cluck,' answers the hen" [21].

Putting aside the depersonalizing usage of the word "it" to refer to the chick, this is a touching recognition of the communication that occurs early in the life of a chicken. The hen looks intently at her egg. They talk to each other. The chick emerges from the egg. But then, "Together, the hen and her new chicks search for food in the barnyard" (31). There it is. These chickens live on a farm. Their lives are one of manipulation, control and a premature and unnecessary death at the hands of the humans who benefit financially from that death.

At the end of the book, the author provides ways to learn more about eggs: "Squeeze an egg in your hand and see if you can break it," "Break an uncooked egg and identify the different parts," "Roll an egg to see how it rolls" (32–33). Shouldn't a book about chickens attempt to increase not only our understanding of them, but also our respect? Does the author *intentionally* gloss over the fact that exploited hens almost always live a life of horror and shortened life spans? Or is she so blinded by speciesism that she doesn't realize that talking about the natural birth of a chick in the same book as eating eggs is ethically contradictory?

Time and time again, overtly speciesist children's media portrays idyllic scenes of barnyard life. The lie of these images is two-fold. The first is a lie of omission. If the images are of chicks pecking the ground for seed, then the images are *not* of the eventual theft of their eggs, the eventual slaughter of them once they become "spent." The second lie is one of scale. The vast majority of farmed animals exist on large-scale farms that bear no resemblance to the scenes portrayed in children's media. The implicit message conveyed by books like *Out and About at the Dairy Farm* and *Where Do Chicks Come From?* is that when you go to a restaurant, the cheese on your burger and the flesh in your nugget came from a happy other-than-human animal on a farm where death at the hands of his or her oppressor isn't even worth talking about.

Overtly speciesist books like this can be a great teaching tool for older children who are able to understand that language can be used as a tool to not only inform, but also deceive. These books can serve as simple, nonthreatening ways to introduce children to the cognitive and linguistic tricks that are employed to mask the routine subjugation and exploitation of farmed animals.

It would be difficult, if not impossible, to adjust the messages in books like these to negate the speciesism contained therein. If a story is about animal use, to change that is dishonest to the story and, more importantly, to the children to whom it's being read. There's no way to make a dairy farm non-exploitative. Consequently, vegan parents can, and should, choose to limit the amount of exposure to media of this type which explicitly promotes animal use. What is routinely done to other-than-human animals is horrifying, but children will find it less so if they're exposed to depictions of other-than-human animal use from an early age. Instead of desensitizing them to violence and injustice, it's best to teach fundamental lessons and let the images of horror come when they're old enough to better grasp that they are indeed horrifying.

If overtly speciesist books are read to children — or they read them on their own once they are able — it's critical that they're accompanied by a discussion about the problems contained within. Unfortunately, speciesist messages are not relegated only to media that focus on direct uses of animals. Even seemingly benign media are saturated with messages that reinforce speciesist norms.

Easygoing Speciesism

"Panda bears come from China and Tibet, "Nancy Parent explains in the children's book *Panda Bears* (2). Pandas don't *live* in China and Tibet, they *come from* there. It's no surprise then that the book also informs children that "[i]n zoos, panda bears eat carrots, apples, and sweet potatoes in addition to bamboo" (4). We can understand the type of speciesist claims made here by employing the term "casygoing speciesism," as coined and defined by sociologist Roger Yates: "The concept defines attitudes and claims-making about human-nonhuman relations and, in particular, highlights the easy assumptions humans tend to make about the *rightful place* and legitimate use of nonhuman animals." As I use the term in this essay, easygoing speciesism can include everything from characters in media eating eggs to a character talking about how much he loves the zoo. Easygoing speciesism occurs outside of the immediate context of overt speciesism. The thoughtless acceptance of other-than-human animal use is the canvas that easygoing speciesist media is brushed upon.

By far, the most prevalent example of easygoing speciesism in children's media is the usage of the pronoun "it" to refer to a being who has a gender. Dunayer writes, "Pronoun use that robs nonhuman animals of sentience and individuality may be the most widespread linguistic ploy by which English-speakers legitimize speciesist abuse. No sentient being is an 'it,' 'that,' or '-thing.' Each is equally someone" (156). In *Michael Berenstain's Butterfly Book*, Berenstain refers to all butterflies as "it." He also writes that, "Butterflies are the most beautiful of all insects," never acknowledging the subjectivity of that statement and thus condemning all other insects to lives of less beauty.

In *Grover's Book of Cute Little Baby Animals*, the author makes the same mistake Berenstain does, deeming some animals to be cuter than others, making them worthy of writing a book about. The book also uses "it" to refer to certain animals — "The baby raccoon can climb up into its home in a hollow tree," — but uses gendered pronouns to refer to others: "Look at the little lamb. Isn't he adorable" (Ford)?

The book, *That's Not My Puppy*, follows a mouse who searches for a dog who apparently belongs to him. Each page presents a new puppy with a different defining feature and the mouse proclaims that "it" is not his. For example, on one page the mouse says, "That's not my puppy. Its ears are too shaggy." Finally, the mouse finds his dog and says, "That's my puppy! His nose is so squashy" (Watt 7–10). The take-away here is that dogs are things unless they are owned, at which point they become gendered individuals.

The television episode "Franklin Wants a Pet," shows Franklin, a turtle, talking with his friends Bear, Otter, Snail, and others about what kind of pet he should get. He eventually settles on a goldfish who he buys at a pet store and names Goldie. The goldfish is kept in a very small bowl, the kind that were made illegal in Rome.[3] Characters like Franklin are meant to act as stand-ins for the young human audience. Kids are supposed to identify with them, and thus take away that it's a good thing to, for example, buy a goldfish from the pet store as opposed to adopting one from a shelter or rescue group.

In *When Is Saturday?*, Grover is excited for his uncle to visit so that he can "show him my new bed, and take him to the zoo" (Kovacs). In *If You Give a Pig a Pancake*, a pig is eventually given a rubber duck that "will remind her of the farm where she was born. She might feel homesick and want to visit her family" (Numeroff). (One can easily imagine that a farm is the *last* place a pig would want to be.)

When watching and reading easygoing speciesist media with pre-literate children, there's no reason vegan parents shouldn't change instances of "it" to "she" or "he." In the case of a character mentioning the zoo in passing, as Grover does in *When Is Saturday?*, there's nothing wrong with just refraining from reading that part or changing "zoo" to "park." In *If You Give a Pig a Pancake*, one could add "sanctuary" after farm, or simply say "forest" instead of "farm." When parents lay the building blocks of language, it's important that they set them down carefully, in a way that reflects and reinforces their values. It's for the benefit of their children that vegan parents thoroughly examine and attempt to root out their own vestigial speciesism and that they take great care in how they speak about other-than-human animals and the institutions which exploit them.

If a piece of media is not explicitly about animal use, then the lie that parents commit when they change words here and there is inconsequential to the story; the integrity of the story is not compromised. In fact, changing those words lends a level of credibility and fairness to something that would otherwise be just another sad reflection of speciesist society. The authors of the above books probably don't understand that they're perpetuating speciesism. It's possible that they don't know better. There are authors, though, whose bodies of work show that they are fundamentally confused and possibly torn about what we owe other-than-human animals.

In *Where the Sidewalk Ends*, a book of quirky children's poems by Shel Silverstein, the short poem "Point of View" could well be characterized as animal rights literature. In it, Silverstein relates that many of the traditional animal-flesh-centric meals such as Thanksgiving and Christmas dinner are quite depressing when you see them from the point of view of the animals being eaten (98). On the other hand, Silverstein's *Where the Sidewalk Ends* also contains "I Must Remember," about a man who tries to remember to eat, among other things, turkeys for Thanksgiving and eggs for Easter, but to not eat them all at once (14). The book also contains "The Silver Fish," which ends with a boy catching a fish and eating him (148). And there's "Melinda Mae," who ate a whole whale because she said she would (154).

Silverstein is not alone in his confusion. Dr. Seuss also doesn't seem to know his position on whether or not animals are ours to use. *Green Eggs and Ham* obviously perpetuates speciesism in that it encourages the eating of pigs' flesh and chickens' eggs. *If I Ran the Zoo* is about replacing the currently imprisoned animals with more interesting creatures. *One Fish Two Fish Red Fish Blue Fish* introduces fantastic characters, some who are objects of use by the children who narrate the book. Given that Seuss's father worked at a zoo, it's no surprise that he saw creatures as objects of utility.

Thankfully, but confusingly, not all of his works are ones of easygoing speciesism. For example, in *Horton Hears a Who*, Horton the elephant risks everything in order to protect small people — Whos — who live on a speck. Horton eventually convinces the antagonists, with the help of the Whos, to protect the inhabitants of the speck instead of destroying them.

The Lorax is an environmentalist story in which the Once-ler clear cuts a forest while the Lorax implores him to stop, speaking for the trees and the various animals who are dependent upon the trees and clean water and air for their well-being. *The Lorax* drives home the point that one should care about the environment in large part because of the sentient beings who are dependent upon it for survival and happiness. Taken alone, this book seems to paint Seuss as not only an environmentalist, but also an animal rights activist. However, the incongruity between this message and the easygoing speciesism of his other books reflects the prevailing thought among the bulk of environmentalists since the movement began: animals who we deem food and entertainment aren't worth protecting, but free-living animals often are.

Silverstein, Seuss and other authors like them can serve as examples of the inconsistencies of cultural attitudes toward other-than-human animals. They can be used as discussion starters with school-aged children who may be trying to come to terms with what they see as the confusing and contradictory beliefs and behaviors of their non-vegan peers.

Unintentional Speciesism

Unfortunately, parents and their children cannot always escape the specter of speciesism just by picking up a book or watching a television program about how great other-than-human animals are. Unintentional speciesism crops up in the least expected places, places where the intention is to foster respect and understanding of other-than-human animals. These attempts often fall short due to the unintentional and unexamined speciesism of the media creators.

The book *Nat Geo Wild Animal Atlas*, appears, at first look, to be a pro-animal book. It's all about other-than-human animals and where they live, as opposed to where they "come from." It contains beautiful photos of animals in their natural habitats. The book also points out which species are on the endangered list and why. On the other hand, as reflected in the title's designation of these animals as "wild," the book focuses only on free living, non-domesticated animals. This designation sets up an artificial separation between the animals we exploit and the animals who are considered worthy of protection. And even this book about other-than-human animals, which attempts to talk about them on their own terms and not about their utility to humans, can't help but refer to some of them as "its."

It's a common thread, mentioned previously in the examples of *That's Not My Puppy* and *Grover's Book of Cute Furry Animals*, that certain animals attain the level of gender — or if not gender, then they at least get the distinction of being referred to as "they" instead of "it"— while others seem destined to be viewed as objects. In *Wild Animal Atlas*, nearly all animals are referred to, not as individuals, but as if the species to which they belong was one homogenized individual. There is precedence of doing this amongst other oppressed groups as well: "Just as racists have spoken of blacks as 'the Negro' and Jews as 'the Jew,' people speak of all members of a nonhuman group as if they were a single animal, implying that they're all the same" (Dunayer 6).

It's written in *Wild Animal Atlas* that, "[t]he North American Beaver, North America's largest rodent, is found throughout the region" (10). But about Bobcats, the book says, "These felines live throughout North America, including desert areas" (13), as opposed to the incorrect "it lives," or "the bobcat lives," which are both de-individualizing phrases. As with more obvious examples of easygoing speciesism, vegan parents should correct these phrases when reading to their children. For example, the above sentence about beavers can instead be read, "North American Beavers, North America's largest rodents, *are* found throughout the region." Parents can also talk with older kids about how these incorrect usages of language perpetuate speciesism.

Moving to television, Diego is a cartoon "animal rescuer." In *Go, Diego, Go!*, he typically hears an other-than-human animal in trouble and, with the help of his rescue pack, camera and ostensibly the children viewing the program, he helps the animal. Along the way, kids learn some basic facts about the animal who needs rescuing. In the episode "Linda the Llama Saves Carnival," Linda the Llama is lost. Diego needs to find her so she can haul party favors to Carnival. Once found, Linda, who is almost always shown with a blanket saddled across her back, is happy and proud to haul treats and instruments up the mountain and to Carnival. Once she gets to Carnival, she is thrilled to pull a float in the parade.

Admittedly, most *Diego* episodes do not reflect the idea that animals are happy to be used for human ends, but they do consistently perpetuate another falsehood. Every episode contains other-than-human animals who speak English and/or Spanish. If the goal of the show is to get children to care about other-than-human animals — almost always "wild" animals, of course — for who they are, they do those animals a disservice by making them all capable of human speech. The show also proffers the idea that other-than-human animals are constantly in need of humans to save them, which has the effect of situating humans in the role of paternalistic protector, as opposed to kin.

Wild Animal Atlas and *Go, Diego, Go!* are two examples of superficially pro-animal media that fail when it comes to ethical and linguistic consistency. It's assumed that neither of these were written by people in the animal advocacy movement, so it's understandable that they would contain unexamined ethical contradictions. Harder to excuse, though, is media produced by those within the animal advocacy community that unintentionally perpetuate speciesist ideas.

A Cow's Life, one of several kid-geared comics produced by People for the Ethical Treatment of Animals (PETA), follows a group of children as they visit a farmed animal sanctuary. One of the kids teaches the others about how badly cows are treated on factory farms, how cows are a lot like them and how they suffer on factory farms. But it doesn't matter, from an animal rights standpoint, that, as the comic says, cows can, "love and feel pain like a human." It doesn't matter that they "form strong lifelong relationships with one another," or "are very devoted and protective of their children," or that "they've been known to walk for miles looking for a lost baby." It shouldn't matter that, "Cows are smart! They can see color and tell people apart by their shapes and the colors that they wear" (Moore 1). When animal rights is sold to children by listing the ways in which certain animals are like us, the idea is reinforced that it is these characteristics in animals that compel us to deem them worthy of consideration.[4]

When talking with children about animal rights, it is only necessary to explain the concept of sentience and the interests that entails. They only need to grasp that, as philosopher Gary Steiner writes in *Animals and the Moral Community*, "the struggle for life and flourishing *matters*, whether or not the being in question has a reflective sense of which things matter or how they matter" (xi–xii). The characteristics of the cow beyond sentience are irrelevant to her basic interest in continuation of life.

It's important here to draw a distinction between what parents should teach their children about animal rights and what they should teach them about other-than-human animals. It's important for children to know about those with whom they share this world. Parents should teach them about other-than-human animals and their species-specific behaviors. Teach them that there are animals who only eat plants, animals who can eat both animals and plants — for example, humans — and that there are animals who have to kill other animals and eat them in order to live. Teach them about how cool it is that bats use echolocation and how fascinating it is that frogs can snatch flies out of thin air with their tongues. Relate to them the examples of interspecies bonding that humans have observed among other animals. Revel with children in the wonders of our animal kin. But once you're done doing that, teach them that the interests of other-than-human animals ought to be respected simply because they are sentient and have an interest in avoiding pain and continuing to live.

In her book, *That's Why We Don't Eat Animals*, Ruby Roth writes,

> Pets are members of our family. They nuzzle us and we play together; we pet them and we both feel calm. Their love is so powerful that it can even help us heal. They can tell when we feel lonely, just as we can tell when they want dinner. We know each other by heart. All animals deserve the care and protection we give our pets.

Putting aside the questionable usage of the word "pet," the suggestion that all other-than-human animals should be given the "care and protection" we give our nonhuman companions is problematic on a few fronts. First, many people don't care much for their pets at all. They treat them as disposable, chain them outdoors and beat them into submission. Many pets aren't loved.[5] Second, most pets are purposely bred to be sold as property for profit. This is not an act of love. Third, by appealing to love instead of justice, Roth starts off on a shaky ground that doesn't withstand logical critique. Should it really be our goal to give turkeys the same love we give our dogs? Isn't the goal to stop breeding other-than-human animals in the first place? If that goal is ever achieved, then wouldn't we, by default, be *unable* to give other animals the same love we give our nonhuman companions?

By appealing to the emotions we attach to the nonhuman animals who live with us, Roth sets the tone for the book: we should care about other-than-human animals because they behave in ways similar to the nonhuman companions who live with us who, in turn, act a lot like us. Roth goes on to explain how chickens play hide-and-seek, turkeys blush, pigs play ball in the sun, and cows play follow the leader. She repeatedly reminds us, after counting the ways these animals are like us, that on a factory farm they cannot do any of these things.

One may ask why this is a problem. Why not teach our kids that other-than-human animals are just like us, feel like we do and have thoughts like we do? Why not focus on the fact that there are horrible places called factory farms where they can't act like us at all? If it will foster in them a sense of kinship with all sentient life, and a sense of the injustice of factory farms, then what is the harm?

An imaginary farm can illustrate the problem. It's one hundred acres of rolling hills, babbling brooks, trees for shade and top-notch grass for munching. There are, at any given time, roughly ten other-than-human animals living on this huge farm. They're allowed to love like humans. They get to play hide-and-seek. They play ball and follow-the-leader. They get to express, as Joel Salatin and Michael Pollan, so-called conscientious omnivores, would say, their "cow-ness" and "pig-ness." And, just because we can, let's say that these animals are killed painlessly right there on the farm. Cows, for example, will be killed at age fifteen, roughly three quarters of the average natural lifespan of a cow and three times longer than a farmed cow usually lives. It's the anti-factory farm, but a farm nonetheless.

Putting aside the fact that a farm of this nature is an economic impossibility, if we take animal rights seriously, we still stand firm that it is an injustice. The animals are controlled, confined — yes, one hundred acres is still confinement — and killed for reasons wholly unnecessary. Their interest in continued existence is violated. The sole criteria that they possess which facilitates them having this interest is sentience.

Roth focuses on factory farms throughout much of the book, missing the chance to oppose all forms of animal exploitation instead of just the most unpopular forms. In ostensibly appealing to the masses, Roth misses a perfect opportunity to show children what language free of hedging and speciesism sounds like. Instead of using language that unequivocally supports the rights of all animals to be free, she qualifies and waters down the message with "factory farm" and "vegetarian."

On the final page of the book, under the heading, "What Else Can We Do?" she writes that kids can "[r]ead books on animals, veganism, vegetarianism, and raw foods." Kids can also "[d]iscover new vegetarian and vegan foods," and, "[l]ook up raw, vegan and vegetarian recipes." What in the world do raw foods or vegetarianism have to do with respecting other-than-human animals? Conflating veganism with vegetarianism and rawism is unnecessarily confusing and distracting. A simple and unequivocal vegan message in a book written by a vegan would make a lot more sense.

An appeal to colloquialism may be made in defense of some of Roth's other word choices. "It" and "pets" are words that most people use when referring to other-than-human animals. "Factory farms" are a well-known evil. One might say that using these words is simply a matter of "meeting people where they are." But this is a book geared toward children. Where *are* children? Books don't need to meet children anywhere. Books *bring* them there.

And if kids *are* anywhere to begin with, it's on the side of letting all animals live and be free. If vegan parents don't give their children an unqualified non-speciesist framework from the outset, then kids may struggle that much more later in life trying to rid themselves of the vestigial speciesism inherited from a most unlikely source: their vegan parents.

Most vegans were not raised as such. Most were indoctrinated into a speciesist culture and have had to consciously root out the speciesist turns of phrase, idioms, incorrect pronoun usage, etc. that comes with it. When crafting future messages, the creators of animal-friendly media would do well to remember that words matter, how we talk about other-than-human animals matters, and all animals matter regardless of their personal and species-specific cognitive characteristics.

Examples of Non-Anti-Speciesist Media

Fortunately, there are pockets of fully non-speciesist sanity in the media landscape, and even some examples of anti-speciesism. Most of these are in the form of books, though it's tempting to think that many children's movies are anti-speciesist. On the contrary, in their paper, "The Conceptual Separation of Food and Animals in Childhood," Kate Stewart and Matthew Cole write:

> Children's films are often about [other-than-human animal] outcasts struggling against their circumstances.... But very often, their salvation comes from

an abandonment of their natural states.... Babe finds acceptance not as a runt but as a sheep-pig; in *Happy Feet* the penguins are saved not for being penguins, but because they get a TV crew to see them tap dancing; in *Chicken Run*, conquering flight is the chickens' escape route from the farm.... The emotional attachment the audience forms is something apart from the animal's animalness. Animals are saved if they ... attain human-like qualities, or quasi-human subjectivity. This phenomenon is ... a ubiquitous feature of the characterization of animals in children's films [465].

Much as is found in other forms of media, there is a subtle message that animals deserve consideration only if they can demonstrate human qualities. Their authentic beings, their features that gloriously set them apart from humans, are dismissed. With this sound critique in mind, I'll leave movies aside and finally focus on two examples of non-speciesist books for children, the second also being anti-speciesist.

If You Were a Penguin by Wendell and Florence Minor puts the reader in the place of a penguin: "You could fly underwater or sing a duet. You could live on the land but get really wet" (7–9). The penguins in this book don't speak a human language and they don't act like humans. Instead, the book simply and elegantly explores the idea that, as philosopher Thomas Nagel has written, "no matter how the form may vary, the fact that an organism has conscious experience *at all* means, basically, that there is something it is like to *be* that organism" (1). If you were a penguin, you would act like a penguin. You wouldn't speak human words, you wouldn't play like a human. You would be whatever it is like to be a penguin and that would be enough.

Finally, there is the anti-speciesist *Garlic-Onion-Beet-Spinach-Mango-Carrot-Grapefruit Juice* by Nathalie VanBalen. This book tells the story of Thora, a character who wears her brain on top of her head and her heart on the outside of her chest, and her two friends Aksel and Krog, who are "totally adventure oriented." Aksel and Krog get very "pumped" about the act of juicing. The two discover on the internet that adding snail shells to their juice will boost the nutritional content.

Thora, a character who "thinks and thinks and thinks and thinks," asks her friends why there are so many snails in their kitchen. "Thora," they explain, "their shells are TOTALLY nutritious! We're going to grind them up and put them in our juice."

A horrified Thora replies, "Yellow spotted snail shells are not for Vikings. They belong to yellow spotted snails."

Garlic-Onion-Beet-Spinach-Mango-Carrot-Grapefruit Juice not only provides a simple animal rights lesson, but also an example of effective outreach. In the end, Thora's friends realize that they shouldn't eat the snail shells. This happens in spite of Thora's feelings of inadequacy about her outreach. Ingvar, the narrator of the book, says, "But sometimes it's hard to know what to say. How can Thora get others to care about little snails? I don't know the answer, and neither does Thora." Vegan parents may feel their heart ache when they read those words with their children, but the lesson is important nonetheless. The fact that Thora's outreach bears fruit in this book is cause for celebration, but also reflection. How do we get those closest to us to care about other-than-human animals? Thora doesn't know the answer, and neither do you.

Conclusion

Jessica Almay cites the *Sesame Street* scene that kicks off this essay as the reason she started a blog that reviews books from an animal-friendly perspective. Vegbooks.org was launched "to assist parents — and aunties, uncles, teachers, godparents, and friends — in finding books and movies that affirm vegetarian and vegan values. Together we can raise children who value life, the connections between humans and other animals, and the need to protect the earth and all its inhabitants." To be sure, many of the books reviewed on the site contain easygoing and unintentional speciesism. Thankfully, the blog's reviewers will often warn parents of the more egregious offenses in the books they review. All told, the site is a great jumping-off point if parents are looking to expand their libraries with books and movies that portray animals as more than mere things.

In the end, much to the chagrin of vegan parents everywhere, Elmo and Zoe found their white food and it was the stolen milk of a cow. Why wasn't it tofu or cauliflower? Would anyone have been offended by that? And if so, should that matter anymore than it mattered when certain viewers were offended that a black man played a prominent role on the same children's television program in the 1970s?

This specific *Sesame Street* example is not an isolated incident, of course. The program is rife with speciesist images and messages. And more than any other book, show or movie, *Sesame Street* is the one that makes my blood boil. It's the gold standard for children's programming. It's supposed to be safe. It's supposed to be friendly. It should know better.

Sadly, children will be exposed to speciesism no matter what. In light of this, how we frame conversations about other-than-human animals in the early years of life is of the utmost importance. Vegan parents should foster a respect for other-than-human animals and a basic understanding that they are like and unlike us in many ways, that the sole characteristic they possess which compels us to respect their interests is sentience and that, simply put, they prefer life over death and we should respect that preference.

If the media that children are consuming don't reflect this view, parents should, when possible, contort them so that they do. They shouldn't hide the fact that they're doing this, especially from older children who can understand the reasoning behind it. They should talk matter-of-factly with their children about why they disagree with what the vast majority of society has to tell us about other-than-human animals. These tasks are as difficult as they are important.

That may sound bleak because it is. But if we vegan parents do our job well, hopefully it will all be a little less bleak for the next generation.

NOTES

1. In this essay, I use the term media to refer not only to TV and movies, but also books, the internet, advertising, video games, etc.

2. I don't touch on "mixed" parenting in this essay predominantly because it is not where my personal experience lies. Many points in this essay may be applicable to all types of guardians whose intent is to raise vegan children, but some may not apply as well as they would if the caregivers were exclusively vegan.

3. This example brings up a peculiar sub-set of speciesism in children's media in which heavily anthropomorphized animal characters subjugate, exploit and even eat other less-or not at all-anthropomorphized animals.

4. It could be argued that this is merely a difference of opinion about what constitutes effective outreach and not a case of speciesism on the part of PETA. While I argue that relying on cognitive characteristics to ground a respect for other-than-human animals is speciesist, I am sure that others disagree.

5. This section's illustration, meant to portray happy pets, includes a fish in a tiny fishbowl, the same kind that Franklin the turtle put his fish in; the same kind that is illegal in Rome. It seems a far cry from care and protection.

WORKS CITED

Almay, Jessica. "About." *Vegbooks*. Web. 21 Sept. 2011.

American Academy of Pediatrics. "Children, Adolescents and Television." *Pediatrics*. 107.2 (2001) : 423–426. Web. 21 Sept. 2011. PDF.

American Dietetic Association. "Position of the American Dietetic Association: Vegetarian Diets." *Journal of the American Dietetic Association*. 109.7 (2009) : 1266–1288, Web. 21 Sept. 2011. PDF.

Berenstain, Michael. *Michael Berenstain's Butterfly Book*. n.p. Racine, WI: Western Publishing Company, 1992. Print.

Dunayer, Joan. *Animal Equality: Language and Liberation*. Derwood, MD: Ryce Publishing, 2001. Print.

Ford, B.G. *Grover's Book of Cute Little Baby Animals*. n.p. Illus. Tom Leigh. Racine, WI: Western Publishing Company, Inc., 1980. Print.

"Franklin Plays the Game/Franklin Wants a Pet." *Franklin*. Writ. Paulette Bourgeois, Brenda Clark and Peter Sauder. Dir. Jon van Bruggen. Viacom, 1997.

Haffner, Debra W. *From Diapers to Dating: A Parent's Guide to Raising Sexually Healthy Children*. New York: Newmarket Press, 2008. Print.

Heyman, Melvin. "Lactose Intolerance in Infants, Children, and Adolescents." *Pediatrics*. 118.3 (2006) : 1280 Web. 21 Sept. 2011. PDF.

Jones, Gerard. *Killing Monsters: Why Children Need Fantasy, Super Heroes, and Make-believe Violence.* New York: Basic Books, 2002. Print.

Kaiser Family Foundation. *Kids and Media at the New Millennium.* Web. 21 Sept. 2011. PDF.

Kovacs, Deborah. *When Is Saturday?* n.p. Illus. Richard Brown. Racine, WI: Western Publishing Company, 1981. Print.

"Linda the Llama Saves Carnival." *Go, Diego, Go!* Writ. Ligiah Villalobos. Dir. Katie McWane. Nickelodeon Studios, 2005.

Minor, Wendell, and Florence Minor. *If You Were a Penguin.* New York: Scholastic, 2009. Print.

Moore, Heather. *A Cow's Life.* Illus. Ken Cursoe. Ed. Ingrid E. Newkirk. Norfolk: PETA, 2004. Print.

Murphy, Andy. *Out and About at the Dairy Farm.* Illus. Anne McMullen. Mankato, MN: Picture Window Books, 2003. Print.

Nagel, Thomas. "What Is It Like to Be a Bat?" *The Philosophical Review.* 83 (1974) : 435–450. Web. 21 Sept. 2011. PDF.

National Association for the Education of Young Children. "Learning to Read and Write: Developmentally Appropriate Practices for Young Children." *Young Children.* 53.4 (1998). Web. 21 Sept. 2011. PDF.

National Geographic Kids. *Wild Animal Atlas.* Washington, DC: National Geographic Society, 2010. Print.

Nowatzki, Al. "My Daughter the Monkey Eater." *These Little Piggies Had Tofu.* 17 June 2010. Web. Sept. 21, 2011.

Numeroff, Laura. *If You Give a Pig a Pancake.* n.p. Illus. Felicia Bond. New York: Scholastic, 1998. Print.

Parent, Nancy. *Panda Bears.* Weston, FL: Paradise Press, 2008. Print.

Roth, Ruby. *That's Why We Don't Eat Animals: A Book About Vegans, Vegetarians and All Living Things.* n.p. Berkeley, CA: North Atlantic Books, 2009. Print.

Sapon, Stanley M. "To Tell the Truth, the Whole Truth ... or Perhaps a Little Bit Less: Challenges to Psychological and Emotional Well-being Related to Lifestyle and Diet Choices." *North American Vegetarian Society Summerfest.* 10 July 1998. Web. 21 Sept. 2011.

Sesame Street: Guess That Shape and Color. Writ. Anne Evans. Dir. Ken Diego. Sony, 2006. DVD.

Silverstein, Shel. *Where the Sidewalk Ends.* New York: HarperCollins, 1974. Print.

Steiner, Gary. *Animals and the Moral Community: Mental Life, Moral Status, and Kinship.* West Sussex, UK: Columbia University Press, 2008. Print.

Stewart, Kate, and Matthew Cole. "The Conceptual Separation of Food and Animals in Childhood." *Food, Culture and Society.* 12.4 (2009): 458–476. Web. 22 June 2011. PDF.

Seuss, Dr. *Green Eggs and Ham.* New York: Random House, 1988. Print.

_____. *Horton Hears a Who!* New York: Random House, 1982. Print.

_____. *If I Ran the Zoo.* New York: Random House, 1978. Print.

_____. *The Lorax.* New York: Random House, 1971. Print.

_____. *One Fish Two Fish Red Fish Blue Fish.* New York: Random House, 1960. Print.

Sklansky, Amy E. *Where Do Chicks Come From?* Illus. Pam Paparone. New York: Collins, 2005. Print.

VanBalen, Nathalie. *Garlic-Onion-Beet-Spinach-Mango-Carrot-Grapefruit Juice.* n.p. Nashville, TN: ThoraThinks Press, 2010. Print.

Vegetarian Resource Group. *How Many Vegetarians Are There?* Web. 21 Sept. 2011.

Watt, Fiona. *That's Not My Puppy.* Illus. Rachel Wells. London: Usborne Publishing Ltd., 1999. Print.

Yates, Roger. "Easygoing Speciesism." *On Human-Nonhuman Relations: A Sociological Exploration of Speciesism.* human-nonhuman.blogspot.com, 11 May 2009. Web. 21 Sept. 2011.

On Cheese, Motherhood
and Everyday Activism

CHELSEA YOUNGQUIST HASSLER

Once upon a time, about three years ago at the age of 28, I was a clueless, meat-eating, cheese-loving Midwesterner. I wasn't particularly fond of meat. I ate it because that's what everyone ate. I knew no vegetarians, knew no one even questioning the health of a diet so rich in meat and dairy. Also, as so many of my generation, I tended to eat out more often than not. My now-husband Eric and I subsisted primarily on a diet of McDonald's, deep-dish pizza, and Taco Bell. I wish I knew our cholesterol numbers from those days.

My best friend Hillary led a very similar lifestyle, but arguably even worse. She detested nearly all vegetables, though I think she liked corn. Her food groups were unapologetically meat, carbs, and cheese. You can imagine my astonishment when she called me with no discussion or prelude to say, "I'm going vegan." I was shocked and a little annoyed. I'd heard of and vaguely understood vegetarianism. Going vegan, however, sounded like she'd joined a cult. It was so far from what I saw as normal, so far from anything anyone I knew was doing. I probably even tried to talk her off the ledge. I thought it was just another weird phase in a series of weird phases my friend was going to try out. She has always been more experimental than me, more open to trying new and radical things, and this certainly seemed radical to me.

In our discussions, I learned that she had read *Skinny Bitch* and found the commentary surrounding cruelty to animals so compelling that she went completely vegan overnight and remains so three years later. I wasn't prepared to hear or see what she was so eager to share; it was new and shocking to me. The information sank in very quickly, however, and I had to do something with and about my new knowledge.

I found (and still find) Hillary to be so cool, that I wanted to be just like her. I expressed my immediate interest in going vegetarian. There was no way I was willing to give up "my" cheese and ice cream, but I would half-ass the attempted change. (It's telling how many people refer to animal products as *my* cheese, *my* meat, *my* ice cream. It's so obvious to me now that those products do not belong to humans, but I did, and the majority of people still do, feel some sort of ownership over animals and their assorted secretions.) I asked for some information on vegetarianism, and Hillary promptly emailed me a reading list and a vegetarian starter kit. I knew in the back of my mind that I could, and should, have been doing more, but I wasn't ready to take the vegan plunge. In hindsight, I'm not sure why. I think I had a pretty strong fear of confronting others who might question my choice. I thought they wouldn't care, I thought they'd be mean, and I thought they wouldn't like me. I also had a really hard time believing that all the nutritional information (i.e., milk builds strong bones and teeth) I'd ever heard or read about was false, as Hillary was telling me.

And so began my year of vegetarianism. I still primarily subsisted on pizza and Taco Bell. I added in all sorts of processed vegetarian foods: chik'n nuggets, Boca burgers, Smart Dogs, etc. I had traded my standard American junk food in for more expensive meatless junk food. I did like some of these items, but I knew that I couldn't subsist on these processed, preservative-laden foods forever. So in between eating all that junk, I was starting to experiment in the kitchen. I tried baking with soy milk and egg replacer. I learned to prepare tofu. Eric was wonderful throughout this process. He liked almost all of the meat analogs and was also willing to try pretty much anything I made. He would even brag to his coworkers about my cooking when they made fun of him for "not being allowed to eat meat."

During this stage of my "vegvelopment," Hillary would invite me to vegan events, ask me to participate in protests, and try to engage me in activism. I wasn't interested. I still sort of saw veganism as fringe-y and super difficult to sustain while living in the suburbs. I'd read *Skinny Bitch* by Rory Freedman and Kim Barnouin, I'd read *Eating Animals* by Jonathan Safran Foer, and I'd read any number of other books documenting the abuse against animals, but I still couldn't get over my apathy. I finally read a book that changed my mind: *The China Study* by T. Colin Campbell. I wasn't sure how anyone could read *The China Study* and defend the average American diet. It framed the argument for veganism in totally different terms than all the other books I'd read. It was coming from a scientific point of view, rather than an emotional one. I found the science compelling in a way that the emotional pleas weren't. I felt validated by it. I felt that I could go out and tell the world what I learned because it isn't just some touchy-feely hippie stuff. It is solid science.

And so I became a vegan evangelist (vegangelist). I lent that book to anyone who was remotely receptive. My brother, my sister, my friend from work. I talked about it with my parents, grandparents, my boss, and my friends. I thought since it was such a light-bulb moment for me, it would be for others too and they would also instantly go vegan. Yeah, I'm a little naïve. I learned how Hillary must have felt after she'd read *Skinny Bitch* and had her own light bulb moment. This experience highlights that what hits home for one person doesn't remotely impact another. For some, change comes from emotion, others from science and still others for the environment. If one angle doesn't work, we can always try others when discussing veganism with omnivores.

At this point, I still wasn't all that interested in doing activist work such as taking part in protests, tabling at events, and distributing leaflets. I concentrated mainly on my friends and family and felt at the time that that was enough. Talking to strangers about animal rights wasn't my thing.

I loved my new vegan lifestyle. I loved how I could eat and eat and not get that heavy too-full feeling that I used to get during the holidays. I felt a sense of lightness. Most importantly, perhaps, I loved the food, and emotionally, I felt very free. It was wonderful to live according to my values. I didn't need to be defensive anymore when people asked why I would eat eggs and not hamburger. (Trying to point out inconsistencies in vegan living is a favorite pastime of the many omnivores in my life). I gradually started eating better, less processed meals. Vegan cooking, especially baking, became one of my greatest passions during this time. My husband, while not vegan, ate whatever I chose to cook up, and he loved almost everything I prepared. We kept a vegan house, and everything was going great until ...

Pregnancy — Ugh!

The myths surrounding pregnancy are many and legendary: pregnant women are "eating for two," if you swell up everywhere you are having a girl, and if you if you carry low you are having a boy. But the cravings, oh the cravings; they are no mere myth. My old nemeses, cheese and ice cream, were back and the pull was strong. Throughout my first trimester, I stubbornly ignored their call. I proudly told my doctor that I was a vegan and the baby would be too. During my second trimester, I was not as successful. I tried every vegan cheese on the market in an effort to satisfy the craving, but to no avail. Unfortunately, I caved, and my husband ordered us one of our old favorites: pizza. While he was a little confused by my change of heart, he knew how I had struggled with the cravings, and he wasn't about to argue with his pregnant wife, especially since he loves cheese.

It was interesting to go back. I hadn't had dairy cheese in about a year, and it didn't taste the way I remembered. I could taste, separately, all the different components in it. The milk, the salt, etc. I think when we eat processed foods all the time, our taste buds get used to super strong (artificial) flavors, and they just become normal. When we eat a whole foods diet, we become more adept at tasting subtle flavors.

Reflecting back on this time, I wish I would have had a stronger network of vegan friends. I knew no one navigating a vegan pregnancy or raising vegan kids. Had I, they may have been able to point me to resources to help ensure a successful vegan pregnancy. However, I had no one holding me accountable. In fact, it was quite the opposite. It felt like most were cheering for me to stray from the vegan lifestyle. Most people in my life still thought veganism was crazy, a passing interest, a fad diet, stupid, or even unnatural. Maybe part of this mentality is that, underneath it all, most people have an inkling that what they are eating hurts animals, and they don't want to be confronted with it. A vegan among them forces them to look in the mirror. So my consumption of cheese once again made them feel all right with their choices.

I wish I could say that it was just that one pizza, but that was not the case. My abandonment of veganism was comparable to cheating on a weight loss diet and eating a bunch of cookies. After the binge, one might say, "Well, now I've screwed up, might as well eat the rest of the box and try again next year." Dairy was back in my life in a big way. I was at Culver's or Dairy Queen at least twice a week for the duration of the pregnancy, with pizza once again a weekly treat.

I felt bad that I was eating this way. I had all sorts of excuses in my head, though, to make myself feel better: "I'm pregnant, I deserve it. It's just cheese, it's not like its meat or anything. If this is the worst thing I do, I'm still a good person." Each excuse was a load of crap. I knew that I didn't "need" cheese. It wasn't going to make the baby any healthier or make me any better off in the long run. I just wanted it. It makes me sad thinking back. I definitely think the cravings were real and strong, but they weren't insurmountable. Should I have another child, I will be more prepared by being stronger in my vegan values. In fact, I've recently heard of a book titled *Vegan Pregnancy Survival Guide* by Sayward Rebhal. Books like this will be a great resource next time around.

Eventually, I had a healthy, strapping baby boy, Cole, who is the very light and love of my life. Was I really going to feed him this junk, knowing the truth and consequences about the Standard American Diet, animal abuse and environmental destruction?

My postpartum diet was much healthier than during my pregnancy diet, but it still contained some amount of cheese and ice cream. I think I kept eating it because my husband and family found it easier, and I was rationalizing away all the cognitive dissonance I was feeling. While my heart and my brain were telling me these dairy products were both hurting animals and bad for my health, I continued to eat them for many reasons/excuses: they tasted good, I was a tired new mom and this made cooking less time-consuming, and my husband seemed to really like that I had returned to my cheese-eating ways.

As luck would have it (a strange way to put it, I suppose), my son had a pretty severe intolerance to the milk I was ingesting. It took a few weeks to determine that as the problem. Consequently, I was able to return to veganism relatively easily, with little pushback from annoying family members since it was for the baby's health.

It was terrific to finally get around that chatter in my head. During the first weeks of his life, I had wondered how I would explain to Cole, once he was old enough to ask those types of questions, the hypocrisy around eating dairy products but not meat. Of course, I will still have to address those issues for him with other family members, but I won't be a hypocrite, and that feels comforting for both me and my son.

So, why did I allow myself to backslide, and what do I do to prevent this from happening again? I needed a support network in a bad way. I had only one vegan friend and one vegetarian sister. This does not constitute a support network. I also needed to revisit my reasons for going vegan in the first place. I wanted to "re-shock" myself, so to speak. I accomplished both of these goals by reading Melanie Joy's *Why We Love Dogs, Eat Pigs and Wear Cows: An Introduction to Carnism.*

This book seriously pissed me off, and that is exactly what I needed. It starts by describing a delicious dinner in detail, the smells, tastes, etc. Then, the people who are enjoying it are told its Golden Retriever stew. The diners are shocked and repulsed. She then goes on to describe the concept of carnism as "the belief system in which eating certain animals is considered ethical and appropriate" (30). This belief system is why some people are very attached to cats and dogs, but don't think twice about the cruelty inherent in meat production. These concepts articulated exactly how I felt about several of the people in my life, especially those who are staunch "animal lovers" except when they are at Burger King. Reading and thinking about the issues discussed in Joy's book led me directly to a more activist role in the animal rights community.

My Vegangelicalism and the Categorization of Potential "Converts"

At this point, I was a recharged, angry, committed vegan. I reached out to Hillary and asked how I could get more involved with the local vegan community. Ever-helpful, she put me in touch with a local animal rights organization and sent me a calendar of events. I got on the list for volunteer opportunities. I have had the good fortune to meet many interesting, thoughtful, wonderful vegans in the area. This has been so psychologically uplifting for me, given the lack of support in my direct circle of family and friends.

I've also become far less afraid of identifying as a vegan and discussing the topic with any and all who will listen. I used to feel that people would be mean, or at the very least, not interested. Now, I don't give a crap. If one person isn't interested, the next person might be. I feel like it's my job to find that person.

I'm approaching my activism from a new perspective, a less unsophisticated perspective. I have given people tools in the past (*The China Study*, Veg starter kits), assuming they would see what I saw. They didn't, but I don't let that dissuade me. Many are resistant to this information at first. I know I was. It's very hard to believe that what you've been told your whole life is fundamentally wrong and also nutritionally bankrupt. Carnism is very much at play here. Joy discusses the process of psychic numbing, explaining how we are numbed from feeling empathy towards the animals we eat. People "don't see meat eating ... as a choice ... rather, we see it as a given, the 'natural' thing to do, the way things have always been and the way things will always be" (29). This underlying belief system is the reason I was so resistant to veganism at first and why so many others remain resistant to taking on a vegan lifestyle.

Understanding carnism has made my perspective stronger and more confident, but less idealistic. I now realize that not everyone will change. Not everyone will even understand. There are many who won't care. But some will! Along the way, I've learned that the best way to be an activist is within my own daily life, not just going to protests or tabling at events. Many people tend to be more receptive to what you have to say if they know you personally. As detailed in the sections below, my family and friends (a.k.a. prospects for conversion) fall into several categories on a continuum from "jerk face" to "supportive." I've even won a few people over.

1. The Respectful but Uninterested: "I barely eat any meat and/or my meat is free range"

Most people I know fall into this category. These people know me; they find me to be passionate, liberal, thoughtful, opinionated, and "crunchy," so they primarily respect and understand my decision to go vegan. They may even agree with me on the treatment of animals, nutrition, and/or environmentalism, but for whatever reason, they are not interested in making a change.

My dad is a perfect example of the "respectful but not interested" individual. He ascribes to what he calls a "lifestyle of personal physical fitness." He works out every day. He maintains a fairly healthy weight, has reasonable blood pressure and cholesterol readings without medication, and he has remained free of any diet-related diseases. My father also enjoys large cuts of meat every day. Until recently, more than once a day.

Of course, through my research on nutrition, I wanted to discuss with my father, whom I love, the detriment of a diet rich in animal products. This is a man who absolutely loves to debate, as long as he is sure to win, regardless of the facts presented him. His favorite arguments against going vegan are as follows: (1) I hardly eat any red meat; (2) And when I do, it's buffalo, which are free range and virtually fat free; (3) I'm too old to go vegan, and I don't want to anyway; and (4) by the way, Amish chickens have really good lives and are demonstrably healthier than the crappy chickens you can buy in a grocery store.

I am probably not going to win Dad over. I doubt even his doctor could. He admires and respects veganism and agrees with its core tenets, but he's just not interested. This does not discourage me, however, as I can still help my dad to live more healthily and with less cruelty to animals. I've suggested ways in which he can incorporate more vegetables and fiber into his diet and lessen the amount of meat on his plate. He now only eats meat once a day and in much smaller portions. In addition, my dad is an amazing cook, and we love to prepare dishes together. We are always trying to impress each other with our cooking adventures. He loves the "challenge" of preparing vegan dishes for me. I think it's great that when I visit him, I don't need to bring a case of Clif bars because there will be no other food options. I know there will be plenty for me to eat. In fact, he makes a better vegan pizza than I do.

My former boss, Mark, is similar in that he respects my veganism while not being personally interested. I remember when I first went vegan; I came in and announced it to the office. Mark thought I needed an intervention. He marched me to Barnes and Noble and bought Michael Pollan's books for me. I'm not certain they had the desired effect, as they convinced me even more that I was on the right path. I realize I'm probably the only vegan who will go on record as admiring Pollan's books. At least Pollan is honest about why he eats meat. And despite his intimate knowledge of food production, he is not vegan or even vegetarian: "I'm not a vegetarian because I enjoy eating meat, meat is nutritious food, and I believe there are ways to eat meat that are in keeping with my environmental and ethical values." I don't ascribe to Pollan's conclusion, but I still learned a lot from reading about his journey. The process of following a steer through his entire life, from the farm to the slaughterhouse to the plate, really affected me. I learned through Pollan's experience that there was no way I was willing to participate in that food system, no matter how mitigated.

Mark and I meet up for lunch a few times a month, and if he's choosing the place, he makes sure there are things I would want to eat. He even orders the vegan option once in a while. He also bought and read, at my suggestion, Joy's *Why We Love Dogs, Wear Cows and Eat Pigs*. We've had several great discussions on the book, and although he agrees with Joy, I'm not going to win him over and neither is she. I can't waste my emotional investment on people who say, "Yeah, but I *would* eat Golden Retriever." While I certainly wish I could convince him, I've learned that I cannot be so personally invested in people coming to the same conclusions about food that I did. It's too hard to be so consistently disappointed.

2. The Detached Intellectual: "I agree with you completely from an intellectual standpoint, but I just don't care"

My husband and brother fall into this category, the most difficult category that I've had to deal with, especially because in the case of my brother and husband, I highly respect them from both an emotional and intellectual perspective. It's hard when they just won't become vegan.

My brother is a genius science nerd, so when I was a new vegetarian reading *The China Study*, I wanted to share it with him. I knew the science behind "why vegan" would appeal to him. And it did. He was amazed at the consistency in the study, from mice to humans. He agreed that a plant-based diet was the healthiest, even stating that the way our country raises animals for food is egregiously inhumane. So, I had a new vegan on my hands, right? Hardly.

My brother would still eat at McDonald's despite what he knew. I think this is why it's tough to convert people to veganism for health reasons alone. Veganism can't just be a diet. Any "diet" tends to be difficult to stick with, and many people, my brother included, just don't care that much about their personal health. On the bright side, however, he does stick up for me when I am accosted by bullies hostile to veganism, and with his big giant brain, I'm glad to have him on my team. He's especially useful at family functions when it's "pick on the vegan" time and declares — sadly, usually with some kind of animal carcass on this plate — "No guys, you're wrong. She's absolutely right." He will then discuss the medically-sound aspects of veganism with the bullies until they lose interest. Their goal, after all, had been to frazzle me, not to get a science lecture.

My husband, Eric, is trickier to handle because I have to live with him and we are raising a child together. People often ask me, "Does your husband eat meat"? And I always say, "He's a good sport." I hate wording it that way because it is like I am apologizing for myself, but I have seen and read about veg/non-veg couples where the omnivore of the pair is not a good sport. I have read about women who make one meal for themselves and one meal for their husbands and kids. I don't mean to reinforce gender stereotypes here, but I've only read about women doing this. The husbands and kids eat meat that the mom prepares. That sure as hell is not going to happen at my house. I'm not sure how, if eating meat goes against one's value system, buying and cooking it for someone else is acceptable.

In sum, I appreciate my husband's understanding even though he does not share my passion for the cause, though my appreciation is not without its frustrations. I have a fundamental belief, a core value, something I see as completely lacking moral ambiguity; it is black and white to me, almost like a religion. Meanwhile, the person I love and respect the most in this world agrees with me, but just doesn't care very much about what he agrees with. However, we still work as a pair because he eats what I cook and he accepted me even after my evolution from meat-eating, cheese-loving Midwesterner to vegan wife and mother of his child.

Eric understands that we will raise our son vegan, fully agreeing that it is a healthier and more compassionate way of life. While Eric may be primarily a dietary vegan because of his choice of spouse, he won't be a full on subscriber to the ideology. I'm still trying to determine why he feels the way he does. It seems that perhaps he may be concerned about how others would perceive him as a vegan man. A man who doesn't eat meat, especially here in the suburban Midwest, is seen as less masculine. He is like my brother in that he thinks a vegan diet is best for one's health and for animals, but he doesn't quite care enough to change. Of course, I am not completely at peace with his decision, but I have come to terms with the reality that my husband is not vegan.

My in-laws also fall into this second category. I pretty much won the in-law lottery, as my mother- and father-in-law are very respectful of my veganism. Alice, my terrific mother-in-law, barely batted an eyelash when I went from meat lover to cheese lover to vegan. As the cook in their household, she simply started adding a vegan entrée whenever we'd swing by for dinner. Oftentimes we would have two entrees, one with meat, one without. Once in a while, she will make just one vegan option and everyone will have it. She's also purchased several vegetarian cookbooks for new ideas on what to serve when I am visiting. Maybe she feels it's just another phase "kids" tend to go through, or maybe she just sees it as a fun cooking challenge. Either way, it's great that she is so supportive.

I think my in-laws' lack of interest in becoming vegan has to do with their growing up in a small Midwestern farm town. Many people of my parents' generation grew up on or near family farms. For example, my mom comes from a family of hog farmers, and so when we discuss cruelty to animals, they don't understand how much farming has changed over a generation. They don't understand the cruelty inherent to factory farming. In their minds, they think animal products are produced in the same manner they were thirty years ago, or at least they convince themselves that that is the case (think Joy's "carnism" here). In *Eating Animals*, Jonathan Safran Foer reports that, aside from what he calls "some vibrant alternatives," the truth about farming today is that "[f]or each food animal species, animal agriculture is now dominated by the factory farm — 99.9 percent of chickens raised for meat, 97 percent of laying hens, 99 percent of turkeys, 95 percent of pigs, and 78 percent of cattle." Despite what folks may remember about farming, or aside from how "humane" they claim their meat consumption to be, these numbers show that the small family farm is more of a quaint notion than anything else, and the overwhelming majority of Americans are getting their meat from the living hell known as factory farms.

I believe that if people would take a few minutes to actually see what goes on in Concentrated Animal Feeding Operations (CAFOs) and slaughterhouses, they would feel compelled to make changes. However, my family members are not even close to willing, so they do not understand what I am so upset about. They don't comprehend why I call myself an abolitionist activist, meaning that I will not eat or use animals, to the best of my abilities, no matter how well they were treated prior to becoming dinner; nor will I support campaigns that make animal abuse marginally less abusive. My family still tells me: "Well, Chelsea, they *are* animals, so that's what they are here for." So, I'm not winning them over either, but I do appreciate the vegan enchiladas and French toast, thank you very much.

The last type of person I place in this category is the one which enrages me the most — the "animal lover." These people volunteer for the Humane Society. They foster animals. They post adorable pictures of their companion animals all over Facebook. They're enraged by dog fighting. And they abhor animal cruelty ... right up to the moment they sit down to eat, that is. My brother's girlfriend was this exact way. She is a kind and generous person. She does, in fact, foster animals. She posts pictures of them to her Facebook page nearly every day, alongside status updates such as, "Lucky me, free coupon for a Wendy's cheeseburger!"

Though others may, I had no advice on dealing with people like this. I just roll my eyes and move on. This meat-eating/animal-loving perspective angers me so much that I stopped even talking about veganism when she was around. However, maybe I did inspire them in some way, for in a *very* surprising twist, my brother (the aforementioned genius) just recently announced to me that the two of them are going vegetarian! I certainly wish they were going vegan, but I understand that everyone's journey is diverse. I'm hoping that they will be able to stick with it, especially due to his previously apathetic nature on this subject. You never really know where and when your message will be heard and internalized, and I am so happy that I was able to help them reach this more compassionate decision.

To sum up, while you might not win this type of person over to veganism, you can enact incremental change through everyday activism. You can prepare amazing food — I find baked goods especially effective, cheesecake in particular; yeah, make them cheesecake — and respectfully and non-judgmentally answer any questions they have.

3. The Almost Interested and/or Super Trendy: "I could be semi-vegan, or 'Oooh, I hear that Alicia Silverstone and Tobey Maguire are vegan, and I want to be like them!'"

I really like this type of prospect. They can be recognized by comments such as, "I've always thought about going vegan, but I could never give up cheese." Or fish, or buffalo wings. More often than not, it's cheese, at least in the Midwest.

My journey to veganism started this way. I thought there was no way in the world to give up cheese and ice cream. Really, I thought it was impossible. As it turns out, I was probably addicted to dairy. Citing Dr. Neal Barnard's *Breaking the Food Seduction*, the Physicians Committee for Responsible Medicine (PCRM) reports that cravings for cheese linger longer and are more intense than cravings for other foods. This is due to the presence of casomorphins, an opiate compound contained in concentrated levels in cheese. Yes, there are opiates in cheese, as in opium, as in an addictive drug. Not as bad as heroin, I admit, but still an addictive substance. My sister Caitlin felt much the same way about cheese. When I became a vegetarian, she did as well. She's quite sensitive, and animal suffering really upsets her. When I made the jump to veganism, I hoped she would follow suit. She didn't. This frustrated me beyond measure. I knew that she agreed with me in theory. I knew that she didn't want to hurt animals, and I knew she was aware that dairy products hurt animals too. It is just that the allure of dairy was too strong.

I didn't give up on her, though. Instead, I would gently bring up things I'd read, podcasts I'd heard, etc. Eventually, she too read Melanie Joy's book, and it turned out to be an effective resource for Caitlin, just as it had been for me. A few days after reading *Why We Love Dogs, Eat Pigs and Wear Cows*, she decided to go vegan. I still remember the hesitancy in her voice when she told me, and I understand why. Going vegan is saying goodbye to a familiar way of life; it means saying farewell to a level of ease at many common places: family dinners, in restaurants and on business trips. For some, it is a major transition, but this big sister is very proud that Caitlin made the brave choice. I know most vegans don't see being vegan as a matter of bravery, for it seems like an easy and obvious choice. But I still think it's brave, especially in the suburbs where the local restaurant choices are Applebee's, T.G.I. Friday's and Perkins.

On the other side of this category are those who are genuinely interested, but not for what ethical vegans see as the right reasons. Honestly, I really don't care why people go vegan or how they go vegan, but I do care about how long they stay vegan. When one adopts a vegan diet for appearances, s/he is not likely to stick with it, and the broader implications of what seems like a mere food choice can become lost (i.e., picture someone eating a seitan sandwich in a leather jacket and Ugg boots).

Veganism is quite trendy these days. Celebrities have been going vegan and "Meatless Mondays" are all the rage. Flexitarian is actually a concept where people try to eat vegetarian or vegan only for a certain number of meals per day or days per week. People who tend to be concerned about their image experiment with vegetarianism/veganism so they can appear hip. I have a close friend who is just this kind of "vegan."

My friend dislikes most meat, especially when it takes the form of an actual animal part (ribs or chicken wings). Steak, however, is acceptable. One might think that if a person was astute enough to connect the animal flesh with the sentient being it came from, then that person could easily make the leap to veganism, but that has not been the case with this friend. She just avoids meat that looks like body parts, though she was very interested when I declared that I was going vegan. She asked me a million questions and was particularly concerned about how she would make two meals since her husband would never eat a meal that didn't contain animal protein. Also, she was worried about how people would perceive her. She didn't want to be seen as "high maintenance." This is a decidedly Midwest phenomenon, and I have seen this fear among several of my friends. They worry so much about what their husbands or coworkers or strangers will think about them going vegan while at the same time being enticed by the vegan trend. I assume this attitude is less prominent on the coasts, with their myriad vegan/vegetarian restaurants and mainstream acceptance of many things seen as counterculture here.

So, this friend decided she would try to go "vegetarian," except she would still eat seafood, and she would never be able to give up cheese or eggs. I find it aggravating when people like this identify as vegetarian simply because it's trendy or they like the sound of it. Not to get too bogged down in terminology, but "vegetarians" who eat fish are the reason that vegans are still occasionally asked, "So, you're vegan, but you can still eat seafood, right?" Annoying, yes, but there are worse categories of responders to deal with ...

4. The Uninterested and Disrespectful: "Yum! Meat, delicious, yummy meat!"

Sometimes, being vegan makes me a target for ridicule. I'm talking about people who try to catch vegans in ethical inconsistencies, who say "mmmmm ... ribs" as they sink their teeth into animal flesh slathered in BBQ sauce, and those who tell activists to "get a job." Do they really think none of us have jobs? Basically, these individuals are akin to schoolyard bullies. Unfortunately, my stepdad falls into this category. When I first became vegetarian, with my sister following suit, and my brother defending the lifestyle without actually embracing it, my stepdad asked a lot of questions, but he was not actually interested in the answers. He just likes making fun at our expense. To use a cliché, Randy can dish out the taunts, but he cannot take them. This seems to be a theme with the older generations in my family. They don't want their beliefs challenged by a younger person. Perhaps they feel like new ways of doing things mean their value system is wrong and they themselves are being rejected, not just their values.

In many other ways, my stepdad is a very funny, caring, wonderful person. He's loyal and always willing to lend a hand to help with home improvements, watching the baby, etc. But he does tend to relentlessly make fun of anything and everything that he perceives as weak or different, or that he doesn't fully understand. For him and others, vegans are easy targets.

So, during a typical family weekend at the cabin, the script goes something like this:

RANDY: So you won't eat [whatever non-vegan stuff] either?
ME: No, Randy, it's not vegan.
RANDY: But what would happen to the animals if we didn't eat them?
ME: Nothing. What happens to bald eagles? We don't eat them.
RANDY (flustered): That's just ridiculous.
ME: (silence)
RANDY: You always bring this up. Don't bring this up when your grandparents get here. You will make them feel bad. Why are you so confrontational and defensive?
ME: (exit stage left)

Yes, loads of fun. Randy also quite often asks me when Cole will get to go fishing with Grandpa. My mother and Randy are *amazing* grandparents, and Cole is the absolute delight of their lives. But Cole is not going fishing with Grandpa. My mom asked me about this once when we were alone.

MOM: So, we were thinking about getting Cole a fishing rod for next summer.
ME: Why? He won't be going fishing.
MOM: Why not?
ME: Mom, we don't eat fish. We are vegan. Why would he go fishing?
MOM: Well he doesn't have to eat them; he can just throw them back.
ME: So he can injure the fish and throw them back to die, but it's okay
   because he isn't eating them?
MOM: I just don't know how Randy will feel about that.
ME: I DON'T CARE HOW *HE* FEELS ABOUT IT! I'M THE MOM!

Yes, I can get defensive and angry. Although I understand that fishing is something that my entire family has enjoyed as a wholesome bonding activity, and my parents would love to share that special time with Cole, he's *my* son, and I should set the parameters around his activities and food intake, especially if it goes against my value system. It is difficult contending with this issue with my parents. I try to be non-confrontational, but no matter what, it seems that my honest responses are deemed hostile to my family's very life fabric. I'm not sure if that's because they simply don't like what they are hearing, so they pick on the messenger, or if it's because I am an opinionated woman, and they are nostalgic for a time when women were silent and didn't cause trouble.

My biggest concern is that one day, when Randy is so generously watching my son, that he will slip him a piece of cheese, a hot dog, ice cream or cookies. I am realistic enough to know that at some point, Cole is going to be given something that isn't vegan, probably by mistake. However, if a family member or anyone else does it *on purpose* because they find his mother's beliefs to be silly, that is inexcusable and blatant disrespect. If Cole and I ate kosher, would Randy slip Cole some lobster? If we were Muslim, would a family friend give Cole a bacon sandwich? Those would be violations of another's ethical beliefs, and it feels the same way to me, although veganism is not a religion.

Internet trolls are another lively addition to this category. I tend to play it pretty low key on my Facebook page. When I was a new vegan, I never posted anything because I didn't want to offend anyone. Looking back, I see how ridiculous this was. Lots of people are offended by lots of things, but it's important for me to stay true to my beliefs, even if I am worried about how others will perceive them. However, even now, I don't post graphic factory farm images or anything of that nature. I might post a funny quote or sign, such as the time I was in Columbus, Georgia, on business and noticed a sandwich board touting a restaurant's vegetable of the day as "Mac 'n' Cheese." Those kind of gems need to be uploaded, but I consciously post nothing that would offend a sensitive omnivore.

I've had two particular situations on Facebook which have led me to believe it's probably not the best venue for constructive debate. The first time, I had been traveling on business in Fort Lauderdale, Florida, and had to order room service for lunch. There wasn't much on the menu, so I asked for a few modifications. I told them that I was vegan and would like the turkey sandwich with no meat or mayo. Basically, I wanted some vegetables with mustard on the bread. When it arrived, the turkey and mayo were nowhere to be seen, but it had several slices of bacon on it. I posted on Facebook something to the effect of this: "Just ordered a vegetable sandwich. It came with bacon. Pretty sure a pig is not a vegetable." The comments were to this effect: count your blessings; mmmm, bacon; and without meat, it's just a snack.

Another more recent post featured a picture of a tabletop advertisement from Subway. It had happy smiling pig faces asking that you add bacon to any sub for only fifty-nine cents. I posted it along with the comment: "Yes, I'm sure sub-eating pigs would love you to add bacon to your sandwiches, as they evidently do with their own sandwiches." The responses were infuriating: "I don't like a sub unless there are three kinds of meat on it" and "You're going to feel pretty ridiculous when you start eating delicious and tasty animals again."

I hesitate to bring this up, but I must: each and every one of these comments was made by a man. I don't mean to be sexist, just honest. I've never once had a woman make a rude Facebook post back to me. I'm not sure if this is because women in general tend to be more polite or more compassionate by nature, but women are often more receptive to my vegan message than men. This goes back to the mythical belief that eating lots of meat equals being a manly man.

These guys might say that I'm asking for it by posting in the first place. Maybe to a degree that's right, but I still don't understand why anyone would post something rude in response to something you know the other person feels strongly about. So while I don't post things on Facebook to start debates, they are sometimes inevitable. So, what do you do? First, you can refuse to read the comments. I've found myself wasting a lot of time and resources on boorish responders. You can also make them vegan goodies or debate them until someone gets bored, but I find refusal to engage to be the best course of action. Argue and debate if that's what blows your skirt up, I just don't have the patience or the interest.

5. The Respectful but Unsure: "I respect your decision, but I don't get how this whole thing works."

Before you finish this essay thinking that everyone I know is a complete jerk, I wanted to touch on this lovely category of people, the "respectful but unsures." In my life, these individuals are aware of how I feel about things and do their best to accommodate me. They aren't interested in changing their lifestyles, but they love me and want me to be comfortable. There just needs to be a bit more education.

My mom has absolutely no interest in going vegan, and she honestly asks me all the time, "Don't you miss hamburgers and hot dogs? I would really miss them." Needless to say, "Um, eeew, as if I would eat such nasty foods anyway." However, my mother loves having family around her, and that means making sure we have plenty to eat. For example, we were having a small family reunion at our lake house last summer. My mom made her favorite Three Bean Hotdish with Boca Crumbles instead of hamburger. We were all enjoying it out on the deck when my cousin noticed something suspicious:

> COUSIN: Isn't this ... bacon?
> ME: Couldn't be, my mom made it vegan.
> COUSIN (eats it): Yep, that's totally bacon.
> ME (to mom): So ... bacon?
> MOM: Darn it, I thought I picked all the bacon out.

She genuinely didn't understand that picking out the bacon didn't magically make the meal vegan. Another time, we were having morning coffee, and the following scenario took place:

> MOM: I bought you this delicious biscotti at the store the other day.
> ME (glancing over the label): Wow, thanks! Sounds good.... Wait. Mom, there's milk in this.
> MOM: Yeah, but it's at the end of the list of ingredients, so there's barely any in there.

At these moments, I sometimes just have to laugh. My mother-in-law is very similar to my mother. Both are in need of some vegucation. My mom tends to buy anything in the hippie section, as I call it, of the grocery story, assuming that it's vegan. For example, she has served Morningstar Farms products that contain eggs and/or milk, or she'll buy a cheese product labeled as "soy," but it contains casein, a milk derivative. Luckily, there are a lot of vegan products out there making it easier for people like my mom and mother-in-law to cook tasty stuff for me. Considering the other categories of naysayers, bullies and hipsters, I am just so grateful that people are even trying to feed me and my son appropriately.

Conclusion

This has been a long journey for me. I've gone from unapologetic meat lover — I actually, embarrassingly enough, uttered the phrase "People Eating

Tasty Animals" as my version of People for the Ethical Treatment of Animals — to vegetarian to vegan. In the beginning, I fell into several of the categories I've described. There were times I was not interested and not respectful, even to my close friend Hillary. When she attempted to veganize me, I poked fun, I made jokes. This is not something I'm proud of. Looking back, I'm not sure there's much she could have done differently with me. I came to veganism in my own time.

I've progressed from apathetic to fired up to annoyed to animal rights activist. To those who cannot make it to protests and outreach events, I encourage you to practice the everyday activism that I have detailed above. This has made me much more effective at discussing animal-related issues with the various people in my life. Since my path wasn't black and white, I don't expect theirs to be. I understand and applaud small steps that people can and do make towards better health, a cleaner planet, and less animal cruelty. I will keep gently pushing them further and further as much as possible. And I do all this as a geographical anomaly: a proud Midwestern mom who doesn't eat cheese.

WORKS CITED

Foer, Jonathan Safran. *Eating Animals*. New York: Little, Brown/Hachette Digital, 2009. eBook.

Joy, Melanie. *Why We Love Dogs, Eat Pigs and Wear Cows: An Introduction to Carnism*. San Francisco: Conari, 2010. Print.

Physicians Committee for Responsible Medicine. "Breaking the Food Seduction." pcrm.org., n.d. Web. 7 May 2012.

Pollan, Michael. "Animal Welfare: FAQ & Useful Links." michaelpollan.com, n.d. Web. 6 Apr. 2012.

Till Vegan Do Us Part?
Personal Change, Interpersonal Relationships and Divorce
ELIZABETH COOK

In 2008, *The Vegetarian Times* reported that there are approximately 7.3 million people following a vegetarian-based diet, with 1 million of those being vegan. This means that about .5 percent, or about one million Americans, are vegan ("Vegetarianism in America"). So what does this mean? Well, aside from meaning that it is still extremely important to explain the difference between vegetarianism and veganism to family, friends and food servers, it also means that if you identify as vegan, you are in the minority and that you walk among meat eaters.

This is obvious to many, and as those who have made the compassionate choice, we have accepted this reality even as we try to change meat eaters' perspectives through education and outreach. However, this also means that our friends, family and loved ones are omnivores, and most of them knew us before we went vegan. (And if you were raised vegan, I salute your parents.) These are the people who went out to happy hour with you to share a plate of nachos. It's the mom who makes grandma's famous green bean casserole every Thanksgiving. It's the father who thinks vegans are a weird subset of people who must be perpetually starving. It's your husband, your wife, and your best friend. As Carol J. Adams states in *Living Among Meat Eaters*, when one makes the choice to become vegetarian or vegan, "we see death" in the meals of the omnivores we are used to eating with, and "they see death in ours" because many cannot imagine how the human body can function without animal protein (6). Adams goes on to compare this change in one's lifestyle to the "shifting of the tectonic plates when an earthquake occurs" (6). While her metaphor is intentionally hyperbolic, I get where she is coming from.

At first, the excitement, commitment and compassion about going vegan can come on very strong. Along with new delicious foods, many new vegans can also be found devouring information related to animal agriculture and the environmental and health implications of an omnivorous diet, wanting to share all of this information with the meat eaters in their lives. While comparable to an earthquake, as Adams suggests, going vegan can also be compared to a moment of calm once the rain ends and the mist clears. Thus, it can be particularly hurtful when, in the midst of your epiphany, your omnivore friends are not impressed with your decision. Even worse, some may push back with inaccurate health information arising from years of being brain washed by the Food and Drug Administration's food pyramid as well as hurtful comments and veiled, as well as not-so-veiled, jokes.

The new vegan is left to ask: "Why?" Why is the friend who has never once had a conversation with you about dietary needs, suddenly a self-professed expert on iron, calcium and protein? Why do you hear, for the first time ever, about a sickly vegan your uncle once knew? Why do your friends and family refuse to accept your new lifestyle? Were they not your true friends and family to begin with? Were you switched at birth? No. Your best friend really is your best friend, regardless of what you are or are not eating. And while at times it probably doesn't seem like it, he or she really does still love and care for you. The real reason you feel such a pushback from friends and family is because going vegan is a change, and change can be scary, even when it is a change you observe in someone else. The foreign nature of veganism may confound those closest to you, and this manifests into jokes and/or sarcastic comments because they love you, so there is a natural tendency to want you stay the person they have come to love. They want you to stay exactly the same, which means that you still eat the same foods and share the same viewpoints that made you friends to begin with.

For example, let's say that while growing up, you and your best friend were both Republicans. Over coffee, you'd talk politics and agree with each other about all of the hot-button political topics. What would happen if one day over coffee you explain that you are now a Democrat? That bond of shared ideology is no longer there. Such changes can often end up going one of two ways. Your friend can go out of his way to say things to get a rise out of you. Conversely, instead of saying anything, that same friend can decide to just remain quiet and standoffish out of fear of an argument or that you will now negatively judge him.

Of course, vegans may also suddenly feel differently about friends and family. I now bristle at the hypocrisy of someone viewing their companion animal as family or engaging in cat and dog rescue work while they still drink milkshakes and eat turkey sandwiches. Before going vegan, I would not make the connection between people saying how much they love animals yet acting in a way, through their food choices, that cause direct pain and suffering to other animals. In my activist and personal life, I face this dissonance from strangers and those closest to me. I always want to point out this discrepancy, but I remain on the fence about making such accusations. Do I say something with the hope that my friend will make the connection, or do I stay quiet in fear of hurting her feelings and starting an argument?

Either way, deciding to say something or not, veganism can come between friends. Saying something could make my friend think I'm judgmental or turn people away from animal rescue and adoption. From here, negative thoughts can start to spiral, and everyone can end up defensive. However, silence causes stress, too. This catch-22 is why so many succumb to the common misconception that vegans are always negatively judging omnivores. This is something I believed back in college, which was the reason I would make negative comments about students who worked with the on-campus animal advocacy group. I assumed that those students could see through the hypocrisy of how much I loved animals yet was still contributing to animals' misery through my food and other purchasing habits. With this presumption that vegans are always passing judgment on omnivores, friends may think that since you are already judging, making fun of you is somehow justified.

However, the truth is that as a vegan, I am not judging omnivores. Sure, it'd be nice for all my friends to go vegan, but I'm not thinking negatively of them for still eating animals. In fact, I'm actually somewhat sympathetic, as I too was once there, eating animals and animal by-products, not realizing the effect I was having on myself and all other living beings. But all of this being said, many might start to wonder if vegans and omnivores can even be friends. My answer? Yes. There is nothing which makes veganism a special case when compared to other life shifts. In these situations, while it may be hard to understand why a friend wants to keep eating meat, accept that he or she just hasn't come to the same conclusions as you, and may never.

That said, just as if you were to switch religions, take up a new passion for human rights or start a new career, true friends should be encouraging and supportive. This means that it is not acceptable for a friend to make hurtful comments to you about your vegan lifestyle or make inaccurate comments about vegans in your presence. Additionally, friends who you've had since you were younger should expect that you are both going to grow as individuals and be different than when you first met.

Personally, I've had the same best friend since I was fourteen years old. She's was there when I decided to go vegetarian and later vegan. And while sometimes there are jokes between us about this shift, there have always been jokes, which is a benefit of our relationship. She's teased me about my taste in music, hair color, and now my food choices, but the jokes have always come within a context of respect and support. Other relationships, however, are not so easy to navigate.

Veganism and Divorce

When it comes to friends and family, it is normal for us to expect that they will be accepting of our lifesty'e choices. However, what about our significant others? What is the effect on a relationship when one spouse goes vegan and other remains an omnivore? We've all heard the common wedding vows: "For better or for worse" and "'Til death do us part." For most, those vows have deep meaning. Despite this initial intention, however, many marriages end in divorce. In fact, for first time marriages, the divorce rate is 41 percent, and it increases as one marries for the second and third time ("Divorce Rate"). Of course, these statistics don't account for how many of those divorces occur because of veganism. Therefore, below is simply my story and not indicative of a nationwide trend.

When I went vegan, I had high hopes that all of my family and friends, especially my husband, would all wake up the next day and go vegan. Of course, this didn't happen. Instead of congratulating me on my positive decision, I was put in a position where I was constantly answering a slew of questions regarding how I could ever live without bacon (easy, it's disgusting) and whether or not I was getting enough protein to work out. And while this was surely annoying and would cause anxiety when going to family members' houses for dinner, I was expecting that my husband was going to support my decision. I didn't think this would be something I would also be battling in my own home. Boy, was I wrong.

Before I continue, I need to clearly state that my decision to go vegan did not cause my divorce. There were other issues at play. As with any relationship, there were complexities that are outside the purview of this essay, and I don't want anyone to get the misunderstanding that my going vegan broke up my marriage. However, the interactions between my husband and I, and especially his friends, certainly put a great deal of stress on our relationship.

My veganism overhauled every aspect of my life. I didn't just stop eating animals, I started reading not only food labels, but also labels on everyday supplies like body soap, detergent and dishwasher fluid. Asking my husband to make a quick stop in at the grocery store turned into a pop quiz. This is a story so common as to be cliché, and with it came the further cliché of the threatened spouse.

Quite often, when one spouse goes vegan, the omnivore becomes unnerved, wondering if sudden changes in shopping and eating habits will lead to other changes. Will the vegan spouse wake up one day and realize that she simply cannot live with a meat eater? The "what abouts" come on full force. What about dinner dates? What about our shared love of chicken wings on Friday evenings? Oh no! What about dinner with the in-laws?

Many of these fears manifest because eating is not as simple as it seems, but this only becomes apparent when one in a pair begins eating differently. So much emotion, tradition, and ritual is tied up in food. Many couples cook romantic Valentine's Day dinners together, while others go to the restaurant where they had their first date every year for their anniversary. For others, as in my situation, there are local restaurants that couples frequent to share appetizers. Whatever the situation is, by one spouse going vegan, those routines will change. No longer will you split the same appetizers over a few beers after a rough week at work. (Indeed, many beers aren't even vegan!) This change can end up feeling threatening and scary to the omnivore spouse. For him or her, the act of no longer splitting that same appetizer is not necessarily a reflection of your compassionate choice, but a decision to break the bond that the two of you shared. It's no longer about the food, but it's a change of routine, a change of scenery and a change of the ties that led to your marriage in the first place. It's as if your decision to order the hummus plate is saying, "I'm breaking our connection." Who knew hummus could be so powerfully symbolic?

When I first went vegan, this change was something I simply did not understand. I wasn't aware that not only would it require an overhaul of my entire life, but it would also affect my husband. Throughout our marriage, he and I had found ourselves at our local sports bar at least once a week sharing boneless buffalo wings or mozzarella sticks and talking about our jobs and what had gone on over the past week. It was something we both looked forward to doing. However, when I went vegan, after I ordered an animal-free option, he was forced to pick only one choice from his two old standbys. Aside from food orders, our conversation topics changed as well. I wanted to share all of the information I was learning, talk about the upcoming "pet" store demonstration, but I suspect he just wanted everything to go back to the way it was before I went vegan. He wanted that same common ground of sharing food and talking about our jobs and plans for the weekend.

Like many who make the compassionate choice, I did not grow up thinking that one day I would be vegan. As previously mentioned, I was one of those who made fun of vegans and used to openly say that I would never in a million years go vegan. Just as I could not anticipate this change, neither could my omnivore spouse. This initially led him to believe (indeed, hope) that my new found veganism was just a phase, not something to which I was committed for the long haul. His reaction was not without cause.

Admittedly, I go through phases. In the past, my husband listened as I would go on and on about wanting to go back to school for public health. I even took the GRE. I would spend hours researching public health schools, degree tracks and constantly talk about how one day I was going to become a registered dietician. However, I then woke up one day, got a job I love, and gave up on the whole graduate school thing. This is just one of many examples of my interests that are quickly put aside. There was the time I wanted to learn French. The time I wanted to become a certified personal trainer. The time I wanted to enter physical fitness competitions. All of these were things that I had once felt so passionately about, but they ended up being short-term whims that I eventually gave up on.

In contrast, going vegan is different than wanting to train for a contest or learn a new language. When I was taking French classes through community education, besides the once a week two hour class and looking over some class notes at the end of the day, learning a new language really didn't consume a large part of my life or my husband's. In contrast, being vegan isn't something I only do or think about a few hours out of my day. It is something that is always there, something that affects the decisions I make throughout my day. Still, not everyone accepts that veganism can be more than just a phase or hobby, which is why people, spouses included, say frustrating thing such as, "Oh, she's vegan today," as if tomorrow you are not going to be. While the spouse may believe this to be true, the downplaying of one's life choices by a loved one can be quite hurtful.

When two people are married, there is an expectation that spouses will stick up for each other. This means that if a friend starts to make fun of your spouse, you would stick up for that spouse and say, "Dude, stop. This is not okay." So what happens when the inevitable poking fun starts and the omnivore spouse does nothing?

Unfortunately, I can take you on a trip down memory lane to answer that question. My husband has a group of friends that he's been extremely close with since his early teens. On weekends, it was commonplace for us all to get together, have some food and drinks and catch up. This was always fun. It was something that I looked forward to doing ... until I went vegan. People I had previously thought of as *our* friends, I began to think of as *his* friends. I even remember one time when one of his friends continuously made fun of me and kept saying "bacon" every time I would try and say anything. On another occasion, one of his friends made the tired comment that "Liz is vegan today." Or, to be more specific, he kept making the comment over and over. This was just one of many times that I ended up on the verge of tears at one of his friends' houses. Sometimes I even found myself in the bathroom splashing my face with water to try and hide my tears. What did my husband do upon seeing me, red-faced, emerging from the bathroom with a shaky smile, knowing how hurt I was? Nothing. Nothing at all. His inaction felt like the ultimate betrayal. I would have never let someone put him down until he was in tears without coming to his defense, so how could he ever let this happen to me?

My reaction came to be about more than just veganism. My significant other, the person I was supposed to spend the rest of my life with, was picking his friends over me, and ultimately showed me a side of himself that I had not known was there. By not sticking up for me, I wondered if he was always going to bail whenever I made any meaningful changes in my life. This push-back from him and his friends led me to find a community where I was no longer the outcast. I needed a place where I, too, belonged. A quick Google search of "vegan Minneapolis" led me to the Animal Rights Coalition, an abolitionist animal advocacy organization.

I've since learned that any kind of animal rights group is very important for new vegans. New vegans who are having their views picked apart at home do not yet have a handy repertoire of come-backs and tools to help cope. Thus, they are particularly ready for these informative and nourishing connections. I still remember going to my first volunteer meeting and actually feeling like I was being selfish because I wasn't truly there for the animals or to instill change in others. I was there because I really needed support. I needed to be treated with respect. I needed a break from being the butt of jokes. I needed to be able to talk to others who shared my viewpoints. Fortunately, no one judged me about why I was there. Further, I later learned that while fitting in was my original intention, helping animals and my fellow humans become vegan quickly took over as a primary goal. By being with like-minded people, I, in turn, was getting the support I needed to stay vegan, which is necessary if one is to stand firm in his/her newfound compassionate beliefs.

However, while the Animal Rights Coalition was a lifesaver and got me involved in activism, it did not help my marriage. In that arena, getting more involved as an activist led to my feeling like even more of an outcast on the home front. At one point, when explaining that I was going to go bring some vegan outreach literature to leave at a nearby coffee shop, my husband compared it to the North American Man/Boy Love Association (NAMBLA). He actually compared literature on ethical living to literature that promotes pedophilia. That's right, I was with someone who was making a comparison between vegans and pedophiles. I still don't understand how he made that leap in logic, so I won't try to explain it here. That one remains a head-scratcher.

Over time, while I don't like to admit it, these comments did break me down, and I bounced back and forth between being vegan and omnivore once or twice. I would tell people that I just no longer wanted to be vegan or that I was losing muscle mass, but neither of these things were true. Really, I had gone back to being an omnivore because it just seemed easier. By my eating the same way as my husband and his friends, I would no longer be made fun of, and in turn, I would no longer have to deal with the stress of my husband not sticking up for me. It seemed a win/win situation, except that I never felt at ease with returning to omnivorism. Looking back now, I'm not even sure what hurt more, that I was hurting helpless animals for my own benefit or that I was not being true to my authentic self and acting against everything I believed in.

As I emphasized before, going vegan did not cause my divorce, and my no longer being vegan didn't save it. Eventually, after many long talks and arguments, including a brief time apart, my husband even did start to somewhat stick up for me and tell his friends to stop when they starting picking on me again — this time, for having been vegan and then eating meat again. However, in retrospect, it was too little, too late. It simply took him too long to be my champion in front of his friends. The previous damage remained stuck in my brain. It was not something I could forget, though I honestly did try.

Over time, both of us ended up wanting different things in life and the marriage continued to disintegrate. After a little more than three years, we both asked for a divorce. He promptly moved out, and I promptly became vegan again. Moving forward in life, I made the decision to always be true to who I am and not change that for anyone. I immediately started going back to volunteer meetings with the Animal Rights Coalition and got re-involved with the community of animal advocates who had once so warmly welcomed me and then warmly welcomed me back, no questions asked, no jokes made. Even when I told them I had briefly returned to omnivorism, my fellow volunteers did not judge or ridicule me. In fact, I was made featured volunteer in the organization's newsletter. Rather than make me feel guilty, they celebrated my return to compassionate living by allowing me to tell my story and, quite possibly, to inspire others.

Conclusion: My Post-Divorce Perspective

Now, months later, I am a divorcée, and I am happy. I'm vegan and living my life fully in accordance with my morals, and I no longer have to deal with unsupportive people in my life. And while I sometimes still remember how much it hurt to be made fun of and to have someone yell "bacon" every time I would try to speak, I can honestly say that I'm pleased that everything happened the way it did, as it led me in the right direction when it comes to my own activism. Now, I take what I wish I had originally known about veganism and relationships and use that to help others who are transitioning into veganism and need tips on how to deal with family, friends and significant others. While everyone's story is different, I have found that my experiences can help others, and this helps me, budding vegan activists, and the nonhuman animals whom I so greatly wish to liberate.

WORKS CITED

Adams, Carol J. *Living Among Meat Eaters: The Vegetarian's Survival Handbook.* New York: Lantern, 2008. Print.

"Divorce Rate." divorcerate.org, n.d. Web. 10 May 2012.

"Vegetarianism in America." *Vegetarian Times.* Cruz Bay Publishing, 2008. Web. 10 May 2012.

Introducing Speciesism
to the Rescue Community
MELISSA E. MAASKE

In order to stay engaged in the work of being an activist, I have found working in dog rescue a tangible way to recharge my belief in animal equality and feel like I'm actually making a difference in the lives of nonhuman animals. Being able to move a dog from a bad situation into a loving home has kept my motivation and spirit for animal advocacy alive. For the last couple of years, I have volunteered with a local dog rescue, and due to my hard work and dedication, attained a leadership role within the organization. As the event and foster team leader, I focus on facilitating adoption events in the community to raise funds for our group and give people the chance to meet dogs. I also interact with the public on behalf of the rescue to raise awareness and to bring in/retain foster homes to care for dogs during their time in the program.

As a vegan activist in a mostly omnivorous rescue community, I have experienced many reactions from other people in the general public and rescue community through their comments on my veganism. In this essay, I will discuss the ethical detachment within people who volunteer their time to help one species, while consistently consuming other species on their plates. Therein, I face a contradiction I find within the area of rescue advocacy: the people I work with are so outraged when a dog is kept in a cage yet get upset when I remind them that the someone they are eating for lunch was kept in a cage before being murdered for food. Through the exploration of specific experiences I've had, I will share ways in which I have been able to engage people within the rescue community to begin examining their own beliefs on animal welfare in our society.

My ultimate goal with this essay is not just to narrate my story. Rather, I write in the hopes of engaging other vegan activists to participate in all types of rescue, advocacy and outreach for all animals. Too often, the animal liberation movement makes stars of those individuals who break the law and/or go to jail because of their rescue work (i.e., releasing mink from a mink farm) while undervaluing the work of rescuers acting within the law. Quite often,

139

those famous individuals are men, and thus the day to day activities of the women who dominate the movement become overshadowed by feats of derring do (Gaarder 11). But the work of vegans within traditional animal rescues can be just as significant. In fact, if working within the rescue culture helps non-vegan dog and cat lovers see their own culpability in the neglect and downright abuse of other nonhuman animals, this form of outreach could perhaps have an even greater impact on animals by saving individual lives, shifting the conversation within an already receptive audience, and preventing burnout.

Rescue work also helps the rescuer. Fostering animals has rewarded me with friendship in my darkest hours. Ali was taken out of a horrible breeding situation in Missouri where dogs are seen as a means to make money and little else. Ali had lived most of her year-long life in a cage, forced to have litters of puppies and given little exposure to humans. Ali had neurological damage in her leg, which she held up off the ground, unable to move the stiff limb. It was assumed that she had been hurt after getting her leg caught in the cage, but I never really knew for sure. Although her leg did not seem to bother her in the least, I was upset that she had not received the medical care needed. I was relieved that someone had gone out of her way to get Ali into a rescue where she could be fostered and eventually adopted. It was late on a warm summer afternoon when I went to pick up Ali. It was like any other transport day: sit and wait, talk with other foster parents and wonder how the dogs will behave when they arrive. The heat of the day was starting to wear off as the transport van filled with a dozen excited dogs pulled up. I was concerned that Ali would be timid and uneasy given what I knew about her situation. I was nervous for Ali, knowing this would be her first night away from her three young puppies. I vowed to make her transition smooth, since she had traveled so far, and I imagined she would be confused going to another new place. I wanted her new life to begin with her knowing that she was safe and would never again have to live in a cage.

Ali was a Chihuahua mix with soft, dark eyes and a tail that would swish seemingly faster than a hummingbird's wings. Her fur was soft and thick and it swirled around her body in rich browns and tans. I nicknamed Ali "the little husky" because she looked very much like a timber wolf and she even howled like one when she barked. She quickly became friends with everyone in my household, including the resident dogs, both large and small. Ali would entertain me by running circles around the dining room table with the other dogs. It was fascinating to watch her keep up with them, despite her only having three properly working legs. When she would lie down, Ali would kick her hind legs out, stretching in the sun laden grass to take a much deserved nap. Ali also enjoyed indoor comforts such as sleeping with her head (or entire body) on a pillow. She would smile in her canine way when she was happy and would lean in to give her humans kisses. At night, Ali would lay right next to me in bed and nestle her head in the crook of my neck. I felt so connected to her that at times that it seemed she became my caregiver instead of the other way around.

Ali was, to my surprise, well-adjusted and seamlessly transitioned to our routine. She was not the traumatized, scared little puppy I had expected. I never imagined a little girl of seven pounds could give so much love and acceptance to a human she just met. Although Ali was only with me for a short time before being adopted, she opened my heart at a time when I was convinced it was broken for good. She taught me that no matter what the circumstances in your life or how many times you've been hurt, you can still love and be loved in return. Since Ali was adopted, there's not a week that goes by that I do not miss her face and sweet demeanor. But it makes my heart swell with joy that Ali is now with a lifelong guardian who is able to provide her with love, care and the freedom she so deserves.

Such advocacy may not earn foster homes places on the animal liberation hall of fame, but Ali would have died as surely as any mink on a fur farm had our group not stepped in to save her. I feel that although it is useful for activists to liberate animals (such as the mink discussed earlier, released into the wild), it is also rewarding to know that Ali will live out the rest of her days with guardians who would do anything for her and for whom she will bring as much joy and love as she offered me.

Finding the Disconnect Between Rescue Work and Veganism

So, how can it be that vegan rescuers find themselves in this thankless position, unheralded by the animal liberation movement and resented by their omnivorous rescue colleagues? Let's begin by examining the underlying cultural "belief system" called carnism that causes humans to value some species over others (Joy 29). Through volunteering at the rescue, I have become distinctly aware of this disconnection between animals who society calls "pets" and animals who are called "food." As I have met other people committed to dog rescue and rehabilitation, I have learned more about the dichotomy into which people put animals: animals to eat /use and animals not to eat/use. Although intellectually I understand why people create these "files" in their brains, to avoid thinking of the reality of where their food comes from, emotionally, I have remained disgusted. How could rescuers, who advocate daily for dogs, stop by a fast food drive-thru to eat another species while transporting their foster dog from an adoption event? Even those who take time off of work, time away from their families and fill their homes with supplies for the rescue, appear unaware of, or unwilling to acknowledge, the lack of value they put on the lives of other species.

I became increasingly more frustrated and confused as the people I was volunteering with continued their detached, omnivorous behavior while I was digging more deeply into animal rights and activism. I started to resent the other volunteers because I could not understand them. I had forgotten what it was like to be so disconnected from the animals on a dinner plate, since I had made the decision to no longer eat them.

With a commitment to not allow my frustration to overtake me, I decided to find a way to make sense of this issue. I began talking to other vegans in the community who had dealt with similar dilemmas. I realized that our experiences were similar, and I felt relieved to have my observations confirmed. Many of my fellow vegan rescuers shared the same sentiment of how frustrating it was to watch non-vegan rescuers be so contradictory in their ways of caring for one species while consuming another. It was not surprising to hear that other organizations, even ones promoting a vegan message, had rescuers dealing with the same contradictions, judgments and stereotypes that I had observed. It was nice to know that I was not alone in my confusion and frustration. Yet I was still very stuck on "why?" I had so many questions with no answers. I was not content with feeling "this is just the way things are."

Melanie Joy's *Why We Love Dogs, Eat Pigs and Wear Cows: An Introduction to Carnism* helped me think about this disconnect in a different manner, by naming behaviors I could not concretely identify or explain. She states,

> [O]ur relationship with dogs is, in many ways, not terribly different from our relationship with people: We call them by their names. We say goodbye when we leave and greet them when we return. We share our beds with them. We play with them. We buy them gifts. We carry their pictures in our wallets. We take them to the doctor when they're sick and may spend thousands of dollars on their treatment. We bury them when they pass away.... We love them. We love dogs and eat cows not because dogs and cows are fundamentally different — cows, like dogs, have feelings, preferences, and consciousness — but because our perception of them is different. And, consequently, our perception of their meat is different as well [13].

According to Joy, we have protected ourselves from the moral discomfort and incongruence of eating animals (when we know that they suffer) by a system which she refers to as "psychic numbing" (19). Joy goes on to explain that psychic numbing is a process by which humans disconnect themselves emotionally and mentally from what is occurring around them. She further explains that people will just flat out deny the abuse of animals because their lives and deaths are such an invisible reality. This invisibility, in turn, allows humans to stay entrenched in the omnivore lifestyle. Furthermore, Joy contends that many people do not even know why they love dogs, eat pigs and wear cows. That is simply the way things are and the way that things have always been. Joy makes the case that as mainstream culture perceives things, eating meat is normal, natural and necessary.

Her book really helped me to clarify why I was so confused and helped to define what I was angry about. I was empowered and re-energized after reading her book. She helped me to conceptualize, in a way I had not been able to before, how our society is entrenched in eating farmed animals, enjoying "exotic" animals for entertainment and loving companion animals as family. The judgmental side of me that could not understand why these rescuers were hypocritical was diminished. I no longer felt that they were putting on a masquerade, but realized that people perceive their dogs as part of the family, unlike the carnal animals who have been on their dinner plate or the supposedly entertaining animals at the zoos they visit. Using this framework, omnivorous behavior can be understood because it is learned, and taking it a step further, it can be unlearned by choice. I felt better equipped to help others deconstruct what they eat by thinking of the animals as individuals.

My Experience in Rescue: Judgmental Opinions from Dog Lovers

My work with the dog rescue has grown over the last couple of years just as my vegan activism has grown. As a volunteer, I was compelled to continue to do more, pushed by the successes of seeing dogs rescued who may have otherwise had their lives ended. Happy endings kept me enthusiastic. During my work, I was never frustrated by dogs, only by humans. I just kept hoping that those I worked with would show as much compassion and consistency for all animals as I was feeling.

When I first began engaging in rescue work, I was vegetarian. During that time, most people left me alone. A few people tried to dissuade me from my diet, but it was never a contentious issue. Since I've become vegan, however, I've faced a litany of shocking, vulgar, judgmental statements made by rescuers. Partially, the intensity of people's reactions to my dietary changes may come from my eagerness to share with others what I have learned about the benefits of a plant based diet, but it seems more visceral than that.

While I expected to find other rescuers wanting to debate "happy meat" and "free-range eggs" with me, I was surprised to find out that this particular group of people, as a whole, seemed uninterested in those ideals. In the greater community, it appears, when I share with a stranger or acquaintance that I am vegan, they will often respond by telling me that they "do not eat that much meat," as if asking me to absolve them of their guilt for the occasions where they do engage in the violent and destructive practices of meat and dairy consumption. In my animal rights activism, I've spent hours with people who want to discuss issues of organic farming, humane meat and free-range practices. They justify their omnivore behaviors with a cloak of misleading industry terms. But the circle of rescuers I work with don't even feel compelled to try and justify their behaviors; instead, they put my behavior on trial.

To counter their defensive "rescuer rebuttals" to my veganism, I often bring up the fact that many other countries eat their dogs. People that I share this information with, especially rescuers, are appalled by this knowledge. In *Eating Animals*, Jonathan Safran Foer discusses this topic. Since Foer is a writer rather than activist by his own self-definition, and since *Eating Animals* is such a well-known book, I have found him to be a useful source to enter into this tricky topic. Foer contends that although it's legal in forty-four states, eating dogs in the U.S. is extremely taboo. He goes on to assert the American prohibition against eating dogs says a lot more about us than about animals themselves. Foer also discusses that there are invisible rules that omnivores follow such as not eating animals with significant mental capacities. Obviously this logic is insufficient since pigs and cows are just as playful, mischievous and affectionate as dogs. Pigs and cows (especially those away from the tortures of factory farm life) are also social, friendly, loyal creatures who form close bonds with one another. Therefore, if you extend the suggested framework of only eating beings that do not have significant mental capacities, pigs and cows (and other animals not examined here) should be excluded. Overall, Foer argues that engaging in a discussion of eating dogs as meat will help to challenge ideals in our society and make the necessity of an animal liberation movement more apparent.

On my first extended ride transporting dogs from one part of the state to the other, a conversation about my current diet came up. I shared with my traveling companion, whom I had known merely an hour or two, my thoughts on the ethical, health and environmental reasons why I was being persuaded towards a vegan diet. He responded by asking why I would want to make a choice that would affect my health in a negative way. He went on a rant about the dietary supplements I would need in order to get enough nutritional value to be healthy if strictly eating a plant-based diet. I stayed quiet. I knew he was inaccurate, but I didn't feel confident enough about the facts to respond to his overconfident bluster.

He went on to share with me his perspective on deer overpopulation and how hunters are a vital part of managing our ecosystem. While he questioned me about how I would feel if deer starved to death instead of being hunted,

I thought about all of the deer who are injured or killed by cars after hunters frighten them out of the woods and onto the road. I also thought about the wildlife management agencies that intentionally keep deer (and other species populations) high to ensure the sale of hunting permits (Luke 140). Mostly, I just kept thinking that deer would be much better off if humans stopped interfering with their individual lives, social structure and habitats.

I was outraged by his approach and arrogance, so I emotionally shut down. Before the drive was over, he attempted to further discourage me from participating in a rescue-linked event against puppy mills that I had been excited about. He stated that he would rather focus on helping dogs in a positive way, than focusing on the negative aspects of the system. It was a wonder that I even stayed with the rescue after this conversation. Instead of quitting, though, I realized that I needed to stand up for my lifestyle and myself. I was lucky that the president of the rescue at the time was vegan and really set the standards for the group, ensuring the rescue practices were never speciesist. But once she left the rescue and some volunteers "turned over," there came a new set of people to address my lifestyle with. As expected, I got the usual questions when others found out that I was vegan: "What do you eat? Where do you get your protein? What would happen to all of the animals if we stopped eating them?" Although I expected to get these sorts of questions from others inquiring about my lifestyle and diet, I did not expect the judgmental, passive aggressive comments and innuendos that I continued to receive from within a dog rescue community.

Once the leadership of the organization left vegan hands, the group began to feel like an omnivore's playground. As my vegan ally was preparing to resign from the rescue, there was talk of making me an addition to the Board of Directors for the organization. I was apprehensive about joining the board because of the nature of such a large responsibility. However, I was also excited at the prospect. In the end, I was not added to the board. I did not inquire into the reasons for my rejection, but chalked it up to the leadership feeling that replacing one vegan board member with another would do nothing to limit the influence of the "vegan agenda."

Around this time, I received a heatedly written email using just those words. In no unclear terms, I was told to stop pushing my vegan agenda on the rescue. I again wondered if I even wanted to continue volunteering when I felt isolated and unwanted. I realized, after much consideration, that for me rescue work was about helping dogs and feeling good about that choice, not about what anyone else thought about my choices. The email (which addressed a host of other concerns common to any volunteer-based organization in tumult) galvanized me to no longer sit back as people discussed my diet and lifestyle choices in front of me. I decided to stand up and say what I was really thinking instead of keeping quiet in the hopes of maintaining the peaceful status quo at the rescue.

Then came the suggestion that we hold a barbeque fundraiser. This notion had been raised several times prior but was immediately dismissed when our vegan president was still with the rescue, as she made clear that it was unconscionable to raise money to help one species by killing another. But as soon as a new board took control, plans for a barbeque began moving forward. As I was presented with the idea, I could feel myself growing anxious, shocked to hear that the new leadership team was willing to allow this event to occur. I was interested to hear what this particular rescuer would say in response to my declining her idea and the logic behind it. Surprisingly, she listened to the reasoning that I could not justify selling one dead species to raise money to save the life of another species.

I felt that the conversation was over, until she asked if I would reconsider. She stated she would be willing to bring me a veggie burger if I would attend the event. I knew that she was just hoping to increase my comfort level, but since she was planning the sale of animal meat solely, I asked if she would be willing to provide veggie burgers for a public option on the menu. She stated that she would not do that. I reminded her of the inconsistency and reiterated that I will not be present for the event. I have vowed to continue to share my distaste for such an affair.

My veganism has also become an issue in my decision making for the behind-the-scenes events with the rescue. In Minnesota, meat-centric restaurants are the ones most easily accessible, and event after event seems to be held at them. I had to attend one planning meeting because I wanted to be on the same page as the rest of the leadership team and get an update on the rescue's plans and goals. Guessing that there would be nothing I wanted to eat on the menu, I ate a meal before I left and brought a snack. Just as I suspected, the menu at the restaurant consisted of country fried steak, bacon cheeseburgers, and the like. Though some other people also didn't order food, I still felt out of place and awkward. When the suggestion to hold a volunteer appreciation party at the same restaurant was suggested a few months later, I graciously declined. I feel that my lack of presence was a greater voice than my being there, not eating anything.

Judgmental Opinions Continued: Criticizing the Abolitionist Message

Despite what feels like personal attacks against me from the other rescuers, I also feel that since I have been a volunteer, there have been attacks against the basic notion that animals must not be regarded as possessions or be used for such purposes as food, clothing, research or entertainment. My abolitionist animal rights activism promotes bringing animal welfare issues into the light and strives to make individuals aware of their ability to choose to not use animals. Due to nature of the work, I'm given ample opportunities to do just this.

Rescuers often spend a lot of time together at planning meetings, on long car rides doing transports, and at adoption events and fundraisers. Time gets filled with conversation. Since discussions and questions come up about why I live a vegan lifestyle, I am able to guide the conversation towards a discussion of abolitionism and speciesism. When explaining veganism in the context of abolitionism, I always begin by informing rescuers why I believe what I do. I explain that my convictions are more than just a matter of diet, but a moral commitment to end the exploitation of all animals. As a human slavery abolitionist could not continue to be a slave owner, an animal slavery abolitionist cannot continue to consume animal products, so I don't. Overall, my greatest goal is always to send a consistent message of choosing "no animal usage" in my life and explain why that makes sense to me on an intellectual, emotional, moral and spiritual level.

While I try to present my perspective as concretely and straightforwardly as I know how, I still get responses from "Your approach is self-righteous; people expect meat at fundraising events," to "You are not a hero just because you are vegan," and "We are at the top of the food chain."

Of course, these comments infuriate me because they are illogical, judgmental and ignorant. The idea that the rescue would not be able to raise money at a large fundraiser without having meat is unfounded. For years, this statewide rescue had a large budget and received national recognition for its extraordinary work. During all of that time, there were never any practices that were outside the scope of abolitionism. So for that to all change and others to suggest that there is only one way to make money — by fundraising via the flesh of other species — was preposterous to me. Consequently, there have been times when I felt burnt out doing this work because of the lack of understanding from other rescuers. Yet, I have realized (and I focus on the fact) that these comments are not about me specifically but how my choices and lifestyle have raised questions and concerns in the other rescuers' minds about their own values and relationships with all animals. Getting them to have such strong emotions in reaction to my values means that something uncomfortable has arisen inside of them. Perhaps it's the knowledge that they're contributing to the same kinds of violence and oppression that they advocate against for dogs.

Perception: Determining the Value of Life

Let's further examine my experience working with other rescuers and the greater public in the adoption of hundreds of dogs. There are many misperceptions that I have been made aware of that I would like to discuss here. I feel this will give a greater context to determine where people are coming from in terms of examining their relationship and values around animals. I know that if I was not a vegan abolitionist, I would not be fully equipped to respond to such issues that arise in this work. These topics include the perception of rescued dogs being "broken" or "unadoptable" and the possessive language used to refer to other species.

One of the things that I love about the rescue that I volunteer for is that they are willing to take dogs into the program who come from really difficult situations, dogs who other rescues or shelters may deem unadoptable or too resource intensive. Unfortunately, while the leadership is often strongly committed to these dogs, the volunteers do not always see the value in these lives. I have frequently overheard conversations wherein volunteers question why a given dog is in the rescue. More often than not, these are the dogs who are sick, old, puppy mill survivors or extremely fearful. One volunteer commented that the rescue was going broke because we were paying for an extensive set of surgeries for a dog who was older and may not even be adopted. When I hear these comments, although infuriated, I am reminded that this is the same justification people use for consuming farmed animals. I am reminded of times I have heard people justify eating farmed animals by saying "pigs are dirty" and "cows are dumb." I always try to calmly remind the volunteers that older or sick dogs need rescue more than anyone else. They deserve care, rehabilitation and life just as much as well-adjusted, cuddly little puppies. I remind them that there are many other groups focusing strictly on younger, healthy dogs. That discussion can often lead to the dignity and worth of every life, regardless of species.

Running a non-profit rescue can be challenging, as we must ensure that there is enough money to pay the bills and taxes and keep up to date with best practices. So when the rescue implemented a plan to have a few "highly adoptable" dogs in care at a time, I was not surprised. Adoptable dogs help the bottom line. But after noticing the kind of attention the "highly adoptable" dogs were getting, I worried that this was reinforcing the volunteers' perspective that only cute, young and well-adjusted dogs in good health deserve the attention of rescuers.

There are many dogs that I have encountered over the years who don't fit the "highly adoptable" benchmarks but became the epitome of a rescued dog. To wit, Patch came to the rescue when he was saved from a hoarding situation in Tennessee where hundreds of dogs were living in a barn. As homes were foreclosed in the area, one kind neighbor was collecting the dogs left behind. After a while, he was unable to care for all of the dogs in his barn and, of course, they began to increase in number as many of them were not spayed or neutered. Patch, a Jack Russell with a docked tail and a lot of spunk, came to the rescue as a ten-year-old senior and was in the rescue for a long time, almost two years.

He was a black and white, much like a Holstein cow, and his pointy ears and big dog smile made my heart melt. Patch loved to ride in the car and would stand tall to stick his head out the slightly cracked window. Patch loved to meet new people and they loved to greet him too, yet a lot of people overlooked Patch because of his age and his one cloudy eye. His eye problem did not seem to bother him, as he ran around, basked in the sun, played with toys and cuddled with his humans. He loved to go on walks and would gladly do tricks to receive treats. I was constantly discouraged as people would meet Patch at events. No one felt a strong enough love connection with him to ensure his adoption. As I got to know Patch more, I knew that he was the special kind of dog that comes around very rarely, similar to my experience with Ali. Patch and I became close, and I found myself inviting him to every adoption event that I was hosting, talking about him to anyone I met who wanted to learn more about rescued dogs. Finally, Patch got adopted into a loving and caring home. I never felt more satisfied with a job well done than when I knew Patch would have love, access to lay in his spot in the sun and lots of treats for the rest of his life.

Just like the concern over Patch's eye, there are many issues that come up in the public perception of rescued dogs. Often people believe rescue dogs are broken, come from bad situations and cannot be "fixed." Many people within the general public make it seem like they are doing these dogs a great favor by adopting them. They complain about the process of applying, supplying references and explanations of how they plan to care for the dog. And, if approved, they gripe about paying an adoption fee. I try to engage these questions with a discussion of the worth of all dogs' lives and that these dogs deserve one final home to live out the rest of their days when they've often been through so much already. I remind people of the dog's personality traits that compelled them to apply to adopt in the first place.

Rescuers can also help sway the public towards a less speciesist view of dogs by moving away from "owner" language. Our rescue has taken all speciesist terms out of its dog profiles, contracts and overall language. Instead, we discuss dogs and their guardians. I know that this small semantic shift has created a bigger discussion to move away from animals as property. In addition to the battle around ownership language, I struggle with rescuers and the general public who use speciesist language to refer to dogs as "its" instead of by their names or genders. Referring to a being as "it" shows a lack of respect for his or her very presence as an equal species and individual. One way that I handle this issue is to simply correct the person by calling the dog by his or her name or gender. I have found that if you do this consistently enough, people do start calling the dogs by their names and/or genders as well. My hope is that people will generalize this to other species. The more the community begins to look at the animals as individuals, the greater the capacity for change in behavior towards them.

Why I'm Vegan: Suggestions for Beginning the Paradigm Shift within the Rescue Community

As discussed earlier, I have spoken with other vegans who participate in companion animal rescue work and have found that I am not alone in the struggles and complexities narrated in this essay. I know many grow weary from combating the opinions of the omnivore rescuers, leadership and donors. I have come to the conclusion that for me, doing rescue work is futile if not done in conjunction with the promotion of anti-speciesism. I have theorized that the best place to start discussing and endorsing talk of this framework is with fellow dog lovers. I contend that a love for dogs and other companion animals can be an avenue for extending compassion to other species. Omnivores who deem themselves animal lovers have a capacity, even more so than the general public, to begin shifting towards compassion for all species.

This is why I believe vegan rescuers are able to engage the greater rescue community in a paradigm shift. I suggest using the moral clarity of an abolitionist vegan perspective when talking to other rescuers about messages that hit close to home for them. Attempting to engage a rescuer in these conversations can be complicated. Although discussions of factory farming and its lasting impacts on the animals, our environment and human health can be informative, I have found that beginning discussions with rescuers about dog related issues can bring about a much more appealing conversation. These have been useful initial points of conversation for me to begin talking about my beliefs.

The three main topics that other rescuers will often hear me discuss include ending puppy mills, ending the usage of dogs for research purposes and informing others about the reality of "no kill" shelters. We know that the segment of rescuers who consider themselves "animal lovers" (meaning they love cats, dogs, and guinea pigs) are often distressed when they learn of the plight of companion animals in mills. For this essay, I will focus specifically on puppy mill advocacy work, and for my purposes, I define puppy mills as the substandard breeding conditions of dogs focusing on production, sale and profit. Avenson v. Zegart established a legal definition of puppy mills in 1984: "a dog breeding operation in which the health of the dogs is disregarded in order to maintain a low overhead and maximize profits."

Just as abolitionist rescuers advocate for the nullification of puppy mills, without knowing it, non-vegan rescuers frequently take a stance against a welfarist approach to puppy mills as well. In most cases, omnivore rescuers would not protest outside a mill to ask for larger cage sizes or more hygienic conditions for the dogs inside. They would ask for mills to be shut down, for people to adopt companion animals instead of purchasing them and for rescue work to get the limelight. This is an example of how an abolitionist mindset may not be that far off, even for those who are speciesist in that they see the value of certain animals but not others.

Another topic where I often like to point out the inconsistencies of rescuers' views is within the issue of dogs used in research and testing. When discussing this problem, I often reveal that I no longer use shampoo or face wash that a dog was forced to drink or have rubbed in his eyes. I use statistics to show the magnitude of this issue. The U.S. Department of Agriculture's Animal Welfare Report for 2010 shows that 64,930 dogs were used in USDA-registered facilities in that year ("Annual Report"). This number often surprises people, especially when I mention that dogs are being tested on for not only medical and cosmetic purposes but also other household products. This is an area where many are horrified when presented with the facts. They would not want their "pet"—whom they deem a part of the family—to be shaved, injected, poked and prodded in the name of research. This shock creates an easy transition into the greater issues of animal testing on other species and the exploitation that goes along with it. It appears that it may not be a far leap for rescuers to care about companion animal testing, and my hope is that they will take the next logical step and make those connections to other sentient species exploited in the name of scientific research.

The last area where it is easier to begin presenting an abolitionist anti-speciesist message to rescuers are the major concerns about shelters themselves. Many times when I am attempting to engage someone in the community about shelter dogs, I will reference the Animal Humane Society's Annual Report whereby in 2009, 30 percent of the animals coming through intake were euthanized ("About the Animals" 14–15). As a society, we are led to believe that all animal shelters are helpful, safe places. This data disproves that theory. Furthermore, I emphasize that animal shelters and rescues are a big economic industry and that the Animal Humane Society in Minnesota earned almost $100,000 in 2011 ("Financials"). After a discussion of the immoral care and unethical practices in the shelter industry, people are often shocked.

Other times, rescuers come into the work already demoralized from mainstream shelter practices. Several of the volunteers I have worked with at the rescue did volunteer at the Animal Humane Society. Almost all of them report having to quit abruptly due to the number of euthanized animals they bore witness to. One volunteer recalled seeing so many dead animals that the number of bodies filled an entire room in the basement. These discussions can become highly emotional for rescuers, and they often report that they would not be okay with euthanizing any of the dogs in our rescue, let alone in numbers of that quantity.

I feel that these conversations are great ways to begin engaging rescuers, and even the larger community, in a consistent, abolitionist message beginning with the area where they feel most comfortable: companion animals.

Now What? Calling All Vegans to Rescue Work

I encourage other vegans who are working or volunteering in rescue groups to not shy away from tackling and discussing these issues. I know it can be frustrating, especially knowing that there are so many animals out there to help. There are many within the animal liberation movement who suggest that activists should stick to advocating for animals tortured, enslaved or slaughtered for food or other uses. I agree that activists should focus on fighting against issues like vivisection and animals used for entertainment. I also think that there is a time and place for abolitionist activists to engage in rescue work. Activists are well equipped to challenge the "norms" that some rescues abide by, such as holding meat raffles as fundraisers. The rescue movement needs our presence in the community to advocate for *all* animals, constantly bringing abolitionism and anti-speciesist messages to every aspect of the rescue world. Also, I have found that having a strong support system of other abolitionist-minded fellow vegans has helped me to stay strong and not give up, even when I wanted to. Therefore, it would be great to have other vegan rescuers working beside me, providing strength in numbers.

As you interact with animal lovers and rescuers, I encourage you to become friends with them and get to know their values and beliefs. Volunteer to walk their dogs, attend adoption events, help transport supplies or do home visits to check for appropriate lifelong guardians. Ask them to have a meal or coffee with you and ask why, since they love dogs so much, they aren't vegan.

I would suggest that even if you do not get involved with a specific rescue, to continue to promote the work of rescuers in the community. Talk to others about their relationships with animals, specifically the illogicality between how they love dogs and eat cows. Although these topics can be tough and even emotionally painful to talk about, the more we engage in them, the more we build community and get people to think about their choices. Mostly, I would encourage you to take part in the types of conversations outlined in this essay with others who deem themselves animal lovers.

Regardless of your presence in rescue work or not, I would also suggest that people talk to others about their food choices and the roles of animals in their lives and our ecosystem. Never take the approach that you think they are "bad" for their choices, but simply remind them that at one point you probably believed what they believe and behaved how they are behaving, but you found a new way. Focus on how any form of animal exploitation is inconsistent with their love for companion animals. Use language to stop the objectification of animals, remind them that animals are not property, but living creatures who can bring joy and fullness to human's lives or who need to be kept away from human contact because they belong in their natural habitats, not in zoos and aquariums. Don't apologize for inconveniencing others with your lifestyle and food choices. Use language like "I *can* eat that meat, eggs and cheese, I just *choose* not to."

Speak about the truth you know: fairness and respect for all species. Challenge the myths and stereotypes about pigs being "dirty," rescued dogs being "broken" and chickens being "stupid." As Joy states, "Recognizing the individuality of others interrupts the process of de-individualization, making it more difficult to maintain the psychological and emotional distance necessary to harm them" (120). Along with rescuing dogs, the duty of abolitionist rescuers is to enforce the interruption of which Joy writes. It is not the only starting point, but a good one, as part of the work is already done because we are working with people who see some value in another species. Our task now as abolitionist rescuers is to get other species into the conversation.

WORKS CITED

"About the Animals." *Animal Humane Society 2009 Report*. Web. 21 Feb. 2012. 1–34. PDF.
Adams, Carol J., and Josephine Donovan, eds. *The Feminist Care Tradition in Animal Ethics*. New York: Columbia University Press, 2007. Print.
"Annual Report Animal Usage by Fiscal Year [2010]." *United States Department of Agriculture*. Animal and Plant Health Inspection Service. 27 July 2012. Web. 21 Feb. 2012.
Avenson v. Zegart. 577 F. Supp. 959 (1984). *United States District Court, D. Minnesota, Sixth Division*. Web. 14 Mar. 2012.
"Financials." *Animal Humane Society 2011 Report*. Web. 21 Feb. 2012. 1–31. PDF.
Foer, Jonathan Safran. *Eating Animals*. New York: Little, Brown/Hachette Digital, 2009. eBook.

Gaarder, Emily. *Women and the Animal Rights Movement.* New Brunswick, NJ: Rutgers University Press, 2011. Print.

Joy, Melanie. *Why We Love Dogs, Eat Pigs and Wear Cows: An Introduction to Carnism.* San Francisco, CA: Conari Press, 2010. Print.

Luke, Brian. "Justice, Caring, and Animal Liberation." *The Feminist Care Tradition.* Adams and Donovan 125–152.

Tales of an Animal Liberationist

DALLAS RISING

As animal rights activists, we are a distinct subculture. Sure, most of us can choose when to reveal the fact that we are part of this subculture, but that doesn't change the fact that many of us often feel as though we don't belong. We are stuck in a world we feel is cruel and twisted. Some of us even have trouble reconciling the fact that we are of the same species that perpetuates so much violence and terror on other species, and it can be horrifying at times. We often feel isolated, different, and at times, even defeated by the omnipresent violence in the world. We see violence when most people see a snack. We see injustice when most people see a purse or a sweater. Where many people hear about a circus coming to town and get excited about a fun-filled afternoon featuring cotton candy and tigers leaping through rings of fire, we only think of torture and forced labor. Not only is it hard to see these things so often, but it is especially hard to feel the emotions that come along with the things we see and not be able to share our feelings with someone who will truly understand and not just be sympathetic, but really empathize because they feel those same feelings, too.

Personal narratives have proved to be a powerful way for individuals who feel separate or misunderstood to gain a sense that they are heard. They have also been great educational tools to help people who are not part of the writer's community gain a better understanding of that person's experience, and by extension, the experiences of that group to which the narrative writer belongs. I have found this to be true in my recovery from anorexia. Reading about what other people with eating disorders went through helped both me and people who cared about me in a way that clinical explanations and treatment plans could not. There is also something to be said about being able to pick up a book whenever there are immediate emotional needs that cannot be addressed in other ways for one reason or another. One can read another's written experience at any time and get the satisfaction of an emotional connection even when physically alone.

I have wanted to share my personal narrative from the perspective of an

155

animal rights activist for years, but I let my fear of being perceived as ego-centric stop me from pursuing a way to share my writing with others. This suppressing of our own pain and suffering is common in the animal rights movement. The common disempowering and dangerous mantra, "The animals have it so much worse, my pain shouldn't matter," stood in the way of me writing and sharing my story for fear that I would be criticized for attempting to take attention away from the animals: the ones who truly suffer. Feeling like my own pain is the equivalent of a first-world problem is something I continue to wrestle with, even as I speak against that notion in advocating for personal narratives in an anthology about animal rights activism and theory.

I suspect I am not alone in my denial and suppression of my own traumas and pain stemming from violence inflicted upon animals and my attempts to challenge and confront that violence. My husband jokes that I should have been put in charge of marketing for pattrice jones' book *Aftershock* because I take every opportunity to tell people about the only book I know of written by an activist for activists that deals with the under-discussed topic of trauma in activist communities. This denial of our own pain and experience is not a noble sacrifice that helps animals in any meaningful way. In fact, it hurts them and us because it leaves silenced the very people who are reacting appropriately with strong emotion to things that ought to elicit strong emotion by the effort it takes to keep feelings hidden and secret. We perpetuate the myth that what is being done to animals is acceptable on some level if we don't acknowledge how deeply disturbed we are by it. We suffer alone and leave others who share our grief to suffer alone, too. When we speak and share our truths, however, we give ourselves the chance to figure out how to live with them in a more empowering way.

My intention in sharing my stories with you is to take a step in the direction of breaking that silence and suppression. At the very least, I am breaking it for myself and walking my talk that being real is the key to getting us out of this disaster we're in. Connecting to another's experience is what animal rights is all about. There's a saying, "What you resist persists," so maybe it's worth stopping and taking a moment to sit with the truths that we stuff deep down with the false belief that our own pain shouldn't matter. Maybe if we take some time to stop resisting it, it won't persist and escape in inconvenient ways such as aches and pains, nightmares, angry outbursts that feel out of control rather than healthful and cathartic, depression, and a pervasive, relentless sense of isolation.

The following vignettes are loosely chronological, but they show the many manifestations that liberation can take, from childhood fantasy, to familial frustrations and inspirations, to daring missions in the dark of night to unplanned rescues of those sentient beings who might otherwise have been killed. In sharing and receiving our stories and experiences, we become more open, hopeful, and compassionate. Softer and stronger. And it will take all of these things to achieve liberation.

Not What I Imagined

I remember walking down by Lake of the Isles with my best friend Ana when we were girls, pointing at the gigantic houses (how big does a house have to be before it's called a mansion?) and imagining that we lived in them. Unlike many girls, we didn't talk about future husbands and what we would name our children. Instead, we talked about how many rooms we would have and what kind of animals would live in each of those rooms.

"I'm gonna live in that one," I say, pointing to a sprawling white stucco home that reminds me of somewhere warm and by the ocean. It has a huge green lawn and lots of tall windows. I imagine a gigantic staircase inside and tons of good places to stash yourself during a game of hide and seek.

My rooms were always chalk full of animals, categorized by species. I imagined having an entire room full of budgies. Colorful small birds with small trees scattered throughout and large branches artfully hanging from the ceiling for them to perch on. I would put them in a room with skylights so they could have lots of natural light, but not too many windows because I had a budgie who flew right into a large window and crashed to the floor, stunned. I felt terrible. I imagined having dozens of dogs, cats, guinea pigs, rats, hamsters, frogs, turtles, rabbits, birds (doves, budgies, cockatiels — none too big), and a potbellied pig.

I didn't think about how I could afford to feed them, or how I would ever manage to keep the house clean. Kids don't think about things like that. I just imagined being in my gigantic yard with my pack of dogs, all of whom would be playful when I felt like playing and cuddly when I felt like cuddling.

Now I am grown and own a small house nowhere near a lake. My husband and I have two dogs and two cats, and this relatively small number of furry companions feels barely manageable. Of course, I am the one who lobbied for them all. I argued and negotiated. I did the research and filled out the adoption applications. I made the travel arrangements to get them, ranging from borrowing my brother-in-law's jeep to booking a flight to California complete with overnight stay at a friend's home and a vet appointment to get a health certificate so our new little dog could fly home with me in the cabin of the plane. One at a time, I was working toward a grown-up vision of my mansion filled with animals.

It's not really anything like I imagined, being responsible for these lives. When I was little, I never imagined any of them getting sick. Or fighting. Or destroying things in the house. I never thought about what would happen if there was a fire, or how much time it would take to scoop litter boxes and pick up poop in the yard. I never thought about how I would keep those dogs and cats off the counter when cooking, or off the table when company was over. And while my real life dogs and cats do all of those inconvenient things, I also never imagined loving any of the imaginary menagerie members as fiercely as I love my real life boys.

The dogs in my childhood imagination would prance and swarm around me in every scene. My real life dogs spend most of their time zonked out on the sofa; they often completely ignore me when I call for them to come in from the yard, and I have to clang their food bowls together to give them some false hope that they might score an extra meal if they come inside. Maybe it's because kids see the whole world as revolving around them that I always imagined myself as a Santa figure with my imaginary dogs clamoring for attention and treats from me 24/7. But in the real world, while I have no doubt that my boys love me deeply, they have their own interests and agendas and motives. I'm an important part of their world, but I am not the sole part. And I wouldn't have it any other way.

Chicken Sandwich

I'm sitting in the car with my sister, whom I might actually love more than any other person in the world. She is my savior, my confidant, my solace, my rod to cling to. I trust her and she understands me like no one else and I look to her for comfort, guidance, and understanding in all things. She's my safe place.

It's an ordinary afternoon. The sun is shining, and I am just old enough to be in the driver's seat. For years my sister claimed that she hated to drive and would always offer me the opportunity to climb behind the wheel when I was with her. Whether she really did hate driving or she just knew that I was dying to, I don't know. I'm behind the wheel and have just pulled into the double driveway of her two story brick home in the suburbs. I don't remember what we're talking about. I'm holding my breath, and focusing hard to keep myself together.

My sister is eating a chicken salad sandwich. The chicken salad between the slices of bread is a light gray color, and she's being careful not to spill any, craning her neck forward and down and twisting her head a little to get a clean, tidy bite. I feel conflict and confusion as my allegiance to my sister is suddenly challenged by my rage and heartbreak from the knowledge of what happened to the animal she's chewing. I'm furious with her for eating a bird, and furious with myself for not knowing what to say to make her stop. I start trembling. Helpless and overwhelmed with pain of the violent knowledge I carry and having absolutely no clue how I could communicate my feelings about having this knowledge or what one teenage girl could do to stop it.

I remember an awkward outburst of tears and then laying on her guest room bed, sobbing. She knocked on the door a few minutes later, wanting to comfort me, I'm sure. Over the years, I have had a lot of practice accepting what little comfort I can from people whom I am sure cannot grasp what it is I am wrestling with. It's a lonely feeling to have the very person you blame for violence, who you abjure for her indifference, who is, in fact, the source of your pain, stroke your back and express her earnest concern for your well-being.

At the time, I thought she was missing the point entirely. What I wanted most of all was for her to care about the chicken she'd just eaten, not me. But she wasn't the only one missing a point. I was missing the fact that her concern for me was valid. I was unaware that I had just been re-traumatized and that I was, in fact, vulnerable and wounded myself.

This afternoon happened half a lifetime ago. My sister and I continued to remain close. I am so grateful to her for the dozens of conversations we have had over the years about animal issues and often struggle to find adequate words to express my appreciation to her for her unwavering support and love for me as I struggled (and continue to struggle) with the pain and anger I feel about the way animals are treated. And I could not be more proud of her for going vegan fifteen years after that first breakdown over the chicken salad sandwich. I have also learned that the ways in which we inspire others may not cull immediate results, but if we are consistent with our beliefs, those beliefs inspire others, even fifteen years later.

I love you much, Stasia, and I always will.

Walking to the Sheds

I remember walking across the frozen field to the shed. I remember following my team mates, Christy and Sarah, and how our boots crunched through the ice that formed a crust over the snow. It was the middle of the night, and it was dark, but the moon reflected light off of the snow and it made our way easier. I remember being afraid, but needing to concentrate on following my companions and walking in their footsteps. There just wasn't room for the fear to grow. There wasn't time for it to overtake me, and what would I have done anyway? Turned around? Never. This was an opportunity I hadn't even dared to hope for. There was no way I was going to be stopped by my fear. This was what my life was for.

It was so cold, and we were crunching our way through that cornfield. The ground was rough and bumpy and it was hard to keep my balance. It was giving my legs a workout. I remember thinking that I am usually asleep in my bed at this time of night, but at that moment, I felt so awake and alive. I remember the smell. I made some broccoli the other day and it smelled a little like that — acidic, sour, rotten — and I couldn't eat it. It was foul. I was blown away by the smell, even more so because of the cold. Scents travel better in heat, so how could the smell from the sheds make me feel ill an acre away on a freezing winter's night? My nose was being scorched by the stench while I was surrounded by snow and ice and my toes were going numb.

It was hard to trudge across the frozen field in the boots I was wearing. We all wore Wellington-style boots with rubber guards over them. The boots were stiff and heavy, so we had to lift our knees up high as we walked. Each time a foot came down it scraped and crunched on the ice. Tiptoeing was impossible. It was odd to be sneaking and making so much noise at the same time.

It took an enormous amount of trust to follow these people across that field and into the shed. We had only met a few months before through our animal advocacy work and it didn't take long for them to invite me to join their team. Our bond was our shared conviction and commitment. It was as simple as that for me back then. This was in 2000, before the abolitionist/welfare split in our area, before September 11, before animal activists had been labeled "terrorists," before we'd all had time to feel betrayed by, disappointed in, and angry at other activists and all of those things turned us into wary people reluctant to take risks with relative strangers.

We shared a mission, a common goal, and that was enough. We were driven by the same values and beliefs that would have us willing to take such enormous risks to fulfill. It's atypical, being in that unfamiliar physical and emotional place with unfamiliar people. Knowing that you could be thrown in jail, pressed with all sorts of charges, fined, maybe even attacked or shot at, and knowing that the state, the government and the public most likely wouldn't support you. It made me feel like a revolutionary. Or a radical. When I think back and remember all of this, I'm still proud of myself for it.

Back to the field. It seemed like it went on forever. I wasn't used to walking that far in heavy boots that don't bend at the ankle, and carrying loads of gear across a field full of bumps and ruts. Cameras, tripods, video cameras, flashlights, head lights, trash bags, water bottles, cardboard carriers, pillow cases.

Before we reached the sheds, we first came to a huge cesspool of waste.

They fit the exact description of the gigantic manure pits I had read and heard about when I worked for a non-profit focused on water conservation. I used to go door to door telling people about how awful these lakes of manure were and the damage they caused when they leeched into nearby freshwater streams and lakes, but I had never actually seen one before. That was why I was here, though. So I could see firsthand what I had been trying to tell people about for years.

We had to walk a little ways before we found a shed with an open door. It didn't take long, though. I remember following the two others, trying to do exactly as they did, trying not to make any noise and not complain about how cold it was. It was my first time out and the others had been out as a team before. I was the "newbie," and I wanted more than anything to be worthy of this task. Even though I was painfully cold, I kept mentally coaching myself, reminding myself that at least I could walk and stretch and stand upright. The girls imprisoned in the sheds couldn't do any of those things. I just waited for my teammates to tell me what to do and tried to stay out of the way.

When we found a door that was unlocked, we stood outside and took off our coveralls. We helped one another with the boot covers and put them all in a huge plastic bag. We shed our outer layer before entering the shed to protect the desperately weak immune systems of the occupants, doing what we could to minimize the risk of bringing anything into the shed that might further compromise their health. Getting the boot covers off was really hard work. They were extremely tight and our fingers were mostly numb, burning and aching from being in fierce cold for such a long time. On top of that, we had to remove the covers while balanced on one foot with our coveralls hanging half off our butts and legs. I really didn't want to fall over, because it was disgusting and the ground was full of feces, dirty feathers, and blood.

We took a moment to video tape and shoot pictures of a wheelbarrow filled with dead hens sitting a few feet from the door to the shed. The poor birds probably died in their cages and were pulled out by some rough-handed worker days after they'd died. Their stiff, dirty bodies jutted out of the dead pile in awkward, unnatural directions. Some had blood frozen on their beaks and feathers. Their wings were either pressed up against their cold bodies or sticking out at odd angles, like they were broken or twisted, and they had frost on them. We could see their bodies, tiny and bare from where their feathers had rubbed off, or from the weeks-long starvation forced on them to shock their systems into another egg-laying cycle. They looked ragged and awful, and the wheelbarrow was covered in dirt, feces, feathers, and cobwebs. We circled the dead pile and took a bunch of pictures, looking to each other for support in the face of this ugliness. We looked carefully to make sure all of the birds were dead. I don't know what we would have done if we had found a bird still alive in the pile.

When we finished with the wheelbarrow, we slowly opened the door to the shed. It was flimsy and not well secured. We were careful not to break anything or let the door fall off its hinges because we wanted all of the focus of our actions to be on the birds, not on something like property destruction. We slipped into the darkness of the shed one by one. I remember being in there and having huge machines in front of me right away and being disoriented by that. I don't know what I had expected instead, but I remember thinking it felt more like I was in a boiler room than a chicken shed. Even after all of the videos and books I had read, I was unprepared. It hit me that I am in. I am in the shed. I have made it. *Now what?*

When it was my turn to enter, I was scared but determined. Once inside, I wondered were we to be caught inside if the charges would be higher than if we had been caught outside. I have never been a person who breaks the law. I was caught shoplifting when I was fifteen and the fear and shame I felt when I was caught was enough to deter me from committing any more petty crimes. But when the law allows for violence against vulnerable and innocent persons, those laws are ones I feel justified in challenging. But I still didn't want to get in trouble.

The sudden heat in the shed caused my glasses to fog up. It's one of the hassles that go along with wearing glasses. Having to wait for my glasses to adjust to the temperature shift when I came in from out of the cold had always irritated me, but I was especially impatient with them because I wanted to get on with seeing what there was to see in there.

Someone shined a flashlight and I could make out the gigantic machine. It was filthy and had large, thick cobwebs hanging from it. There were feathers and dust clinging to the dirty metal. The thick dust drifted through the beam of the flashlight, and I was grateful for the flimsy hardware store filter mask I wore. I have been concerned about my lungs filling up with microscopic sediment ever since I was in seventh grade when I took Human Anatomy. I was amazed to learn about the tiny, fragile vessels in the lungs and how red blood cells went through those tiny tunnels one at a time to fuel up with oxygen. I always wondered how each cell knew when to let the oxygen go. How did it know when it was time to put that precious resource into action? It's amazing how many things we take for granted in life. Our physical heart pumps automatically, but our emotional heart sometimes needs to be deliberate in actions of love. I just needed to trust that my emotional heart would know what to do that night like my physical one.

I had to breathe through my mouth because the stench was so great. Constricting the back of my throat to protect my nose from the inside, from the back as well as from the outside and the front. I tried to trick myself into thinking that I was only breathing the air that was closest to my face, on the inside of the stiff paper mask covering my nose and mouth. I didn't want to think about the air in there being in my body, in my lungs. The thought of it scared and disgusted me. It was bad enough being in that air. I didn't want to think about that air being in me. But the birds trapped in this shed had no choice, no masks. They had tiny lungs, much more vulnerable than my bigger ones. I thought of the ads I'd seen about secondhand smoke and babies. I felt a pang of guilt for worrying about *my* lungs when the vast majority of the time I breathe cleaner air than the imprisoned hens and have so much more lung capacity than they do.

Disoriented, I moved with my teammate, not knowing which shed we were in or if we're in the tunnel connecting all of them. At the first row of cages, we split up into pairs to look for birds in the most need of immediate vet care. But how are you supposed to do that when every single one of them needs medical attention? How does a person pick 14 out of 1.5 million?

I used to play a game with myself when I was little. I loved my cat Luna more than anything, and when she would go outside at night to roam the neighborhood, sometimes I would worry that the cat who came back might look like her but not *really* be Luna. What if the cat who came back just looked a lot like her and sounded a lot like her? I would study Luna to look for tiny details that set her apart from other cats. The scar on her ear from when she laid in the sun too long and got a blister. The exact shape of the white patch on her chest. It wasn't perfectly symmetrical, so I would look for specific distinguishing features where the black fur overlapped the white fur. I studied the shade of tan on her belly. I imagined a field full of cats that looked like Luna and would look for any little thing that might help me identify the true Luna if I was ever faced with the challenge of picking her out of a field of look-a-likes. No matter how much we may look like someone else on the outside, we each experience life in a completely unique way and are one-of-a-kind individuals. Each one of us is irreplaceable.

But in the shed, I wasn't looking for someone I already knew. I was supposed to pick unknown birds from an unknown mass.

Yes, any of them would be lucky to come with us. And their cage mates would be lucky for the little bit of extra room in the cage when their companion was picked. But that still left a barely conceivable number of birds whose chance for a better life would have come and gone. And the pressure was on. We didn't have a long time to make a decision. We had to hurry up and get the job done so we could get out without getting caught. Every minute in this place was another minute we were risking someone discovering we were there.

The aisles between cages were so narrow that only one person could walk down them at a time. In order to pass one another, we'd have to turn sideways. Cages were stacked six tiers high so that the heads of the birds on the bottom cages were at our feet and we couldn't see the feet of the birds in cages above our heads. The rows were so long that when standing in the middle of the row, I couldn't see the end of either aisle. Egg laying hens are kept in total darkness for much of the time in order to manipulate their bodies into forced molting, and without the flashlights, we were completely sightless. The dark pushed in from every direction, filled with misery and despair. Our tiny lights illuminated only a small space around us and allowed us to absorb small portions of this immense hell one piece at a time. One cage at a time. One bird at a time.

They were remarkably quiet, these small creatures with stained, ragged feathers. Their combs were pale and hung limp on their heads. Their eyes small, black, and wide — pupils dilating to adjust to our lights. Their beaks were mutilated, cut off when they were babies with a hot blade to prevent them from killing their cage-mates. Many of their nostrils had dried mucus or blood surrounding them. Several of their beaks had healed poorly and left them with swollen growths that looked vaguely like grotesque lips. As they breathed, their bodies expanded into their cage-mates' because of the overcrowding. Feathers pressed against wire. Their toenails curled long through the wire floors of their cages or bent their toes sideways as they lay across the wire grids the birds were forced to stand on. Their bodies kept growing those nails from toes that had never scratched the ground, just as their bodies kept laying the eggs that rolled down the slanted wire floor to a conveyer belt, to a factory, to a machine that boxed them up, to a truck, to a store, to a person who would likely never think of the curled toes that egg once grazed as it rolled away from the pained hen who'd laid it.

Split into pairs, we began our search for hens who needed "immediate medical care." We knew they all did, but we looked for those suffering extremely on this skewed bell curve of pain that we were forced to use to measure who was deserving of rescue that night. I found three of the fourteen chosen to take with us when we left.

The first girl was Abbey. She was huddled in the back right corner of her cage on a blackened pad of waste and she was missing the majority of her feathers, especially around her neck and face. She had growths that looked like a cross between boils and warts all over her skin with dark flecks on them that made her look unsightly and diseased. Whereas most of the other girls we saw that night looked scared, depressed, or just plain driven mad, Abbey looked pissed off. Her feather loss and the crusty growths on her face gave her a menacing, furious expression, and I was a little bit nervous to reach in and touch her. But the moment I saw her, I knew she was one of the girls I'd come looking for.

I worked the stiff cage door open and slowly reached into the cage with my latex gloves on. I didn't want to startle her and imagined that every hen in the area's heart sped up the moment they heard or felt the cage door being pulled. In all likelihood, these birds had never had a gentle touch from a human in their lives. I didn't expect to be trusted. I also didn't want to scare anyone into harming herself further by thrashing into the metal sides of the cage or getting twisted in the surrounding wires. Abbey just sat very still and threw daggers at me with her tiny, fierce eyes. If she were to fight, she'd give it all she had.

I touched her gently with my fingers, on her back, where she had the most feathers, and she stayed still. She was in the very back, so I had to reach past the four or five other birds in her cage, and working my hands under her belly was difficult with both of my arms stuck through a tiny space between the door of the cage and the floor, but I managed it and kept her wings pressed firmly to her sides while I slowly lifted her up and out of the cage to my chest. It was then that I realized she hadn't been sitting on a matted bunch of fecal matter, but on a decomposing, flattened cage-mate. The dead bird she'd been sitting on bore little resemblance to a chicken, but it was unmistakable: Abbey had been forced to stand or lay on a dead, rotting body for who knows how long. For a moment, I felt a new intensity of queasiness but pulled it together quickly. I could feel Abbey's heart beating hard and fast in her chest, but she didn't struggle. I don't know if she was too weak to fight or if she knew that I was there to help, not hurt, but I was grateful she allowed me to cradle her tiny, battered body. I mentally promised her that she had someone to help her from now on, that we would take her to a safe place where she could be warm and comfortable, and we'd do our best to make her well and happy. I placed Abbey on a flannel pillowcase in a cardboard carrier and slowly closed the lid before moving on to find her a traveling companion.

There were several of us searching the aisles for birds to rescue that night, so we each were able to pick out two or three to liberate from that awful place. I was aware that time was moving quickly and we had a few more open spots, so I continued my search for another girl to bring home. When I laid eyes on Wren, there was absolutely no question that she was leaving with us. She was so ill that I was afraid she would not live through the ordeal. But her chances of surviving if we left her behind were zero, so we had to try.

At first I thought she had an infected eye, or maybe a tumor growing out of her eye. Chickens' eyes are small, maybe the diameter of a pea, but the growth coming out of Wren was huge; about the diameter of a quarter. It looked like a hardened version of what you'd expect to see come up after snaking a clogged drain. The skin around it was inflamed and sore. Wren was collapsed onto her feet and her toes were curled under her so the tops, where there is very little padding between the scales and bones, were pressed against the wire floor with her full weight atop them. She was laboring to breathe and she had blood coming out of her nostrils on her beak, forcing her to breathe through her mouth.

When we removed her from the cage, we realized that what we had thought was an infected eye was actually an infected ear, and the infection was so huge that it was pushing against her eyelid, and Wren couldn't open her left eye completely. Now, if a chicken's eye is small, her ear is even smaller and the quarter sized mass became that much more horrific in an instant. We had to get her to a vet immediately. We were all worried she might not survive the trip home, as we still needed to walk back across the frozen field and drive back to Minneapolis, and every breath looked difficult and painful for her. But we would do our best to see that she made it through.

And we did. And she did.

Fish Hands

My hands retain the trauma ... the pain. The numb. After scooping up the flopping fish or the dead squirrel in the road, my hands and my arms feel strange and foreign to me, as if they've been infected with that pain and terror, or that tragedy that the nonhuman animals felt before their deaths by the lake or road side. My fingers feel deadened after touching a fur coat or trim. My hands complain when I pick up meat. My hands are clammy and the muscles in my palms, in my wrists, are heavy and frozen, even though they still work like they should. It's a feeling, an energy, an aura that's different.

And tonight, even Warren knows that there's something wrong with Mommy. He's come to be my sentinel. Laying close to me, he's forsaking his habitual and coveted spot, the stinky, faded throw pillow from IKEA that no longer goes with our new sofa. He's lying next to me while I sit here, attempting to make sense of what happened earlier tonight. What I did, and what it means. The dogs always know when I'm not okay. Earlier that day, we had tried to unwind. We tried to have a leisurely, wholesome, relaxing evening like so many families seem to do effortlessly. Couples celebrate the end of a work week by going out for a drink. Parents may order pizza and pop in a kid-friendly movie, curling up under blankets as worries sink to the back of their minds for a few hours.

The start of the Labor Day weekend is the perfect time for this kind of wholesome family activity. I insisted that we do something out of the ordinary to pull our attention away from the stress of that week and toward something, anything, hopeful. I tried to enjoy a holiday like other people, but because I don't see the world in the same way as most folks, it's a challenge to let go and enjoy in the way I imagine they can. We tried to take a walk around the lake. Brandon, me and the dogs. I wanted to enjoy the end of summer's days, to soak up the green before it gets cold and going outside isn't relaxing anymore. It was a gorgeous evening, as balmy and pleasant as it ever gets in Minneapolis. It appeared that lots of other people were ringing in the holiday weekend with a visit to the lake. People are riding bikes, walking their dogs, jogging ... and fishing.

The fishers look innocent enough, almost Norman Rockwell–esque, that is, until they're dragging fish in with their barbed hooks. Often I just see people standing on the shore, or casting an empty lure into the water. But tonight was different. I saw a fish being reeled in, ripples in the water trailing behind her as the weight of her body cut through the water. The panicked animal being pulled by metal that had pierced her sensitive flesh. This image flashed in my mind. It's like lightning, there one moment and then a trace of it as I quickly tried to redirect my attention to the happy dogs on the ends of the leashes my husband and I hold. I forced myself to focus on their feet. Max's deliberate plodding and Warren's speedy skittering across the black asphalt. I watched their feet and kept my own moving along with them. We kept walking.

What else was I going to do? I was determined to relax. I needed it so badly after a week of sifting through hundreds of emails about dogs on death row, watching footage of baby chicks being ground up alive that had made headline news (finally), and reading a book about animal experimentation and the horrors inherent within; I was desperate to relax. The night before, I had even taken a sleeping pill to help me get to the morning. The serial nightmares that plague me were back, always leaving me exhausted and tense. I couldn't let the fishing ruin the ushering in of what was supposed to be a holiday weekend. Holidays are for restoration, and I felt like I had been running on fumes for weeks. *Just walk. Keep moving. Feel Brandon's hand in yours. Look at your babies enjoying the outdoors. Warren's smile. Max's tail straight up in the air while his nose grazes the ground, smelling things you can't even imagine (and probably don't want to).*

Then I saw it. It didn't jump out at me right away. I noticed it as I notice countless other insignificant objects every day. I probably see thousands of items every day, every hour, that leave no impression on me whatsoever. The white plastic bag lying on the ground didn't register as important at first. There was nothing remarkable about it. It was just a plain white plastic bag laying in the grass. Until it flopped and crinkled. Once, then twice, and somewhere in between, my adrenaline kicked in. There was a fish in that bag. Struggling. Suffocating. Dying. For a moment, I panicked. My heart rate sped up, my senses peaked. I was terrified. I was furious. I had to do something, but what? Part of my brain and body was telling me to get out of there. *Just keep walking: look for the dog feet, grip Brandon's hand, and shut it out. Just keep moving. Don't fall down the rabbit hole of anguish again. It's a holiday and you just need to keep going. Whether it's happening in front of you or out of sight, these things are happening every moment of every day and you can't let it destroy you. You have to just get yourself out of here and do it now.*

But another part, a primal part, wasn't going to walk away. Yes, it's risky to intervene. It's scary, uncomfortable, and maybe even illegal. But it's the right thing to do. Yes, these things are happening every day out of my sight. Out of my reach. But this was happening right here, right now, and I might be able to stop it. What actually happened is a blur. I gave Brandon Warren's leash, and I walked over there — it felt like I was running, but I could have been going slowly, afraid of what I was doing. It was like a dream where the physical experience and your surroundings don't match up the way they should. I saw the fish's scales. I saw a tail. Yellow and brown and green like the beet leaves in our garden that are getting old or dying or maybe got too much water. My face and neck started to swell and close up. I'm panicking. I know this fish can't stay in that bag. "What's going on here? This fish is still alive!," I hear myself say. The two women with the fishing poles look at me without saying anything, and I realize they don't speak English. "This fish needs to go in the water. In the lake. Right now," I say as I point at the bag and then at the lake. I'm gesturing, my hand making a frantic swimming motion. My heart is swollen and feels like it's straining in my chest.

A man in dark clothing gets up from the blanket he has been sitting on with his wife and toddler. He comes over and tells me I'm not being sensitive to the women's culture. I tell him if he were the fish in the bag that he wouldn't care about cultural sensitivity; he would just want to be dead already or back in the water. I'm aware that a small crowd has gathered and is watching the spectacle, but I can't care about it right now. Then I see a little fish, flopping on the ground, on the dirt and the weeds. A new surge of nervous energy surges through me and I see a second fish flopping near the first one.

I dismiss the man and squat down to scoop the small, flat fish up off the ground. As I scoop them up in my hands, I worry I might hurt them. Don't fish have a protective coat of slime on them or something? Isn't that why my parents told me I couldn't pet my fish when I was little, that it was bad to touch them? That it could make them sick? I bring one to the railing the women have been fishing from and toss him or her into the water. I worry that the free fall could be scary. That the impact on the water could hurt. But it was only about three feet, and when I saw her swim away, I felt immediate relief. I rush to scoop up the other and hurry to toss her, too. They have a chance now.

I try to offer the younger woman money for the fish in the bag, knowing I have none, knowing that every moment I spend trying to reason with her is terror and agony for the fish. I don't know what to do and I'm really freaking out. She finally takes the bag and I think I have lost. I think she is trying to keep her catch away from what must appear to her to be a very unstable woman. But then she reaches over the rail and empties the fish back into the lake. I immediately start to cry. I'm so grateful. I put my hand on her shoulder and say "Thank you. Thank you. Thank you." I cannot move. My knees are shaking; my hands are trembling and numb. And all I can do is keep saying, "Thank you, thank you, thank you." I slump on the railing, trembling violently. I'm hardly in my body. It's like I'm caught inside somewhere tiny and caged and my body doesn't know what to do without me. I'm stuck. Slowly I get my legs to move; I get them to walk to my husband and my dogs. Brandon has been out of sight the whole time. I don't think he saw any of it. I think he's embarrassed by me.

It's been hours now and the parts that haven't come back yet, even while I type all of this, are my hands. They touched the fish. I still can't reach them. They still don't feel like mine yet. But the memory of that fish hitting the water and swimming for her life makes it all worth it. Even if she died from shock or the wound, at least she would die in the water, where she belongs.

Aala

I dreamed once of a woman who was furious with me for "wasting so much precious time" on one dog when there are "real issues" that need my attention. Boy, was she ever mad. But her bitterness was familiar to me — I've accused others of this same thing in the past. It still haunts me when I find myself stretched to the limit in the name of a stray dog who just happened to cross my path or times when my life felt upside down because of commitments I had made to the rescue I ran for four years after I realized that rescuing dogs and cats *is* direct action, and every bit as important as releasing animals slated for killing or destroying the weapons used against innocent creatures every single day. Rescue work isn't as sensational as Animal Liberation Front (ALF) style direct action and there isn't a lot of machismo bravado associated with companion animal rescue. Most people who run and volunteer with rescues are women who invest their time and personal funds into saving animals who are considered by many in society to be of little to value. Regretfully, I was once among the arrogant animal rights people who idolized the anonymous, masked liberators of the ALF, but had no genuine appreciation for the direct action that (mostly) women in my own community were taking daily to save the lives of animals who would have otherwise been killed because no one else was willing to make the sacrifices necessary to intervene. I wouldn't show it outwardly, but I felt resentful when someone wanted me to spend time on one dog or cat, and I felt superior to these women because I was focusing on the unpopular animals, not the "cute, fuzzy puppies and kittens."

My ignorance of the severity of the situation was partly to blame. After all, name one animal rights activist who isn't aware of the incomprehensible number of farmed animals killed for food annually. I didn't stop to consider that the fear and loneliness each of those animals felt as they huddled in the backs of metal cages and concrete kennels long enough to recognize that their fear and misery was just as worthy of attention as any turkey or pig slated for slaughter. There is no central data reporting agency in the United States for animal shelters to submit their kill counts, but a conservative estimate would be about 4 million per year. I am so grateful that I swallowed my pride enough to see the value that people doing companion animal rescue were bringing not only to the individuals whose lives they saved, but also the fact that they were laying an important foundation for a larger conversation about regarding animals as individuals who are deserving of safety and love, each and every one.

Kill rates eventually became just as traumatic for me to confront in my companion animal activism as they had in my farmed animal activism, if not more so. It's easier to find mainstream sympathy and support for dogs and cats than it is for chickens and cows, and the chances of being directly responsible for an individual who's very survival depends entirely on you are much greater when it comes to dogs and cats. I have found myself making emotional, physical, and financial sacrifices for the sake of one dog at a time to the degree that I never have for a farmed animal. I was shocked to realize that even though there are a lot more people out there who are sympathetic to a dog's story, there are nowhere near enough people who are willing to take on the responsibility that goes along with that same dog — not animal rights activists and not mainstream self-professed animal lovers.

I can't pass by an animal in danger or pain and not intervene. I just can't. That's how my life ended upside down over a pit bull I saw across Park Avenue one morning while my husband, Brandon, and I were out for our morning walk with our boys, Max and Warren.

It's been suggested to me that "animal people" probably notice things that other people don't notice, which would explain my consistent surprise when I am the person who so frequently spots a lone dog wandering the streets. Are we drawn to help animals because we notice them, or do we notice them because we're either consciously or unconsciously always on the lookout for an animal in trouble? I feel as though I'm always asking, "Why didn't someone see her sooner?" when I see an animal in need. It can't be that I'm *always* the first to notice the dogs I find.

She was across a five lane one way street, trotting through yards, no leash and no person to be seen. I crossed the street and watched her carefully for any signs that she might bolt. It's common for loose dogs to be wary of strangers approaching them, and given that I was on foot, if she were to run, chances are I wouldn't be able to catch up to her before I lost track of where she'd gone. Luckily, she let me approach her with no problem and she was curious and friendly. She was big, compared to my dogs, maybe 60 pounds, and had rippling, solid muscles. Her body was nearly all white with a brown spot just over the base of her tail and another on one side of her ribcage. Her head was almost all brown, with a white blaze down the center. One ear pricked up while the other flopped playfully when she moved. It was a very hot day and her huge spoon-shaped tongue lolled out of her gigantic smiley jaws and dripped a steady rhythm of slobber on the grass.

After knocking on doors and asking neighbors if they recognized her, I slowly steered her the two blocks back to my house. She guzzled water and food while I reported her as found to the Humane Society and Animal Control. I had doubts that anyone would call around looking for her but made the reports just in case. In truth, I was sort of scared that someone *would* recognize her and I wouldn't want to give her back for fear that she wouldn't be treated well. We live in a part of town where pit bulls are popular accessories for wannabe tough guys and are not treated as valued family members so much as they are status symbols. The stores near our house have bars over the window fronts and police cars frequently park in our neighborhood just to attempt to deter crime. A nineteen-year-old boy was stabbed to death a block and a half from our place last year. Whether people get pit bulls to intimidate or protect, most of the pits around here have short lives, and they live them with chains around their necks. The chances that she may have been living with someone who wasn't treating her right were too high for my comfort.

Generally, when I find stray dogs, I will do my best to keep them until I can either reunite them with their family or get them into a rescue program, so I can be sure that they will end up going to a good home. I do whatever I can to keep them from going to a shelter where they could end up being killed because of overcrowding or a treatable medical or socialization issue. That was the plan for this dog, but there were a lot of obstacles to keeping her at our home. We had recently adopted a senior cat who was still overcoming the trauma of his re-homing. We have a seven pound dog with a Napoleon complex who likes to pick fights with larger dogs and scares Brandon and I half to death in the process. We have a room in the basement where we tried keeping the pittie we found, but she was so sad to be left all alone in a room that she cried and scratched at the door—which would have been tolerable if Brandon hadn't been on the other side of a shared wall in his home office on the phone with clients. After only a couple of hours, this energetic and emotional girl had exhausted our options.

I got online and started looking for alternatives. I couldn't reach anyone else who could take her in on short notice. I wasn't going to bring her to the Humane Society because in all the trips I've made to that shelter, I have never seen a pit bull on the adoption floor, and there are far too many pits who are abandoned each year. Plus, the Humane Society kills half of the animals that come through their doors. I was afraid to take her to Animal Control, but read on their website that they work with a number of rescue groups to place as many animals as possible, including pit bulls. With her charming personality, I was certain she would qualify as adoptable and she would be a likely candidate for placement with a rescue group. Brandon and I decided that I would take her there and offer to pick her up again if they were unable to place her in a rescue program after her five day required holding time for being found as a stray dog.

The closer we got to Animal Control, the stronger my sadness at the inevitable goodbye grew. I tried to calm myself by noting how well this dog rode in the car and how mild mannered she was. But, regardless of her excellent behavior, she was still a pit bull and that increased her chances of being put to death. There are thousands of animals with phenomenal personalities who are put to death every month simply because trying to figure out a permanent housing solution for them is inconvenient or difficult. I tried not to think about it as I pulled into the parking lot, but it was a lot like trying not to think about what your sentence was going to be when the jury files into the courtroom after a deliberation.

I brought her up to the front desk and filled out the paperwork required to surrender her as she strained at her leash to smell the lobby. Before the guard took her away, I asked for a moment to say goodbye. I led her to a bench and did my best to reassure her that things would be okay; she would be out of the heat and be seen by a vet, which wouldn't happen if she stayed with me. She completely ignored me and craned her neck to try and catch a glimpse of the dogs barking in a back room somewhere.

Before I handed her over to the guard, I asked for reassurance that they would do their best to place her in a rescue group if no one came to get her within five days. The woman looked me in the eye and said, "We get a lot of pits in here. I can't give you any kind of guarantee." I quickly added that if they couldn't find a group to take her, I would come back and get her if she had run out of time. The guard said, "No. This is the final goodbye." My throat clenched tight and I said, "I'll need another few minutes to call my husband and make sure this is still what we want to do."

As the phone rang, I didn't know that when I opened my mouth to tell Brandon what had happened that I would be crying. My stomach was knotted as I gripped the leash and Brandon said, "Bring her back home. We can't leave her there; it's too risky. Just bring her back home." As I passed the guard to the door I called over my shoulder, "I'm bringing her back home." I couldn't get her out of there fast enough.

Once outside, I crumpled down against the red brick of the building and wept. I wept for all of the sweet and innocent pit bull puppies who are beaten and yelled at in an effort to make them mean. I wept for the ignorance that surrounds this misunderstood breed. I cried for all of the homeless animals who face death every day because there aren't enough people to care for them. I cried with shame that I had ever stood in judgment of the people who choose to make dogs like this one a priority in their activism.

As I sat, a crumpled up lump, this dog stood over me and licked the tears streaming down my face, her tail swooshing gently side to side in gentle sympathy. She, the homeless one at risk of being killed, was the one who comforted me. My heart felt as though it were cracking as she unquestioningly offered what she could of herself to this upset person on the ground. My heart was breaking for this precious dog who could have easily come out of that building dead had I left her there, while at the same time opening up and letting in the tenderness that I'm always reluctant to feel for animals whom I know will only be a part of my life for a short time. It hurts to love them strongly and suddenly (which is the way this love so often shows up) and not be able to keep them with me for the rest of one of our lives, especially when chances are that I'm the only one who feels that way about them at that moment.

I piled her back in the car and brought her home again. On the way, the sky opened up and rain poured down harder than I had seen in years. We were inching along the freeway, wipers going at full speed. I thanked the universe that I found her before she was caught out in this weather all alone. She sat next to me and smiled as she watched the world go by, completely at my mercy, and protective feelings toward her steadily grew inside of me as I thought about her vulnerability and trusting nature.

In rescue, it's often a "go big or go home" kind of game. All in or nothing. This girl needed a name and I chose Aala because it was pretty and strong, just like her. We got Aala the shots she needed so that we could board her in a top-notch facility where she could play with other dogs for half the day, and we went to visit her daily while we worked to find an opening in a pit-friendly rescue, which ended up taking about four days. When it was finally time to say goodbye, I cried again. Only this time it was because I knew her and would miss her. It was because I didn't want to put her through yet another new place to be with more strangers. I didn't want her to be knocked out and wake up with a cut in her belly from being spayed and not know why someone would do that to her, and I didn't know who would nurse her through her recovery. I also felt relief that she was safe and my part of keeping her safe was done.

Several months later, I was in a local shop buying dog food and saw a flier recruiting foster parents for the rescue that took Aala. And right there on the flier was that big jowly smile and the one floppy ear. I just stood and looked at her photo for a while, surprised to see her photo in this unexpected place, but not surprised that she must have won over some hearts in order to literally become a poster dog for the rescue.

I just stood there and looked at those shining eyes and her one floppy ear, feeling those familiar love pangs that will never stop me or make me apologize for being an animal liberationist in the smallest and largest of ways.

An Oral History of the Animal Rights Coalition

Thirty Years of Grassroots Activism

MARY BRITTON CLOUSE,
CHARLOTTE COZZETTO, HEIDI GREGER
AND VONNIE THOMASBERG

People will often talk about either the history of a social "movement," as though it's some monolithic entity, or the history of national groups who do all the fundraising and get all the public relations for a movement. There is a tendency to look at everything from a macro perspective of, "We're going to try to blanket the media with the message and make an impact on a national scale." However, many other groups are asking, "How can we change our community? How do we change things at the local level?" The Animal Rights Coalition (ARC) is possibly the longest, continuously running group to have a basis in one city — Minneapolis, Minnesota — without trying to explode into a bunch of national satellite offices or change their mission and message, which is to approach animal liberation from a micro perspective. And with national groups most frequently in the spotlight, very few talk about how work such as ARC's is done.

Grassroots groups are seen to have little staying power. In our experiences, the lifecycles of such organizations can be short, and one may think about people picking up, slipshod, three or four campaigns and doing them for five years at the most. Some members move out of town, others move in, and still others lose interest altogether. Another group will come up three years later, often affiliated with a college or university, and the cycle begins again.

These realities of the animal rights/liberation movement led us, as co-editors of this anthology, to an exploration of how ARC has been able to sustain itself for so long while maintaining a core group of members over the past thirty years. What follows is the story of the Animal Rights Coalition through its current and former members' own words.

The Animal Rights Coalition:
An Early Timeline

Vonnie Thomasberg (founder of the Animal Rights Coalition [ARC] and former President): I worked with the civil rights movement; I worked against the war in Vietnam. I was very active in that. I was very interested in working with animals, but I couldn't find any groups, so I kind of was on my own. I would stop abuse here; stop abuse there; get stores to quit carrying animals as part of their inventory; getting into schools to change attitudes about goldfish swallowing and some of the other wonderful things that they had kids doing.

Then my mother picked up a brochure at Southdale for one of the large national [animal rights] groups. I saw there was a local group here, so I joined it, but they didn't do anything. A bunch of us that went to these meetings every month decided to ask the state coordinator if we could form a committee and start a campaign. Well, as it turned out, she didn't like that one single bit and told us that wasn't appropriate. We decided to go off on our own.

It's much more complicated than that, but we got all people that were interested in protecting animals together for a large meeting at Powderhorn Park and thought we could form a coalition where we could all work together. That went over like a lead balloon. We got seven people together and we each threw in $25 — that was our bank account — and then went from there. [In 1980], ARC was formed primarily because the three areas that were not being covered nationally were farm animals, lab animals in cosmetic testing, and animals used in entertainment. There were people working on wildlife, there were people working on domestic animals. We decided not to mess with that because that was being taken care of, but we, of course, picked the three hardest and that's why they probably weren't being worked on. That's how, actually, it started, was for those three things the animals are used for.

The first year, we had National Day for Lab Animals. We joined that on April 24, and we got enough people from around the state and in Wisconsin and northern Iowa to come and form a band around Diehl Hall at the University of Minnesota, but we couldn't get any news coverage. The second thing we did was a three-day conference. We brought people all the way from Florida, and it was a very successful first year. Of course, we were living from hand to mouth, but we survived and grew from there. Our mailing list grew and the office was in my basement.

Well, we were and we consider ourselves a national group located in Minnesota, with Minnesota ties and with Minnesota interests, but we did draw from people like Alex Hershaft, Alex Pacheco, and those people. We coordinated with them all the time, but we were in Minnesota because there wasn't any [local groups]. It was like we were the vast wasteland, you know? They have from East Coast to West Coast, and we just were, yeah, the vast wasteland. That's all I can say.

A lot of people that we brought in from the Midwest were lured away to the coast, which was too bad. I think it's the passion and the fire in the belly — I don't know how else to put it — of a few real dedicated people that kept things afloat. We almost did lose our identity because we joined a national campaign for the Mobilization for Animals. We brought in so many people to go to Chicago, and it was confusing to the new people that Mobilization for Animals and the Animal Rights Coalition were two separate things, that we were only coordinating for the national group. I had to explain to these people that, no, we weren't Mobilization for Animals; we were coordinating Minnesota for them for the campaign. So we almost did go under at that time [1983], but we didn't.

We were not the only grassroots group. Animals' Agenda, every month or two when their magazine came out, had a listing of all the new groups that were forming all over the country. I saw to it, of course, that was before computers or anything like that, to either call or write them to tell them, you know, if they wanted any help, suggestions, or that sort of thing. To make them feel welcome, because we weren't at all when we started. We weren't felt welcomed by anyone. All of these hundreds of groups were springing up all over the place, so we weren't the only ones.

PETA, of course, was founded about the same time. I met both Alex and Ingrid [Newkirk] in upstate New York when I went to the Vegetarian Conference up there. It was in the late '70s that I went to those conferences two years in a row, and that's when I met Jim Mason and all of these people: Alex Hershaft, Ingrid, Connie Salamone, and all of these wonderful activists. That was really something that got me going, too.

Charlotte Cozzetto (early ARC member and current President): I honestly didn't join because I really knew what it was about. I joined because I worked with Women Aid [and someone] who was on the ARC Board ... asked me if I liked animals. I said, "Yeah," and she said she worked for this nonprofit organization that needed a secretary, and you can be a secretary without being a voting Board member. I went to a couple of meetings, and I had never heard of animal rights. I don't know where I'd been, but I hadn't heard of any of that stuff. I just got sucked into it. I mean, I wasn't vegetarian or anything. I was close to it, just by virtue of taste. I'd never liked eating [meat] that much, so I just kind of fell into it because of her.

Mary Britton Clouse (early ARC member and former President): And then Bert and I got involved when we landed in Minnesota. We moved up here from New Mexico, and we knew not a soul. We landed in North Minneapolis, and all the other people said, "You've got an apartment *where?*" We've always lived in really poor neighborhoods, even in Albuquerque; animal cruelty and poor neighborhoods go hand-in-hand. Our first summer we spent watching, out the window, this asshole across the street and his beer belly and white T-shirt beating puppies that he was weaning. He had just bred [them], and he was weaning the puppies with a baseball bat. I called Animal Control thinking that was going to do something, and it did nothing, and I got pissed off.

At the time, Minneapolis was contracting out their Animal Control services. It wasn't a city-owned agency. It was contractors, and they were strangling dogs in their own backyards. I mean, every scum of the earth was working for this agency that low-bid the contract, and it was just one disaster after another. I was so outraged that I contacted — I think it was my counsel person; I forget who I contacted — and I said, "Isn't there a group that's doing something about this?" Lo and behold, the Animal Rights Coalition's name came up. They said, "Well, yeah. I think the Animal Rights Coalition is pissed off about this." So I tracked them down. Bert and I went to a couple of meetings and suddenly realized that the world was a lot bigger than just dog and cat issues, just from our exposure to ARC.

We became vegetarians prior to that. We didn't get involved until '86. We moved into this house in 1983 and became vegetarians the very night we saw *The Animals Film* on Channel 2. Public TV — *The Animals Film* — can you wrap your head around that? I mean, they won't even give out John Robbins' books for premiums now because it's too controversial. It changed our lives.

In '86, that's when our awareness started to come together and we realized that it went beyond the dog and cat issues. We've considered ourselves to be reasonably well-educated people. We had not a clue until we connected with ARC and really realized the breadth that we were able to step back and understand from a really global perspective. Then we just started getting more and more involved.

Heidi Greger (early ARC member and former Vice President and Treasurer): I moved to Minnesota in 1990, and that's when I started with ARC. I was in graduate school at Purdue in Indiana, and I had gotten involved with an animal-rights group there. A little, tiny one from Indianapolis called CHEETAH which was the Coalition of Hoosiers for the Ethical Treatment of Animals — or something like that. And then we started a little, tiny group, there were three of us, at Purdue, and we would do tabling events, like on Earth Day we would go to different venues. Very small, it was nothing that cost any money — you know, in parks and things — and just handing out animal-rights literature. I had become a vegetarian — I think that was 1988, maybe. I had been giving money to groups — many, many groups — since I was thirteen. I had gone on a list when I was thirteen for giving my allowance to Save the Seals, you know, from being clubbed in Canada. From then on, I would get mail and I would always give money, but I didn't know that much about the issues.

Then PETA sent some little pamphlet on if you have a cat or a dog, why don't you eat your cat or dog? Something about the illogical nature of why you eat some animals and have some animals — call them pets. I just went, "Oh, my God!" because I'm a very logical kind of person. At that, I became a vegetarian from that. PETA was offering an Activism 101 seminar in Fort Wayne, Indiana, so I drove hours to go to that thing, and then I really became committed to becoming an activist.

[After calling the Animal Humane society and being told they didn't need volunteers], I kept looking in the phonebook and I found Animal Rights Coalition in the white pages, and I was stunned. I thought, "Oh, my God. There's an animal-rights group." I went right to the meetings, and the rest is history, as they say. The organization was in shambles at the time. That was 1990. Things were falling apart. I came in, I attended a board meeting to see what they were like, and everything was just imploding.

CHARLOTTE: Personally, this is my take on it. ARC was transitioning from kind of a small organization that the president did a lot of the work and a few key people, into an organization that was more strategy-driven. It was getting a little, I don't know, more mature. There was a meltdown, kind of, with one of the presidents. It was personalities ...

MARY: That's typical of the organizations, I think. It's part of the growing pains, and that actually is why ARC survived: it did change.

CHARLOTTE: Yeah, and none of us were really involved in the meltdown.

HEIDI: We were coming into it as it was melting down. It was perfect timing, because Mary became president, I became vice-president. We went out to dinner after one of these meetings.

MARY: We're sitting there and Heidi and I are looking at each other ...

HEIDI: We hardly knew each other then.

MARY: We didn't know each other at all, and it was obvious that something really bad was going to happen and ARC was going to close if we didn't step up to the plate. Heidi and I looked at each other, and I said, "I don't have a clue what a President does."

HEIDI: "Or what a vice-president does. I don't know what to do." You said, "I'll do it if you'll do it." And I said, "I'll do it if you do it."

MARY: We had just discovered ARC, and it was really great, and it had changed us. We recognized how important it was, and here it was about to fall apart. That was really the motivation [for saving it].

HEIDI: We'd seen that they'd done so much good work and we couldn't let it die, so we just came in at the right time. The right people at the right time.

CHARLOTTE: I had got burnt out. I had been on a leave of absence from the board for a few years, and I came back to a board meeting in 1999 and Vonnie was still on the board. I was so disgusted with how some of the Board members treated her, where I went, basically, "Fuck this." You know? By hook or by crook ... we wrested control of the board back.

For a time [1999], it was just a group of people who thought it was great fun to spend their Saturdays protesting. They'd all go out to eat after- wards — big social event. While they're protesting, they'd spend more time yakking it up with each other than worrying about [the issues]. It was silly, and they were the most disrespectful group of people. I was incensed at the way they treated Vonnie. They totally marginalized her, like, "No, we don't need to hear from you."

Engaging the Public and Transitioning to the Age of Technology

CHARLOTTE: An issue that public sentiment really did help, I think, was the gas chamber at the Animal Humane Society, because we closed that down. As recently as 2000, they were still gassing animals. We got them to switch to lethal injection, but I think the public played a major role in that. We took out ads in the local newspapers, and we paid an online search service to get the unlisted phone numbers of the Board members. After consulting with our lawyer, we published their unlisted phone numbers and addresses which, clearly, we couldn't do today.

HEIDI: I feel pretty cynical about [the] public — it sort of goes in peaks and valleys. You can't really count on it, although there's so much information out there and it's so easily accessible now. I think when you approach peo- ple about an issue, they're more likely to know something about it or just say, "Oh yeah, I kind of heard something about that." Which is nice, but I think people are so concerned about their own economic situation that stuff like animal issues takes a back seat. I'm just very cynical.

MARY: It's been really interesting to consider the impact of technology and the accessibility of information that's had on the movement. I can still remem- ber the day Bert and I went out and bought the first fax machine for ARC..., and that was a big deal. We had a old fashioned telephoned deal when somebody would have to sit and write out in longhand what the caller [was saying] in the logbook. It really opened up the whole world in terms of being able to not only get information in, like documentation — the amazing array of information that you can get on stuff you want to know about, and particulars — and also outgoing ways to disseminate informa- tion. There was a tipping point, and I think that the [recent] information overload has made it more difficult to engage people.

[Today,] I'm actually talking about the amount of information you're bombarded with from sunup to sundown. You wake up with the radio, and then you're on the computer and you're going on the Internet and email.

You're just bombarded [with information], and I think that it's had an effect on us as a species, at least in the civilized world. You can only grieve so much. You wake up every day and there's a new tsunami, or earthquake, or tornado ...

CHARLOTTE: I think it's diluted the shock factor.

VONNIE: [But] thank God for the video camera, because all the abuses and all the confinement farming are being brought [to the public], and people are starting to look at it, and the stockyards, and the slaughterhouses. I don't know; it's a wonderful time. It's a wonderful time, the fact that the newspaper will call us for information. One of the first times that happened, I just fell off my chair.

HEIDI: ARC is still a kick-ass organization.

MARY: In our experience, when we were still with ARC, there would always be one thing that brought somebody in, and it was the meeting place. You didn't have to buy the whole package. [One gentleman] came because he had purchased a puppy who was a puppy mill puppy who had all kinds of horrible health issues. Once he learned about everything else, his world opened up, and he wound up being the main organizer for the Green Party for many years. It was a window, it was a meeting place, and people could come in with very narrow concerns and learn about everything else.

CHARLOTTE: Well, it still is. We get asked constantly, or questioned, about why we're still a multi-issue group. We're still a multi-issue group because I, for one, don't believe that personal veganism is the path to salvation. Everybody has their tipping point, or trigger, or what. Some people are going to come in because fur really bothers them. Some people are going to come in because they can't stand seeing elephants in the circus. Once they get there, they're going to be exposed to this other stuff. I still resist — kicking and screaming — this emphasis on veganism. I'm not saying we shouldn't do a lot of it, don't get me wrong. It's not the end all and be all.

HEIDI: Because most people aren't [vegan] when they come to us.

CHARLOTTE: I answer the ARC email, and I do get emails that start out with, "Well, I'm not vegetarian but" — they feel like they have to explain — "I'm interested in this or that." We respond and say, "Well, that's great." In the meantime, thinking, "We'll rope you in."

ARC Campaigns

Dog Labs and Pound Seizure

VONNIE: After World Day for Lab Animals [began], they started shutting down all the labs on the 24th of April every year because they were afraid they were going to get infiltrated and people were going to start sitting in and stuff. So they just closed them down. Then, actually, we put on a campaign, because I had asked to see all of the minutes from all the meetings that the Animal Care Committee (ACC) [at the University of Minnesota] was supposed to have regarding animals used in research. I got all of the records, and there wasn't any mention of animals in it. It was cage size, duration, how many, that sort of thing.

When that was brought to my attention, I decided that we needed to change the ACC. They were meeting twice a year, and they were just rubberstamping and saying okay to just about anything that you can imagine. So they started meeting every two weeks instead of twice a year, and they also even trimmed down a couple of awards. They were being a lot more careful, not so cavalier.

HEIDI: [And there] were protests every February against the dog labs.

CHARLOTTE: Right, but [we] also had some people who were kind of on the down-low, who were feeding [us] information and minutes, even subscriptions to the U's lab newsletter. We used to get a packet in the mail periodically with that kind of stuff. [We] had some sources — two or three people that I can think of.

HEIDI: But nothing was really being done with it. That's where it would stop because things were starting to get sour.

CHARLOTTE: Well, they did try to get people on the Institutional Animal Care and Use Committee (IACUC) [at the University of Minnesota]. There were some efforts around that, but it didn't happen. I know they did put some work into that.

HEIDI: We instituted long-term strategic planning, we went to a conference, but that was the big thing. We brought somebody in to help us with strategic planning.

CHARLOTTE: We went on from the dog labs to ... doing data practices requests from the University of Minnesota, and they weren't giving us the information we'd asked for or responding. They were saying maybe a lot of it was lost in the mail.

HEIDI: Or, "We just don't have those records."

CHARLOTTE: We went to a conference and met an attorney who suggested how to do it, and we brought him in. He kind of started the whole thing, and then we ended up hiring a local lawyer. As luck would have it, we got in a large donation at the time so we were able to afford it because [the lawyer] did charge even though it was about half his normal rate. We sued the University for access to the records we were denied, and we won, and we won big time. The U had to pay our legal expenses. It was considered a big public records lawsuit.

HEIDI: [That was from] '95 to '97. I think we won the actual lawsuit in '96.

VONNIE: Shutting down the dog labs at the U was really a nice thing to have happen. It was a lab that they used for teaching that most of the other labs like that in the country had already been shut down because they were deemed unnecessary. The University of Minnesota just held on, held on, and held on. We finally just shamed them into [closing down]. Of course, they said they did it because they looked into it, the usual rhetoric, not because of any outside pressure. That's a biggie. I think that the ACC meeting more often and being more thoughtful about the way they look at the studies that are being introduced; I think that's a biggie.

HEIDI: I mean, we slogged through boxes, and boxes, and boxes of paperwork.

MARY: And copied, and copied, and copied. This was before there was scanning, computers, barely faxes.

HEIDI: If you wanted to scan something, you had to rent this giant machine.

MARY: We wound up with these cases full of records. Bert and I drove back East that summer, and I took the records with me and read them on the trip. Coming home with this stuff, and then it had to [be] organized, and it had to be read through. They had us in this little, tiny room. We'd get there, and there'd be these boxes stacked out in the hall, and they had somebody keeping an eye on us the whole time. We had a form copier in there, didn't we?

HEIDI: No, we had to flag everything that we wanted.

MARY: We would show up and we'd be treated like dirt. They'd be sneering up their sleeves. We'd be going through the records, and every time something looked interesting, we had a shopping list of things that we knew that we wanted to see. What we really wanted to do was match up the United States Department of Agriculture's (USDA) tag numbers with what those dogs got used for.

When the University acquired them, they would be assigned this number, and that number followed them all the way through whatever the dog — mostly dogs, but some cats, some primates — was used for. You could follow that animal.... [One] dog was taken under false pretense in Missouri and wound up being sold to the University of Minnesota. He was retrieved this date. Here's his tag number. Here's the department that requested a dog, so he was transferred to that department. Then you've got the name of the researcher who was doing the research project, and then we had the link of what was being done. The ACC reports, where they had to spell out what they were planning to do.... They had to have approval to do it. We'd found the records that were kept while the animal was in the lab, and we were finding blood on them. It went from being this abstract concept to a document that had this animal's blood [literally] smeared all over it.

HEIDI: Yes, literal ... literally, blood-spattered. Horror stories of finding, "Oh, we came in today and found So-and-So dead" or "Oh, somebody forgot to feed them over the weekend and they're dead now."

CHARLOTTE: Because they never thought anybody would be reading that.

MARY: Yeah, so that was a real eye-opener. The impact of learning the importance of primary sources, investigating stuff, and being able to put it to use once you've got it. That was huge.

CHARLOTTE: Also, I think the University learned to ... take us a little more seriously because we would get really flippant with lies. Like the letter. Do you remember the letter, when we asked for video tapes? [We] got a letter back from their lawyer that said, "We have a videotape of some little fishes swimming around. If you're interested in seeing that, we can copy it for you." I mean, even [our lawyer] was appalled.

MARY: They denied the existence of photographic records, but then I actually had a client for our business that was one of the photographers.

CHARLOTTE: [The number of animals used at the U] continues to increase, but what's noticeable is the dog and cat numbers are going down but the agricultural animals — like pigs — that's exploding. They're not going down. A couple years ago, we considered picking up where we'd left off, and we were talking about possibly suing the U again to gain access to the IACUC meetings, which now are closed. We do get the minutes now if we request them, which we didn't used to before, so that's a plus. Going forward, that's the next issue.

We were fighting the pound seizure at the same time. A lot of this ended up translating to the Pound Seizure Campaign, because the animals seized from the pounds were being used at the University.

HEIDI: When Judith Reitman did her book *Stolen for Profit*, we were able to show that they were [knowingly] using stolen animals.

MARY: The University was purchasing from Julian Toney, and Julian Toney had a historic judgment against him for ...

CHARLOTTE: 1,200 counts.

MARY: Oh, I think it was 1,500 hundred counts, 1,500 violations of the Animal Welfare Act. He was the primary supplier for the University of Minnesota. I can still remember Patrick Manning, he was the head of Research Animal Resources — that's the department that procures the animals that are then sent off to the labs — and, "Well, those aren't stolen animals. We buy our animals from him."

CHARLOTTE: I was just going to add, as far as pound seizure, what we did at the time is we weren't able to outlaw it, but we got the cost of the dogs raised significantly by the Saint Paul City Council. So the dogs cost, what was it, two or three times what they used to cost, which was a real deterrent to the U purchasing them.

What's going on [now] is there's the "End Pound Seizure Minnesota" on the End Pound Seizure Minnesota website. That was done by ARC, but it doesn't have ARC's name on it because we didn't want to bring up the specter of animal rights. ARC worked with a local attorney, and she did a lot of the historical research. It's a combination of her and ARC doing all the data practices requests and all that kind of stuff. That's where all that information came from. The Humane Society of the United States (HSUS) approached us because Howard Goldman is their [Minnesota] State Director. On their agenda suddenly appeared pound seizure as an agenda item.

We were working on it and we were starting to have some success with this, and Howard approached us about working with us. So [our lawyer], Howard, and I, and Heidi met a number of times. Basically, we agreed to let Howard run with it and we'd stay kind of in the deep background. Howard did do a bang-up job talking to everybody and getting a proposed bill, which is a proposed bill that [our lawyer] wrote, to go on the record, with just a few tweaks from HSUS. Of course, we've been running into what we knew we would run into, which is [credit thieving].

HEIDI: All the work, and it's all our money, our people, our resources. And then somebody swoops in at the end.

CHARLOTTE: We knew this was going to happen. Why I think it is because we were willing to do all the work, and when there was an actual chance of HSUS taking it over and getting a bill introduced, we were willing to step back and say, "Okay, we do care about the animals more than the organization. Here's all the work we've done. Here is the bill we've written. We're turning this over to you. We will stay in the background. We just ask that you would give us some credit when it's all passed."

I think ARC's non-expansionist tendencies were on purpose. We've never thought [of] emulating, like, say Mercy for Animals or something. Growth in and of itself is a good thing. I think we've made a conscious decision to be locally-based. I personally think when growth is your goal, you start worrying more about the organization than the animals. Your goals are promoting the organization, and the work you're doing to help animals gets left in the dust. Your angle becomes self-promotion of the organization, you know, and you kind of tend to forget why you're doing it.

MARY: Yeah, pretty much any organization with a name and it's particularly tragic for the animals, the animal organizations, because really, the grass-roots people are all they got. That's the frontline between what's happening to that animal and the possible redemption, that national groups don't even answer emails, you know? I can't tell you how many people I hear from on a daily basis: "I contacted HSUS, and they won't do anything." Well, duh.

HEIDI: We decided, when we took over, we saw the opportunity for long-term strategic planning, and we needed to do this project, this project, this project, and set goals [and] strategies of how to meet those goals. One of them was closing the dog labs at the U of M, and we did it. They had been protesting there every February for, like, ten years or something — no strategy. We laid down the strategy, and then three years, you know, we shut them down.

CHARLOTTE: Well, but we did it through research. I think we need to say that. We did it through compiling copious amounts of information on the suppliers ... and showing that not only were [the labs] probably operating illegally, but also showing that the U was taking in animals with tattoos, collars, and obviously stolen animals, and that kind of thing.

Bird Trapping

MARY: The agricultural plots on the Saint Paul campus [of the University of Minnesota] used to have these bird traps, and they were randomly catching [birds]. They claimed that they were threatening their experimental plots. They were catching ... to the tune of, gosh, I think it was about 3,000 birds a season, and feeding them to the raptors. They would trap them, and they were right out where the public could see this happening, and the public hated it. We managed to get one of the TV stations out there and got some footage of birds in one of these traps, and that just turned everything around.

I and a couple of other people from ARC met with the University officials, and they had to negotiate a real PR nightmare. Learned a lot on that project. Ultimately, what they discovered was that they had uncovered complaints from plant pathology professors who said that the current methods of deterring the birds was not working. What we ultimately did was to get them to investigate non-lethal means of controlling the predator, which they were able to do. They determined that the birds who might have been influencing the crops feed at the perimeters of the areas. What they did was they cut paths through, and then they were doing some experiments with different types of caspase and other types of things that could be put on the plants to make it distasteful for the birds.

Anyway, that whole department blossomed into all of these really progressive, non-lethal means of understanding urban wildlife and working with the information instead of just trapping and killing the animals. Learned a lot, not only about birds and about deterrents, but also learned a lot about how to put together a strategy that backs people into a brick wall ... and that was huge. I mean, up until then, it was real easy to dismiss all those little-old-ladies-in-tennis-shoes types. Once we figured out how to use public records and we started to figure out how to use the media ...

HEIDI: That illustrates why we wanted to stay a local group. I mean, we're working on local issues that are affecting the animals in our community, but it can have a national effect. These people at the U talked to other people. The professors talked to other professors.

MARY: Yeah, one of them actually developed a course using the bird trapping as an example. It was an environmental ethics course on conflict resolution, and so they stepped back and they looked at the whole bird-trapping issue right from the get-go and documented the part that ARC played in negotiating as a means of teaching other people in similar positions as the people in plant pathology. You know, when someone raises an issue, it can't just be dismissed; you have to look at it and deal with it. Because up to that point, it was just real easy, you know, they had the media wrapped around their little finger and, "Oh, we're saving the world with those crops. What's more important, feeding the hungry or a few crap sparrows?"

Changes, Progress and New Concerns

VONNIE: It's been two steps forward and one step back, and two steps forward and one step back. I think [the movement's] progressing, slowly but surely. Now that Britain has banned circuses using live wild animals, I mean, things are happening. Yeah, dancing bears now are being banned just about everywhere.

Getting back to Minnesota, I really think we can make an impact here. Things are changing. I watch the news occasionally, not very often, and people are saying things like, "Well, that police officer shot my dog, and he's a member of my family." If you would have said that twenty years ago, the little men in white coats would be coming up to your house.

People are also taking the law into their own hands in many instances and deciding that that creature is not being treated well and needs to find other surroundings to be in. People are stepping forward and having lawsuits and deciding that the animals that live with them are not things but part of the family. That, I see, is a huge change in the past thirty years, almost 180. I mean, amazing.

The young people are the ones that have to carry this forward. It also really upset me when Obama said, "We can't look backward." I think we have to look backward to see where we've come from because we keep making the same mistakes over and over and over again. I've even seen that in thirty years in ARC. When new people come, they start making the same mistakes that were made by people previously because they don't know that those mistakes were made.

I expect, but I don't know whether [or] how soon it will be, that people will start thinking about releasing all of these animals that are in confinement situations: hogs, pigs, cattle, calves.... Maybe that might change because it has such an impact on human health. I'm sorry to have to add that.

The lagoons are ruining communities. People are having to move, and if they can't move, they've got to hope the wind comes from a different place. It's polluting our waterways. The animals are fed so many antibiotics that that's unhealthy. We're finding that there's a recall of tons and tons of animal flesh. I don't know where they're putting it, but they're recalling it.

I think people are going to get sick of being sick. Maybe if we can get doctors and nutritionists to quit pushing meat. One thing that has happened, you know, the food pyramids were always done by the Food and Drug Administration (FDA) and were run by the Egg Institute and the Meat Institute. That has changed, you know, that's a good step.

It impacts humans, and that's what's going to change it. That's a sad statement, to talk about our species as being so insensitive, but we really are. We're not sensitive to any living thing on this planet, whether it's flora or fauna, including each other. It all comes back to "me." How is it impacting me? Well, we've got to quit doing that because I'm sick. I remember the time we were protesting on the streets and marching, whether it was feminist rights, civil rights, animal rights, the war in Vietnam. That was the thing that people did, you know? Everybody says they're so busy, and they're no busier than they have ever been anywhere. They're not making their own soap; they're not scrubbing clothes by hand or hanging them outside. They're pushing a bunch of buttons, and they're not as busy as people were a century ago.

CHARLOTTE: [The] most positive [change] would be, I think, we've made a lot of forward progress; it's just hard to realize because there's still so much shit going on. If you look at how we've kind of become part of the mainstream culture; [vegan] is a recognizable term now. People know what it means. They may not agree with it, but they know the concept. I think there's been huge strides, because when I read what Vonnie's written about having to make tofu in buckets at one time, you know, it's huge.

MARY: I especially like seeing "vegan" on convenience foods because that's what we live on.

HEIDI: Yeah, and that just wasn't true even ten years ago, so that is a big deal.

CHARLOTTE: We are [also] starting to narrow down [campaigns again], and pick some that we might go forward with. Also, I think it's part of what we've been talking about. We're deciding to maybe do fewer activities because it's been feeling that some of us, like, we're doing too much. It's frantic, it's frenetic energy. Yeah, people are having fun and stuff like that, but it's not necessarily accomplishing [anything] ...

I also think we're partly creating a market [by opening a vegan boutique in Minneapolis called Ethique Nouveau] because we get a lot of people in from the neighborhood who aren't vegan and want to look around. We talk to them, and I think it's a real welcoming space.

HEIDI: It's a way to be non-threatening and not scary, and say, "Hey, these things aren't tested on animals, and they don't have animal products."

CHARLOTTE: Well, that's what we say on [the] Ethique Nouveau website. We want to show that you can [be], I don't really like the word "fashionable," but you can be fun and fashionable, have fun stuff, and not have to live in Birkenstocks and plywood.

[We purposely designed] the store to go against the stereotypical "this is what people think a vegan store should look like." It's funny because a lot of our earlier views from mainstream media, like the big shopping blogger lady from *Minneapolis Saint Paul Magazine* [said], "Well, I had a little bit of trepidation going over there, because I thought I'd find, blah, blah, blah." [But she found it to be] a cute little store, so that's what we were trying to do, make it seem less like we're all a bunch of oddballs.

HEIDI: It's not a store for vegans. That's not our "business plan," if you want to call it that. It's supposed to be for the general public, vegan or not vegan.... Obviously, we want to convert people, but in a subtle way. It's not just for the vegan community, it's for everybody, and then you get to learn about why this is better.

CHARLOTTE: I think the store has been extremely successful. It can always make more money, but it's helping. I also think the store gives us a little more credibility, like, we're not this "fly-by-night." We have a store, an office. It's a more permanent "we can afford to do this" kind of picture.

MARY: I would love to take the opportunity to discuss the sustainable forward movement and the impact that this locavore movement is having on encouraging former vegetarians and vegans to go back to not only raising livestock in the city but slaughtering them themselves in the backyard. It's not just here. We started Chicken Run [Rescue] in 2001, and in 2009, the numbers spiked [to a] 780 percent increase in the number of birds we've been asked to take. We can't take them all, but it's just exploded, and the condition of the birds is atrocious. You've got these people who are utterly ignorant who decided that they are going to save the world by being sustainable and raising their own eggs, [saying] "Kids should see where their food's come from." Utter ignorance that they are supporting exactly what the commercial agriculture industry does in the terms of exploiting the female of the species and disposing of the males of the species.

I'm talking about the fact that if they're purchasing from hatcheries, which most of them do, fifty percent of those birds are being ground up. The males are being ground up either at the hatchery, or they're shipped off as packing material. When it arrives here, the roosters are disposed of as soon as their sex is apparent. It took many years to put it into perspective, but a two-year old hen has ovulated as many times as a menopausal woman. Chickens only lay one clutch a year in the wild, and they've been selectively bred to lay constantly. They're worn out by the time they're two-years old, and they have a life expectancy of fourteen years. Now, my favorite way to close an email from somebody looking to dump a rooster or some other bird is, "Please ask the next locavore that you meet who claims that they're sustainably raising animals in their backyard, 'Sustainable for who?'" Certainly not the roosters and certainly not the hens that are done laying after two years.

HEIDI: This would go in your "least-awesome change" category?

MARY: I think it's a whole new bag. There's all these people who, "Oh, I used to be vegan, but then I figured out that the food miles is really more important to the environment." The animal is lost. The animal has become utterly invisible. *The Daily Planet*, it's a publication, they just had an account of this poor guy that had forty-nine birds on that parking lot, in a parking lot in Seward. People were breaking in and clubbing the birds with baseball bats, stealing the eggs, just insane. No permit. All of the locavores are gathering around him supportively, "Oh, it's such a shame that zoning turned him down, that he can't have his poultry farm there in the middle of the Seward neighborhood."

I did an interview last spring with a woman. She contacted me from the … what's their newspaper? I can't remember the name of the publication. It's the free thing that they give in the stores. Anyway, she was writing an article on keeping chickens. I spent three days compiling sixteen pages of, "What should people know before they decide to have chickens?" Cut to the chase, the conclusion was that people shouldn't, that a plant-based diet is what people should be looking at for sustainability. It's a hell of a lot of work to have chickens and to do it properly. There's all the shit that people don't know about predators and health problems. All the reasons that would make a sane person think, "Maybe a plant-based diet really would be a lot simpler." They said, "Well, that isn't the article my editor wanted me to write. He wanted to tell people how to do it, not if they should do it." They completely obliterated any reference to Chicken Run Rescue, with the exception of one link that was tacked on to the end of the article. That kind of blatant censorship; I see it as nothing but censorship. We've got all of these people who it used to be that we thought we're kind of aligned with.

CHARLOTTE: The Co-ops *were* our friends.

MARY: Yeah, and what we discovered [is that] we were involved with the Green Party Animal Caucus. Bert and I did that for a couple of years. You would not believe the hostility from the Green Party to animal [concerns]. It was an eye-opener for us, the absolutely antithetical relationship between animal rights stuff and [the Green Party].

CHARLOTTE: The locavore thing though, it brings up an interesting thing because I do think that's one area where ARC is still kind of, "By God, we're going to do it this way." I mean, we're not caving into this whole "cage-free egg" thing. No, and we never have. We've never been like other local groups — which will remain nameless — "Okay, we've convinced So-and-So restaurant to go "cage-free," and blah, blah, blah." No, it's abolitionism, and that's what ARC is all about, so "cage-free" is not an option.

Editors' post script: In April 2012, approximately one year after this oral history was recorded, pound seizure, which allowed laboratories to take animals from shelters for medical research if they were not claimed within five days, was officially banned in Minnesota thanks to the work of the women interviewed for this oral history, their lawyer, Howard Goldman (the State Director for Minnesota of the Humane Society of the United States), and Governor Mark Dayton who signed the Omnibus Agriculture bill, HF2398/SF2061.

Killing Them Softly

Marketing a Movement, Marketing Meat

M. RYAN LEITCH

Marketing and words. These things matter. I learned this as a student, and I learned this through the ways in which veganism and animal rights have been marketed to me. I am an activist with a background in critical marketing studies. This perspective has offered me a unique position from which to critique the marketing of meat and the animal rights movement. As a marketing expert, I know how important words are. In some cases, one word, be it on a billboard or a bottle of hair gel, can make all the difference between someone purchasing or not. In kind, activists from all backgrounds may find themselves using different terminology when referring to the animal rights/liberation/ advocacy movement. Therefore, I feel it's important to define some terms as they will be used throughout this essay. When I speak of animal liberation, I consider that to mean the cessation of animal use in all forms. An abolitionist is a person who participates in activities that are consistent with this term, meaning all of the campaigns, rescues, and outreach in which she engages specifically request that people never participate in activities that hurt animals in any way, in what they eat, products they buy, or experiences they seek.

Therefore, from my perspective, the opposite of abolition is welfarism, or more recently termed protectionism, indicating individuals who intentionally participate in activism that asks people to regulate their treatment of animals, such as campaigns to legislate better treatment of chickens, but not the cessation of chicken consumption. Unfortunately, in my experience, welfare tactics sometimes include attempting to help one animal while hurting another. For instance, I am aware of "pet" adoption days where a group may serve food for attendees made from animals or their byproducts. This sends a contradictory message telling the public that animals have value and are deserving of a good life or home, but only the cute, domesticated animals with whom we're used to sharing our lives. While welfarists may find themselves working on abolitionist campaigns, an abolitionist will never knowingly work on a project that doesn't promote animal liberation in its entirety.

This is how I define these terms, which may differ from others in the movement or even in this book. But it is my background in marketing that allows me to see how much these terms and definitions are products of advertising. Similarly, as a marketing student years ago, I was introduced to concepts and terms that horrified me as a young woman. These concepts created ideas of normalcy and ideal appearance or behavior (i.e., it is ideal to be slender and attractive). I found myself speaking out against these concepts when I realized that the marketing industry was trying to define me when what I really wanted was to live an authentic life where actions are consistent with values, not filtered through the lens of commodity culture.

Despite my best efforts to eschew the marketing machine, my entry into veganism was a product of advertising premised upon the idea that it is normal to be thin. A slender little book with an impossibly slender cartoon woman on the cover beckoned to and seduced me, saying, "Beyond this cover lies all the information you need to become skinny enough to feel good about yourself; so buy it, Fatty." Though I had felt above such marketing influences, I bought this idea like other consumer zombies buy various other products. I was prized out of my money by an engaging book alerting me to the dangers of the Standard American Diet when suddenly I was caught off guard by this diet book exposing the lies I'd been told my entire life about what it really means when we pay others to treat animals like products and machines to get their meat to market. While some good came out of my feeling bad enough about myself to pick up this book and immediately become vegan, I realized very quickly that *Skinny Bitch* uses language that is completely speciesist with its overreliance on "pig" to describe culturally unworthy women. I then learned that the authors are women affiliated with arguably the largest animal welfare organization in the world, People for the Ethical Treatment of Animals (PETA), an organization that notoriously uses women's bodies to sell animal liberation.

Activism as Marketing

Our job in this lifetime is not to shape ourselves into some ideal we imagine we ought to be, but to find out who we already are and become it. — Steven Pressfield

Despite problems with *Skinny Bitch*, my vegan evolution had begun. I stumbled hard and made lots of wrong turns into welfarism, many proponents of whom introduced me to the phrase, "Oh, I'm an abolitionist at heart." (Yes, I heard this phrase quite often early on.) While I never actively participated in a welfarist campaign, I did spend a lot of time volunteering with a welfarist group. My experience solidified my belief that working on campaigns to convince companies and universities to switch to cage-free eggs, for example, is inconsistent and does more harm than good, especially in terms of how they support marketing terms such as "cage-free" and "free-range" that make people not only feel better about eating animals and their byproducts, but also make consumers willing to pay a premium price for such products.

As a nascent activist, I became familiar with the notion that vegans in general and abolitionists in particular are militant, lacking a sense of humor, and strict. My direct experience tells me that while these notions may be true sometimes, abolitionists are morally consistent, serious about equality and dedicated to what they know is right. After weighing the perspectives, my conclusions left me with a burning question. When a "free-range" animal processor claims the moral high ground, we lose what morality even is. If it is moral to give the animals a "better life," isn't it more moral to not kill them at all? In an essay for *The Atlantic*, James McWilliams states about the animal food industry: "It's difficult to imagine any other issue where such a basic sense of right and wrong is so thoroughly perverted. But when it comes to slaughtering animals, even animals raised under the strictest welfare standards, a twisted ethical logic prevails." McWilliams also refers to free-range farming as a "carnival of ethics" and, as I've come to learn, this "twisted ethical logic" finds its way into the animal rights movement as well.

When I went vegan, I had no support system. I had no one telling me what to eat, advising me about nutrition, or explaining the difference between abolition and welfare. I was motivated but with nowhere to turn. Then, serendipitously, having never done so in my life, I turned to iTunes and subscribed to every podcast on the subject I could find. I sifted through dozens and was drawn to one in particular called New Zealand Vegan Podcast, recorded by Elizabeth Collins. Perhaps what hooked me at first was her accent. I'm not ashamed to admit that I'm an American with a soft spot for beautifully spoken accents. More important than her soothing tone, however, was the pain in her voice because of frustration she felt in dealing with insensitive co-workers and family members. But she held firm to what she believed, no matter how dangerous the storm.

She suffers through the pain of being fully awake to the horrors of animal slavery, but she perseveres. Sometimes she does this all on her own, dealing with hurtful comments by family members or rude co-workers, and sometimes with friends she's made who face the same injustices she does, like a peer who was almost suspended from school for refusing to wear the leather shoes required for his school uniform. I came to realize that her messages and actions, while not always easy or popular, were strong and clear. There was no confusion about what she was trying to do in her activism. This was such a different message than what I received from reading *Skinny Bitch*. Elizabeth marketed her activism by teaching me that I can be consistent and not participate in activities that hurt not only animals, but women as well. Her activism is empowering and fearless because it's an honest, direct reflection of her experiences and doesn't trade one injustice for another, sending the right kind of consistent message that doesn't start with the "cute" animals and end with topless models and pornography sites.

I am thankful that I found Elizabeth soon after reading *Skinny Bitch*. I learned through her consistency that I don't have to compromise my dignity and participate in activities that are hypocritical, like a vegan food giveaway at a zoo. (Indeed, in 2011, an animal welfare group based out of Minneapolis gave away free vegan food at a local zoo, despite concerns of activists that their message was incongruous and possibly confusing to the public, as their actions indicated that animals used for food matter but animals in captivity for entertainment or education don't.) I learned that I did not have to spend my time campaigning for incremental changes that result in marginally less suffering at best but contribute to markedly more animals being tortured and slaughtered. My introduction to animal rights had taught me that welfarism *is* speciesism. Supporting the notion that animals should at least be treated better as slaves still condones slavery, particularly in a society where financially advantaged people pay more money for animal products that are perceived to have been humanely produced.

Selling Social Norms

What is the difference between unethical and ethical advertising? Unethical advertising uses falsehoods to deceive the public; ethical advertising uses truth to deceive the public. — Vilhjalmur Stefansson

As previously noted, during my marketing coursework, I stumbled across something terrifying yet liberating. Besides learning how to market products or ideas, I was shown what marketing does to the society we are obligated to participate in. As someone who always felt like she never quite fit in, like I was always on the fringe of normalcy, my discoveries during my marketing coursework put things into perspective for me. I found Jean Kilbourne and her life-changing thirty-four minute presentation "Killing Us Softly 3." I subsequently read her book *Deadly Persuasion: Why Woman and Girls Must Fight the Addictive Power of Advertising*. I learned that the advertising we're exposed to thousands of times per day not only tells us what we should buy in order to be "normal," it tells us what "normal" is.

Admittedly, Kilbourne's work has not made me immune to the effects of advertising, much to my dismay. Fortunately, I am now usually able to look at what ideals are being sold to me from a critical perspective, which makes me feel a little bit better when "effective" marketing gets its stranglehold on me and starts chipping away at my self-esteem. Unfortunately, even with my education, I still have experienced over thirty-one years of being treated in commodity culture as a consumer rather than an individual, so while I'm able to externally rationalize my negative self-worth, the marketing wounds are deep and may never heal. I can critically view an ad and understand that it's deceitful, but that doesn't change that the rest of the world still operates as though advertising's ideals of normalcy are natural. Therefore, when I see most of the people I encounter every day buying into the lies, it's extremely difficult to be so hyper-rational and pretend that I too am not constantly affected by messages that make me question my "normalcy" as a woman in Western culture.

Women are not the only casualties of advertising, for people of color are sent similarly destructive messages. For example, a 2010 Coca-Cola commercial exemplifies this normal vs. abnormal dynamic. A high school football game is being played, white versus green. Almost every player in a white jersey is Caucasian, and almost every player in a green jersey is African American. A white jersey-ed Caucasian tackles and knocks down the African American student in the green jersey, and while someone drinks a Coke in the background, the white student finds his humanity and extends a hand to pull up the black student he's just knocked over. This is no coincidence.

The ad implies that whites are the dominant race, and they can knock you down or pick you up as they wish if you are among the oppressed. This analysis may seem far-fetched at first, but every person, every gender, every race, every age you see in an advertisement is painstakingly selected to portray a very specific message. Until very recently, if ever there were men and women or boys and girls shown together in ads, the males were shown as active and the females passive, unless race was involved; in that case, the female would be in a dominate posture if she was white and the male was a person of color. As a student, I found all of this fascinating, but it was not until years later that the significance of Kilbourne's analysis would become newly relevant to me when considering how the animal food industry peddles meat eating as "normal," thereby reinforcing human dominance over nonhuman animals. Her comment in the book's introduction that she "saw that women's bodies were often dismembered in ads — just legs or breasts or torsos were featured" (18) unknowingly applied to my later life role as an animal advocate who would protest the dismembered animals parts that our culture considers elements of a normal diet.

In her documentary, Kilbourne references a magazine advertisement depicting a woman's body as a bottle of tequila. She states in "Killing Us Softly 3":

I'm not at all saying an ad like this causes violence, it's not that simple. But it's part of a cultural climate in which women are seen as things, as objects, and certainly, turning a human being into a thing is almost always the first step toward justifying violence against that person. We see this with racism, with homophobia. It's always the same process. We think of the person as less than human and violence becomes inevitable.

Obviously, Kilbourne is concerned with violence against women, but her words are directly applicable to nonhuman animals as well. To wit, in *The Pornography of Meat*, Carol J. Adams discusses "the *thingification* of beings" in much the same way (22). Kilbourne continues in the lecture: "At the same time that we have all of these blatant sexual messages, there's no emphasis on relationships or intimacy, and we have to fight to get accurate sex education into our schools. No wonder we have the highest rate of teen pregnancy in the developed world."

These impassioned words could easily be turned into an argument against animal welfarism by changing just a few words, as I have done here: "At the same time that we have all of these 'humane' welfarist messages, there's no emphasis on veganism or speciesism, and we have to fight to get accurate health education into our schools. No wonder we have the highest rate of osteoporosis and obesity in the developed world." When a living being becomes a thing, that being is targeted for violence, and this is true for nonhuman animals more so than for any other species. Kilbourne's research, once so important to me when I was an impressionable college student trying to find my authentic self as a woman in commodity culture, also shaped my worldview on the issue of animal rights and liberation.

Marketing a Movement, Marketing Meat

Health makes good propaganda.— Naomi Wolf

It's entirely possible that my outrage at being marketed to at every turn and my disgust for advertising, as opposed to ignorance about marketing, is why abolitionism makes so much sense to me and why the welfare approach seems so shortsighted. Essentially, welfarism, as it is currently advocated, actually green lights animal consumption, confinement, and slavery. We already have such cognitive dissonance when it comes to speciesism (just think about the number of people who reportedly "love" animals they call pets while eating animals they call "food" and wearing animals they call "clothes"), and the welfare message muddies the water even more. Take, for example, a commercial for a fast food restaurant specializing in dead chickens' flesh where cows are in a tall office building late at night. You see them wandering around on various floors while office workers exchange confused glances. At the end, they emerge outside where a shot of the building reveals that the cows have turned on the lights inside the building to spell out "Eat more chicken."

Though clever enough to be memorable, this ad offers a disturbing and confusing message for an badly informed public. The advertising agency exploits cow sentience by acknowledging that cows do not want to be eaten, so eating more chickens means eating fewer cows. But despite the shocking honesty in this commercial, consumers don't realize how serious that message is. Viewers are amused, and very likely doing exactly what the commercial told them to do, much to the detriment of the chickens who, we may imagine, do not want to be eaten either.

Even organizations that seemingly send the right marketing message have a tendency to pander to both sides of the eat animals/don't eat animals issue. Compassion Over Killing (COK), a national animal advocacy group, has been running advertisements on MTV. In one particular ad, a woman pulls into a fast food drive thru, and as she's placing her order, the voice booming through the drive thru narrates it back while graphic images of commonplace cruelty related to factory farming flash upon the screen. The consumer is disgusted and no longer wants to eat at the fast food restaurant. While I was excited to see this commercial presented to a mainstream audience, my excitement was short lived when I visited their Web site and found this verbiage: "Granted, living in cramped conditions is better than living in even more cramped conditions. Laying hens who have 67 square inches of space per bird likely suffer less than those who have only 50, and giving even 10 out of 10,000 turkeys access to sunlight and the outdoors is better than denying all of them such basic needs" ("How Free Is 'Free-Range'?"). While they do follow up this commentary with a statement against "commercial 'free-range' farming," I'm left to wonder why they would not make a declaration against any and all farming. Instead, they tacitly show support for moderately less animal suffering. Their ad identifies that people are doing something harmful when eating fast food, but they then countermand their own message by supporting animal byproducts if they are ostensibly nicer. COK's message is confusing to consumers, to new advocates, and worst of all, it maintains animal commodity culture.

Admittedly, not everyone will go to COK's website to witness this paradoxical message. However, some will. Were someone affected enough by that commercial to consider its significance, chances are she would use COK as her first search on the subject of animal cruelty considering that COK is the messenger. When that's the case, COK's commentary may actually undercut their own message because a person moved to change (while possibly reluctant to make such a "dramatic" lifestyle alteration as going vegan) could come across the page quoted above and decide that while commercial farming is to be avoided, eggs from local backyard pens are acceptable. This is problematic. It confused me, and I can imagine that it will confuse others with the wherewithal to investigate COK's website.

Animal welfare campaigns are dangerously similar to the aforementioned racist and sexist advertisements in that they provide an inconsistent and confusing message to an uneducated public. One look at a relatively current welfarist "victory" shows just how convoluted their messages can be.

In 2007, the University of Minnesota's dining services switched to cage-free eggs after pressure from a local animal advocacy group who presumably supports veganism. Although the organization responsible for the so-called victory addresses the limits and lack of regulation around cage-free eggs on their Web site, stating that "cage-free doesn't have much legal meaning," they still applaud this change and report the backing of other welfarist industries such as the Humane Society of the United States" ("Frequently Asked Questions"). To make matters worse, the University of Minnesota touts cage-free eggs on their annual "Green Report Card," so what was originally a misguided attempt at humane treatment is now a selling point for this school, additionally allowing them to appear environmentally-minded and concerned about non-human animals ("University of Minnesota"). However, *cage free doesn't mean cruelty free*, and it doesn't mean that chickens aren't still subjected to de-beaking, forced molting, extremely cramped and filthy living conditions, barbaric transport and cruel and unnecessary slaughter, especially of newborn male chicks who are deemed useless to the industry. It just means the chickens didn't live in a cage, and that is not enough to be considered humane.

In reality, the term "free-range" means that birds are "free" to share cramped living conditions with thousands of other birds whose conditions "range" from dying to dead. The welfarist approach doesn't take into account that the beings people eat are individuals. Advocates of the approach presume that nonhumans like to be treated better in general without actually giving them the individuality they deserve, while ignoring that they should not be property at all. At the very least, the problematization of animals as property is too regularly left off the table.

In forgetting about the totality of the chickens' lives, either intentionally or ignorantly, the welfare group responsible for the University of Minnesota cage-free egg "victory" rejected one more extremely crucial concept best exemplified via analogy. Imagine you're eating a large chocolate bar. You've gotten halfway through it and are starting to feel a little bit guilty about how much you've eaten when someone tells you that it's a special kind of diet chocolate bar with no calories. Most people would then finish eating the candy bar and maybe even have another since the consequences of ingesting that food item have been eradicated. In the case of animal consumption, welfarist messages essentially tell people that they aren't doing anything wrong when they eat "cage-free" or "free-range" animals. In effect, they have slapped a bogus marketing term on this product so that all can enjoy their dead animals guilt free.

Sadly, animal producers have caught on to the success of welfarist campaigns without even being pressured to by animal advocacy organizations. During the 2009 Animal Rights Conference in Los Angeles, Dallas Rising speaks to this dangerous trend. She says:

> Animal welfare improvements in the British veal industry resulted in a new product called Rose Veal. This product differs slightly from conventional veal in that it's produced in a slightly less cruel fashion, that there's no confinement of calves in veal crates. Now, after some media attention and the applause of a large animal advocacy group in Britain, veal sales increased by 45 percent in the first supermarket to carry it.

UK veal producers have applied welfarist standards to their own dirty marketing campaigns. Borders Rose Veal has this to say about their product: "Holstein Bull calves, a by-product of their 150 head Pedigree Holstein Dairy herd, are reared with high welfare standards, with access to light, water, fresh solid feed, with the ability to stretch, move and exercise to around 6 months of age" ("About Us"). Borders is not saying that the veal calves have light, water, fresh solid feed, the ability to stretch, move and exercise. They just say the calves have "access" to those things. This producer brags about a calf's ability to move and then be slaughtered at six months of age, as if it is a benign act of generosity to the calf and the mother from which he was stolen. To an animal advocate, this is an outrage, but to a somewhat sensitive consumer who misses eating veal but was guilted out of consuming it because of traditional production methods, this marketing campaign puts veal on the table once again. Between welfarist messages and animal marketing, the third option of not eating veal is taken out of the equation.

Sophie Morris of the *LoveFood* online journal, states the following in her oxymoronically titled entry "Ethical Veal":

> I haven't eaten veal for a long time, because I thought the moral argument against eating calves was black and white — eating the meat of male calves reared on milky water in tiny crates was cruel, and should be avoided.... As it turns out, there is a third way, and buying British veal reared humanely saves these calves from an early grave.... [Now] You don't need to rule out foreign veal altogether.

For this person, and for many others, marketing worked. (For instance, consider a 2007 *New York Times* article called "Veal to Love, Without the Guilt"). Consumers may hear that rose veal is more humane without ever looking into what the seemingly lovely term even means. When applied to veal, the word rose — normally reminiscent of flowers, romance and spring — refers to its pink color rather than the white of an anemic calf. As Borders Rose Veal explains, their calves are slaughtered at about thirty-five weeks. If cows can live up to twenty-five years and thirty-five weeks is barely over half a year, I'm curious as to what Morris thinks an early grave is! To anthropomorphize my point, the Center for Disease Control suggests that human life expectancy is 77.9 years ("FastStats"). Compared to a veal calf, it's like killing a child who is less than two years old — not even a toddler! In what world is killing a toddler *not* an early grave?

People are duped by the clever words of marketers, and it is up to abolitionist vegan activists to offer alternatives. We live in a culture that thrives on the marketing of products, images and even ideologies. Therefore, the animal rights/liberation movement must also consider issues of marketing if we are to enact change in people's perceptions of nonhumans. So, how shall we market ourselves? Two words immediately come to mind: *Consistency matters.* Consistency is what ultimately drew me through welfarism to abolitionism. I know that consistency matters because when outsiders learn that one is a vegan animal advocate, questions of consistency naturally arise. Ideological opponents try their damnedest to find inconsistencies in pro-animal arguments, or even inconsistencies in one's behavior. They will try to frustrate advocates with comments about driving a car, buying non-local produce, wearing diamond rings, using electricity, etc. Obviously, this is to try to point out that we, as vegans, are not perfect. The fault in those comments lies in that vegans aren't claiming to be perfect; we're just trying to do our best to not cause harm to beings capable of feeling pain.

This is where ideological and strategic stability is of the utmost importance. Animal activists often get into debates with individuals who have no real interest in veganism and ultimately just want to catch vegans being hypocritical so they feel better about eating meat. However, even moderately astute observers can see the inconsistency in something like campaigning for cage-free eggs while maintaining that chickens should not be property and their by-products should not be consumed. In cases such as this, the debater doesn't care as much about animals as they care about pointing out vegan hypocrisy. We can help ease such uncomfortable conversations by being consistent in our actions, advocacy and campaigns.

Conclusion

> Our society's values are being corrupted by advertising's insistence on the equation: Youth equals popularity, popularity equals success, success equals happiness.— John Fisher

After being empowered by fellow abolitionist activists and Elizabeth Collins' podcast on veganism, I have found myself engaged in a type of activism I've never expected. On Midwest Vegan Radio, a podcast I host with Dallas Rising, we had initially intended to talk about what it's like to be vegan in the Midwest, but after only a few episodes and countless write-ins from all over the world, I finally understood what vegan podcasters really do: we offer refuge for those who feel marginalized by both commodity culture and sometimes even within the animal rights movement. We receive messages from people spanning the globe saying that we are their only vegan friends. It's an honor to now be on the giving end of that relationship and to support people in this technological way.

I do believe there is a place for the welfarist perspective in the animal rights movement, but only as stop on the path toward abolitionism. I have known a few people who actually made it to veganism by way of cage-free eggs, meaning that these clever marketing fallacies actually made them think about animal treatment to the point that they eventually got the larger message that not eating animals at all is better than eating animals who are suffering moderately less than others. However, too many people get comfortable at that point and do not move on toward veganism. Episode 17 of Midwest Vegan Radio asks: "Is it better to go vegan immediately or gradually?," and I think this is where the confusion comes in. It seems as though people think that if you're abolitionist, you don't allow for and respect others' journeys if they make incremental changes. The way I see it, it's not a matter of better, it's about making the transition easier. What we have learned from our fans is that it's easier to go vegan immediately and reap all the amazing benefits of living vegan instead of baby-stepping through various stages, which, for someone not extremely motivated or strong willed, can lead to excuses for sliding back into negative patterns that perpetuate animal suffering and slaughter. It's also important to consider that while many people consider welfarism to work on reforms rather than toward abolition, there are particular exploitation industries where legal intervention can be considered abolitionist, as in the case of banning puppy mills or exportation of products such as bear bile.

Albeit anecdotal, my experience with welfare groups is that they market humane concepts without ever asking of people what they really want: for others to go vegan. Some vegan activists are afraid of scaring people who cannot imagine life without meat and dairy. Even national groups that support veganism promote vegetarianism in their literature. PETA does this, as does Mercy for Animals. PETA's *Vegetarian Starter Kit* reports: "Leading health experts agree that a vegetarian diet provides optimal nutrition for both children and adults. The largest nutritional and medical organizations, including the American Dietetic Association, confirm that balanced plant-based diets are healthier than diets that include meat" (4). However, PETA does not report that the ADA said the exact same thing about *vegan* diets as well (1266). PETA is an animal advocacy organization with more media power than any other, but they chose to market vegetarianism over veganism. Admittedly, all of the recipes in their starter kit are vegan, but they choose to express that message in misleading terms. In contrast, as advocates, we need to get people comfortable with the word vegan. It is not strict vegetarianism, it is not a plant-based diet, it is veganism, and it is a healthy way to nourish one's body and life. Even the ADA, who has no animal rights agenda, agrees. This is what these national groups need to market.

Instead, they tiptoe around what's really important without giving people the benefit of the doubt when it comes to knowing the truth of where their food comes from and what it does to their bodies. It's not fair to make assumptions about another person's capacity for empathy, and it's not our job as advocates to shield them from the truth of what is happening for the pleasure of their palettes. For me, the only way to be an affective activist is to live and promote a clear, consistent, unapologetic message. Let us remember what's most important, summarized beautifully by Jean Kilbourne in her analysis of marketing and women:

> We have a long way to go. And the changes have to be profound and global. And what they will depend on more than anything else is an aware, active, educated public that thinks of itself primarily as citizens rather than as consumers. We need to get involved in whatever way moves us to change, not just the ads, but these attitudes that run so deep in our culture and effects each one of us so deeply whether we're conscious of it or not, because what's at stake for all of us is our ability to have authentic, freely chosen lives, nothing less ["Killing Us Softly 3"].

So many people chose veganism because it's consistent with their values and makes them feel whole. You can decide to fight the marketing choke-hold and draw the parallels between how we treat animals and how we treat all beings that are uniquely different than us, whether you like animals more than people or don't feel any connection to animals at all. *You* get to determine if your actions will mimic your values. Chose to be consistent. Decide to live an authentic life, and in the meantime, let the nonhumans live their own authentic lives as well.

Works Cited

Adams, Carol J. *The Pornography of Meat.* New York: Continuum, 2003. Print.
"About Us." *Borders Rose Veal.* A Shaws Fine Meats and New Heaton Holsteins Partnership. n.d. Web. 9. Nov. 2011.
American Dietetic Association. "Position of the American Dietetic Association: Vegetarian Diets." EatRight.org. American Dietetic Association. 2009. Web. 18 Oct. 2011.

Center for Disease Control and Prevention. "FastStats: Life Expectancy." CDC/National Center for Health Statistics/USA.gov. Web. 9 Nov. 2011.

"Frequently Asked Questions About Cage-Free Eggs." *Compassionate Action for Animals.* n.d. Web. 9 Nov. 2011.

"How Free Is 'Free-Range'?" cok.net, n.d. Web. 21 May 2012.

Kilbourne, Jean. *Deadly Persuasion: Why Women and Girls Must Fight the Addictive Power of Advertising.* New York: The Free Press, 1999. Print.

_____. "Killing Us Softly 3." 4 Oct. 2006. Youtube.com. Web. 16 Mar. 2012.

McWilliams, James. "An Inconvenient Truth: Free-Range Meat Isn't 'Natural.'" *The Atlantic.* 8 Apr. 2011. The Atlantic Monthly Group. Web. 9 Nov. 2011.

Morris, Sophie. "Ethical Veal." *Love Food.* 28 Dec. 2010. Web. 9 Nov. 2011.

People for the Ethical Treatment of Animals. *Vegetarian Starter Kit.* Peta.org. Web. 11 Nov. 2011. PDF.

Rising, Dallas. *Animal Rights Conference 2009 in Los Angeles.* 30 Sept. 2009. *YouTube.* Web. 29 Oct. 2010.

"University of Minnesota." *The College Sustainability Report Card 2010.* Sustainable Endowment Institute. Web. 9 Nov. 2011.

How "Humane" Labels Harm Chickens

Why Our Focus as Advocates Should Be Egg-Free Diets, Not Cage-Free Eggs

MELISSA SWANSON

We've seen the images of cages upon cages stacked in dim and windowless sheds. We've seen the hens in those cages: feathers worn away, combs pale and drooping over eyes that are either brightly frightened or dull and hopeless. We've seen the images of dead birds left to rot where they fell and hens with feet and nails entangled in the wires of the cage floors, starving or dying of dehydration literally inches from food and water. We've seen the videos, heard the eerie quiet of the dark barns, have heard hens going mad with fear when the barns are lit and they are being caught for transport to slaughter or for on-farm disposal.

We know, in our guts, that what we are witnessing in these images and films is wrong. It is powerful imagery, damning imagery, and it is being used astutely to bring attention and outrage upon the battery egg industry. What many do not realize, however, is that it is not just factory farming, nor just battery cages, that cause this level of suffering. No method of modern egg production is guiltless; all are complicit in almost unimaginable levels of suffering for chickens. Even the most graphic video cannot show us how it feels to be the hen caught on camera, to endure those conditions, to be treated merely as a production unit, to die afraid, confused and surrounded by the calls and scents of fellow beings in pain and terror.

In response to these images from various animal welfare groups, the general public — everyday people who may not have given the origins of their food much thought, as well as consumers who are educated on current food production issues — have been mobilized in a pushback effort against the egg industry. They are vocally opposing battery cages, urging legislators to pass laws to protect hens and support the implementation of less inhumane systems of egg production. They are writing college campuses, prepared food producers and restaurants urging a switch to non-caged eggs. While these activities are usually fired by a desire to prevent animal suffering, the facts about ostensible "humane" egg production show that this relatively recent drive for "cage-free" and "free-range" eggs is not ending the painful and unethical mistreatment of chickens.

Increased demand for "happy meat" and "humane" eggs and dairy by "conscientious omnivores" (those who want to eat animals and their by-products but who do not wish for those animals to be raised or killed in overtly cruel ways) may be hurting more animals than it is helping. The pervasive marketing by companies and producers for these "humane" animal products have the unfortunate ability to cause people who are sympathetic to animal suffering — potential vegetarians and vegans — to purchase "humane" animal foods rather than avoiding consuming animal products at all (Joy).

If one's main concern is that the animals who are eaten merely avoid obvious torture before becoming the burgers, chops, omelets and cheese on the plate, the humane myth goes a long way towards appeasing a guilty conscious. If, as Michael Pollan states during an interview with Oprah Winfrey, "most all animals (on small, local 'humane' farms) live a happy life and have one bad day" then those who are concerned only with animal welfare can eat those "happy" animals' parts and sleep easy that night. For those of us who see animals as more than commodities, this is not enough. It is impossible to raise living creatures as products, use them to make a profit, and still put *their* needs first. When animals are production units, they suffer and they die needlessly. Even in the idealized perfect system, a fantasy world where animals experience no discomfort or distress while being raised as food, they are still killed prematurely. That "one bad day" is one bad day too many for activists fighting against speciesism, which indicates prejudice against nonhumans in deference to human needs and desires.

While those in the "humane" farming movement set out with the admirable intentions of dismantling factory farming and Animal Feeding Operations (AFOs) — defined by the Environmental Protection Agency (EPA) as operations where "animals are kept and raised in confined situations. AFOs congregate animals, feed, manure and urine, dead animals, and production operations on a small land area. Feed is brought to the animals rather than the animals grazing" — their efforts fall well short of truly improving animals' lives or altering their status from products we can control and sell to one of beings that have worth independent of monetary value.

Locavores who prefer to source their food from nearby farms and producers, so-called "conscientious omnivores" and other welfarists, who I define as those for whom animal use is not a moral problem as long as said animals are kept in non-factory conditions and killed with a minimum amount of suffering, fill the ranks of supporters for these alleged improvements. "Cage-free" and "free-range" eggs are a very visible and a major part of the "humane" myth which is "an idea being propagated by the animal-using industry and some animal protection organizations that it is possible to use and kill animals in a manner that can be fairly described as respectful or compassionate or humane" ("Humane Myth").

Even many groups that promote veganism as the ideal have gotten on board with "cage-free" initiatives and have plugged large amounts of money into these campaigns, all in the name of reducing suffering while seemingly ignoring the inherent impossibility of a "humane" system of animal exploitation. In cases such as these, I feel like these groups are doing so in an attempt to meet people half way. Most of these organizations are directly supported and kept afloat by donation money. There are more vegetarians (who eat eggs, dairy or both) and "conscientious omnivores" than there are vegans. I imagine that animal rights groups, who'd ideally prefer people adopt a vegan diet, give some attention and support to "humane" initiatives in order to retain their non-vegan supporters, seem non-threatening and avoid looking like the stereotypical pushy, preachy, holier-than-thou vegans. It is understandable, from a public relations viewpoint, but unfortunate for the animals impacted by those who chose to eat "humane" eggs and dairy rather than avoiding those things entirely.

The euphemisms "free-range" and "cage-free" suggest an idyllic pastoral scene. Perhaps we imagine a clean, sawdust-floored barn with wide spaces for the hens to roam, eaves for them to roost upon, straw nests scattered about. In our minds, we fill these "humane" farms with hens with clean feathers, clucking to themselves as they root for food, rest or bathe. Perhaps "free-range" evokes images of glossy white birds in grassy fields, chasing insects and pecking the earth. In either case, we imagine a peaceful Old MacDonald-esque form of farming, one that is not a complete mockery of the word "free." This sort of idealized fantasy is a major hurdle for animal advocates working to show others how eggs, *all eggs*, are harmful and unethical.

In this essay, I hope to show how alternative methods of commercial egg production, from factory farmed "cage-free" eggs to the growing urban farming movement, continue to cause unnecessary harm to chickens. Urban farming, "cage-free" and "free-range" eggs are not the answer for those looking to avoid causing animal suffering. Only a vegan diet that completely eschews eggs truly helps chickens. As animal advocates, we should vocally and publicly discuss the pitfalls of all these so-called "humane" farming systems. While it is tempting to give credit to the small improvements involved in switching from intensively raising hens in battery cages to these other systems, it is not the most effective use of energies for the abolitionist-minded vegan. To be clear, when I use the term "abolitionist," I am referring to those who think that any animal exploitation or use is not ethical. As long as animals are being used for human gain, entertainment or convenience, that use is not morally defensible. "Nicer" exploitation is still exploitation. Abolitionists are looking to empty cages, not to make them larger.

I will outline the specific animal welfare issues inherent in all these commercial egg production systems (by commercial I merely mean "for profit or human gain" on either a large or small scale). In doing so, I hope to give my fellow grassroots activists an arsenal to call upon when the subject of "humane" farming is broached. By educating ourselves about the industry standard practices, production methods and supply chain, we are better able to explain why the answer is not purchasing and consuming "humane" eggs. We should not be advocating for the consumption of "humane" eggs but rather for the cessation of egg consumption. The message should always be that the only way consumers can avoid harming chickens is to boycott eggs entirely by adopting a vegan diet.

The producers of "humane" eggs help to paint one picture for consumers via advertising and marketing, on the packages and in their commercials — it is a bucolic scene shaped in part by our childhood story books and songs about family farms and sunny barnyards — but reality for those "cage-free," "free-range" hens is much grimmer. Reality for the invisible victims of "humane" egg production, male chicks, is even more tragic. Before the hens, before the "cage-free" eggs on the grocer's shelves, come the hatcheries.

Hatcheries and Male Chicks: The Unseen Victims of Egg Production

Hatcheries are enormous commercial breeding operations that supply chicks to nearly every farm involved in egg production, from factory farm battery operations to urban farmers with backyard coops. "Free-range" and "cage-free" hens are born in the same hatcheries as those chicks who end up in caged systems. These hatcheries are chicken mills where the approximately 200 million egg-laying hens born in the United States each year begin their lives. It is also where around 200 million male chicks have their lives ended, many less than one day after hatching and all within 72 hours of hatching ("Chicken Care Information"). In egg production, the male chicks are typically disposed of or composted.

Modern chicken farming uses chickens bred for specific traits. There are chickens intended for the meat industry that are selectively bred to be heavier, put on weight faster, and grow larger in less time; there are those bred for egg production who were selected for laying proficiency and smaller, lighter bodies that take up less space in the barns or cages ("Understanding Heritage Poultry"). A rooster of the egg-laying breed is of no financial value. He is too small, slow growing and lightly muscled to be used as a meat bird. He is unable to produce eggs and is not needed for breeding hens. Hatcheries, for all their meddling with chicken genetics, still have not managed to manipulate the sex of chicks. This means that roughly half of all the chicks hatching each year are males.

These scores of economically worthless male chicks must be disposed of in the least time-, money- and labor-intensive ways possible or else the hatcheries lose profit. The industry standard is to macerate male chicks in wood chippers, gas them or leave them to suffocate in dumpsters or plastic garbage bags. Statistically, for every laying hen, including those in "free-range" or "cage-free" facilities, one male chick has been killed in the hatchery ("Chicken Care Information"). All chicks, male and female, in the hatchery are born in artificially lit and warmed plastic trays. When the majority of eggs in each tray have hatched, they are transferred to a fast moving conveyor belt that separates egg shells, chicks and unhatched eggs. Some chicks end up trapped in the egg trays. These chicks suffer intense pain as they are sent through the scalding water spray intended to clean and disinfect the trays. The hatched chicks who are successfully transferred to the belts move down the line for debeaking and sexing ("Hatchery Horrors").

Chickens are animals with sophisticated social structures. Given proper space, they will work out a system of comparative ranks, a "pecking order." When chickens are crammed tightly together, as in battery cages or in the thickly populated "cage-free" barn systems, they are unable to respond in appropriate ways to other birds. Lower ranking birds usually stay out of the way of higher ranking ones. When approached aggressively, they retreat submissively. In natural, unconfined situations, a flock of chickens is a peaceful group (Davis, *Prisoned Chickens* 29).

In the egg production systems, these social balances are not possible. Lower ranking hens cannot avoid their dominant flock mates or cage mates and are sometimes pecked to death. Other explanations for the hens cannibalizing their flock mates relate to the stresses of being in such tight confinement. Hens are sensitive and intelligent animals, so when they are cramped and confined, whether in cages or packed closely in "cage-free" barn systems, they suffer mental anguish and react to that emotional distress. Such violent actions are not inherent in hens' personalities; rather, these behaviors are prompted by the living situations they are forced to endure.

The egg industry resolves the issue of cannibalism by altering the birds' bodies via debeaking. Debeaking or, as the industry calls it, "beak trimming," is a process in which a chicken's beak has the tip seared off with a hot blade, laser or wire. Chicks born at hatcheries, whether destined for battery farms or "free-range" farms, are debeaked to prevent feather picking, when one hen pecks at another, normally drawn to a wound or similar stimulus, and which can commonly end in cannibalism. As noted by Sheila E. Scheideler and Sara Shields in "Cannibalism by Poultry," these "vices," as they are called by the egg producers, are a stress reaction to instinctive and normal chicken behaviors being thwarted and overridden by a life for which the chickens have no coping mechanisms in place.

Debeaking is done quickly, hundreds of birds per hour is the average in most hatcheries. As one would expect, the procedure is done with varying degrees of success due to the sheer mass of animals who go through the system, the experience levels of each debeaker and the reaction of the chicks themselves to the process. In many big hatcheries, the procedure is largely mechanized. Chicks are placed head first into a rotating machine that removes the beak tips via laser ("Hatchery Horrors"). Ideally, the beak has only the sharp tip removed, leaving the wound to the underlying tender and nerve rich tissues cauterized and the tongue uninjured. In reality, as reported by United Poultry Concerns' Karen Davis, many chicks suffer grave injuries to their tongues, have beaks unevenly amputated and/or have terrible trauma to their mouths ("Debeaking Birds").

Even the most textbook case of debeaking leaves the chicks wounded, in pain and with a greatly reduced ability to use their beaks. Chickens' beaks are equivalent of human hands. They use their beaks to explore, interact with their surroundings and take in sensory information. Debeaking handicaps the individual birds and gravely affects their lives and how they experience and understand the world. Chicks can die after the procedure, either due to a botched debeaking that causes extensive bleeding or trauma, stress from the procedure itself or starvation and dehydration from being unable or unwilling to eat or drink due to the pain in their mouths (Davis, *Prisoned Chickens* 64–70). The debeaked chicks are then sorted and any chicks who are deformed or sickly are disposed of.

Chicks can be shipped via the United Postal Service without any special sort of guidelines to ensure their safety, comfort or survival. There are no laws in the United States regulating poultry transport. The Animal Welfare Act excludes animals sold for food and the Twenty Eight Hour Law, which states that animals must be given food, water, and rest every twenty eight hours, typically applies only to animals shipped via trains and ships (Davis, *Prisoned Chickens* 138–139). The fatality rate during transport is so high that hatcheries use extra chicks as "packing peanuts," thus avoiding too much open space in boxes and ensuring buyers receive enough living and healthy chicks to fulfill their orders. Of the chicks who arrive alive, some are mortally injured or ill. Chicks who arrive dehydrated will die. Their organs, once shrunken, cannot bounce back ("Reasons Not to Purchase Chicks"). The young hens who arrive relatively unharmed are transferred to barns or cages and begin the process of becoming egg production machines.

"Cage-Free" and "Free-Range":
Different System, Same Cruelty

The animal welfare and, to a lesser extent, the animal rights movement have been sold on the idea that simply removing barren battery cages will cause actual, important changes in how hens are raised. In actuality, the only thing we can be sure is changing with the adoption of "cage-free" or "free-range" systems is the removal of the physical bars around the hens. Some of the biggest welfare concerns in battery egg production are crowding, the inability of hens to express their natural behaviors, forced moulting via starvation or food deprivation, debeaking and the fetid living environment caused by so many animals kept in such small, enclosed areas without fresh air flow. These problems also exist in "cage-free" operations — lack of cages does not mean all is well for hens.

It is important to note the definitions of "cage-free" and "free-range" and what, if anything, those terms legally require regarding hen husbandry. "Cage-free" is an unregulated term with no third party auditing. The birds are not caged but are not guaranteed outdoor access. As the Humane Society of the United States (HSUS) explains, "free-range," also sometimes called "free roaming," is another unregulated term ("Egg Carton Labels"). The United States Department of Agriculture (USDA) has set some standards for "free-range" poultry but none for egg production; their guidelines read: "typically, free-range hens are uncaged inside barns or warehouses and have some degree of outdoor access, but there are no requirements for the amount, duration or quality of outdoor access" (quoted in "Egg Carton Labels").

As J.A. Mench and J.C. Swanson report in "Developing Science-Based Animal Welfare Guidelines," during production, chicks are raised in small pens until they are large enough to safely live in the barns. At around eighteen weeks of age, the chicks are transferred to the sheds. Each young hen is about 3 lbs in weight and the barn is relatively uncrowded. Hens reach adult size at 30 to 32 weeks and adult weight averages at 4 to 5 pounds. As they grow larger, space per bird reduces equally. The United Egg Producers (UEP) claim each hen has 1.3 square feet (187 square inches) in their "cage-free" systems; however, hens need up to 262 square inches to turn around completely. They require up to 420 square inches to perform normal comfort behaviors like wing flapping and preening.

Most "free-range" or "cage-free" commercial egg producers keep hens in near or totally windowless aluminum sheds. While Americans almost never see hens outside anymore, it is quite common to see these sheds in fields on the sides of highways. You could never tell from the exterior that they are filled with laying hens. They look rather like equipment sheds for farm machinery — which is, in a sense, exactly what they are. The sheds are dimly lit, if they are lit at all. Confusing the hens by altering their perception of day/night cycles to increase laying productivity is common in the industry (Daniels).

At the most extreme end of this practice of disrupting hens' natural circadian rhythms is a process the industry calls "forced moulting." In *Prisoned Chickens, Poisoned Eggs*, Karen Davis explains that hens, like other birds, naturally moult their feathers and grow new ones cyclically. Typically hens moult in the fall, when daylight hours shorten. The moult is a reaction to environmental factors with the addition of stress, such as that caused by egg laying and brooding (incubating eggs and hatching chicks). They eat less and body weight drops. Their reproductive systems take a break and egg production ceases while their bodies use the energy normally expending in laying to grow new feathers. After the moult, egg production starts again at a slightly reduced level. Egg producers, even "humane" ones," thwart this natural behavior to try and increase egg yield of hens whose production has dropped below profitable levels. Such hens are referred to as "spent" by the egg industry (75–77).

The food and water supply is either completely removed or greatly reduced for upwards of two weeks and the shed lighting is manipulated. The hens respond to these stimuli by ceasing egg production and dropping feathers. As discussed by United Poultry Concerns, while hens naturally moult when broody or in response to seasonal changes, and naturally show anorexia during these moults, that is dramatically different than what is being done in these egg production facilities:

> Force-molted hens do not stop eating because they lose their appetite or don't want to eat, but because their food is taken away from them.... Naturally-molting hens do not go for days and weeks without eating.... Fasting originates within an individual or a species as part of a larger purpose or activity that is meaningful to that individual or species ... and has no resemblance to the frightening experience of being arbitrarily deprived of food ["Forced Moulting"].

If the process is successful, the nearly "spent" hens will be induced into another laying cycle. Production will be slightly lowered but still profitable. Most hens in all types of egg production settings are moulted once or twice in their lives. This is done not only to get more eggs out of each hen but also to reduce the costs incurred by completely repopulating the laying houses every 72 to 80 weeks. With a forced moult cycle or two, producers can get more than 105 weeks of laying out of the hens before sending them to slaughter or otherwise disposing of them via composting on site. Most farms keep hens for 1 to 3 laying cycles; once feed costs trump egg production profits, the hens are disposed of and new chicks are brought in to fill the barns (Meuiner and Latour).

Forced moults weaken the hens, many of whom are already stressed and bordering on ill, and mortality can be high. Hens in any of these confinement systems, from battery to "free-range," are dealing with large amounts of strain and the addition of starvation and thirst proves to be too much for many of the weakest of these already weakened birds. Hens become more prone to succumbing to infections as their immune response drops. During the moult, birds are either not being fed at all or are being fed low-quality foods. Birds who die during the process aren't eating up resources and, as the moult is a last effort to squeeze more eggs out of nearly spent hens, cost/benefit favors the process.

Egg producing hens are so ravished by their short, physically demanding lives that their flesh is considered low-quality and has little monetary value. Most hens sent to slaughter are sold for companion animal foods, processed items like chicken nuggets, TV dinners or canned soups. Some farmers will "euthanize" hens via suffocation or maceration on farms and compost their bodies rather than paying to have them shipped to slaughter (United Poultry Concerns, "Forced Moulting").

Hens, like other birds, produce a large amount of waste, including ammonia, a very harsh and potentially corrosive chemical. Ammonia is acrid and hens have sensitive respiratory systems. The stagnant, polluted air makes for an unpleasant, painful and unhealthy environment for both the hens and the workers. The hens, unlike the staff, endure it throughout their entire lives. At levels above 50 parts per million, more birds are seen with eye and trachea/lung damage. The trachea and lung lesions cause the hens to be more susceptible to bacterial infections such as E. coli. Ammonia levels have also been associated with a high incidence of skin problems including foot, hock, and breast burns. If the foot lesions are serious, lameness and leg problems may result (Estevez). Such problems are found in both "cage-free" hens and those from battery cages — birds raised without cages still live in dirty and dangerous conditions that cause them physical pain, injury and illness. Hens in all these systems who are sick or hurt will not receive veterinary assistance. Medical care for these short-lived birds is not profitable nor is it likely that individual hens doing poorly will be noticed in the flock of thousands.

"Cage-free" hens, like their caged battery brethren, live a mockery of a chicken's existence. They are unable to function socially, breed normally, nurture chicks, dust bathe to remove parasites, stretch their wings or forage. Jewel Johnson, who visited a "cage-free"/"free-range" system with the permission of its farmer, describes the conditions of these putatively more humane farms:

> Upon opening the door — it was dark. Only one bulb was on in the very far off distance ... not enough to light up this metal Quonset hut used to house the ... ten thousand birds that were crying inside. The floor under my feet was cement, and the building was freezing cold with no heat in early April. I couldn't see much for hens at all down the shed.... All I could see was black, all I could hear was crying of hens, all I could smell was ammonia — it was a cold, black cement hell.

These hens are still tragically abused; their lives aren't greatly improved because they are crowded on dark, ammonia laced open floors in a shed rather than surrounded by cage bars in that same shed. Hens do not think in terms of square inches or via comparisons. They do not find themselves lucky to have ten more inches or to be spared battery cages. "Cage-free" hens just know that they cannot spread their wings without touching another bird, cannot express certain natural behaviors and cannot truly be chickens. They do not think in terms of this life being better than the alternative; they just live in the moment and deal with the stress of having their basic needs thwarted by the situation in which they find themselves, for reasons they cannot understand.

Smaller Farms Don't Equal Humane Treatment

Many consumers who are shocked at the treatment of battery hens choose to buy only "cage-free" or "free-range" eggs. Some, upon realizing industrialized "humane" farming is doing next to nothing to alleviate animal suffering, try to remove the "industry" aspect of eggs by choosing to buy eggs from small farmers via Farmer's Markets, direct sales at the farms, Community Supported Agriculture (CSA) programs or food co-ops. While some of the "better" farms in these systems may provide hens with marginal welfare improvements, they are still supporting the suffering and death of both chicks and hens.

Even in those rare situations where hens have access to outdoor spaces, as in Polyface Farms — the darling of Pollan and other sustainable farming advocates — we ask: where are the chicks coming from? Where are the male chicks? What happens to those "happy" hens once their bodies can no longer produce eggs in profitable numbers? The hens come from hatcheries. The male chicks are killed almost at birth. The hens are slaughtered. The idea that eggs are a deathless food is a pervasive one. Vegetarians will eat eggs and dairy, but not flesh, due the flawed idea that eggs are not the product of suffering and slaughter. Hens do not need to die to produce eggs. This stance willfully ignores what happens to all hens who no longer lay enough eggs on any farm that is profit-driven.

On Polyface Farms, the hens are slaughtered on the farm in an open air abattoir. As shown in a company-produced video entitled "Polyface Processing Overview," the hens aren't stunned (Schafer). They are placed, head first, into cones and their carotid arteries are slit. They kick and bleed out while the other hens wait nearby in crates. The living hens can smell the blood and hear the cries of their flock mates as they are killed. The chickens are scalded and their bodies are put into automatic pluckers, where they are tossed around like stones in a polisher. Their denuded bodies are dismembered and gutted. We cannot let the end of these hens' lives be glossed over when talking about egg production. These pastured eggs are still the products of a system that chews animals up and spits them out in price-tagged pieces.

The Problems with Urban Farming: "Do It Yourself" Exploitation

With the push for "cruelty free" animal products has come a large upswing in people choosing to raise their own food. Urban farming is part of the relatively recent locavore movement, which focuses on food miles, the distance food travels from farm to plate, as well as avoiding factory farming and promoting "humane" animal agriculture. As distrust of our food system grows, more people are taking up small scale farming in their own yards. Raising chickens for eggs is, unfortunately, a common addition to these backyard gardens and is becoming ever more popular.

Many urban egg farmers buy their chicks from the same hatcheries that supply the large and small commercial farms. Some buy chicks at feed stores, which function as an intermediary between the hatcheries and the consumers. The chicks acquired for urban farming experience the same mistreatment, stressful shipping methods and mortality issues as those purchased for commercial farms. These urban farmers are removing the factory from the egg production, but they are purchasing a product of those factory cruelties. Many do so without fully realizing the extent to which they are still paying into the system they are trying to avoid.

Once the chicks are in these backyard coops, other problems emerge, many of which new urban farmers are woefully unprepared to deal with. Due to the exploding interest in urban egg production, scores of websites and message boards for prospective new farmers exist. Many websites and forums for urban farmers insist that raising chickens is quite simple; they are low-maintenance and require little care. In reality, hens require very specific care and are prone to some common illnesses and problems. Most of these are due to breeding practices that select for high-quantity egg yields rather than longevity and will result in the hens needing veterinary attention some time in their lives.

Finding a vet who will take care of poultry, which are commonly considered "exotics," can be problematic in certain areas. If beginning urban farmers are not aware of this, they can (and often do) find themselves with a sick bird and no idea who to turn to for help. The fact that chickens, being prey species, mask illness also adds a layer of difficulty to making sure they are healthy. As most humans have not spent a lot of time around poultry, it can be difficult to detect symptoms until the animals are quite ill. Combine all these factors and you have a recipe for suffering hens with lingering illnesses that too often go untreated.

Improper shelter is another issue that can plague urban farming systems. Improperly constructed coops that aren't secure can result in heavy predation of the hens. Even the most well maintained coops attract unwelcome visitors like insects and rodents. Chicken feed, droppings and bedding are appealing to these creatures under normal circumstances. Poorly maintained, dirty coops can draw in even more pests, causing problems for the hens, farmers and their neighbors.

As summed up by Mary Britton Clouse, of the Minneapolis-based Chicken Run Rescue (CRR), "the 'urban ag sustainable' crowd races to (the) same bottom of cheap and easy standards of care as the commercial producers *sans* any experience" (personal email). CRR posts photographic evidence that underlines the shamefully inadequate care some urban chickens receive. Foot deformities, untreated wounds, infected eyes and injuries abound (Chicken Run Rescue Facebook Page). Many come to CRR with bumble foot, a painful foot infection that is caused by dirty conditions and wire flooring. Many have grossly overgrown nails from being kept in barren pens or cages, unable to wear the nails down with regular movement. Others have scaly leg mites, a sign that they were kept in unsanitary environments at their previous homes. As the rescue is located in Minnesota, they also receive many birds who are suffering from frostbitten feet and toes due to improper housing during the region's cold winters.

Many of the urban farming websites also gloss over what to do with older hens who are not producing eggs at a high enough rate anymore. Given the number of hits you can get when searching for "chicken slaughter classes" online, offered by a variety of organizations in many states, at least some people are experimenting with killing their own hens. Uneducated, inexperienced urban farmers — even those who have the foresight and funds to attend the aforementioned slaughter classes and demonstrations — are not working with professional equipment or knowledge. Given the number of botched slaughters that happen even in factory slaughterhouses, we can only imagine how many backyard hens are victims of the prolonged misery of a crude attempt at butchery by the hands of urban farmers.

Even those who insist that they love their hens and consider them family often end up with chickens they cannot support and do not want. Thomas Kriese, a blogger on Urban Chickens Network, writes in the dismissively-titled post "What to Do When Chickens No Longer Lay Eggs":

> While some urban chicken keepers seem content to keep the old chooks around for amusement, the more economically minded ... seem less than enthralled with the idea of all those extra mouths to feed. And those of us who live where there are tight restrictions on the number of hens allowed in a backyard can't really keep a flock of non-layers around if we're in it for the omelets, can we?

He goes on to suggest that those with unwanted chickens adopt them to other urban farmers via Craigslist or other such outlets.

Some urban farmers choose to place their unwanted chickens personally. Others simply abandon them outside. This is most common with unwanted or unexpected roosters, but older hens are not immune to being abandoned. Still others contact farmed animal rescues, if they are available in their areas, or surrender their birds to local "humane" societies, basically removing any sense of responsibility and passing the responsibility to already inundated animal rescuers. In the case of birds surrendered to Animal Control agencies or local Humane Societies, urban farmers are merely outsourcing the slaughtering of their birds, as those agencies euthanize nearly all chickens they receive.

CRR, the only urban chicken rescue of its kind, has been in operation since 2001. From 2001 to 2009, the organization averaged thirty-five surrender inquires for poultry (ducks, chickens and others, mostly chickens). Between 2009 and June 2011, they had 616 such calls, 308 a year. *That's a 780 percent increase in abandoned poultry.* CRR's Britton Clouse states that "the urban farming fad has created an epidemic of unwanted chickens, ducks and other species who are being callously killed or abandoned" ("Adoption Chronicles").

Animal Place, a farmed animal sanctuary in California, has also experienced an upswing in surrender requests in recent years. Their Education Manager Marji Beach explains that "many of those [surrenders] are from people who bought day-old chicks at hatcheries, only to discover the birds were inaccurately sexed and were roosters, not hens.... In the past three years, we've seen a dramatic increase in the calls for chickens, especially roosters." Farm Sanctuary, possibly the best known farmed animal rescue in the United States, also has seen an increase in surrender calls. Colin Henshock, Farm Sanctuary's Placement Manager, explains that "the biggest problem that we deal with in regards to the backyard chicken issue is trying to place the unwanted roosters. We average around 20 requests per month.... The companies that send chicks through the mail are a huge problem, with ... many chicks turning out to be roosters after being improperly sexed."

Urban agriculture, while trying to overcome the problems with traditional commercial farming, merely succeeds in producing other issues for chickens. The "humane farming" mythology is perpetuated as consumers try to find the ever elusive harm-free way to both exploit animals for their bodies and bodily excretions and respect them at the same time.

The Humane Society of the United States and United Egg Producer Agreement

Consumers who desire to continue eating eggs chase that elusive "ethical" source. Egg producers respond by trying to convince the public via marketing, labeling and public relations that their eggs are not like those factory farmed eggs we've heard about. They continue to advertise that their eggs can be eaten free of guilt for their hens are treated well. As the industry races to prove themselves to their customers and to increase consumer confidence while public awareness of some of the worse abuses grows, they are willing to do new and seemingly out of character actions on animals' behalves. One example is the recent, and highly publicized, UEP and HSUS agreement regarding battery egg production.

The news that UEP agreed to phase out barren battery cages nationwide is seen by many as a victory, even amongst vegans, animal rights organizations and sanctuaries. All of the specific details of the agreement are still not public knowledge as of this writing. What we do know regarding the proposed legislation sounds, on the surface, like a large step forward for hens. The federal law, if accepted as it is currently presented, would:

> Eliminate new construction of barren battery cages, and replace the existing cages, through a phase-in, with new "enriched colony cage" housing systems that provide each hen nearly double the amount of space they're currently allotted.... [The agreement requires] that these new cages provide environmental enrichments that will allow hens to engage in important natural behaviors, such as perches, nesting boxes, and scratching areas [HSUS, "Details of the Animal Welfare Agreement"].

There are multiple problematic issues with this agreement. The maceration and suffocation of male chicks is not addressed. Debeaking is not addressed. While it prohibits forced moulting via starvation, nothing is mentioned of the other, less harsh forms of inducing moults. Reduction of food and manipulation of light and dark cycles, presumably, are still allowable. The hens are still in cages with no outdoor access. Given the details of this agreement, that is where the majority of hens will stay — in cages.

The term being used for these cages is "enriched," but a more accurate term would be "furnished." The argument for these cages seems to fall down to three differences between "enriched" or "colony" cages and the traditional battery cages. One is that the cages are larger than a standard battery cage, but larger cages do not mean happy birds. While

> it's natural to think that if a hen is moved from 68 square inches to 144 square inches she will feel like she's gained something ... that isn't how it works.... She simply finds that she hasn't got enough room to move...; a bird requires an average space of 198 square inches to turn; stretching wings requires 138 square inches; and flapping wings 290 square inches [Gunther].

In other words, the additional space still confines birds within unnatural restrictions and succeeds only in making human animals feel better about their egg consumption.

The other differences are the inclusion of perches, nest boxes and possibly areas for dust bathing. Proponents of these cages insist that the perches and boxes provide the hens with valuable opportunities to express natural behaviors. United Poultry Concerns and other farmed animal rescues disagree:

> [A]n "enriched" cage has a tiny perch and nest box, and maybe a little box of sand or wood shavings for the hens to scratch and dust bathe in, within the confines of their cage. The hens have "extra" space, about the size of a postcard, in a metal-plastic environment containing a clutter of tiny dollhouse items.... Depending on size and design, each cage holds from 10 to 60 hens ["'Enriched' Cages"].

The perches in these cages are small, only about three inches off the ground and hens are disinclined to use them. The nest boxes and areas for dust bathing are also problematic. Hens prefer to lay at certain times of the day. One nest box in a cage with multiple hens means that hens will either be waiting to lay in the box or the majority of hens in the cage will not have access to the nest box. Dust baths in these cages are also inadequate. As the box is small, shallow and shared amongst many hens, the birds will often go through the motions of dust bathing, rather than actually using the baths properly.

The sham baths involve the birds sitting outside of the bathing areas, on the cage wires, while doing the physical motions of a true dust bath. The hens are, in effect, pretending to bathe. Mimicking and going through the motions of tossing "dirt" over their shoulders, fluffing up, whirling their wings, but there is no dust available to clean them. The birds are not grooming their feathers or skin and are not affecting parasites that may be infesting them. In these cage systems, sham dust bathing is common with two-thirds of dust bathing happening outside of the designated bath areas (United Poultry Concerns, "'Enriched' Cages").

United Poultry Concerns also raises the issues of environmental pollution being worsened by the addition of the bathing substrate: "Industrial chicken houses are densely polluted with toxic gases and airborne debris—floating feathers, dander, and pathogens. Thousands of little 'sandboxes' will increase the airborne debris in the caged environment ... [and] increase respiratory and eye irritation" ("'Enriched' Cages"). In the end, a cage is a cage. The addition of furniture and token attempts at enrichment do not change the fact that no cage system, especially one that is developed specifically to be profitable, can ever be adequate or truly "humane."

As part of this agreement, HSUS agreed to a list of demands by UEP, these include ceasing the push for a complete ban of caged systems in favor of phasing in "cage-free" or "free-range" systems and no longer doing undercover investigations of egg product facilities unless they are aware of egregious cruelty. Rod Smith of the agribusiness trade journal *Feedstuffs* notes, "As part of the agreement, HSUS and UEP said *they will not 'initiate, fund or support' any ballot initiatives or local or state legislation that would define hen space*, and they will not 'initiate, fund or support' investigation of or litigation against each other or UEP members" (emphasis added). This sounds like a good deal for UEP in terms of public relations, but still an inhumane decision for the animal "products" the UEP produces each year.

If this legislation passes, it will become even harder to convince the general population that egg production is not a harmless industry. Consumers, having heard battery cages denounced loudly and at great length, will see that the HSUS supports this new system and will be less apt to realize how problematic any cage, enriched or not, is for hens. HSUS is one of the most well known and well-funded animal protection charities. In many ways, non-vegans see the HSUS as a stand-in for the animal rights and welfare movements. When HSUS puts their stamp of approval on these new cages, that will hold weight in the eyes of the public.

When activists draw attention to the many flaws in the newly adopted system, when we continue to ask more of the consumers and the producers, the public may simply shut down. This occurrence is similar to how new data on carcinogens in our food supply elicits the now common "everything gives us cancer, so why bother" reaction, and we risk creating a mindset of "why bother" in those who eat eggs. With the HSUS saying that these eggs are acceptable to eat, with egg cartons having labels that rank them in regards to how the animals were treated, it makes it that much harder to convince consumers to eliminate eggs entirely. Incremental change, in this case, is not our strongest weapon.

Also problematic is the fact that this federal law, if passed, will trump state laws which may provide more protection for hens. Humane Farming Association founder Brad Miller says that the "agreement would not even go into effect for another 18 years, if ever ... [yet] immediately, the industry gains positive publicity and avoids the negative publicity of a ballot measure media campaign.... [S]tates would be explicitly prevented from outlawing cages — *or doing anything to help laying hens beyond what the egg industry happily adopts on the federal level.*" (quoted in "Humane Society of the U.S. Cuts Deal," emphasis added). Miller's points about what the industry has to gain from this proposal are razor keen. Make no mistake: the UEP has agreed to this deal because it serves their purposes and is in their benefit. Eggs, especially battery produced eggs, have a definite public relations problem and it keeps getting worse. Undercover videos, graphic photos and multiple single-issue campaigns from a score of animal groups and environmental groups have made battery eggs *the* issue. Pollan and the locavore movement, the slow food movement, sustainable farming — all have taken the intensive nature of caged eggs to task as an example of the problems inside our broken, industrialized food system.

If we accept and support this agreement, we are unintentionally assisting the egg industry in their attempts to market their products as anything but inhumane. By promoting the idea that a move to these "enriched" cages is a victory, we're doing hens a disservice and shooting ourselves in the foot. If our real desire, the thing we are fighting for, is the abolition of the animal industry, then offering support to this legislation that is so utterly inadequate is a step in the wrong direction.

What We Can Do to Help Chickens Now

It is reasonable to want to make welfare improvements for hens who are currently alive and suffering. It is natural to be concerned for the hens who will be killed in the years, perhaps decades, before real victory — the elimination of eggs from our diets and the end of egg production — is achieved. However, the way to make those lives better is not to gloss over the problems in the current stop-gap "humane" farming systems. We have a duty to the chickens, both those currently living and those who are yet to be born, to loudly and emphatically speak the truth about the pitfalls and myths of "humane" animal products.

If our goal is the cessation of egg consumption and chicken exploitation, then ending the demand for those eggs is the path we must take. Only by increasing the number of consumers who will *not* buy eggs do we help chickens. The sooner demand is removed, the sooner the supply will cease in response. The industry is large and powerful and has many voices — advertisers, industry spokespeople, the government, celebrities, notable authors and even so-called animal advocates — soothing the public, telling them half truths and feeding them fantasies of Old MacDonald's farm, albeit modernized. We must be just as vocal about the problems with all egg production systems.

We have a duty to speak out for the hens, for the chicks, for the roosters. We owe them nothing less. One of the best ways to do this is to use the many forms of social media to share information about and imagery of "humane" farming's victims. I understand it can be difficult to rock the boat, especially face-to-face with our friends and family. Many vegans and animal activists are all too aware of the stigma of the "preachy vegan extremist" or the "vegangelical" spouting rhetoric and insults. How we come across to those outside our circles is always a concern. Framing our arguments so that the industry is the villain, not the individuals whom we are speaking with, goes a long way towards keeping them from shutting down out of defensiveness. Every person who disregards the information we provide due to the tone of the message is a potential ally for animals lost in the carnage of modern industry.

It is imperative that we consistently speak up. Keep your arguments factual and support them with sources. The animals are depending on us. Share links, post statistics backed with scientific research, spread videos and images from undercover investigations. Volunteer to table and leaflet with local abolitionist minded groups, donate money and time to organizations who are doing valuable work promoting veganism as the moral baseline and, above all, do not remain silent when those around you reiterate the industry's myths, half truths and lies. Spread the truth, speak out. We have so much passion and so many strong voices in our movement; we need only harness them and hone them by presenting a unified message that no animal use is ethical. There is no such thing as an ethical egg when it is produced for human consumption and industry profit.

WORKS CITED

Beach, Marji. Email to Melissa Swanson. 5 Aug. 2011.
"Chicken Care Information." animalplace.org. n.d. Web. 15 Dec. 2011.
Chicken Run Rescue. "Casualties of Urban Agriculture." Facebook.com. 12 Apr. 2011. Web. 18 Apr. 2012. JPEGs.

Clouse, Mary Britton. "Adoption Chronicles." marybrittonclouse.com. Chicken Run Rescue, June 2011. Web. 20 Aug. 2011.

_____. Email to Melissa Swanson. 6 Aug. 2011.

Daniels, Tim. "Light for Laying Chickens." poultrykeeper.com. 4 Nov. 2008. Web. 15 Dec. 2011.

Davis, Karen. "Debeaking Birds Has Got to Stop." *Poultry Press*, Winter (2007). United Poultry Concerns. Web. 21 Feb. 2012.

_____. *Prisoned Chickens, Poisoned Eggs: An Inside Look at the Modern Poultry Industry.* Revised Ed. Summertown, TN: Book Publishing Co., 2009. Print.

Environmental Protection Agency. "What Is a CAFO?" epa.gov. United States Environmental Protection Agency, 17 Jan. 2012. Web. 15 Apr. 2012.

Estevez, Inma. "Ammonia and Poultry Welfare." *Poultry Perspectives* 4.1 (Spring 2002). University of Maryland: Department of Animal and Avian Sciences. Web. 17 Apr. 2012.

Gunter, Andrew. "Rotten Eggs: HSUS and United Egg Producers Enter Agreement That Bird Cages Are Here to Stay." *HuffPost Food Blog.* TheHuffingtonPost.com, Inc., 14 July 2011. Web. 12 Aug. 2011.

"Hatchery Horrors: The Egg Industry's Tiniest Victims." mercyforanimals.org. n.d. Web. 21 Feb. 2012.

Henshock, Colin. Email to Melissa Swanson. 5 Aug. 2011.

"Humane Myth." *Humane Myth Glossary.* Humanemyth.org, n.d. Web. 21 Feb. 2012.

Humane Society of the United States. "Egg Carton Labels: A Brief Guide to Labels and Animal Welfare." humanesociety.org. 8 Oct. 2010. Web. 15 Jan. 2012.

_____. "Details of the Animal Welfare Agreement Between the Humane Society of the United States and the United Egg Producers." humanesociety.org. n.d. Web. 2 Jan. 2012. PDF.

"Humane Society of the U.S. Cuts Deal with United Egg Producers to Seek Federal Law." *Animal People Online.* 30 July 2011. Web. 17 Apr. 2012.

Johnson, Jewel. "A Rare Glimpse Inside a 'Free-Range' Egg Facility." *The Prairie Progress* 8.8 (Spring/Summer 2007). Peaceful Prairie Sanctuary. Web. 18 Apr. 2012.

Joy, Melanie. "Understanding Neocarnism: How Vegan Advocates Can Appreciate and Respond to 'Happy Meat,' Locavorism, and 'Paleo Dieting.'" onegreenplanet.org. One Green Planet, 29 July 2011. Web. 21 Feb. 2012.

Kriese, Thomas. "What to Do When Chickens No Longer Lay Eggs." urbanchickens.net. 24 Jan. 2011. Web. 3 Mar. 2011.

Mench, J.A., and J.C. Swanson. "Developing Science-Based Animal Welfare Guidelines." *Avian Science Website.* University of California, Davis: Animal Science Dept., n.d. Web. 17 Apr. 2012. PDF.

Meunier, Ryan A., and Mickey A. Latour. "Commercial Egg Production and Processing." *Avian Sciences Net.* Purdue University, n.d. Web. 11 Feb. 2011.

Pollan, Michael. "Michael Pollan Talks Meat." Oprah.com. Harpo Productions, 1 Feb. 2011. Web. 15 Dec. 2011.

"Reasons Not to Purchase Chicks from Hatcheries." marybrittonclouse.com. Chicken Run Rescue, n.d. Web. 21 Feb. 2012.

Schafer, David. "Polyface Processing Overview." Uploaded 8 June 2009. *YouTube.* 17 Apr. 2012.

Scheideler, Sheila E., and Sara Shields. "Cannibalism by Poultry." *NebGuide.* University of Nebraska, Lincoln, Feb. 2007. Web. 10 Dec. 2011.

Smith, Rod. "HSUS, UEP Reach Agreement to Transition to Colonies." *Feedstuffs.* Miller Publishing Co., 7 July 2011. Web. 20 Aug. 2011.

"Understanding Heritage Poultry." yellowhousefarmnh.com. n.d. Web. 16 Apr. 2012.

United Poultry Concerns. "'Enriched' Cages for Egg-Laying Hens in the US and EU." upc-online.org. 10 July 2012. Web. 16 Apr. 2012.

_____. "Forced Moulting." upc-online.org. 23 Sept. 2003. Web. 16 Apr. 2012.

The "Dreaded Comparisons" and Speciesism
Leveling the Hierarchy of Suffering
KIM SOCHA

People who advocate for nonhumans sometimes face hostility and ridi-cule from a public who assumes that showing concern for animals indicates lack of concern for humans. In response, activists make direct connections amongst oppressions, arguing that animal and human oppressions are allied, even equal. In the annals of critical animal studies, two works stand out as being especially provocative for daring to compare suffering: Marjorie Spiegel's *The Dreaded Comparison: Human and Animal Slavery* (1996), a comparison of the African slave trade and animal exploitation, and Charles Patterson's *Eternal Treblinka: Our Treatment of Animals and the Holocaust* (2002). While "holocaust," "genocide" and "slavery" are used in animal liberation rhetoric, skeptical audiences are often hostile to expressions that attempt to expose ani-mal exploitation through the filter of human suffering; they are more willing to acknowledge animal abuse if it remains differentiated from that of humans because in a speciesist world, human suffering matters more. Nonetheless, if attended to appropriately, these correlations can guide people to more com-passionate perceptions of nonhumans. But first, the concept of speciesism needs greater integration into popular vernacular.

Spiegel and Patterson's works remain significant not just because they level the hierarchy of suffering for the sake of animals, but because they identify the aspects of *human* nature that lead to hierarchical thinking. However, it is not my intention to offer an overtly academic analysis of these texts, for I want to explore how the dreaded comparisons have succeeded and faltered in both personal and national activist contexts, to come to some final determi-nations as to their ability to help liberate animals, both human and nonhuman. Therein, *The Dreaded Comparison* and *Eternal Treblinka* can be envisioned as books that are just as much about emancipating humans from oppressive behaviors as they are about freeing nonhuman animals from literal bondage.

223

The Veracity of the Dreaded Comparisons

To best understand the dreaded comparisons, I want to start with basic terminology, for although "holocaust," "genocide," and "slavery" have been integrated into animal liberation vernacular, the words' meanings need revisiting to go beyond images of the early American slave trade and World War I, for slavery and genocide are not limited to those historical occurrences. Slavery is almost as old as humankind, as is the ethnocentric (clan) mentality leading to the Holocaust of World War II. Initially, holocaust indicated a sacrifice by fire and has also come to indicate the intentional annihilation of a group of people. I am aware of the controversies surrounding the use of "Holocaust" to refer to the World War II concentration camps because of this early association with sacrificial/religious burnt offerings. However, as noted by the United States Holocaust Memorial Museum, the term, when capitalized, has generally come to be used in reference to the annihilation of European Jews between 1933 and 1945, and that is how I will use it in this essay.

Slavery indicates that one being is the legal property of another. Animals remain legal property today, they are slaughtered en masse, and they are compelled into submission by dominating forces, but their destruction is not toward the ultimate goal of annihilating "in whole or in part, a national, ethnical, racial or religious group," which is how the United Nations General Assembly defined genocide four years after World War II. Nonhumans are destroyed by the billions on a yearly basis not because their oppressors hate them, but because their oppressors are *indifferent* to them.

Consequently, animal activists must destabilize indifference, not hatred. In a 1999 speech, renowned author and Holocaust survivor Elie Wiesel explored that word's import:

> Of course, indifference can be tempting — more than that, seductive. It is so much easier to look away from victims. It is so much easier to avoid such rude interruptions to our work, our dreams, our hopes. It is, after all, awkward, troublesome, to be involved in another person's pain and despair.... Their hidden or even visible anguish is of no interest. Indifference reduces the Other to an abstraction.

Hatred caused the mass killing of Jews during World War II. Nazis were not indifferent to the Jews' fate, yet indifference manifested through worldwide refusal to acknowledge that genocide, with German citizens going about their lives and other countries ignoring rumors of extermination camps or denying admittance to Jewish refugees. (And there must have been some level of hatred in those decisions to ignore the genocide as well; thus, the terms are not so easily differentiated.) Those who eat animals are not acting like Nazis, who exemplify an extreme case of human degeneracy; rather, they seem to be acting like average humans who follow the standard social mores of their society without question. That said, the idea that German soldiers were "just following orders" and that ordinary citizens were unaware of the carnage has come under scrutiny as well. In *Hitler's Willing Executioners*, Daniel Jonah Goldhagen challenges the myth that the Holocaust was an anomalous example of human depravity gone awry. He argues that although German culture did "roughly mirror" the rest of the world, there is much in their history and culture that set the stage for the events of World War II (28–29).

Although the nature of the German people pre–World War II remains nebulous, the numbers in which nonhumans are exploited proves the extent to which the average person in the United States is at least indifferent to nonhuman animal suffering. Even those who claim compassion for animals while still eating them in their abstract states tune out talk of the brutality that led to their food. Food industry animals are not destroyed because profit makers want to eradicate them; rather, they are bred and destroyed by industries that must keep producing them to make money. Generations of sentient beings are born so that another species can slaughter and ingest them. In this way, the trans-species comparisons, while sometimes suitable, are far from ideal.

As Melanie Joy candidly states in *Strategic Action for Animals*, "Animal liberation is *not* human liberation" (16). The animal liberation movement differs from other social movements in three ways: first, the public has a "personal investment" in maintaining a speciesist culture; secondly, animals do not have human voices with which they can attest to their abuse; and lastly, animals are property, in the legal sense (Joy 16–17). Joy's first and last points could apply to Blacks during American slavery. Southern Americans, and some Northerners as well, had personal and financial investments in preserving the slave trade, and their slaves were legal goods. However, as humans, African Americans could speak their oppressor's language. They could bear witness to atrocities perpetrated against them, and even during the slave trade's peak, slaves were declared to be three-fifths person (in other words, partly human) (Joy 20). When the myths of racial difference were challenged, some individuals would not and still do not renounce their bigotry, yet that remaining prejudice does not assuage the reality that there is little to nothing besides external characteristics that differentiate one group of human being from another. We are all *Homo sapiens*.

But other animals are not, and we eat them. We also wear their skins, and their material derivatives surround us. This is unique in the annals of oppression, of both human and nonhuman animals. As an animal advocate, I do not seek elevated legal status for oppressed beings so that they may share cultural space with their past subjugators, as is the case with many historical human liberation movements. (There are exceptions, of course. Marcus Garvey's Black Star Line/Back-to-Africa Movement called for a return to Africa away from Western colonizers.) I want animals to be left alone. Animal abuse is abhorrent regardless of its associations with human abuse, and global animal cruelty is different from slavery and genocide. It is foundational and invisible in a unique way divorced from issues of ethnicity and race.

"Race," as in ethnic identity, is a relatively new concept, coming into wide use during the Enlightenment — though oppression due to other types of dissimilarity did manifest earlier in Europe than the eighteenth century — when the compulsion to classify living organisms and dominate the world were ignited anew (and racism justified that domination, of course). George Fredrickson argues that racism is ultimately about "difference and power," and the concept of "rac*ism*," a term now applied to centuries old injustices, did not develop until the early twentieth century, coming "into common usage in the 1930s when a new word was required to describe the theories on which the Nazis based their persecution of the Jews." When contemporary activists appropriate this terminology of human oppression to inform the public of animal oppression, they may offend or confuse their audiences who do not yet understand the concept of speciesism.

C. Richard King asserts that when activists use the dreaded comparisons, they are "literally trading upon past horrors and dehumanization in hopes of securing rights in the present.... In this context, the marginalized, maligned and maimed compete with one another claims of injury and victimization, a perverse combat takes shape, known colloquially as the Oppression Olympics" (8), a term first coined by Chicana feminist Elizabeth Martínez in the early 1990s. In a speciesist culture, humans will always win the gold medal in the Oppression Olympics. Thus, loaded trans-species terminologies attempt to shed light on animals' current woes without showing any understanding of the historical and contextual circumstances of other oppressed groups. I am not claiming the comparisons invalid in every situation, but acknowledging their limits and looking for ways to make those powerful associations more nuanced and productive.

These considerations evoke another question: Do I (or others, if they are vegan) believe that meat eaters support slavery and genocide, or is such word choice a rhetorical embellishment? My gut response affirms the comparisons. However, this affirmation leads to uncomfortable truths, for this means that some of the people I love and care for are akin to Ku Klux Klaners of early twentieth-century Alabama and Nazis of 1930s Germany. And what does this say of *me*? Although an animal advocate, I also enjoy leisure activities purposely not related to animal issues. I have attended social events with activist friends who forbid "shop talk." We eat at restaurants with vegan options but that also serve animals and their byproducts.

But how can someone become distracted from slavery and genocide? Would I have been, in Wiesel's terms, "indifferent" to Black and Jewish suffering had I been alive during the 19th century and World War II? Does a German citizen's going about her life while Jews were being piled onto transport cars parallel my seeing pigs on a transport truck but doing nothing to stop it at that moment? How many activists are willing to face jail time if they did attempt an on-the-road pig rescue? These are difficult questions to which Tim Wise offers an interesting retort:

> But of course, whether they admit it or not, most all believers in animal rights do recognize a moral and practical difference between people and animals: after all, virtually none would suggest that if you run over a squirrel when driving drunk, that you should be prosecuted for vehicular homicide, the way you would be if you ran over a small child. The only basis for a distinction in these cases is, at root, recognition of a fundamental difference between a child and a squirrel.

Wise offers the caveat that "most," not "all," animal advocates would agree with him, as I am apt to do as well. However, he does not completely answer the question: why do we "recognize a moral and practical difference between people and animals"? I have run over a squirrel while driving, but I have yet to run over a child. When I ran over the squirrel, I cried, I felt terrible, and I've yet to forget having made that mistake, but there were no repercussions in a culture that hunts nonhuman animals — squirrels included — for fun. If I had run over a child, I am sure that I would have cried, felt terrible, but also faced legal sanctions against my error, especially if I was drunk. In other words, despite being vegan, I am speciesist, but I am not willing to accept Wise's proclamation as an ultimate truth as much as it is an observation on *current* cultural norms that need to be challenged and problematized. This is a norm that I and other activists attempt to disrupt, sometimes by using the dreaded comparisons, but more often by getting the word out on speciesism, as detailed in the next section.

The Dreaded Comparisons in Praxis

Last year, I was leafleting anti-rodeo pamphlets in Minneapolis, offering the literature to a man and two women walking down the street. The two women took it and quickly handed it back, explaining that they opposed rodeos and would never attend. Their companion, an African American man, did the same, and he explained why by shouting back to me as he walked away, "I'm against the rodeo because there was a time when Black people were treated like those animals. *We were the rodeo!*" There it was — the dreaded comparison: nonhuman animals are thought of and treated similarly to humans during periods of slavery and genocide, and the oppression and slaughter of nonhumans is as unethical and immoral as that of humans. I yelled back to the man about a book that explores the connection he had made, and I wanted to tell his female companions about *Sistah Vegan*, an anthology by vegan Women of Color who expose the Standard American Diet, widely adopted by Black Americans, as imbricated in our country's racist history and current neo-imperial contexts.

This gentleman made a connection that fueled my activism, yet it is a connection that I am loath to make outside of my restricted activist circle because as a middle-class Euro-American woman, the potential to offend or amuse seems greater than the potential to enlighten. Lisa Kemmerer makes a similar admission in her introduction to *Sister Species: Women, Animals, and Social Justice*: "I am one of those many white, middle-class, female vegans whose voices dominate Western animal activism. My whiteness ... limits my effectiveness as an activist" (3). I fear coming across as patronizing, as yet another guilty white person intent on helping the "less fortunate" because I have the time and resources to do so. And therein lies the ability to amuse as well, for as that person, I am a parody of the self-loathing white activist intent on bridging "the [outmoded] black and white racial paradigm — victim vs. victimizer, the patron and the patronized" (Walsh). My self-censorship is not completely altruistic, however, for it prevents me from having to acknowledge the ways in which I truly am a victimizer and a patronizer by nature of my cultural status as a white-identified person.

A similar instance of dreaded comparison self-censorship occurred when another activist and I were holding a workshop at a local college. A Holocaust survivor would be answering questions during a simultaneous session. My colleague and I felt guilty for taking potential attendees away from this man's assembly, and we wondered if we should tell them to listen to him answer questions instead. We digressed, as the point of this event was for individuals to attend panels they found most interesting. Further, as my colleague suggested, "We have our own Holocaust to expose." I cringed when she said it, and although she felt free to say it because she is Jewish, we decided that this was not the crowd upon which to lay that term, although it felt apt, for the news at that time was reporting stories from South Korea of animals being buried alive by the millions to prevent spread of foot-and-mouth disease and bird flu.

Images of screaming pigs piled upon each other in earthen pits were fresh in our memories. One picture showed an open mouthed pig amongst others of his/her kind staring in horror from an online news source, and I was reminded of Paul Celan's poem "Tenebrae" in which he describes Jews in gas chambers as "clawed and clawing" against each other. I then wondered if that cognitive association was ethically appropriate, for I was comparing the suffering of humans and nonhumans in a culture that sees human animalization as vilification. Likewise, artist Sue Coe writes of her visits to slaughterhouses: "The Holocaust keeps coming to my mind, which annoys the hell out of me ... I am annoyed that I don't have more power in communicating what I've seen apart from stuttering: 'It's like the Holocaust'" (quoted in Patterson 70). Animal advocates may feel guilty for making dreaded comparisons, even when the associations go unspoken. This is because we are speciesist.

Less restrained dreaded comparison projects have failed, but activists can learn from these disappointments. In 2003, People for the Ethical Treatment of Animal's (PETA) began the "Holocaust on Your Plate" campaign, juxtaposing images from concentration camps and factory farms. The traveling demonstration included the words of prominent Jewish activists and writers such as Isaac Bashevis Singer who wrote in his novel *Enemies: A Love Story*: "In relation to them [animals], all people are Nazis, for them it is an eternal Treblinka" (quoted in "Group Blasts PETA"), hence Patterson's book title. Public response to PETA's campaign was largely hostile. The Anti-Defamation League (ADL), with a stated mission to fight "anti–Semitism and all forms of bigotry," was especially critical. Eventually, PETA President Ingrid Newkirk issued an apology, though not a retraction of the project's message. Further, Spiegel wound up suing the organization for appropriating her idea for a similarly controversial campaign that compared the animal-industrial complex to the Euro-American slave trade.

Another PETA staff member, Kathy Guillermo, stated that "we would rather trouble people in the hope that they may consider that there is not a hierarchy of suffering" (quoted in King 4). But there *is* a hierarchy of suffering, and in the end, PETA's campaign inadvertently confirmed rather than challenged it. When a Cornell University student yelled "Jews are not pigs" during one of PETA's installments, s/he was right (King 3). Jews are not pigs. No human is a pig, but pigs still matter. PETA's desire that there wasn't a hierarchy of suffering does not make it so, and comparing troubling photos of transspecies anguish does not ensure that people will make the cognitive and ethical leaps needed to unite the images.

In defense of PETA's dreaded comparison campaigns, for they also campaigned using images of slavery and Native American genocide, Joi Marie Probus argues that its critics are missing the point, for the images are meant to "evoke compassion, to help people empathize with" animals as they would with humans (56). This was undoubtedly PETA's objective, but humans don't work that way. Rather, the majority of viewers just got angry. In *Eternal Treblinka*, Patterson observes that "[c]alling people animals is always an ominous sign because it sets them up for humiliation, exploitation, and murder" (28). Angela P. Harris echoes this contention by noting that "[t]o be moved from the human to the nonhuman side ... is to be made a being with no moral claims, a being whose body is only flesh, vulnerable to any kind of treatment for any reason, or for no reason" (22). In Western cultural, to animalize humans is to denigrate them, and pretending that we do not live in a speciesist world is unproductive. When speciesists saw "Holocaust on Your Plate," they saw Jews being compared to animals in a culture that views animalization as degradation. PETA skipped the necessary qualifying and contextualizing needed to make the comparisons valid and meaningful. In other words, they've yet to effectively introduce their audiences to the term "speciesism."

PETA inarguably believes that "any publicity is good publicity," but they'd be hard pressed to prove it in this case. In her analysis of the campaign, Carrie Freeman, who *does* believe in its message, concludes that it did little to promote positive dialogue, for when media outlets addressed the campaign, they reported on "the public's outrage over the comparison of human lives to animals rather than a willingness to deeply investigate the ethics of their own dietary choices or the destructive logic of the constructed human/animal dichotomy" (21). King agrees, noting that while it does "cause trouble," the campaign's reliance on shock almost assures that the *import* of its message, though not necessarily the campaign, will soon be forgotten (1; 2).

I spend the majority of my social time with vegan animal advocates. This causes me to forget how the rest of the world thinks about, or does not think about, animals. Therefore, it is jarring when I come across unwitting speciesist behavior and rhetoric. Although a tricky prospect, activists should occasionally think like speciesists. If PETA had done so, they "would not have mocked the public's current humanist value system (often based in religion) which prioritizes human life over nonhuman animal life" (Freeman 20). In an ironic sense, the very need for a "Holocaust on Your Plate" campaign should have alerted PETA to the reasons the campaign would not work. In the end, they enforced rather than troubled the assumption that animalization debases human dignity. It was successful in that they got attention and people are still discussing the campaign, but they have yet to report, likely because they cannot, the number of people who went vegan or challenged their own speciesism after seeing it.

PETA also failed to consider the possession question: who owns the memory of the Holocaust? Despite there being non–Jewish victims of the Nazis, King argues that due to the vast numbers in which they were persecuted, Jews have made the commitment to safeguard "the memory of those who sacrificed so much, while protecting exceptionalism of the Holocaust from trivialization" (5). In an analysis of artistic representations of the World War II genocide, artist Ruth Liberman likewise asserts that using Holocaust imagery to evoke alternative, non–Holocaust implications will be seen as trite to contemporary viewers, and the alternative meanings that the artist hopes to suggest can easily become lost in the intense emotional and psychological weight of the Holocaust (93). Liberman continues by noting that the viewer will ask one question only: "[H]ow does the work represent the Holocaust?" (97). The other topic that the artistic image attempts to highlight vanishes. During PETA's campaign, people saw Holocaust representations in much greater numbers than they saw animal abuse. In our current cultural contexts, perhaps in any situation, "Holocaust on Your Plate" is a trivialization of human suffering, and it is ineffective in emphasizing animal suffering.

It is also disingenuous. In one image, an emaciated Holocaust survivor is posed against an emaciated nonhuman (so emaciated that it is hard to determine what type of animal s/he is). This dreadfully neglected animal is not reflective of the overfed, plump creatures regularly slaughtered on farms. "Food" cows' lives are deplorable, and they are often internally ulcerated and diseased from corn overload, but "food" animals are most certainly fat when slaughtered. PETA used an excessive image to entrance viewers, but it is not always the extreme that shocks people into action. The ordinary, mundane consistency and invisibility of animal exploitation is more horrifying than isolated images of extreme abuse that can be easily countered with alternative photographs of healthy-looking cows chowing down on grass.

A final problem with the campaign is the messenger. After years of outrageous publicity stunts, PETA is not a credible organization (Freeman 17). They cannot have naked women in cages on Monday, naked celebrities on billboards on Tuesday, naked women on grills on Wednesday and still be able to foster solicitous, responsible reconsideration of the most horrific genocide in modern Western history on Thursday. In kind, their reputation makes them incapable of recontextualizing Native and African American history with photo comparisons and quotations from prominent individuals who may or may not have ever cared about animals. As A. Breeze Harper affirms, "I feel that PETA's campaign strategies often fail to give a historical context for why they use certain images that are connected to a painful history of racially motivated violence against particular nonwhite, racialized humans" ("Introduction" xiv). The dreaded comparisons are difficult to speak and to hear, and audiences will naturally consider who is doing the comparing. As Harper reminds us, when a predominately white organization from a predominately white movement offers "racialized humans" as metaphors, viewers will likely be more upset than transformed. Further, it is likely to assume that PETA simply did not care what "racialized humans" thought, if such humans were not their target demographic.

The man who proclaimed to me that Black people "were the rodeo" echoes another man quoted in Spiegel's book: "My people were the first laboratory animals in America" (70). For the dreaded comparisons to have meaning, those who feel that historical connection to an oppressive history need to voice them. When made by "nonwhite, racialized humans," as opposed to the so-called racially "unmarked," the comparisons are not dreaded, they are legitimate and compelling. When PETA appropriates the experiences of Native and African Americans, they are trading on tragic histories while also limiting those cultures to tragedy alone. It is painfully obvious to any observer that PETA is not interested in the rich cultural traditions of people indigenous to the Americas and Africa; they are just interested in the analogical possibilities of their subjugation. When white activists hijack other oppressions, they may face (not necessarily unwarranted) accusations of insensitivity. This does not help animals.

In Harris's "Should People of Color Support Animal Rights?," she notes, as I have argued above, that the dreaded comparisons ignore historical specificities as they pretend that all oppressions are the same. However, she goes a step further by explaining that when the animal rights movement enters the Oppression Olympics, it does so with the subtle implication that those historical subjugations—of Blacks, Native Americans and Jews—no longer exist, thereby emphasizing the image of animal advocates as unrefined, unaware single-issue activists who are ignorant of the ways in which racism has not been eradicated as much as it has been reformatted and recast (25). The distorted worldviews and social ills that led to slavery, the Holocaust and the destruction of Native American tribes prevail today. Rather than disregard the continued culture war upon, for example, the African American community, animal activists may want to consider volunteering their time to the struggles from which they are so willing to borrow their metaphors.

For example, I workshop with incarcerated youth on a weekly to bi-weekly basis to contest the school-to-prison pipleline that plagues Minnesota's urban areas. These youths, almost without exception, come from Black, Latino/a and Native communities. I am a member of the Minnesota branch of the National Organization for the Reform of Marijuana Laws (NORML) because drug laws in the U.S. unfairly target young black males for imprisonment. Finally, having worked in the past with survivors of sexual abuse and domestic assault, I currently volunteer with a restorative justice program that supports recently paroled sexual offenders to lower recidivism rates of sexual violence. Even volunteering with one of these types of organizations can help animal advocates see that oppression does not begin and end with nonhumans, and by working directly with other oppressed groups, we can see that our activism is, whether we know it or not, intimately connected to other forms of domination.

Although PETA's campaign has passed, the imagery and the metaphors have not. I regularly encounter "slavery" and "genocide" rhetoric in both scholarship and activist commentary. Continued use of these terms is what led me to consider how "dreaded" these comparisons are/should be. I have not rehashed PETA's campaign only to admonish past wrongs, but to nurture responsible outreach for others and myself, for I admit to irresponsibly wielding the dreaded comparisons in the past.

After a speciesism presentation that I gave at my college, a young man approached me to contest closing factory farms, noting that the meat industry is important to the economy, and too many people would be out of work if it was destroyed. I explained that the same was said about the abolishment of American slavery, that the economy would collapse if slaves were emancipated. I argued that financial motives do not justify enslavement. Ownership of working bodies is always good if you are not among the oppressed nor sensitive to their situation. Free labor beyond upkeep costs benefits profit makers financially, but that does not morally justify slavery. The animal consumption industry is based on the ownership and exploitation of bodies upon which one group of animal claims ownership of another. I concluded by declaring, "This is slavery, and if you eat meat, you support slavery." To some activists, this comment may not sound scandalous, but it was to someone attending my lecture primarily because his anthropology teacher told him to. He was offended by my remark, but I pressed him anyway: "Do you agree that factory farms claim animal bodies as products to be bought and sold?" He affirmed that reality. I concluded, "How is that not slavery?" While I was sure he would say "because they're animals," he didn't, simply concluding, "I have no response to that. I'll just shut up." I felt triumphant for a moment, a reaction that soon gave way to the regret of lost opportunity. My activism is premised upon fostering compassionate perception of sentient beings, not shutting down dialogue with sensationalistic accusations.

In *Speciesism*, Joan Dunayer argues that to treat nonhuman suffering "less seriously than human suffering and death is speciesist" (57). This is true, but we should not pretend that they are the same thing, as Dunayer herself uses many casual references to slavery and genocide in her study while dredging up the nagging problem posed, again, by Wise: if "factory farming and eating the products of factory farming are literally the equivalent to human genocide,.... [T]hen, to be consistent, [animal advocates] would have to argue for the criminal prosecution of all meat-eaters, and War Crimes Tribunals for anyone even remotely connected to the process." I do not believe that either Dunayer or most other advocates are calling for tribunals. This is why our use of such history-laden references needs to be more thoughtful. Animal advocates absolutely have a duty to treat animal suffering as seriously as human suffering, but we must also acknowledge that it is serious in a extraordinary way, and we are challenging a different set of cultural assumptions than were abolitionists in nineteenth-century America.

Slavery and ethnocentrism are possibly congenital to the human condition, however much we now know them to be inexcusable, but slavery and genocide concern the human animal, and Western culture has not yet experienced an enlightenment period through which the human/animal binary has dissolved. Indeed, there is evidence of slavery and oppression in the history of nearly all cultures known to anthropologists. Even today, battles for human dignity continue to be fought in the name of social justice, and when won by the righteous, once-warring human factions have a chance of coexistence; this is not the case with animals. Animals do not need integration into human society. Rather, humans need humans to get their forks, scalpels and prying eyes out of nonhuman animals' lives.

As explored above, animalization debases humans, but once the smog of ignorance clears, all humans are of the same species. We can reproduce with others of our species, no matter how dissimilar we look, and we can discover each other's languages. We can also learn how speciesism uniquely manifests in other cultures, from Zulu torturing and mutilating bulls, to South Koreans beating dogs to death for their meat, to Mexican cock fighting, to American dog fighting and fast food indulgences. Throughout history, both oppressors and oppressed have been speciesist, and this word needs more press before campaigns such as PETA's have a chance at lasting significance:

> I hope that the word speciesism soon will be as familiar to the general public as racism and sexism are today.... Enslavement is wrong, murder is wrong, and causing innocent beings to suffer is wrong. Fully as much as humans, all nonhumans are entitled to life, freedom, and other basic rights. Humans deny this for only one reason: speciesism [Dunayer 160–61].

Animal advocates must subvert human perception of nonhuman animals, but before using the dreaded comparisons to do so, we have to consider ways to introduce people to speciesism. With that term more widely understood, activists pave the way for the cognitive association that occurs between the image of the emaciated human and the emaciated cow.

Activists must continue to reflect on the animal liberation movement's singularity, as opposed to plugging the word "animal" into past oppressions, which feeds the stereotype of the politically and intellectually unsophisticated advocate. In the introduction to Michael Bakunin's *God and the State*, Paul Avrich comments on the revolutionary's refusal to accept "the view that social change depends upon the gradual unfolding of 'objective' historical conditions," and he cites Bakunin's warning that "'[n]o theory, no ready-made system, no book that has ever been written will save the world'" (vi). Bakunin's vision of liberation limits over-analysis of the past. More recently, *Green is the New Red* author Will Potter explores the U.S. government's repression and stigmatization of animal and environmental activists. Although his title alludes to 1950 America's "Red Scare," he restricts the association in terms comparable to Bakunin's: "There is much to be gained by putting [things] in historical context and recognizing patterns of government repression, yet there is a danger in trying to fit contemporary experiences into a historical mold — the analogy must end when change begins. There is nothing inevitable about history repeating itself" (248). Potter also cites expressive passages from Martin Luther King, Jr.'s "I Have a Dream" speech and "Letter from a Birmingham" jail, encasing King's eloquent rhetoric in ideas and situations particular to the animal liberation movement. These wisely chosen passages emphasize aspects of human nature that allow tyranny to thrive: indifference, apathy, ignorance, denial. Potter does not use King's words to compare Black humans to non-humans, but to expose the human attributes that foster domination. This is a productive use of history. Similarly, Spiegel and Patterson's studies remain relevant because they offer what disconnected quotations and image contrasts cannot — extensive analysis and contextualization of the past.

Enduring Messages of Spiegel and Patterson's Texts

The Dreaded Comparison primarily covers the African slave trade in the U.S. It does not offer an all-encompassing overview of slavery from ancient civilizations onward. Thus, it lacks the sweeping historical focus that could better emphasize how embedded the "right" to own other bodies is in human history. Slavery did not start in seventeenth-century Europe and America, and it is not the shame of the U.S. alone, but of any culture that took part in slave trades. Further, Frederickson argues that the "presumption that dark pigmentation inspired instant revulsion on the part of light-skinned Europeans [in the late Middle Ages] is, if not completely false, at least highly misleading." Spiegel does not offer this history. Instead, she begins with the European conquest of the Americas. In kind, *Dreaded Comparison* often falls into the trap of fetishizing all cultures as Edenic before the arrival of Christian explorers, tacitly inferring that animals lived in harmony with humankind and that they were not exploited by anyone except Euro-Americans. This is not true, further enforcing the mission of activists to subvert assumptions as old as humanity, assumptions with no cultural or geographical boundaries.

Still, Spiegel's comparisons are more effective that PETA's because she has textual support to explain the photographs of dog muzzles and slave muzzles (39), dog collars and slave collars (42), a syphilitic chimpanzee and a casualty of the Tuskegee Syphilis Study (69). Imagistic moments such as these successfully demonstrate "that the slavery-related sufferings of black people are often paralleled by the sufferings of animals lost in the machinery of modern institutionalized cruelty" (Spiegel 44). Spiegel proves that the methods used to contain and restrain nonhuman animals have been used upon humans, but the similarities do not end there:

> Both humans and animals share the ability to suffer from restricted freedom of movement, from the loss of social freedom, and to experience pain at the loss of a loved one. Both groups suffer or suffered from their common capacity to be terrified by being hunted, tormented, or injured..... And both blacks, under the system of slavery, and animals were driven to a state of total psychic and physical defeat... (With animals, of course, this continues today in its most extreme form.) [31].

When I think of my failed dreaded comparison with the student who attended my lecture, I wish I had paraphrased Spiegel because hers is the message I want to spread, not accusations. I could have even loaned the young man a copy of the book, encouraging his understanding of interconnected oppressions. Martin Rowe's appraisal of Spiegel's book summarizes its lesson that "we should recognize the abuse of power wherever it is and whoever it is upon, unmask it, and stop it" (Rowe). Sharing that truth is more useful than calling someone a pro-slavery Nazi. The lesson in *Dreaded Comparison* is a challenge to oppression, more palatable to speciesist audiences, and it opens the door for coalition building with human-centered social justice organizations.

This coalition building must go beyond mere rhetoric, as noted. In "Challenging Whiteness in the Animal Advocacy Movement," Anthony J. Nocella II speaks to "the value of being intersectional, multi-movement based, and engaged in challenging all forms of domination in theory and practice," as effective animal advocacy "is as much about being vegan as it is about actively reflecting and engaging against all forms of oppression, including racism ... prisons and poverty" (143). He further emphasizes that this intersectionality should not be used to pave the way to the more/most important issue of animal liberation, nor should our other-than-animal-rights activism be used to recruit new vegans. To wit, when I work with young Black males in a local prison, certain situations arise that cause me to identify as a vegan animal liberation activist, as when we talk about our favorite foods. At those moments, I do not reprimand them for missing the animal entrees that await outside the prison walls. In contrast, I rally *with* them in the hopes that they will be given an opportunity to leave their confinement and enjoy the steak and gravy or chicken parmesan that their mothers will lovingly prepare for them. However, when my turn comes to discuss my favorite foods, I *do* extol the virtues of vegan pizza and fresh fruits and vegetables. Quite often, my feedback elicits questions such as, "What's vegan?," and "Is it hard not to eat animals?" I also get comments such as, "That's really cool," "You must really love animals!," and "I wish we had better food to eat here in the jail." If nothing else, moments like this open up discussion of issues such as food justice, causing these young men to consider why their communities are rife with liquor and convenience stores, rather than fruit stands and community gardens.

Consequently, I believe other activists of all sorts would do well to consider how their main advocacy focus is buttressed by other forms of domination and exploitation and reflect on volunteering their time to issues that initially appear outside of their purview. And the animal advocate in me hopes that once humans see their connection to nonhumans, speciesism has a better chance of being identified and subverted.

Trans-species analogies are not fast food activism. The dreaded comparisons can work in select activist contexts when there is time for historical perspective and careful word choice. A recent interaction confirmed this for me when a non-activist friend told me that she still doesn't buy the connection between women and animals that Carol J. Adams establishes in *The Sexual Politics of Meat: A Feminist Vegetarian Critical Theory*. When I asked my friend if she had read the book yet, she admitted she hadn't. We laughed, neither of us surprised that she wasn't getting a connection explored in a book she hadn't read. Sometimes, activism means persuading people to put in analytical groundwork to make new cognitive associations. Images only go so far, especially when people would rather look away from tragedy.

Patterson's *Eternal Treblinka* tells a similar tale. He gives a more holistic view of human history than Spiegel, arguing that animal exploitation began when hunter-gatherers started domesticating plants and animals (6). His more comprehensive historical narrative demonstrates speciesism's trans-cultural quality, showing that it even exists among those victimized by colonial expansion. Like Spiegel, he explains that industrialization has appreciably increased oppression of all species. For example, Patterson charges anti–Semitic auto mogul Henry Ford with inventing the technology, originally used to manufacture cars, with which Germans killed Jews (73). He compares the similar means by which Jews and nonhuman animals were slaughtered, noting that

> [o]ne bitterly ironic feature of killing operations [in concentration camps] is their attempt to make the killing more "humane." By "humane," the operatives mean they want the killing to be done more efficiently and to be less stressful on the killers. The truth is, of course, they're not really interested in being "humane." If they were, they wouldn't be killing in the first place [132].

Patterson's message is that you can't have killing and be humane too. Animal advocates agree, and just as we want speciesism to become more widely understood, we should enrich our own understanding of racism and ethnocentrism so that we do not diminish the reality of human oppression by whittling it down to mere metaphor. A critique of Patterson's point can do just that. For example, it is often the most marginalized American workers (i.e., immigrants and those living in poverty) who work in slaughterhouses, a work environment with the "highest employee turnover rate in North America" ("Slaughter-houses"). This high turnover rate was not the case with Nazi henchman. (Again, see Daniel Jonah Goldhagen's *Hitler's Willing Executioners: Ordinary Germans and the Holocaust* for further exploration of that issue.)

Like Spiegel, Patterson compares and contrasts human and animal suffering, but also like Spiegel, he is more successful when exposing the shortcomings of a humanity that lets tragedy occur unhindered. As Harper says of his book, "Patterson's research conveys an example of how we in the West constitute a society based on violence, oppression, misery and domination that has led to an ongoing societal trauma from the micro-scale to the macro-scale for all of us — whether we are the oppressors, the oppressed or both" ("Social Justice" 34). Harper homes in on the dreaded comparisons' power: they can level the hierarchy of suffering by considering not just the victims of oppression, but the victimizers, both those directly responsible for inhumanity and those indifferent to it. Harper also emphasizes that one can be both an oppressor and of the oppressed. This breaks down the typical victim/perpetrator binary, and it is useful in encouraging others to expand their ideas of what abuse of power looks like, from slavery, to the massacre of indigenous peoples, to the overt barbarity of concentration camps to the subtleties of our diets.

With this change in focus, the "Oppression Olympics" may decrease, and frustrated activists would do well to remember that the "liberal rights project has a constantly moving horizon: as we continually 'widen the circle of the we,' we learn to recognize that the social arrangements taken for granted today as normal, natural, and necessary are always historically and socially constructed" (Harris 25). In the meantime, rather than fetishize and analogize suffering and wield loaded terms without proper context, the most inspiring lessons from Spiegel and Patterson's books are about human nature, the good *and* the bad.

The hierarchy of suffering can begin to level when "speciesism" is more widely understood. In the activist/public dynamic, the dreaded comparisons should be suggested through dialogue focused not only on violence, but on human response (or non-response) to violence. As Rowe explains, Spiegel does not argue that "we need to 'raise' animals to a condition of being human or that we should 'lower' ourselves by recognizing that we are all brutes to each other." Rather, Spiegel and Patterson use the dreaded comparisons to help readers recognize our ability to confront oppression because we know that the world doesn't have to be this way. Only then do we have something positive to propose, as opposed to more images of suffering.

WORKS CITED

Anti-Defamation League. "About the Anti-Defamation League." Adl.org. Anti-Defamation League, 2011. Web. 12 Aug. 2011.

_____."Holocaust Imagery and Animal Rights." 2 Aug. 2005. Web. 15 May 2011.

Avrich, Paul. Introduction. *God and the State.* By Michael Bakunin. 1871. Mineola, NY: Dover, 1970. Print.

Celan, Paul. "Tenebrae." Trans. Michael Hamburger. *Art from the Ashes: A Holocaust Anthology.* Ed. Lawrence L. Langer. New York: Oxford University Press, 1995. Print.

Dunayer, Joan. *Speciesism.* Derwood, MD: Ryce, 2004. Print.

Feinstein, Steve, ed. *Absence/Presence: Critical Essays on the Artistic Memory of the Holocaust.* Syracuse, NY: Syracuse University Press, 2005. Print.

Frederickson, George M. *Racism: A Short History.* Princeton, NJ: Princeton University Press, 2003. N. pag. Kindle file.

Freeman, Carrie. "Who's Harming Whom? A PR Ethical Case Study of PETA's Holocaust on Your Plate Campaign." Unpublished paper presented at the annual meeting of the International Communication Association, San Francisco, CA, 23 May 2007. *Allacademic.com.* All Academic, Inc., 2011. 15 May 2011.

Goldhagen, Daniel Jonah. *Hitler's Willing Executioners: Ordinary Germans and the Holocaust.* New York: Random House, 1997. Print.

"Group Blasts PETA 'Holocaust' Project." CNN.com. Cable News Network, 28 Feb. 2003. Web. 20 June 2011.

Harper, A. Breeze. "Introduction: The Birth of the Sistah Vegan Project." Harper xiii–xix. Print.

_____, ed. *Sistah Vegan: Black Female Vegans Speak on Food, Identity, Health, and Society.* New York: Lantern, 2010. Print.

_____. "Social Justice Beliefs and Addiction to Uncompassionate Consumption." Harper 20–41.

Harris, Angela P. "Should People of Color Support Animal Rights?" *Journal of Animal Law* 5 (2009): 15–32. Print.

Joy, Melanie. *Strategic Action for Animals: A Handbook on Strategic Movement Building, Organizing, and Activism for Animal Liberation.* New York: Lantern, 2008. Print.

King, C. Richard. "Troubling Images: PETA's "Holocaust on Your Plate" and the Limits of Image Events." *Enculturation: A Journal of Writing, Rhetoric and Culture* 6.2 (2009). Web. 20 June 2011.

Kemmerer, Lisa. "Introduction." Kemmerer 1–43. Print.

_____, ed. *Sister Species: Woman, Animals and Social Justice.* Urbana: University Illinois Press, 2011. Print.

Liberman, Ruth. "Matters of Interpretation: One Artist's Commentary." Feinstein 93–106. Print.

Nocella, Anthony J. "Challenging Whiteness in the Animal Advocacy Movement." *Journal for Critical Animal Studies* 10.1 (2012): 142–154. PDF.

Patterson, Charles. *Eternal Treblinka: Our Treatment of Animals and the Holocaust.* New York: Lantern, 2002. Print.

Potter, Will. *Green Is the New Red.* San Francisco: City Lights, 2011. Print.

Probus, Joi Marie. "Young, Black and Vegan." Harper 53–57. Print.

Rowe, Martin. "Buck Fever." *Boston Book Review* 1 June 1998. Martin-Rowe.com. Martin Rowe, 2011. 15 June 2011.

"Slaughterhouses: Overview." *Global Action Network.* n.d. Web. 5 Dec. 2011.

Spiegel, Marjorie. *The Dreaded Comparison: Human and Animal Slavery*. New York: Mirror Books/IDEA, 1996. Print.

United Nations General Assembly. "Convention on the Prevention and Punishment of the Crime of Genocide, New York, 9 December 1948." UN.org. United Nations, 2011. Web. 18 June 2011.

United States Holocaust Memorial Museum. "Frequently Asked Questions." USHMM.org 14 Jan. 2008. Web. 26 Oct. 2011.

Walsh, Joan. "Confessions of a Former Self-Hating White Person." Salon.com. Salon Media Group, 17 Feb. 2000. Web. 20 Oct. 2011.

Wiesel, Elie. "The Perils of Indifference." 12 Apr 1999. Americanrhetoric.com. American Rhetoric, 2011. Web. 18 June 2011.

Wise, Tim. "Animal Whites: PETA and the Politics of Putting Things in Perspective." *Tim wise.org*. 13 Aug. 2005. Web. 2 Dec. 2012.

Animal Enterprise Acts and the Prosecution of the "SHAC 7"
An Insider's Perspective
AARON ZELLHOEFER

The history of cancer research has been a history of curing cancer in the mouse. We have cured mice of cancer for decades, and it simply did not work in humans.— Dr. Richard Klausner, Director, National Institutes of Health

All of the studies are so screwed up all the time because no one cares. No one cares if stuff gets done right and there's always problems. I feel so sorry for all of the animals. How would you like to be locked in a cage all of the time with nothing to do?—An employee of Huntingdon Life Sciences

The risks posed by SHAC and its ilk should not be underestimated. Imagine the impact if SHAC tactics were used by those opposed to various other industries from defense, to mining, to oil, to timber, to who knows what else.—Mark Bibi, General Counsel for Huntingdon Life Sciences

The No. 1 domestic terrorism threat is the eco-terrorism, animal-rights movement.—John Lewis, former FBI Deputy Assistant Director of Counterterrorism

The following essay is my best attempt to present the context, background, and effects of the passages of the Animal Enterprise Protection Act (AEPA) and the later, even more draconian Animal Enterprise Terrorism Act (AETA). These patently unconstitutional laws, intended to intimidate and silence the animal rights and environmental movements, were tested on the activist leadership and volunteers who would come to be known as the SHAC 7. Part of the anti-vivisection movement that organized campaigns against Huntingdon Life Sciences (HLS) under the banner of Stop Huntingdon Animal Cruelty (SHAC), these defendants were prosecuted as an example to all would-be protesters against animal abuse. The ripple effects of their lengthy prison sentences and the government's continuing confidence in the tactic of scaring social movements into silence are still impacting animal rights efforts today. As a long-time volunteer with SHAC, a co-founder of Support Vegans in the Prison System (Support VIPS), and the partner of Kevin Kjonaas, who was sentenced to six years in prison as the ringleader of SHAC, I have had an insider's view of these fights to protect civil liberties. With this essay, I hope to clarify this complex, frightening, and ongoing chapter in our movement's history so that animal advocates of all kinds understand the powers that we are up against and to motivate my fellow liberators to continue fighting for justice, rather than cowering under our nation's unjustifiable laws.

When an Agent Knocks

In August 2005, an FBI special agent (name redacted) drove to the victim's house. The victim, Pamela Ostroff, was an attorney for Roche Molecular Systems, Inc. She lived in a two story home in Oakland, California's Piedmont neighborhood, an upper class neighborhood on Greenbank Avenue. There had been previous animal rights related activity in her neighborhood. Animal rights activists from SHAC, an international campaign to close the contract research organization HLS, had leafleted in her neighborhood. They knocked on her front door wanting to talk to her, for she would not respond to them at her place of business. She still would not talk to them, so they passed out leaflets to her neighbors detailing the cruel practices at HLS and explaining that their neighbor refused to talk to the protesters. The activists wanted her neighbors to contact Ostroff, knowing her peers would more likely be in the position to have a heart to heart talk with her about getting Roche to pull their business from HLS. The agent drove to the house likely knowing what to expect. Ostroff had called earlier in the day and the FBI arrived even before the Piedmont police (Garretson).

The crime hardly seemed a federal case, or even a crime, for that matter. Activists had hung a banner in the neighborhood with Ostroff's contact information and the words "Stop Huntingdon Animal Cruelty." SHAC activists accompanied this banner hang by the aforementioned handing out of leaflets and protesting in the neighborhood.

Years ago, the FBI would likely have dismissed the request to come out to the suburbs to investigate individuals handing out leaflets. However, the FBI has diverted resources from investigating violent criminals in order to persecute nonviolent animal rights and environmental activists in this country. This shift in focus leads to these pressing questions: Why are some animal rights activists treated differently than other activists in the legal system? Why are activists being charged with laws that would not be available to law enforcement had the "crime" not been committed in the name of animal rights? Why are some of these activists given disproportionately long sentences — *tenfold larger than the sentence of someone who is found guilty of committing the exact same crimes for non-political purposes?* Why are activists threatened with multiple life sentences for crimes of property destruction that never physically harm anyone?

After September 11, 2001, the FBI reassigned 2,400 agents and highly skilled white collar crime investigators to domestic terrorism investigations. An investigation by the *Seattle Post-Intelligencer*, which relied on former FBI officials, revealed that the agency knew of pervasive fraud in the mortgage industry and its potential for national and international economic crises. Instead of having those 2,400 agents investigating a massive fraud scheme, which assisted in the global economic crisis of 2008, they used those resources to investigate a banner hang (Potter 240).

Those who have been on the receiving side of protests from the animal rights movement have lobbied for years for tougher sentences and more laws to restrict protests, campaigns, acts of civil disobedience, and also acts of disobedience deemed to be uncivil. In particular, lobbyists for the pharmaceutical industry looked for ways to dismantle SHAC, the grassroots group dedicated to ending the horrific animal experimentation at HLS.

The Story of SHAC, the Failure of Animal Research and the Cruelty at HLS

SHAC started in 1999 in England. The individuals who formed SHAC had just finished several campaigns which saw victories for animals and doors closed for several breeding companies. In 1996, a campaign was formed against Consort kennels, a breeding facility which bred dogs for vivisection. In July, 1997, after a ten month campaign, the facility was closed and 200 beagles were rescued and put into loving homes. Next targeted was Hillgrove farm, the last UK breeder of cats for vivisection. In August of 1999, after an eighteen month campaign, Hillgrove farm closed and 800 cats were re-homed. HLS was chosen as the next target.

Huntingdon Life Sciences is Europe's largest Contract Research Organization (CRO). A CRO is a facility where pesticide/fungicide, agriculture, industrial, chemical and pharmaceutical companies — basically, whoever wants something tested, but do not have the ability or time to do it themselves — get their products tested on nonhumans. These products are usually *not* required to be tested on animals; the FDA requires only that over-the-counter drugs and food additives be tested on animals. HLS has done tests for some of the world's largest pharmaceutical companies. As many see it, these tests hold little to any scientific value. Dr. Tony Page reports in *Vivisection Unveiled* that "animals do not suffer from all the same diseases as humankind. Of the *30,000* known human diseases ... animals would seem to share only *1.16 percent* of them" (6). So, while animal experimentation may ultimately be useless in bettering human health, this also means that it is fairly easy to find a nonhuman species to pass safety tests and get products on the market as fast as possible for financials purposes.

Some of those who have used HLS are GlaskoSmithKline, Novartis, Bayer, Pfizer and Roche, and some of the drugs they have released onto the market have had disastrous results. Just because the FDA requires new pharmaceutical drugs be tested on animals does not mean that they will lead to positive results for humans. Quite the opposite. During the time they were working with HLS, these pharmaceutical giants released "safely passed" animal-tested drugs that went on to have adverse results in humans. A sampling of those failures follow.

Accutane (or Roaccutane) resulted in at least 240 suicides and Baycol (cerivastatin or Lipobay) caused over 100 deaths. In fact, Bayer AG has agreed to pay $1.08 billion to settle 2,825 Baycol lawsuits out of court. Other failures include Redux (commonly known as Fen Phen) and its sister drug Pondimin (fenfluramine); these notorious diet drugs produced by American Health Products, a subsidiary of Wyeth Pharmaceuticals, have led to 123 deaths in the U.S. ("Fen Phen Recalled"). Duract (Wyeth-Ayerst Laboratories), approved in July 1997, was removed from the market in 1998 after causing 68 deaths; Propulsid, a heartburn medicine released by Janssen Pharmaceutica, led to "381 cases of irregular heartbeats[,] 80 of which resulted in death" ("Propsulid"). In September 2001, a Claiborne County Circuit Court jury in Mississippi awarded $10 million to 155 plaintiffs who sued Janssen and their parent company Johnson & Johnson ("Janssen Pharmaceutica"). Finally, Rezulin (troglitazone) was a diabetes drug manufactured by Warner-Lambert to treat type-2 diabetes, causing at least 400 deaths as of 2002 (Drug Recall Writer).

During the period of SHAC's ascendance, these high profile lawsuits and drug failures led to fast growing knowledge of the fallacies of vivisection and animal testing in general. There is clear reason to be confident that what works for other animals may not work for humans, and vice versa.

Huntingdon Life Science director Dr. Ralph Heywood stated that "the best guess for the correlation of adverse reactions in man and animal toxicity data is somewhere between five and twenty-five percent" (quoted in Greek, Greek and Goodall 56). Translation: animal research, when applied to humans, can have up to a 95 percent failure rate. Likewise, in 2004, former FDA head Commissioner Lester M. Crawford acknowledged this high failure rate of animal research, with a slight variation on the failure percentage: "Just 8 percent of (animal-tested) drugs that enter Phase 1 and 2 trials reach the marketplace and half of products fail in the late stage Phase 3 trials" (quoted in "Animal Experimentation"). Again, in plain English, this means that animal research has somewhere between a 92 percent and 95 percent failure rate. This makes sense. Human and nonhuman animal bodies are different. A dog could drink from a puddle on the street and not get sick — if a human animal did that, s/he could get violently ill. Even Dr. Charles Mayo, founder of the world renowned Mayo Clinic, and one of America's most skilled and highly respected surgeons, once stated, "I know of no achievement through vivisection, no scientific discovery, that could not have been obtained without such barbarism and cruelty. *The whole thing is evil"* (quoted In "Animal Experimentation," emphasis added).

In *Targeted: The Anatomy of an Animal Rights Attack*, two supporters of animal research tell other researchers how to deal with an animal rights attack at any given university. The researchers, Lorenz Otto Lutherer and Margaret Sheffield Simon tell other researchers how to deal with a debate over animal research: "[R]ehearse three to five main points that can be made and repeated; and take the high moral ground, understanding that the debate will hinge upon emotional issues and not upon science" (94). However, it turns out that animal testing is not much about science either.

Animal research causes pain, suffering, distress, and the torture of sentient beings. It is important to stress that animals *are* sentient, although the idea seems self-evident. Similarly, relatively not so long ago in U.S. history, the justification for using African Americans in gruesome experiments was because they were thought of as being non-sentient. In the early twentieth century, Dr. Benjamin Moseley wrote in his book *Treatise on Tropical Disease*:

> Negroes ... are void of sensibility to a surprising degree. They are not subject to nervous disease. They sleep sound in every disease, nor does any mental disturbance ever keep them awake. They bear chirurgical operations much better than white people, and what would be the cause of unsupportable pain to a white man, a Negro would almost disregard" [quoted in Spiegel 65].

It took years for abolitionists to convince society that black people were sentient beings, that they could suffer from both emotional and physical pain. Therefore, it was unjust to perpetuate that pain and violence on them, and it was unethical to use them to benefit white society. Medical science has been wrong and unethical before, and that trend continues now with nonhuman animal subjects.

Elephants weep when a loved one dies. They will bury their dead and visit the grave site for years. In the wild, sport hunters randomly shoot the mates of waterfowl, some of whom pair for life. Often, the surviving mate dies of starvation while mourning. Rats will sing to their partners after mating and mourn the loss of their partners, sometimes being so emotionally weak that they will die. They will also laugh if you tickle them. Prairie dogs utter different warning noises showing that they can count the number of predators entering a field, proof of a language in which we can distinguish 300 different calls. Jeffrey Masson cites the case of a parrot that unquestionably disproves the accepted belief that these birds can only repeat, devoid of context, remembered phrases. Left by his trainer at a veterinarian's office, the parrot pleaded, "Come here. I love you. I'm sorry. I want to go back" (quoted in Spiegel 27). Ironically and disturbingly, a common justification for the continued use of animals in research is they are so much like us that we can learn from them, yet at the same time, researchers claim that animal testing is justifiable because human animals and nonhumans animals are fundamentally different.

Huntingdon Life Sciences epitomizes the worst that medical science has to offer from the outdated practices that are animal research and testing. Even industry insiders agreed that what they saw inside of HLS was disturbing, as I learned when walking into a pharmaceutical conference in Washington, D.C. Another anti–HLS activist disrupted the talk by shouting anti–HLS slogans. In response, the speaker, Mary Hanley, head of the Society of Quality Assurance, acknowledged that what she saw at HLS was disturbing. This was actually acknowledged at a Society of Quality Assurance Conference; this says a lot when even industry insiders are disturbed.

Michelle Rokke, a PETA employee, got a job at an HLS lab to document some of the most horrific abuses occurring inside. She wore a hidden camera in the lining of her glasses and recorded and documented egregious acts of animal cruelty at HLS and glaring scientific failures. All of the following documentation of animal cruelty at HLS is taken from Rokke's diary.

While observing a scientist perform a shoddy scientific procedure, Michelle asked if he was supposed to perform it that way. His response was, "No, not supposed to, never saw it, never did it, can't prove it" (67). During another test, scientists acknowledged the poor results of animal testing. While standing over a primate, after administering a chemical substance to the animal's neck, the scientist states to Michelle's hidden camera: "[Y]ou might as well wipe your ass with that data."

This was the tip of the iceberg of what Michelle saw: HLS veterinarian Terry Kusnir complaining how she did not want to attend a meeting on minimizing pain in animals and she knew others did not want to as well, so she would keep the meeting short, saying that animals would never see joy at the lab (15); dogs having their heads slammed in doors (19); a live animal being cut with a scissor until dead (23; 28); an animal having his head being crushed by a cage door (30); an HLS employee worried about other HLS employees throwing dogs against the wall (34); HLS admitting they will contract with customers that will *not* allow euthanasia for suffering animals (34); technicians bragging about diverting the attention of the so-called quality assurance inspectors (36); employees joking about primates dying in the extra colony because the vet did not knowing about bacteria or cleaning cages (37); employees talking about how they would love to yank out an animal's teeth with pliers (38); employees joking about HLS being a circus because of their own gross incompetence (45); employees laughing at a dog's brain damage due to another worker's incompetence (46); primates being caged in research for years (47); dogs locked in two foot cages for a year (56); HLS workers acknowledging they are not compassionate enough (57); and dogs with only an hour of human contact a day (63). When Michelle asked the employees not to kill one of the dogs, they looked at her and laughed.

Her diary also notes that HLS undertook a study for Proctor and Gamble that did not use euthanasia for suffering primates (65); to prevent dogs from struggling during experiments, HLS uses an (often rusty) alligator metal clip (27); one HLS employee is recorded yelling at another employee who was gentle with the animals, telling him to hurry things up (32). Indeed, jokes and other disturbingly flippant attitudes were common at HLS, with employees finding humor in monkeys dying of lung-shots, which happens when a naso-gastric tube is improperly placed in the animal's trachea and lung instead of his/her esophagus and stomach; the animal receives the test material in the lung and dies within minutes. If an animal is killed via lung-shot at HLS, the employee who killed the animal becomes part of the "platinum club" that lists employee names as if the deaths are a badge of honor. An HLS employee bragged to Michelle that he had the most primate kills. He had also killed a dog with a lung-shot and broke a primate's arm after which the animal was euthanized (67).

Similarly, someone broke a primate's tail from improper handling, leading to the tail's amputation. Employees had to do a total of four different tail operations because of their technical failures, and the primate did not heal properly because the stitches kept coming out (75). An HLS employee complained that she had seen injuries on every single primate in one room, from broken tails, to nearly-severed fingers, all caused from people handling them improperly during tests and procedures (75).

One employee was videotaped talking about how she broke a primate's leg when trying to catch him for testing. She had seen *multiple* tails lying on the ground from people pulling on them. Further, four primates went without water for a week (75), and an HLS employee operated on a primate with a dull razor. He began hacking away at the arm, but his razor was so dull that he took several swipes to remove a chunk of flesh the size of a lemon. *The primate was conscious during the procedure.* Meanwhile another HLS staffer spells out his initials on the table with the primate's blood (85).

While employed at HLS, Michelle was told that a true scientist really has no need for Good Laboratory Practices (GLP) because they're interested in science and don't need documentation (89). She was also informed that HLS uses outdated practices that have been around since the 1960s, saying that it is time to move forward. However, she witnessed no progress, only more brutality.

Further documentation reports an HLS employee lifting up a sick dog by the back skin and shaking her (91). When another "researcher" got mad at a dog for not cooperating, and he took out his rage on "man's best friend" by grabbing his face and twisting his head; another employee is seen smiling when tasked with killing a dog (97). A rack of mice and rats died after being put through a cage washer, with other rats starving to death because staffers forgot to feed them. In fact, a whole room of rats were once killed by mistake simply because an employee erroneously thought that was what he/she was supposed to do, kill them (91). Rats are seen being bled by inserting a glass pipelette deep into their eyes, hitting a vein. They are then held upside down to collect blood (102).

The nonhumans at HLS are more than just research subjects. They are sources of amusement, toys and games to HLS workers, and their treatment of these beings is the stuff of horror films, as when an HLS employee slaps a monkey, saying "He is a bad monkey. He needs to be spanked" and when another staffer grabs a pig by her legs and swings her out of a cage. This same person was also seen grabbing a pig by her hind legs and dragging the animal across the floor on her face (102).

SHAC wanted these travesties to end, and those who wanted them to continue — corporations who benefit from animal abuse and donate to political campaigns — attempted to stop SHAC by labeling them a terrorist group. SHAC was not alone, for organizations that protest the use of animals as research and testing subjects had been in the crosshairs of the government and industry groups for years.

ALEC, Industry and the FBI: A How-to Guide on Turning Activists into Terrorists

To understand how SHAC became a so-called terrorist group, one must understand a brief history of the animal rights movement's relationship with corporate America and the U.S. government. The American Legislative Exchange Council (ALEC), an organization established to "advance the fundamental principles of free-market enterprise, limited government, and federalism at the state level through a nonpartisan public-private partnership of America's state legislators, members of the private sector and the general public" ("About ALEC"), has worked hard to marginalize animal rights activists in America. In 1992, ALEC helped roll out a federal law called the Animal Enterprise Protection Act (AEPA) to further punish the already illegal actions of some activists in an effort to shake up the community of animal rights supporters working within the law. Bluntly, AEPA was created to do just what the name implies: "protect animal enterprises" (Animal Enterprise). AEPA was more concerned with radical activists in the shadows and not so much with the activists in the streets. In fact, this law was primarily developed to stop one individual — Rodney Coronado. In the 1990s, Coronado had been suspected of destroying buildings involved in the fur trade and whaling industries. He was never accused of hurting anyone, but the FBI was on his trail.

United States attorneys and assistant U.S. Attorneys from Spokane, Seattle, Portland, and Michigan gathered for meetings to map out a strategy to stop Rod's direct action. They decided that they might be able to put Rod behind bars for a crime of property destruction in Michigan, but on the other actions, there simply was not enough evidence (Kuipers 229). They needed a tougher law to get Rod for the other crimes — a crime that made it illegal to cross state lines and to merely speak in support of the type of crimes Rod was accused of committing. On August 26, 1992, the Feds got their law to convict any future Rod's the movement would engender — AEPA. (For a detailed review of this story, more than I can indulge in here, see Will Potter's seminal *Green Is the New Red: An Insider's Account of a Social Movement Under Siege* and Dean Kuiper's *Operation Bite Back: Rod Coronado's War to Save American Wilderness*).

Eight years later, in 2000, a mink liberator would indeed plead guilty to violations of AEPA. But even at this juncture, the animal rights movement was still not a pressing issue to the FBI. In fact, FBI Director Louis Freeh told European newspapers in 1998 that crimes by the Animal Liberation Front (ALF), Earth Liberation Front (ELF), and Earth First! were not even on his radar screen (Potter 56). However, ALEC remained persistent in maintaining AEPA and would later have a hand in passing the more stringent and ominously named Animal Enterprise Terrorism Act in 2006, which would "provide the Department of Justice the necessary authority to apprehend, prosecute, and convict individuals committing animal enterprise terror" (Animal Enterprise Terrorism). The former Act is the one under which the SHAC 7 would eventually be convicted and it set the stage for the latter. Obviously, in post 9/11 America, integration of the word "terrorism" to the bill was a strategic move on the government's part.

As the new millennium progressed, however, ALF, ELF, Earth First! and other activist organizations became very much on the FBI's radar. In the case of SHAC, the pharmaceutical industry had a lot to do with this new focus on domestic "terrorism." Big Pharma had their first break at passing a new law on May 18, 2004, marking the first of several hearings into whether or not Congress should pass new laws making traditional protest campaigns illegal. John E. Lewis, Assistant Deputy Director for the FBI at the time, was called by the Senate Committee on the Judiciary to speak at a hearing dubbed "Animal Rights: Activism vs. Criminality." At this hearing, he stated,

> While some ALF activities have involved direct actions covered by this statute, such as animal releases at mink farms, the activities of SHAC generally fall outside the scope of the AEPA statute. In fact, SHAC members are typically quite conversant in the elements of the federal statute and appear to engage in conduct that, while criminal (such as trespassing, vandalism or other property damage), would not result in a significant, particularly federal, prosecution. (United States. Senate Committee on the Judiciary.)

Despite Lewis's opinion, within days of this statement, seven SHAC activists were arrested and charged with breaking the law that the FBI deputy director said they were not breaking.

At one of the first hearings of the SHAC 7 case, the defense immediately brought up that even the Deputy Director of the FBI said the individuals charged with the crime were not breaking laws under the AEPA. As an eyewitness to this case, I can report that Charles McKenna, the prosecutor, stood dumbfounded and stumbled over his words, "Well, I tried to call Washington, but they never returned my calls." The oddity of it all is that the SHAC defendants' rhetoric was relatively tame compared to other forms of verbal protest. For instance, they did not call for breaking anyone's neck, although such verbiage was constitutionally protected by the Supreme Court when used during a strike as someone crossed a picket line; SHAC defendants did not claim racial superiority via hate speech and marches, which is also protected by the Supreme Court. Not only was the SHAC 7 case mild in comparison to the broader political hyperbole of other protest groups, their speech was even tame in comparison to those in the animal rights movement.

Jerry Vlasak, retired vivisector and current heart trauma surgeon, often talks about his transition from using dogs in research himself, to actively working to stop those that do by using extreme measures, as he explained in a June 18, 2006, interview with *60 Minutes* entitled "Whatever Means Necessary." Vlasak justifies his views in his oft-noted statement from a 2003 animal rights conference,

> I think there is a use for violence in our movement.... For instance, if vivisectors were routinely being killed, I think it would give other vivisectors pause in what they were doing in their work.... [I]f prominent vivisectors [were] being assassinated, I think that there would be a trickle-down effect.... And I don't think you'd have to kill — assassinate — too many vivisectors before you

would see a marked decrease in the amount of vivisection going on. And I think for 5 lives, 10 lives, 15 human lives, we could save a million, 2 million, 10 million nonhuman animals [quoted in Best].

I am not arguing that Vlasak should be arrested for his comments, but merely showing the inconsistencies of the Act's enforcement and to highlight what was a full-frontal attack on SHAC because they were targeting Big Pharma's financial interests by attempting to close down HLS. The validity of Vlasak's statements is not the point. Rather, I am attempting to demonstrate a violation of the SHAC defendants' freedom of speech to which other activists, even animal rights activists, appear to be immune.

So, what did the SHAC campaigners do that was so egregious as to made Vlasak's call for assassinations pale in comparison? In addition to one of the defendants stating on a Seattle radio station that she supported individuals entering HLS and rescuing animals, the government also presented the individuals with count 29 of the indictment against the SHAC 7, which read: "On or about October 21, 2002, the SHAC Website posted an announcement relating to signs that were posted in and around the Princeton, New Jersey area, which referred to CA (Carol Auletta, an HLS employee) as 'deluded and deranged' and listed her home address and telephone number" (quoted in "SHAC 7") However, the prosecution failed to mention that the "announcement" was an article reposted from a local online news station. This article was not written by animal rights activists. The prosecution argued that it was illegal for SHAC to *further* post information on an HLS employee that had already been noted online for all to see. In sum, the SHAC 7 were indicted for posting information that was already available to the public.

According to the SHAC 7 indictment, posting public information was an offense. Others outside the animal rights arena have committed similar acts, but with no prosecution to follow. For example, in August 2010, Jane Mayer of *The New Yorker* wrote a scathing article on billionaire David Koch and his family. In that article, she included the home address of one of the family members, with no legal repercussions to follow. The lesson here seems to be that it is acceptable and legal to post home addresses as long as it is not done in the name of animal liberation or *especially* if it is aimed at animal liberation activists. To wit, the website targetofopportunity.com, "devoted to fighting Terrorism and the forced integration of Marxist oriented ideals and values into the American mainstream," lists the home address of Andy Stepanian of the SHAC 7 on their "Hit List" ("Our Mission"). And much like Mayer, but unlike SHAC and Stepanian himself, they face no penalty for posting an individual's home address.

As the SHAC 7's legal fight continued, so did the battle to strengthen the AEPA. Senator Patrick Leahy (D-VT) expressed concerns about the hearing. Refusing to attend, he submitted a statement in which he first expressed approval that the hearing's original title, "The Threat of Animal and Eco-Terrorism," had been abandoned. Leahy wrote: "Most Americans would not consider the harassment of animal testing facilities to be terrorism, any more than they would consider anti-globalization protesters or anti-war protesters or women's health activists to be terrorists.... I think that most Americans would rather that we address more urgent concerns that really do pose a serious threat to this country and to the world" (quoted in Potter "Animal Enterprise"). Indeed, even then–Senator Barack Obama (D-IL) stated:

> While I want these crimes stopped, I do not want people to think that the threat from these organizations is equivalent to other crimes faced by Americans every day. According to the FBI, there were over 7,400 hate crimes committed in 2003 — half of which racially were motivated. More directly relevant to this committee, the FBI reports 450 pending environmental crimes cases involving worker endangerment or threats to public health or the environment [United States. Senate Committee on Environment and Public Works.].

This is the same Obama who also compared ALF to other liberationists such as Denmark Vesey, Frederick Douglass, and Harriet Tubman. In *The Audacity of Hope*, Obama writes of

> slaves and former slaves ... who recognized power would concede nothing without a fight.... Knowing this, I can't summarily dismiss those possessed of similar certainty today — the anti-abortion activist who pickets my town hall meeting or the animal rights activist who raids a laboratory — no matter how deeply I disagree with their views. I am robbed even of the certainty of uncertainty — for sometimes absolute truths may well be absolute [97].

Despite views such as this within the U.S. government itself, pursuit of the SHAC 7 under AEPA continued, as did the pursuit of passing AETA.

At the last hearing on the Act on May 23, 2006, Bill Delahunt (D-MA) asked to make a final comment, noting that the crimes covered by the AETA were already crimes and that "[r]edundant statutes burden the federal government and shift power from the states." With limited federal funds, he advised industry groups to lobby their state officials (quoted in "SHAC 7"). However, the AETA had powerful supporters on its side. The National Association for Biomedical Research (NABR) purchased a full-page ad in *Roll Call*, the paper covering Capitol Hill that is read daily by Congressional staff. The ad featured a black-and-white photograph of a vandalized office. On the wall, in bright red spray-paint-style lettering, it said "Your home is next." At the bottom of the page, it stated: "SUPPORT THE ANIMAL ENTERPRISE TERRORISM ACT." On his Web page, Will Potter discusses leaked "internal documents outlining how corporations and industry groups planned to label activists as 'eco-terrorists'" in their efforts to pass the AETA, effectively turning activists into terrorists. However, while the word "terrorism" may lead most Americans to think of planes flying into buildings on September 11, 2001, killing thousands, these corporations and industry groups had a different concern — money. As Potter reveals, one internal document stated that "[t]hese [activist] tactics have been very successful ... in damaging the financial footing of corporations involved in animal enterprise" ("Internal Industry Documents"). AEPA and AETA were never about terrorism, they were always about money.

The inherent injustice of AETA is so evident that even those who oppose animal activism can see its discriminatory nature. Mike German, a former FBI agent who went undercover to investigate a domestic terrorist hate group, had this perspective on the Act: "[T]o create a law that protects one particular industry smacks of undue influence and seems to selectively target individuals with one particular political ideology for prosecution. Why does an 'animal enterprise' deserve more legal protection than another business? Why protect a butcher but not a baker?" (quoted in Lovitz 98). However, this has not stopped the government, backed by ALEC and corporate lobbyists, from demonizing animal advocates for engaging in the type of activism that they, and other activists, had already been doing for years.

For example, in Minneapolis, two animal rights activists were recently arrested, charged, and convicted for holding signs, chanting, and making comments about animal abuse in front of Ribnick Fur and Leather store. The activists directed their comments at individuals and yelled through a closed window that they knew the owner's license plate number and where he and his mother lived. In this case, the conviction was overturned, for the "court noted that there was no reasonable likelihood that the statements would 'tend to incite an immediate breach of the peace or to provoke violent reaction by an ordinary reasonable person'" (State v. Peter). Unfortunately, this positive outcome does not necessarily mark a trend as more states move to institute bills expanding on AETA. The battleground is moving to the point at which the legislature of ten states, as of April 2012, have introduced bills known as "Ag Gag bills" to criminalize taking photo- and video-graphic evidence of animal cruelty — and it is all cruelty — on factory farms and within other animal industries.

Ironically enough, the Supreme Court ruled differently when it came to people who enjoy images of animal suffering. To wit, Robert Stevens produces dog fighting videos. His audience most likely had no problem watching images of animals in pain. The Supreme Court ruled 8–1 in support of his producing these videos. Commenting on this case, Wendy Kaminer of *The Atlantic* poses the perfect question here when considering who gets to document animal cruelty: "[S]houldn't people who oppose animal cruelty enjoy the same constitutional rights as people who enjoy it?"

Only time will tell. And I maintain the hope that the story of the SHAC

7 and the continual enforcement of the AETA will rouse animal activists to action, not scare them into stasis.

WORKS CITED

"About ALEC." alec.org. Web. 4 May 2012.

Animal Enterprise Protection Act of 1992. Pub. L. 102–346. 26 Aug. 1996. *National Agricultural Library.* United States Department of Agriculture. Web. 3 May 2012.

Animal Enterprise Terrorism Act of 2006. Pub. L. 109–347. 120 Stat. 2652. 27 Nov. 2006. *U.S. Government Printing Office.* Web. 4 May 2012.

"Animal Experimentation." Kinshipcircle.org. Web. 3 May 2012.

Best, Steven. "Who's Afraid of Jerry Vlasak?" animalliberationfront.com. n.d. Web. 4 May 2012.

Drug Recall Writer. "Rezulin Linked to Liver Failure & Heart Disease." DrugRecalls.com. 12 Aug. 2012. Web. 3 May 2012.

"Fen Phen Recalled — Linked to Primary Pulmonary Hypertension (PPH)." *Primary Pulmonary Hypertension.* n.d. Web. 3 May 2012.

Garretson, Con. "FBI Probes Activist Protest at Piedmont Home." *Contra Costa Times.* Freere public.com, 31 Aug. 2005. Web. 14 May 2012.

Greek, Ray C., Jean Swingle Greek, and Jane Goodall. *Sacred Cows and Golden Geese: The Human Cost of Experiments on Animals.* New York: Continuum, 2002. Print.

"Janssen Pharmaceutica, Inc. and Johnson & Johnson v. Robert Bailey, et al." *State of Mississippi Judiciary.* 9 Sept. 2001. Web. 3 May 2012.

Kaminer, Wendy. "'Trust Us' Legislation: When Protest Becomes an Act of Terror." *The Atlantic.* The Atlantic Monthly Group, 28 Dec. 2011. Web. 5 May 2012.

Kuipers, Dean. *Operation Bite Back: Rod Coronado's War to Save American Wilderness.* New York: Bloomsbury, 2009. Print.

Lovitz, Dara. *Muzzling a Movement: The Effects of Anti-Terrorism Law, Money, and Politics on Animal Activism.* New York: Lantern, 2012. Print.

Lutherer, Lorenz Otto, and Margaret Sheffield Simon. *Targeted: The Anatomy of an Animal Rights Attack.* Norman: University Oklahoma Press, 1993. Print.

Mayer, Jane. "Covert Operations." *The New Yorker.* Condé Nast, 30 Aug. 2010. Web. 3 May 2012.

Obama, Barack. *The Audacity of Hope: Thoughts on Reclaiming the American Dream.* New York: Random House Digital, 2006. eBook.

"Our Mission." targetofopportunity.com. n.d. Web. 4 May 2012.

Page, Tony. *Vivisection Unveiled: An Exposé on the Medical Futility of Animal Experimentation.* 2nd Ed. Chicago: Jon Carpenter Publishing, 1998. Print.

Potter, Will. "Animal Enterprise Protection Act." greenisthenewred.org. n.d. Web. 5 May 2012.

_____. "Internal Industry Documents Show Plans for Labeling Activists as 'Eco-Terrorists.'" greenisthenewred.org. 17 Dec. 2008. Web. 4 May 2012.

_____. *Green Is the New Red.* San Francisco: City Lights, 2011. Print.

"Propsulid." Resource4thePeople.com. n.d. Web. 3 May 2012.

Rokke, Michelle. "The Diary of Michelle Rokke." SHAC.net. 1996. Web. 3 May 2012.

"SHAC 7 — Kevin Kjonaas Released." 4strugglemag.org. 5 Aug. 2011. Web. 5 May 2012.

Spiegel, Marjorie. *The Dreaded Comparison: Human and Animal Slavery.* New York: Mirror Books/IDEA, 1996. Print.

State v. Peter and Lawson. A10-1263. Court of Appeals of Minnesota. 3 May 2011. Findlaw. com. Web. 4 May 2012.

United States. Senate Committee on Environment and Public Works. Statement of Senator Barack Obama. 18 May 2005. Web. 5 May 2012.

United States. Senate Committee on the Judiciary. Testimony of John E. Lewis. 18 May 2004. Web. 3 May 2012.

"Whatever Means Necessary." *60 Minutes.* CBS, 18 June 2006. Web. 1 May 2012.

Some Things Get Better, Some Get Worse

On Being Scared, Being Around, and Trying to Be Kind

SARAHJANE BLUM

A map of the world that does not include utopia is not even worth glancing at.— Oscar Wilde

I can't remember a time when I wasn't scared, but I try to imagine, and I act as if I'm not. As I write, I'm living a paradox. The lead plaintiff in a lawsuit challenging the Animal Enterprise Terrorism Act (AETA), I am suing the most powerful lawmaker in the nation to fight my way out of being scared into silence. The story of the lawsuit goes back to 2003, or maybe even to 1978. Like most of you reading this, I was born into an apocalyptic moment, where nuclear annihilation twinned with environmental destruction portended an end for our planet. The fallout shelter in the basement of our apartment building was kept "safe" with asbestos for decades and not too long after the leaded pipes were ripped out and replaced, toxic dust from the Twin Towers permeated our windows. Yet, I was eleven before it dawned on me that death was the passage through which cows, chickens, and fish were transubstantiated into breakfast, lunch, and dinner. Eventually that knowledge led me to help animals. Heading towards two decades later, I'm still trying. I've done every-thing from handing out gray mushy veggie burgers outside of McDonald's to riding jet skis between hunters and whales, and I'm still not sure which tactic is better. What I do know is that what's smart in one case is not always the way to go in another, and that the more we reflect and experiment, the more the movement will thrive.

It was 1997 when I first went to a workshop on the theme of "If we're hoarse from shouting, why isn't anyone listening?" I'm sure it wasn't a new question even then, and it isn't old now. Back then I was six months into the movement, and still learning the chants, statistics, jargon, and how to explain

255

to my mom why she started getting death threats from Macy's security guards angry at me for hanging a banner demanding the corporation stop selling fur. Today, the terms I learned in the 1990s have totally different meanings. Lockdown no longer brings up images of blocking the doors of department stores, rather the vision of friends and colleagues in prison denied what little access they normally have to the outside world. And jokes about eating grass have become as antiquated as the punch line "take my wife, please."

Some things change, and some don't. Some things get better, others get worse. Most of this is outside our control (a hard fact for any activist to accept), but there are things we could do better. We should, and we must. Sometimes that work takes us away from the animals we wish we could scoop up and save today, but it's still necessary work. The incredible rate of change of animal abuse and environmental devastation makes us forget we are an incredibly young movement. The modern American animal rights movement dates back only to the 1970s, and already words like vegan — a coinage dating back only to 1944 — have become common usage. As we celebrate our tenacious, tentative growth, we should applaud the impact we've had on the world around us, yet still recognize how much we simply reflect it.

We continue to model widespread moral hypocrisy, accepting class, race, and gender privilege as givens. Though this has begun to change (most notably with the *Sistah Vegan* anthology and Food Empowerment Project), there remains "an underlying assumption amongst mainstream vegan media that racialization and the production of vegan spaces are disconnected" (Harper 6). Compared with other anti-oppression movements in the country, we are woefully slow at even attempting to institute "safer spaces" policies where discrimination is actively confronted and subject to consequence. As such, retrograde sexual politics infect our gatherings and groups, and prominent men within our movement get away with continuing to exert undue sexual power over women. Interpersonal (particularly sexual) dynamics remain one of the most intractable problems within any social movement, but it is particularly challenging in a movement where "the animals come first," and as such, we are expected to transcend harms done to our own bodies and hearts.

It seems a regular occurrence that a national gathering of animal rights activists will be derailed by accusations of sexual misconduct. Calls emerge to hold a perpetrator accountable for his misdeeds, and the movement endures another polarization. It is good that at these junctures we look at concepts of social justice within our community as well as the wider world and refuse to model misogynistic behavior, but I've seen these conversations die down as soon as the wounds begin to scab. Just as it doesn't inspire change to bring up the corpse in the center of the table in the middle of family dinner, only having conversations about sexual violence in the midst of accusations of it will never move us forward. Whether you are friends with the victim or alleged perpetrator, defensiveness will override both compassion and reason. Instead of trying to reconstruct who hurt who, how, and why, let's see what happens if we say as a group that we recognize a responsibility to demand better norms for our behavior when we get together. Perhaps this call for new standards of accountability takes me far afield from what we typically think of as "movement strategy," but my words come from the same fundamental belief that fuels my work for nonhuman animals.

I am convinced activists can do the most good by being direct and honest as we work on issues we are passionate about, while recognizing that all oppression is interconnected. We can't expect justice for one animal without believing in justice for all. Still, no one person can do everything, and I've seen too many of us broken by the fear that taking up one struggle detracts from other efforts. When activists began staging sit-ins at lunch counters to challenge segregation, no one argued that a lack of access to sandwiches was the biggest injustice faced by black America. And when people volunteer their time at battered women's shelters, advocates for affordable housing and prison reform don't accuse them of doing more harm than good. More often than not, we are all on the same team.

Since 2003, I have been deeply involved with the anti-foie gras and open rescue movements in the U.S. Compared to the numbers of animals farmed for the staples of the Standard American Diet, foie gras can seem a relatively small concern. Likewise, in contrast with the ten billion land-dwelling animals killed for food every year, saving one life might seem a meaningless effort. But my work as a foie gras investigator/rescuer has delivered transformation and kept me engaged in a way a number, no matter how big, never could.

To quickly define the terms, open rescue is the practice — popular in the late 1990s and early 2000s — of investigating and documenting conditions on (primarily) factory farms without any endeavor to hide our identities, and liberating a handful of the captive animals from the those conditions. The action has both symbolic significance, in that it provides a face to the unnamed, invisible animals who suffer in these conditions, and for the animals who are rescued, a new life free from exploitation. Rescuing ducks from foie gras farms also served to debunk a myth continually perpetrated by the industry, and undercut notions of the possibility of "humane" animal agriculture. Foie gras — produced by force-feeding ducks and geese until their bodies are on the brink of death from obesity, disease and injury — is inherently brutal and violent, whether it is done by multinational corporations or one or two individuals. Yet farmers defend the process as "artisanal" and maintain that shoving a pipe down the throat of a penned bird twice a day mimics the natural gorging processes birds undergo before migration.

Oddly enough, though, none of the ducks rescued ever engaged in any sort of gorging behavior. They did, however, learn to play with cherry tomatoes, swim, enjoy gentle petting on their keels, and even fall in love. Two of the birds, Jean-Paul and Jean-Claude, became a devoted same-sex couple living on a chicken sanctuary on the eastern shore of Maryland. Their connection gives insight about any number of misperceptions about what's "natural." But theirs is a different story. I will stick to telling mine.

My story is a story about stories. None of my work has provided such a potent antidote to my own fear and despair, or as much clear change, as my work with open rescue. In the abstract, when we become too involved in the memorial rolls of statistics, activism becomes penance. But it's not possible to repent for what we have done to the animals, nor is there even a group called "the animals." There are only individual animals (although billions of these individuals are killed by and for individual humans each year). And we have never been more cut off from other species and our own. One of the many reasons I was drawn to working with ducks is they were one of the only "wild" animals I had ever had interaction with growing up. I had seen them, so I could see them. I'm not alone in this disconnect.

Recently, psychologists have shown that "[g]iven increasing urbanization and declining populations of wildlife" there is a "paucity of ... children's direct experience of wildlife outside of school. One recent study found that eight-year-old children in Britain were better able to identify artificial Pokémon creatures than real, native ones" (Balmford et al., 2637). The result of this was that children, especially girls, were inclined to think of non-mammalian wildlife in terms of objects. There is a direct connection between non-experience of animals and objectification of them. Being vegan, and/or engaging in animal rights advocacy does not immunize us from the effects of an absence of the non-urbanized world in our experiences.

I have spent as much time as anyone learning statistics and trying to grapple with that blurry drugged feeling that comes from looking at numbers instead of animals. It turns out that my inability to process some of the information is a coping strategy I have little control over. In fact, research has shown that making statistics out of individuals is one way people protect themselves from the cost of emotions that "animate moral judgment and behavior" (Cameron and Payne 15) So we get caught in a double bind; we suffer from the trauma of staring at suffering, and then by trying to wrap our heads around it, we lose our intuitive ability to hold onto compassion.

This can be seen in the increasingly popular idea that advocacy is a numbers game, judged by how many leaflets someone gives out or how many hits a blog post receives. An extreme focus on the number of humans any given activist interacts with moves animal rights away from care. As a movement we internalize the notion that hands-on work with animals is an "innocent" non-political act (Michel 163). It is anything but. In my own experience, hands-on care for animals led to exposure on national television and print media. The work of grassroots groups like gourmetcruelty.com changed law and, to some small measure, culture.

After the rescue, I spent months rehabilitating Harry and Penhall, ducks I named after two characters on *21 Jump Street*, my favorite TV show growing up. Like his namesake, Penhall was big bodied, with a sweet open face. In keeping with *Jump Street's* Harry, whose back-story had him escaping from Vietnam in his youth, Harry was a refugee who took full advantage of freedom. Before their rescue, Harry and Penhall were living in small cages barely bigger than their bodies, being force-fed to the brink of death. They could no longer walk on their own. I took them to vet visits and helped them regain muscles in their legs.

This human interest story became the subject of a half hour episode of *A Pet Story* on Animal Planet. As the episode developed, the producer of the show spent what seemed like forever going back and forth with people within the company trying to figure out just how much footage from the farm she could show without scaring advertisers or viewers away. Today Animal Planet runs three different spinoffs of *Whale Wars*, which bring complex indictments of hunting on the high seas to a mainstream audience every week. Yet, I'm afraid to even screen *Delicacy of Despair*, the documentary about the investigation and rescue that I and others undertook. Under the AETA, showing or even discussing footage from an undercover rescue and investigation can be regarded as a criminal act if it cuts into corporate profits.

The AETA — steamrolled through Congress by the heavy lobbying of corporate interests from factory farming, animal research, and the fur industries — has as of yet attracted little notice. For many of us who have chosen to work to oppose animal abuse, however, it has created a perilous climate where free speech becomes ever more dangerous.

By evoking national fears of "terrorism," big business pushed through a law that renders criminal any work found to have caused the loss of property or profits to a business or other institution that uses or sells animals (or animal products) or to "a person or entity having a connection to, relationship with, or transactions with an animal enterprise" (AETA). But, by definition, no protest against injustice changes anything unless it affects the bottom line of the powerful. Cesar Chavez has been immortalized on American postage stamps for organizing a boycott on table grapes. Today, calling for a boycott on beef or pork has been criminalized by what the Massachusetts ACLU has said "may be the broadest criminal statue in the United States Code" (18).

The AETA is part of a broader effort by corporate interests to constrain social and political activism by making people afraid of being labeled "terrorists." We are singled out for thought crimes — as in the case of Eric McDavid, who at the time of this writing is serving a twenty-year prison sentence after being charged with conspiracy to commit a never committed crime planned and incited by an FBI informant — and chilled from speaking our minds. Some of the peers I began doing activism with in late '90s have curtailed their activism because of fears for their personal safety, and others have decided that the only way to help animals is to work alongside animal exploiters and try to change the system from the inside. Some of the people I have been closest to have gone to prison, and some have turned informant for the government. All of us have had our minds twisted by living in ironic terror of that laden and powerful word.

This is, in part, why our movement is so fragile. To buoy ourselves up as activists, we underestimate the governmental repression we act under and the self-censorship we apply. Instead of acknowledging this climate, we blame our cohort (and often ourselves) for not being convincing enough when we speak out for animals. Despite the perma-shock in which many of us have lived our entire lives, with alarms in our ears made only more shrill by 24 hour news cycles, and unrelenting internet death row photos of dogs and cats at animal shelters, we inexplicably expect our shocking truths — that ours is a society built on oppression, rape and murder — to get heard the first time through.

When the truths aren't heard, we end up beyond frustrated. We butt up against other people's moral hypocrisies and shut down as we hear the same stories about people who are compassionate but still eat animals. We grow weary of taking people's hands and walking them down the road to see the more than 23 million chickens killed for food every day in the U.S. And we forget that people can't see the animals hiding in their words and signifiers; we forget that we can't see them either. Beyond beef and bacon, there are other words that hide animals: deforestation, road construction, housing development, *war*. We must learn to be attuned to those words. And we have to learn how to speak kindly to people who are thinking about them, even if they don't yet recognize the absent referents in their speech (Adams 40).

When we are thinking about how oppressors have guns, prisons, and slaughterhouses, we remember that words are weapons. When we turn them on each other and our potential allies, we forget. Out of frustration over all the things that haven't gotten better, we resort to name calling, dismiss the possibility of bridge building with other movements and within our own, and retreat back to internet cliques to discuss cupcake recipes or bash something we read in the *Huffington Post*. But if there is one thing I have learned from those I've had the privilege to share my home with, it's that humans and nonhumans alike suffer when I use the Internet too much. Change often comes too slowly, but what change has come has almost always been initiated by people who avoid being detoured by online debates and instead did the work they felt called to do.

For a while now, these sidetracking debates have centered around a nebulous construct of "abolitionism." Despite my deep unease about animal advocates working for things we don't want and asking for changes we don't believe in, I am not an "abolitionist." First, the abolition of animal slavery will no more end speciesism by itself than the abolition of American slavery ended racism. To change the world, I think we should aim higher. Second, I'm increasingly convinced that no matter who uses the term, it hides a slur. When used to refer to others, it connotes zealotry and obstructionism, and when taken as a self-definition, it is seen as an attack by anyone who does not apply it to herself. Yes, it's a highly defensible moral philosophy, right up there with Peter Singer's application of Utilitarianism to animal liberation, and Tom Regan's Theory of Rights, but like those other intellectual concepts, it's useful only so far as it engenders right action. As early as 1956, Theodore Adorno said, "philosophy is truly there to redeem what lies in the gaze of an animal" (quoted in Mendieta 147). More recently, ecofeminists like the late Marti Kheel have invited us "to dissolve the dualistic thinking that separates reason from emotion, the conscious from unconscious, the 'domestic' from the 'wild,' and animal advocacy from nature ethics" (251). It's easier said than done, but that's no excuse not to try.

As we ought with so many other fights that seem intractable, lets sidestep this one altogether. Whom does it serve for us to be name-calling when we should be working? It serves only the same entrenched powers who began snitch-jacketing activists to get the Black Panther Party fighting each other until they devolved into self-annihilation. But, whether or not it's the actual industries of animal exploitation that led Singer to remark back in 1998 that "American animal organizations are notorious for wasting more energy in fighting one another than in fighting for animals" (94), only we can stop the infighting. The abolitionist/welfarist argument is only one example of the off the rails defensiveness that keeps popping up when we try to distract ourselves from the despair we feel at the actual odds we fight against (jones 28). Other debates that should be intellectual but become frightfully personal are whether to use the word vegetarian or vegan in our advocacy, and which, if any, extra-legal tactics are justified in defense of nonhumans.

If any of these topics make you crazy, mad, or shut down, try practicing kindness by challenging behaviors, not people. Try out radically different styles of talking and listening, and see if it helps to cultivate a more diverse movement, and one in which the voices of activists are more appropriately represented. Our movement is predominantly female, but more often than not, the leadership is disproportionately male. Instead of accepting this status quo, or even lamenting it, can we try to uncover why this is so? Where is the disconnect between feminism and animal liberation that keeps women from demanding that their voices be heard within our movement? And why does the movement remain so persistently unfriendly to people of color or of different classes? These aren't merely academic or even moral questions. As smart, compassionate, and dedicated as my fellow activists are, I keep ending up in rooms where we all seem to have read the same books or trained under the same teachers. No wonder we keep coming up with the same answers.

This can change. Once it does, there will still be injustice, repression, and our world will still be frail. I will likely still be scared. But some things will be better.

WORKS CITED

Adams, Carol J. *The Sexual Politics of Meat: A Feminist-Vegetarian Critical Theory.* New York: Continuum, 1995. Print.

Animal Enterprise Terrorism Act of 2006. Pub. L. 109–347. 120 Stat. 2652. 27 Nov. 2006. *U.S. Government Printing Office.* Web. 31 May 2012.

Balmford, Andrew, et al. "Why Conservationists Should Heed Pokémon." *Science,* AAAS. 29 March 2002: Vol. 295 No. 5564: 2367. Print.

Cameron, C. Daryl, and Keith B. Payne. "Escaping Affect: How Motivated Emotion Regulation Creates Insensitivity to Mass Suffering." *Journal of Personality and Social Psychology,* 100.1, Jan 2011: 1–15. Print.

Harper, Amie Breeze. "Race as a 'Feeble Matter' in Veganism: Interrogating Whiteness, Geopolitical Privilege, and Consumption Philosophy of 'Cruelty-Free' Products." *Journal for Critical Animal Studies,* VIII.3: 5–27 Print.

jones, pattrice. *Aftershock: Confronting Trauma in a Violent World.* New York: Lantern, 2007. Print.

Kheel, Marti. *Nature Ethics: An Ecofeminist Perspective.* New York: Rowman and Littlefield, 2008. Print.

Massachusetts American Civil Liberties Union. "Brief of *Amicus Curiae* American Civil Liberties Union of Massachusetts in Opposition to Defendant's Motion to Dismiss" Blum V. Holder. No. 1:11-Cv-12229-Jlt. United States District Court for the District of Massachusetts. Print.

Mendieta, Eduardo. "Animal Is to Kantianism as Jew Is to Fascism: Adorno's Bestiary." *Critical Theory and Animal Liberation.* Ed. John Sanbonmatsu. Lanham, MD: Rowman and Littlefield, 2011. 147–160. Print.

Michel, Suzanne M. "Golden Eagles and the Environmental Politics of Care." *Animal Geographies: Place, Politics, and Identity in the Nature-Culture Borderlands.* Eds. Jennifer R. Wolch and Jody Emel. London, Verso, 1998. 162–190. Print.

Singer, Peter. *Ethics into Action: Henry Spira and the Animal Rights Movement.* Lanham, MD: Rowman and Littlefield, 1998. Print.

Afterword
Flower Power
PATTRICE JONES

Everything springs from plants. All animal life, including human life, depends upon the ability of plants to transubstantiate sunshine into calories, creating oxygen in the process. If it weren't for the magic of photosynthesis, none of us would be here.

Where does that magic happen? Not at the ice-capped mountain-tops, but down below, where billions upon billions of tree leaves, fern fronds, and — yes — blades of grass work wonders of transformation every day. Every leaf lives on a particular plant, which is rooted in a particular place, the ecology of which determines whether and how it will grow.

You're getting my point now, aren't you? Whatever would-be leaders might be shouting from their ivory towers, substantial cultural and political change happens — can only happen — when ordinary people collectively transform themselves and each other. Because each of us is somewhere and nothing happens in a vacuum, all of this "grassroots" conversion of ideas and energy into changes in beliefs and behaviors occurs in particular places.

Every place is different. The physical and social ecologies of Minneapolis differ significantly from the topography and demography of Mumbai. Such differences determine not only the problems to be solved but also the methods most likely to make a difference. While an outsider perspective sometimes can be useful, the people who live in a particular place are often best able to see what needs to be done and how best to do it. The standpoint of black women in Jim Crow Alabama allowed them to see that a bus boycott in Montgomery would have an out-sized effect on the local economy. And so Jo Ann Robinson and her students stayed up mimeographing leaflets the night Rosa Parks was arrested and then went out to the bus-stops before day-break, because they knew — as perhaps no one else would have realized — that domestic workers would be on their way to make breakfast at the houses of the wealthiest whites. Robinson's book, *The Montgomery Bus Boycott and the Women Who Organized It*, offers instructive lessons in collective, creative strategic thinking

263

from a specific standpoint at a particular time and place. Similarly, Jane Goodall's book, *Hope for Animals and Their World*, details numerous case examples of audaciously innovative local efforts to protect, preserve, or restore the habitats of members of endangered species in places ranging from the beaches of Bermuda to the deserts of Mongolia.

All of which brings us to the utility of this volume and the many similar books I hope will be inspired by it. Theories are always most sound when they arise from the facts on the ground. When we read the words that begin Dallas Rising's opening essay —*I'm standing in the basement of Coffman Union at the University of Minnesota next to a television playing a looped DVD of the slaughterhouse documentary* Meet Your Meat—we know that what follows will be the product of active engagement with those facts. We may or may not agree with the conclusions she draws from her observations, but we will in either case be educated. When we read the story of how she literally stood up for a mole, we become more likely to behave compassionately when doing so requires courage. That story is now part of *your* memory, and you now know that you won't be standing alone, because Dallas will be standing there right beside you (and that may be lucky, because she knows Muay Thai).

Let's applaud the authors of the essays in this volume both for their activism and for their courage in daring to put their observations and ideas on paper for others to read and assess. Let's reward their efforts by thinking carefully about what we can learn from these essays, as individual works and considered collectively.

Lessons from "Little Old Ladies"

Tom Reagan, Andrew Linzey, and Peter Singer all have infamously derided the women who originated animal advocacy as "little old ladies in tennis shoes" (Adams and Donovan 284; 306). As Greta Gaard and other eco-feminists have amply demonstrated, denigration of the female and denigration of nonhuman animals are just different aspects of the same algebra of ascendency. So, let's not make the same mistake. Let's take the women who founded a grassroots animal rights organization in Minneapolis thirty years ago very seriously, understanding that we have much to learn from their experiences.

I find the oral history of the Animal Rights Coalition to be the heart of this book, and I hope that its readers (including its other contributors) will see it as such. In that chapter, we not only hear the voices — and ideas — of numerous long-term, local animal rights activists but also have the opportunity to listen in as they recall the strategies they used to create change in this particular place. The story of their multi-year struggle against vivisection at the University of Minnesota is inspiring, instructive, and chastening in its reminder that actually ending animal exploitation is never so easy as simply shouting "no compromise." The women of ARC didn't give up or just keep doing the same thing when their initial demonstrations didn't have the desired effect. They thought strategically, trying first one tactic, then another, and then multiple tactics in combination. They didn't end all vivisection, but they did shut down that dog lab, and that's not nothing. They went through literally blood-spattered records to do it, taking incremental steps that did at one point involve working within a system that condones "humane" animal experimentation. And they won. To the dogs who therefore *weren't* tortured in that lab, that means everything.

Vonnie Thomasberg, Charlotte Cozzetto, Mary Britton Clouse, Heidi Greger, and other activists used the same thoughtful, strategic approach in ARC's successful effort to end lethal bird-trapping by the university's agricultural researchers. Here, their careful local efforts reverberated nationally and perhaps even internationally, as the researchers who were forced to think more creatively to solve their problems by non-lethal means then shared their strategies with their peers. That local struggle has since become a case study in environmental ethics, further widening its impact.

Speaking of vivisection and bird-trapping, I want to encourage readers of this book to think seriously about why Charlotte Cozzetto, a founding member of ARC with thirty years of grassroots animal advocacy behind her, says "I still resist — kicking and screaming — this emphasis on veganism." ARC runs a vegan store. Charlotte volunteers to staff that store. And still, she has told me that she worries deeply about the present-day animal rights movement's vegan litmus test for activists and increasingly exclusive emphasis on farmed animal issues. I share those concerns. (For the record, so that I myself am not misunderstood, I do pass the vegan litmus test. Also, I co-founded a farmed animal sanctuary. A cow rescued from the dairy industry ran past my window while I typed that last paragraph.) I'd not thought much about this until the 2005 Grassroots Animal Rights Conference at which, in the midst of a panel discussion on movement strategies, Adam Weismann — another *long-term* animal liberation activist — remarked that the movements against fur and vivisection lost members and momentum as personal veganism became a sort of pre-requisite for engaging in animal advocacy. Since the majority of Americans oppose both fur and non-medical animal testing, he wondered if those struggles might already have been won were it not for that loss of activist energy.

Here's how I see the history: Farmed animal issues had been almost entirely neglected in the early years of the animal rights movement. Farmed animal advocates, justly, complained of insufficient emphasis on the category of animal exploitation responsible for injury to the greatest number of animals. The movement rightly corrected its course but may have overcorrected, going too far in the other direction. Certainly, the emphasis on personal veganism — and on persuading people to "go vegan" as the *sine qua non* of animal advocacy — has created a chilly climate for people who might be ready to devote substantial time and energy to zoos, circuses, vivisection, fur, or other forms of animal abuse and exploitation but are not yet ready to go vegan. When we lose those potential activists, we not only lose the work they might have done but also the possibility of having the kind of low-key conversations among comrades that might lead them more gradually toward personal veganism. I just said that "we" lose their work but, really, it's the elephants in zoos and chimps in vivisection labs (not to mention the cows on dairy farms whose milk those folks might quit misappropriating after extended contact with close comrades who are ethical vegans) who are the real losers. So, let's listen to Charlotte and start thinking about strategies for becoming a more inclusive movement while still giving due emphasis to the struggle to end the exploitation of farmed animals.

Let's also pay attention as Chelsea Youngquist Hassler, Melissa E. Maaske, Al Nowatzki, Dallas Rising, and Aaron Zellhoefer construct typologies and other theories to help them (and us) make sense of the data they've encountered in the course of their adventures in vegan outreach, animal rescue, antivivisection activism, and vegan parenting. As a scholar and an activist, I'm all for what B.G. Glaser calls "Grounded Theory" — a methodology by which theories arise inductively from the facts on the ground — as this keeps us from selectively ignoring data in order to make reality seem to fit our pre-existing hypotheses. Indeed, I came to my ideas about animal liberation and its linkages to feminism by way of my research into the origins of racism. Had I proceeded on the basis of pre-existing theories of racism, I'd never have perceived those connections.

So, while I deeply appreciated *every* essay as an example of a grassroots activist grappling with the questions that vex us all, I was happiest when the authors grounded their own theories in their experiences as activists. Speaking of ground, I was particularly pleased whenever an author mentioned the specific challenges of working in this particular place at this particular time, as everything depends on ecology. Chelsea Youngquist Hassler's achingly honest account of being a "geographic anomaly" in cheese country stood out for me in that respect. But — wait! — before I move on to talk about what we might learn from the book as a whole, I have to give a shout-out to Patrick McAleer's unique effort to read animal rights themes in Stephen King novels. While I don't know enough about those novels to have a clue as to whether he's on the right track, I do know that *millions* of people read Stephen King and that it might be useful to have this way to talk about animal rights with them. Lurking within every grassroots animal rights group are people who have ideas about how to talk about animal rights to people who are like them in some way or share some specific interest or viewpoint. We desperately need such creativity, and I thank editors Kim Socha and Sarahjane Blum for nurturing it here.

Essays in Conversation

What can we learn from the essays in this volume, considered collectively? Let's consider this a snapshot of a subset of Minnesotan animal rights activists. What do we learn from this glimpse into their hearts and minds in this place at this moment in time? We can see that, not surprisingly, animal advocates in the Twin Cities wrestle actively with questions that wrack the movement nationally and that they very much want their own views on those controversies to be heard. We also see — so vividly — the frustration, anger, and anguish experienced by these people who put so much of themselves into their activism on behalf of animals.

That, too, would be unremarkable — animal advocacy is grievously difficult and emotionally demanding work — except for one curious fact: Most of the anger in this volume is directed not at vivisectors or dairy farmers but at people who put their own hearts and souls into working for the immediate reduction of animal suffering. How can this be? How have animal rights activists who exclusively focus their efforts on promoting veganism come to see animal rights activists who also promote veganism but include efforts to improve the immediate well-being of animals in their spectrum of activities as the enemy? Since (according to the statistics in this very volume) only 22 percent of "beef," 5 percent of "pork," 3 percent of eggs, 1 percent of turkey flesh, and 0.1 percent of chicken flesh comes from any place other than factory farms, it cannot possibly be that efforts to eradicate the most egregious abuses perpetrated by factory farms have stalled what would otherwise be a whirlwind ride to worldwide veganism. Yes, those "cage free" egg cartons and "humane" meat labels do introduce new challenges — challenges we might creatively meet if we would put our collective minds to that — in persuading the small sub-set of consumers who care enough about animals to look for such packaging. But they are not the problem.

The problem is that we are frustrated. So many of the activists in this volume report that they've not even been able to persuade their closest friends and family members — the people who presumably are most like them — to go vegan. When they stand on street-corners or in college hallways handing out vegan literature, they are often mocked or ignored. Over time, those insults add up, compounding the (entirely accurate) sensation that the world is awry. What might the problem be? Why won't people listen to the truth? It must be those welfarists!

And so we see how easily our anguish can be turned against our allies. This is not to say that the national organizations do not sometimes behave with reckless disregard of the opinions of grassroots activists or that those organizations have never stepped over the clear line between condemning specific inhumane practices and promoting "humane" exploitation of animals. I, too, have gnashed my teeth and torn my hair when reading about some foolish stunt perpetrated by PETA or some sickening compromise made by HSUS. But I do not make the mistake of questioning the motives of the sincere and steadfast people who staff those organizations. In her famous poem, "Snapshots of a Daughter-in-Law," the late Adrienne Rich writes of "a woman, partly brave and partly good, who fought with what she partly understood." That's all of us animal advocates, including both "abolitionists" and liberationists who work for animal welfare along the way. We all make mistakes. None of us have enough information. We're all trying as hard as we can to do right by animals anyway. We'll be much more likely to succeed if we can learn to set aside dogma and defensiveness in order to strategize together, daring to ask whether our own favored tactics are working and what we might do differently or instead.

Which brings me to my next point. I also notice — sorry, but I do — that almost every essayist feels compelled to recite a variant of some sort of "abolitionist" creed before going on to say whatever they have to say, as if the failure to include such a loyalty oath might result in expulsion from the company of the righteous. I know that an anthology requires authors to define their terms, but still, this troubles me deeply, as it suggests that groupthink — the antithesis of the kind of creative, practical, and ever-evolving problem-solving we need — may be at work in local activist circles. (Please do look up groupthink and its antidotes if you don't know how to spot it. It's insidious if unchallenged but relatively easy to remedy once recognized.) I also notice that the contributors seem to be reading the same books while tuning into blogs and podcasts that will reflect their opinions back to them. That suggests what social psychologists call "group polarization," which leads people to become less and less able to understand or communicate effectively with people different than themselves — a potentially dangerous development for activists who aim to persuade a wide variety of people.

In her book, *Mighty Be Our Powers*, Nobel Peace Prize winner Leymah Gbowee tells the story of how she came to organize a grassroots, multi-ethnic women's movement that confronted a murderous dictator, forced warlords to cooperate in peace talks, and then helped to disarm Liberia after almost two decades of civil war. She prepared herself for this daunting task by reading widely, learning from many different case examples of effective activism. In the documentary *Pray the Devil Back to Hell*, we see Gbowee and other organizers trying one thing after another, sometimes using well-worn tactics like sit-ins and marches but also using methods matched to their specific cultural context. At one moment in the film — which every activist should watch — we see Gbowee frazzled and despondent because "no new ideas were coming," and she knew that steadfastness alone would not be enough: They had to try something new. (They did. Watch the movie and you'll see.) We need that kind of informed, creative, collective thinking. We need to learn not only from those Little Old Ladies who marched against vivisection thirty years ago but also from Liberian peace activists, Latino union organizers, and sustainable agriculture experts from Laos.

As editors Kim Socha and Sarahjane Blum note in their introductory pieces, the contributors to this volume are remarkably similar to one another demographically. Even within this sharply circumscribed group, we read that one contributor was deeply offended by a book that inspired another contributor to go vegan overnight. That being the case, the likelihood that such a narrow set of Twin Cities citizens will know what to say to inspire the entire metropolitan area to become ethical vegans tends to zero. If only for practical reasons, activist organizations ought to roughly reflect the demographics of the region in which they work. If an activist organization in a multi-racial city of people from every economic class is exclusively white and middle or upper class, something's gone wrong. So, let's look more closely at this particular metropolis to see if we can figure out what's happening and how it might be fixed.

The Social Ecology of the Twin Cities

As this anthology was conceived and compiled, I happened to be living in the Twin Cities, teaching psychology and women's studies at a Minneapolis community college and gender studies at a university in St. Paul. The community college has the most diverse student population in the state, with more than half of the students being people of color; the university serves working class adult learners and also is more diverse than the norm in the state. For three years, I rode the bus or my bike to school each day, paying attention to people and neighborhoods along the way.

Let me take this opportunity to share my own observations of the Twin Cities, in the hopes that these may be useful to local animal advocates unused to thinking closely about the dynamics of race and place. Like the rest of the United States, the lands upon which Minneapolis and St. Paul sit used to be the habitat for far fewer people and far more birds. The first people to inhabit this place did augment the wild rice they harvested from the waterways by fishing, but they did not consider themselves to be the owners of the land or its other-than-human inhabitants. It was Europeans who introduced the idea of animals as property.

French fur trappers were among the first Europeans to encroach into this ecosystem. They relentlessly trapped beavers, eventually driving them to the brink of extinction. Next came the soldiers of the newly united States, who built Fort Snelling and began the process of deliberately confining Native American people to less and less land. At this time, genocide of Native Americans was the official policy of the United States, so it is not surprising that much violence attended this process. In 1862, tiny Pike Island (at the confluence of the Mississippi and Minnesota rivers) was used as a concentration camp for 1,600 Dakota people, hundreds of whom died of disease and starvation over the winter. In nearby Mankato, thirty-eight Dakota men were hanged in what remains the largest mass execution in this nation's history.

Also, as happened elsewhere in the United States, the incomplete extermination of the "wild Indians" so often compared to animals — Colonel John Chivington justified killing Native children at the Sand Creek Massacre by stating that "nits make lice" — was followed by a policy of cultural genocide wherein children were forcibly removed from their families and sent to boarding schools where they were forbidden to speak their native language, practice their family faith, or wear the clothing and hairstyles of their tribes. Children spent ten or more years at such schools, at which physical and sexual abuse were rampant, seeing their families only in the summer or — if they had been "farmed out" to white families as summertime slave laborers — never at all.

While this may be news to some readers of (and contributors to) this anthology, it is living memory for Native people living in the Twin Cities. Many Native families grapple with multi-generational trauma dating back to the boarding schools. Native communities struggle with high rates of poverty, and Native girls and women are particularly vulnerable to sex trafficking. Of all racial or ethnic groups in Minneapolis, Native Americans have the shortest life expectancy. On the upside, local Native Americans participated in the American Indian Movement (AIM) in its heyday, and a vibrant array of Native community organizations and projects pepper the Franklin Avenue corridor — on which the Animal Rights Coalition used to have its office.

When I first moved to Minneapolis, I noticed that many of the streets and natural features were named after fake Indians (Hiawatha, Minnehaha) while real Indians went about their daily lives as if on a parallel plane of existence invisible to whites. Nonetheless, Native American activists have shown themselves willing to work in coalition with white activists (including vegan environmentalists), most notably in the struggle to preserve a spring and stand of trees through which a highway was slated to be rerouted. (Mary Losure's *Our Way or the Highway* tells the story of that partly successful and partly failed struggle, which included both direct action, lobbying, and mass demonstrations.) Most recently, local Native elders showed up to support the local Occupy Movement, despite their dismay at its name.

The next wave of European immigrants included numerous Irish Catholics (St. Paul) and Scandinavian Lutherans (Minneapolis). The latter brought with them many egalitarian traditions, along with a commitment to niceness and a conviction of their own goodness. How, you might wonder, could such convictions co-exist with the knowledge that genocide had cleared the land for them? Good question! If we can come to understand that, then maybe we can gain some insight into the duplicities of consciousness that facilitate both factory farming and local consumption of "happy meat."

The Twin Cities are now home to the largest Hmong community outside of their homelands in the mountainous regions of Southeast Asia as well as the largest Somali community outside of Somalia. In both instances, war drove people from their countries and Twin Cities citizens collectively elected to be welcoming. Hmong people are concentrated in St. Paul while the Somali community is centered around a public housing project in South Minneapolis. In this sharply segregated city, African Americans are most likely to live in North Minneapolis — which might as well be a separate city — and also cluster in a few South Minneapolis neighborhoods. In local communities of color, grassroots anti-poverty, anti-violence, and environmental justice activists are hard at work. And, to be fair, they are joined by some whites from other neighborhoods. (You can always count on vegan anarchists to show up at any demo.) But most white residents live their daily lives without any real engagement with people of color. Or so it seems to me.

In my experience, most white residents seem entirely unaware that they are living in such a segregated metropolis, even though the news that Minneapolis has the highest black-white achievement gap in the country and St. Paul has the highest rate of poverty among Asian American children is right there in the local paper. Minneapolis progressives, in particular, feel pride in living in what they perceive as an especially liberal city. They bike the greenway to the co-op to pick up fair trade coffee and organic milk and then sleep smugly in hemp sheets, evidently untroubled by the traffic in Native women in the Phillips neighborhood or the drive-by shootings on the Northside. I suspect these are the same folks whose consumption of "happy meat" so enrages many of the contributors to this anthology. If so, then the problem goes much, much deeper than the superficial labels on those particular animal products, involving a habitual tendency to preserve one's own sense of oneself (or one's community) as righteous by blocking out evidence to the contrary. So, we need new strategies for talking to them. And, maybe, we need to see those folks as particularly difficult nuts to crack and turn our attention to all of the people we haven't even tried to talk to yet.

Since I bring my whole self to teaching, every class I taught included some attention to animals and their exploitation, whether this be a discussion of animal sentience in general psychology, a deconstruction of vivisection in lifespan psychology, a look at the diversity of animal sexuality in a course in GLBTQ studies, a survey of animal abuse (including both cockfighting and factory farming, not to mention attacks on companion animals by perpetrators of domestic violence) in a course on women and violence, or a thorough examination of the uses of animals in the construction of race and gender stereotypes in a course on gender, race, and popular culture.

On the basis of that experience, I am here to tell you that there is no particular antipathy to animal rights among the communities that are currently under-represented (if not entirely unrepresented) within the local animal rights movement. Quite the contrary! Even though none of these students signed up to learn about animal rights, none ever complained about my coverage of those subjects. (And I do set it up so that students can — and do — tell me when they are displeased.) Instead, again and again, every semester, students — most of them women of color — went out of their way to thank me for including attention to animal exploitation, thereby giving them the conceptual tools to link their long-standing sympathies for animals to their opposition to other forms of injustice. Several — again, some every semester — announced their intention either to change their own diets or to initiate or join efforts to reduce animal abuse. One working-class white woman from a nearby small town made a few phone calls and, with the help of her mother, forged a working alliance between that town's humane society and domestic violence project, instantly creating a mechanism to keep companion animals safe if their guardians have to flee for their own lives. One Native American woman began making plans to improve the lives of feral dogs on a nearby reservation. One African American student shifted her long-term career plans from law enforcement to animal advocacy.

These were not students with "nothing else to worry about." Most recently, a former battered woman still grieving the death of her daughter to a drive-by shooting went out of her way to thank me for reminding her of her care and respect for animals. A homeless student told me of her struggle to stay vegetarian while eating at soup kitchens. An undocumented immigrant working under the table to support himself and pay for college told me of his shame at having slipped from veganism and his determination to get back on that track. A Native American student whose relatives include both boarding school survivors and AIM activists was inspired by my lecture about chickens to do his own research and came back to class eager to tell me all about the atrocities involved in factory farming. Hmong and Vietnamese students came up to the front of the classroom to tell me of their own past personal distress at witnessing the violence of cockfighting and egg farming. Alice Walker's essay "Am I Blue?" (which begins with a horse, considers comparisons between animal exploitation and slavery, and ends with the author spitting out a piece of steak) was the hands-down favorite reading for African American students in the popular culture class, one of whom made sure to tell me that she hadn't drunk milk since the day we discussed it.

I could go on. And on. The point is: If the organized animal rights movement in the Twin Cities isn't reaching these students and people like them, then the responsibility for that state of affairs lies with the movement rather than in any supposed closedness of their communities.

Working within Whiteness

White animal advocates in the Twin Cities and elsewhere must make affirmative efforts to educate themselves about race and racism (male animal advocates also ought to educate themselves about gender and sexism, but that's another story). Since racism is a key thread in the network of intersecting oppressions that include speciesism, and since sufficient expertise in the dynamics of race is a prerequisite for effective activism in a multicultural environment, such self-education should be seen not as something that takes time away from animal advocacy but an essential element of animal advocacy.

If we want other people to be more willing to look at the things they don't want to see, we need to be willing to do the same. We can start with white privilege. I would hope that white animal advocates would also feel ethically impelled to confront and begin to think about how to divest themselves of white privilege. The persistence of racism, along with the structural legacies of decades of institutional racial injustice, means that most white people are walking around with extra change in their pockets whilst enjoying a wealth of race-based advantages made all the more insidious by their invisibility to their beneficiaries. However much white, middle-class animal activists may feel identified with the animals for whom they advocate, the fact is that they are not chickens locked down in battery cages. They are white people participating in a culture where people of color are disproportionately locked down in prisons. Editor Kim Socha works with a local restorative justice organization and many animal advocates (especially those vegan anarchists!) engage in similar social justice work, but it has not yet become the norm for white animals advocates to confront their ethical obligation to challenge their white privilege as relentlessly as they challenge their species privilege.

In the course of her honest account of her own efforts to wrestle with race, Kim recounts a time when she wanted to encourage African American passersby to read Breeze Harper's *Sistah Vegan* anthology. I want *every* animal advocate to read it closely and carefully. Lisa Kemmerer's anthology, *Sister Species*, also includes an instructive array of essays by other-than-white animal advocates and thus also should be studied mindfully. But animal advocates shouldn't limit their reading to books that directly address vegan and animal liberation issues. As Leymah Gbowee did, we must read widely — not only in the literature documenting successful social change efforts but also in the poetry, novels, plays, and essays that will help us to understand how race, class and gender shape the people and communities with whom and within which we must work if we hope to effect the structural and psychological shifts necessary for the liberation of animals.

Once such book-based groundwork is begun, how might all-white (or disproportionately white) animal advocacy organizations begin to make contact with potential members from other communities as well as potential allies in coalition efforts? Certainly, leafleting in central locations visited by a diversity of people can't hurt and will go more smoothly if white activists have grappled with the conundrum in the opening lines of the famous Pat Parker poem, "For the White Person Who Wants to Know How to Be My Friend," — which begins, "The first thing you do is to forget that I'm Black. Second, you must never forget that I'm Black. You should be able to dig Aretha, but don't play her every time I come over." — and thus understand that they must simultaneously be able to talk about concepts like the dietary racism implicit in the promotion of dairy by the USDA *and* resist any urge to assume that people of color will only be interested in such race-related arguments. Deep grounding in anti-racist theory *and* practice also helps to allay that palpable physical unease that comes over some white folks whenever they talk with people of color and especially when they talk with people of color about race.

But that's not enough. Representatives of grassroots animal rights organizations also ought to be joining local struggles for social, environmental, and economic justice. It's okay if you want to wear a vegan or animal lib t-shirt and answer any questions about it, but do not bring copies of "Why Vegan?" to pass out at the first meeting you attend. Wait until you've become a trusted ally before initiating conversations about why you're vegan and what connections you see between that and the problems on which you are working together. Become that trusted ally by behaving in a helpful and trustworthy manner. Offer to photocopy flyers — and do it. Offer to do some tedious background research — and do a great job at it. Offer to bring refreshments for the next meeting, and show up with a few dozen vegan goodies from the Donut Cooperative. Don't mention that they're vegan until everyone has enjoyed them.

What kinds of local projects might be the best places to start? Efforts to bring (or expand) community gardens and farmer's markets in low-income neighborhoods are worthwhile in and of themselves — people with access to fresh vegetables (and who know how to cook them) eat fewer animals — while also setting the stage for wider food justice activism. (Check out the Food Empowerment Project for more ideas about that.) Similarly, local environmental justice projects also are inherently worthwhile — animals need us to clean up the planet just as much as they need us to go vegan — while setting the stage for broader coalitions.

If I were staying in town, and particularly if I were a parent, I'd involve myself in efforts to address the achievement gap in local public schools. At some point in that process, I'd bring up the idea of getting a soymilk option into the lunchrooms, so that African American students — the majority of which are lactose intolerant whether they know it or not — don't have to deal with headaches and gassy stomachs while trying to concentrate on algebra. (I'd solicit the help of the Physician's Committee for Responsible Medicine "Healthy Lunches" project on the mechanics of that.)

Whenever you do start talking about veganism or animal rights to people outside the movement, *don't* use the word "abolitionist." Why not? In my view, "abolitionism" (as it is used by those who describe themselves thusly) cannot be separated from the problem of movement whiteness.

First, the very use of the term "abolitionist" presumes the controversial "dreaded comparison" and is thus likely to be off-putting to anyone who doesn't already see and agree with that analogy. If you've read *Sistah Vegan,* then you know that even some African American animal advocates balk at making that particular comparison. We all must guard against any impulse to, in Kim Socha's words, "hijack other oppressions." There are ways that even white animal advocates can draw the parallels in a manner that does not inadvertently diminish the living pain of the legacy of slavery by using it as a mere prop to make a point about animals, but this requires a kind of nuanced rhetoric that is exactly opposite of the *petition principia* involved in the use of the term "abolitionist" when talking to people who don't already see the analogy.

Next, there is a kind of implicit whiteness in the term itself. While some former slaves became known as "abolitionists," abolitionism as such was primarily a white movement — and rightly so, since it was white people who profited from slavery. While some white abolitionists did try to make common cause with enslaved Africans and most did use the stories of former slaves as case examples of suffering and sentience, abolitionism was mostly a process of white people talking with other white people about how to free those other people.

And then there is Frederick Douglass, who is among the most revered icons in African American history, and who "abolitionists" love to quote out of context. I regret being the one who has to say it, but there's something unseemly about a predominantly white movement that has been rightly critiqued for its failures to attend sufficiently to race cloaking itself in the mantle of this hero of Black history.

Finally, "abolitionism" has come to be used primarily as a way for some animal advocates to sharply distinguish themselves from other animal advocates. As such, I wonder whether it sends the message that this is a movement in which a diversity of perspectives (and, thus, a diversity of people) are welcome. In contrast, the term that I prefer—"liberation"—has only positive associations with a wide array of movements while still communicating commitment to ending of ownership and exploitation of animals by people. I suggest that activists who want to build a broader movement use that term instead.

Vitriol Versus Nurture

Melissa E. Maaske and Dallas Rising both defend the rescue of companion animals as a valid form of direct action for animals. I wholeheartedly agree both that such activism constitutes a valid end in itself and that such work brings vegan animal advocates into contact with people who may be open to arguments for animal liberation based on their own observations of animal sentience. I can't help but notice, though, that the end result of any dog rescue is placement of that animal in a home where—whatever the words on the "adoption" papers may say—she or he legally will be the property of a person. I'm glad that Melissa and Dallas are willing to make this compromise and don't demand that we forgo the protection of currently-existing dogs from the most egregious abuses in favor of an exclusive focus on ethical argumentation aimed at ultimately removing dogs from the category of property. Unfortunately, such willingness to take action for actual animals within the compromising context of the real world right now is condemned rather than commended by many of this volume's essayists.

I'm so glad to know that my book, *Aftershock*, has brought solace to many animal advocates. In that book, I stress the importance of being true. And so, I faced a dilemma when writing this afterword. I want to commend every author for their activism and for the courage implicit in daring to write, but I'm lying if I don't admit that I felt literally sickened when reading the many vituperative attacks on people who work to immediately improve the welfare of animals, as if we could shut down the factory farms and vivisection labs tomorrow if only they would quit trying to relieve animal suffering today.

I've written about this before, evidently to little avail. If we are serious about animal rights — any conception of which must include self-determination — then we must be willing to try to figure out what animals might want us to do. In some cases, it's very clear. We are not "the voice of the voiceless." Animals have their own voices, along with various gestural methods of communicating their wishes. If we listen to animals, we will hear many of them crying out for relief from suffering *right now*. Unless we can *prove* that relieving the suffering of one animal will cause the suffering of another, then we ought not refuse to relieve or mitigate that suffering if it is in our power to do so. Certainly, even if we prefer to deploy our own energies otherwise, we may not interfere with people who are sincerely trying to relieve that suffering.

I have rescued and nursed back to health both hens from battery cages and hens from a variety of cage-free egg facilities. It's true that hens in cage-free egg facilities experience deprivations, as described elsewhere in this volume. But the difference in extent and degree of injury between that and battery cages is substantial. Every time I read some screed against the effort to ban battery cages, my hands twitch with the memory of holding the completely defeathered bodies of debeaked battery hens. M. Ryan Leitch argues that people who work for animal welfare don't see the animals. I wonder if she would hold that opinion if she saw a just-rescued battery hen careening crazily as she tries to walk on her crippled feet using her atrophied leg muscles. I wish everybody could stand in the barn with me, looking at a heap of recently rescued battery hens — free now but unable to imagine how to do anything but stand in slumped passivity. They do recover, eventually, but none are ever unmarked by their years in the cages. I've rescued or rehabilitated hens from some pretty awful cage-free facilities but never — except in Sarahjane's footage of caged ducks in the foie gras factory — seen anything remotely resembling the damage done to birds by battery cages.

I do not condone and certainly do not promote any kind of exploitation of hens for eggs. But I would never — ever — interfere with efforts to ban battery cages. Neither the contributors to this volume nor the wider animal advocacy movement know how to convince everybody in the country to quit eggs this year. That being the case, we know for sure that many hens will be confined for purposes of egg production next year. These are real birds with real feelings. One way or another, they're going to be locked up by egg producers. In battery cages or not? You decide.

Please do read my essay "In Defense of Actual Animals: Moving Past the Abolition-Welfare Impasse," as this includes a more extensive explanation of my reasoning than I have room to offer here. In that essay, I suggest setting aside generalized critiques of "welfarism" in favor of careful ethical and strategic analysis of specific proposed animal welfare reforms. By my reckoning, using the method of strategic analysis outlined in my essay "Strategic Analysis of Animal Welfare Legislation: A Guide for the Perplexed," the abolition of battery cages — which would simultaneously substantially improve animal welfare, increase the costs of egg production, and sharply reduce the number of hens that may be kept in captivity — passes the test. The justly controversial "enriched cage" scheme lately promoted by HSUS does not.

You might or might not agree with those analysis, once you do the math. But, please hear *my* cry: Those hens are hurting! Let the people who want to ease their suffering do so. Turn your attention to the ten thousand other things we need to do.

Let a Hundred Flowers Bloom

We need more books like this. Whilst contemplating this afterword, I sat on a boulder in the middle of a farmed animal sanctuary, eating adventurously grilled watermelon and peaches. Working the grill was the sanctuary's animal care-taker, a vegan who grew up on a Midwestern "beef farm" and used to be one of those non-vegan animal-lovers that confound so many of us. How does *she* make sense of those burger-chomping dog rescuers? How does *she* envision a process by which the animal-murdering local economy in which she grew up might be transformed? What does she know that we all need to know? What data and insights are lurking in the minds of other grassroots animal advocates around the country? We need *many* more books like this.

Here are just a couple of the things that will have to happen in order to achieve a world without animal exploitation:

- Since laws have limited effect (even though enslavement of people is illegal everywhere in the world, there are more people enslaved today than at any other time in history), human attitudes about animals will need to be reshaped to prevent anybody from wanting or believing they have the right to exploit animals. People who earn their own bread through the exploitation of animals will have to find other livelihoods. Local economies rooted in the exploitation of animals or their habitats will have to be restructured from the ground up. Governments, which now recognize only people as rights-holding entities and rest entirely on the notion of the living world as property, also will have to be entirely restructured.

• Since animals are endangered not only by what we do to them but also what we have done to their habitats, real liberation of animals from human interference will mean cleaning up the mess we've made of the planet and sharply delimiting "development" of land for human uses. I don't need to list all of the steps *that* will take, do I?

Nobody has *the* answer. There is no one answer. No one person could possibly conceive of all of the different answers we need. Even if we narrow the question sharply — How might we shut down the Wisconsin dairy industry?— we need to hear and fairly consider a plethora of perspectives before selecting a strategy from among the possibilities.

Wheat, barley, rye, corn. All of these and so many more of our dietary staples began as wild grasses. Astute gatherers — women, mostly — took careful note of where and how their favored grasses grew, and in so doing (for better or worse), invented agriculture. They learned which plants grew in which kinds of soil. Through careful observation and trial-and-error practice, they figured out how to nurture the soil so that the grassroots could grow.

Today, many wild grasses are endangered by the same factors that menace animals: industrial agriculture, pollution, climate change, and the incessant encroachment of people into their habitats. Botanists and ecologists understand that preserving beach grasses ravaged by rising tides will require different strategies than protecting the genetic integrity of land races of maize endangered by the pollen of genetically modified corn. They learn from each other but know they must also attend closely to local conditions, the slightest variation in which may mean that a strategy that succeeds brilliantly in one place may fail entirely in another. If they fail, they try something different, rather than doing the same thing over and over again because some philosopher said it should work.

Let's give at least as much nuanced attention to nurturing our own diverse grassroots in all of the different places that other-than-human animals need them to flourish. Let's make sure that our organizations are sufficiently diverse, and sufficiently tolerant of critical and creative thinking, so that all of those grasses — and all of those fruits and legumes too — can bloom.

WORKS CITED

Adams, Carol J., and Josephine Donovan, eds. *Animals and Women: Feminist Theoretical Explorations.* Durham, NC: Duke University Press, 1995. Print.

Gaard, Greta Claire. *Ecofeminism: Women, Animals, Nature.* Philadelphia: Temple University Press, 1993. Print.

Gbowee, Leymah. *Mighty Be Our Powers: How Sisterhood, Prayer, and Sex Changed a Nation at War*. 1st ed. New York: Beast Books, 2011. Print.

Glaser, B. G. *Basics of Grounded Theory Analysis*. Mill Valley, CA: Sociology Press, 1992. Print.

Goodall, Jane. *Hope for Animals and Their World: How Endangered Species Are Being Rescued from the Brink*. New York: Grand Central Publishing, 2009. Print.

Harper, A. Breeze, ed. *Sistah Vegan: Food, Identity, Health, and Society: Black Female Vegans Speak*. New York: Lantern Books, 2010. Print.

jones, pattrice. *Aftershock: Confronting Trauma in a Violent World*. New York: Lantern Books, 2007. Print.

_____. "In Defense of Actual Animals: Moving Past the Welfare-Abolition Impasse." 2008. Web. 2 June 2012.

_____. "Strategic Analysis of Animal Welfare Legislation: A Guide for the Perplexed." 2008. Web. 2 June 2012.

Kemmerer, Lisa A., ed. *Sister Species: Women, Animals and Social Justice*. 1st ed. Champaign: University of Illinois Press, 2011. Print.

Losure, Mary. *Our Way or the Highway: Inside the Minnehaha Free State*. 1st ed. Minneapolis: University of Minnesota Press, 2002. Print.

Robinson, Jo Ann. *The Montgomery Bus Boycott and the Women Who Started It*. 1st ed. Knoxville: University of Tennessee Press, 1987. Print.

About the Contributors

Sarahjane **Blum** has been active in the animal rights movement since 1997 and is the co-founder of gourmetcruelty.com. She currently serves on the boards of Support Vegans in the Prison System and NYC's Empty Cages Collective. She is lead plaintiff in Blum v. Holder, a lawsuit challenging the constitutionality of the Animal Enterprise Terrorism Act.

Mary Britton **Clouse** received a BFA from S.U.N.Y. at Buffalo and an MA from the University of New Mexico at Albuquerque. She served as president of Minnesota Animal Rights Coalition, co-founded the Minnesota Spay/Neuter Project, Legislative Efforts for Animal Protection and most recently founded Chicken Run Rescue and Justice for Animals Arts Guild. She has concentrated her activism and art on animals used in agriculture.

Elizabeth **Cook** has a degree in journalism from the University of Minnesota and has written for several newspapers in the Twin Cities area. She's been involved with the Animals Rights Coalition since 2010.

Charlotte **Cozzetto** works in the computer field and has been active with ARC since 1988, currently serving as president. She worked on the campaign that led to the abolishment of the University of Minnesota's live dog lab for first year medical students, ARC's successful lawsuit against the University of Minnesota for denied access to research records, and ARC's successful campaign to persuade the Animal Humane Society to discontinue use of the gas chamber for euthanasia.

Travis **Elise** is an activist and organizer in Minneapolis. His work has mainly focused on animal rights and community and workplace organizing. A former Catholic Worker and organizer with the Industrial Workers of the World, he is currently pursuing his Bachelor's degree in philosophy.

Heidi **Greger** holds a PhD in sociology and was active with the Animal Rights Coalition from 1991 to 2012, serving on the board of directors as vice-president, president, and treasurer. Her primary interest is animals used in research, and her proudest achievements with ARC have been her contributions to the ending of dog labs at the University of Minnesota and the successful lawsuit against the university to open its animal research records to the public.

pattrice **jones** teaches at Minneapolis Community and Technical College and at Metropolitan State University in St. Paul. She is the co-founder of the Eastern Shore Sanctuary (now VINE Sanctuary), where she sheltered survivors of the poultry and egg industries and developed a method of rehabilitating roosters used in cockfighting. Her book *Aftershock: Confronting Trauma in a Violent World* is a guide for activists.

M. Ryan **Leitch** is a Minnesota grassroots activist with ties to the Animal Rights Coalition. She is also co-host of the podcast Midwest Vegan Radio (MVR). She has also written for the Web site *This Dish Is Veg*.

Melissa E. **Maaske** lives in Minneapolis. Along with her work in the field of dog rescue, she is a volunteer with the Animal Rights Coalition and a vegan mentor with Vegan University. A social worker servicing people who have experienced mental illness, she received her BSW from Minnesota State University.

Patrick **McAleer** is an instructor of English at Inver Hills Community College in Minnesota and holds a PhD in English literature and criticism. In addition to his interest in animal rights, he writes much on Stephen King, including *Inside the Dark Tower Series* (McFarland, 2009) and *The Writing Family of Stephen King* (McFarland, 2011).

Al **Nowatzki** is an animal rights activist from Saint Paul, Minnesota. He is a vegan mentor for the Animal Right Coalition's Vegan University program, volunteers at outreach events and is a coordinator for ARC's family group, VegKins.

Dallas **Rising** is the program director for the Animal Rights Coalition and a founding member of Support Vegans in the Prison System. She served as the board chair and president of Small Dog Rescue of Minnesota, a statewide no-kill rescue, for four years.

Kim **Socha** holds a PhD in literature and criticism and is an English instructor with scholarship on topics such as critical pedagogy, surrealism, atheism, critical animal studies and Latino/a literature. She is an animal liberation advocate who sits on the boards of the Institute for Critical Animal Studies and the Animal Rights Coalition. Her book *Women, Destruction and the Avant-Garde: A Paradigm for Animal Liberation* was published in 2011 by Rodopi through ICAS's book series.

Melissa **Swanson** is an animal rescuer and activist in St. Paul, Minnesota. A volunteer with the Animal Rights Coalition and Second Chance Animal Rescue, she is an advocate for all animals but has a special passion for rats and chickens, two of the least protected species.

Vonnie **Thomasberg** was named president emerita of the Animal Rights Coalition in 2005, and is ARC's founder and past president. For over thirty years, Vonnie has defended the rights of nonhuman animals and has advised, counseled and provided effective leadership and inspiration to others in this ongoing effort.

Chelsea **Youngquist Hassler** lives in suburban Minneapolis. She has a degree in marketing from the Carlson School of Management and works in IT sales.

Aaron **Zellhoefer** is an animal, environmental and LGBTQIA activist living in Minneapolis. He has campaigned with Stop Huntingdon Animal Cruelty (SHAC) and currently serves on the board of Support Vegans in the Prison System. He has appeared in the *Contra Costa Times*, the *Toronto Star*—who dubbed him "George Bush's worst nightmare"—and *No Compromise* and *Hustler* magazines.

Index

Adams, Carol J. 5, 129–130, 196, 237, 260, 264
Animal Enterprise Terrorism Act (AETA) 241–254, 255, 259
Animal Rights Coalition (ARC) 135–136, 175–190, 264, 270

Barnouin, Kim 56–57, 113
Best, Steven 40, 45, 54, 59, 70
bird trapping 185–186

cats 79–82, 163, 183, 243
Cherry, Elizabeth 14
Chicken Run Rescue (CRR) 189, 215–216
chickens 24, 29, 98–99, 106, 108, 118, 121, 153, 159–166, 189, 191, 196–200, 204–222, 260, 273, 277
Compassion Over Killing (COK) 197
cows 11–12, 23–24, 26, 29, 55, 89–91, 98, 104–106, 142, 144, 148, 196–200, 231, 266

Davis, Karen 208–209, 211
dog labs 181–185, 265
dogs 75–79, 101, 116, 139–154, 169–174, 178, 243, 246–247, 276
Dominick, Brian 54, 60
Donovan, Josephine 264
ducks 216, 257–259, 277
Dunayer, Joan 8, 70–71, 85, 98, 100, 103, 233–234

fish 101–102, 124–125, 166–169
Foer, Jonathan Safran 113, 121, 144
Francione, Gary 22–41, 53
Freedman, Rory 56–57, 113
Freeman, Carrie 230–231
Friedrich, Bruce 22, 27–28, 30, 41, 49, 55

Gaarder, Emily 5, 140
Garner, Robert 22, 24–28, 31, 33, 41

Harper, Breeze A. 3, 231, 238, 256, 274–275

Harris, Angela P. 230, 238
Haynes, Richard 49–50, 61
Hribal, Jason 66, 80
Humane Society of the United States (HSUS) 24, 29–30, 35, 49–50, 184–185, 210, 217, 219–220, 268, 278
hunting 24–26, 31, 51, 145

jones, pattrice 4, 8, 15, 156, 261
Joy, Melanie 17–18, 117, 119, 141–143, 153, 205, 225

Keith, Lierre 47–48
Kelch, Thomas G. 53
Kemmerer, Lisa 3, 228, 274
Kheel, Marti 261
King, C. Richard 226, 230
Kuipers, Dean 249

locavore movement 47, 188–189
Luke, Brian 51, 62, 145

Mercy for Animals 185, 201

Nibert, David 13, 32–33, 37
Nocella, Anthony 45, 54, 236

Patterson, Charles 13, 229, 237–238
People for the Ethical Treatment of Animals (PETA) 24, 26–27, 29, 35, 49–50, 55–56, 104, 177, 179, 192, 201–202, 229–235, 246, 268
Phelps, Norm 22, 27–30, 41, 46, 48, 54
pigs 29, 50, 56–57, 106, 121, 126, 144, 148, 153, 184, 228–229
Pollan, Michael 106, 118, 205, 213, 220
Potter, Will 40, 235, 243, 249, 252–253
pound seizure 181–185

Rising, Dallas 46, 199, 201
Rokke, Michelle 246–248

Sapon, Stanley M. 93–94
Scully, Matthew 48

Singer, Peter 22, 27–28, 261, 264
Spiegel, Marjorie 51, 223, 229, 235–
238
Stănescu, Vasile 47
Steiner, Gary 105
Stop Huntingdon Animal Cruelty (SHAC)
241–254

Torres, Bob 50, 56, 58
Torres, Jenna 56, 58

Wise, Tim 227, 233
Wolfson, David J. 51, 54

Yates, Roger 40, 100